GOVERNING
THE
SOVIET
UNION

D. RICHARD LITTLE

San Diego State University

Longman

New York & London

Governing the Soviet Union

Longman Inc., 95 Church Street, White Plains, N.Y. 10601

Associated companies:
Longman Group Ltd., London
Longman Cheshire Pty., Melbourne
Longman Paul Pty., Auckland
Copp Clark Pitman, Toronto
Pitman Publishing Inc., New York

For my Father and Mother in memorium.

Senior editor: David J. Estrin
Production editor: Helen B. Ambrosio
Text design: Stephen August Krastin
Cover design and illustration: Jill Francis Wood
Production supervisor: Judith Stern

*The map appearing on pages 10–11 is reprinted with
permission of Macmillan Publishing Company from*
Comparing Political Systems: Power and Policy *by Gary
Bertsch, Robert Clark, and David Wood. (New York:
Macmillan 1986)*

Library of Congress Cataloging-in-Publication Data
Little, D. Richard.
  Governing the Soviet Union.

  Bibliography: p.
  Includes index.
  1. Soviet Union–Politics and government–1982–
2. Soviet Union–Politics and government–1917–
I. Title.
JN6511.L58   1989   947.085'4   88-7240
ISBN 0-582-28484-8 (pbk.)

88 89 90 91 92 93 9 8 7 6 5 4 3 2 1

Contents

Preface

For anyone familiar with the Soviet Union of Leonid Brezhnev, General Secretary of the Communist Party for eighteen years until his death in 1982, a return trip to the USSR in the late-1980s would be a startling experience. In place of the stable, conformist society over which Brezhnev presided, the visitor would find a country alive with controversy and enveloped in a rapidly changing social environment. With Mikhail Gorbachev leading the Communist Party Politburo, the country is embarked on the most serious path of reform it has followed since Stalin took power in the 1920s.

Whether the Gorbachev reforms will succeed is the central issue for the Soviet Union. The analysis in this book is intended to provide a basis for making a judgment on that issue, and in the process to give students a solid understanding of the operation of the Soviet political system.

The chief focus of this study is the conflict between Soviet society's need for greater initiative, spontaneity and individuality, as called for by the Gorbachev reforms, and the determination of the Communist Party leadership to retain unchallenged political control over the nation. This conflict is explored in several important contexts. Major sections of the book deal with the exercise and distribution of political power by the Party and government, the means of Party control over the legislature, the military, and the police, the nature of the policymaking process, and the management of the national economy, including a chapter devoted to the "second" economy. Because the success of the Gorbachev reforms depends so heavily on the cooperation of the managerial class, the book analyzes the political and personal choices facing representative officials in deciding how far to extend their cooperation to the Party's reforms.

A further section deals with the interaction between the Party and the Soviet people. The Party's efforts to guide the behavior and shape the values of the population are examined in some detail. For those citizens who operate outside approved limits, the coercive forces of the Party and government come into play, and these are also examined. In recent years both of these kinds of public pressures on the population have evolved in response to changing circumstances in the nation as a whole.

In order to place all this in a broader perspective than merely the contemporary circumstances, the book offers a brief interpretation of Russian history and an analysis of both Lenin's and Stalin's contributions to the shaping of the modern Soviet polity. This background is essential for achieving an understanding of the pervasive historical forces that continue to shape Soviet politics.

The overriding purpose of the book is to help students see the complexity of power relationships even in a system as dominated by the top Party leadership as that of the Soviet Union. The limits on the power of the Party Politburo are real and diverse, even if they do not translate into freedoms for the Soviet people. The fact that Gorbachev, for all his authority as head of the Politburo, must struggle against powerful forces to implement his policies, and may ultimately fail, is a matter worthy of study and reflection.

The writing of a book on an extensive subject is always a collaborative effort, and my debt to colleagues, on my own campus and elsewhere, and to my students past and present, is one I am pleased to acknowledge. My special thanks go to several colleagues who perused sections of the book with a critical eye and lent much to whatever quality it may have: Professors Jan Adams, Lyndelle Fairlie, Neil Heyman, Philip Pride, and Peter Vanneman. Professors George W. Rice and John E. Turner read the entire manuscript, and I began to think of them, toward the end, as co-authors. Their generous help and rigorous critiques are greatly appreciated. And to my colleague and friend, Richard Gripp, my thanks for countless conversations on everything to do with the Soviet Union that crossed either of our desks.

Working with Longman has also been a great pleasure. I am indebted to both of my editors, namely, Irving Rockwood, who originally stimulated this project and saw me through the early chapters, and David Estrin, who accompanied me the rest of the way with patience and unflagging encouragement.

Finally and most importantly, to my wife, Linda, and to Greg, Marcy, and Omi, I offer this book as small compensation for the extended periods away from the family circle that it required. Their constant understanding and accommodation are gratefully acknowledged.

CHAPTER 1
Introduction

For many people living in Western democracies, thinking about the Soviet Union arouses strongly negative reactions. They see in that mammoth state not only a threat to their physical security but also a challenge to the values and patterns of life that inhere most deeply in their cultures. President Ronald Reagan once called the Soviet Union an "evil empire" and many would agree with that judgment. And yet there are other, more positive, feelings as well. A performance of the Bolshoi Ballet or the Moiseyev Dancers in London or New York brings out enthusiastic crowds of admiring patrons, and curiosity about the country, as reflected in the growing number of Western tourists who travel to the Soviet Union, remains high.

It would be encouraging to believe that the apparent contradiction represented in these feelings could be resolved through education, through a deeper understanding of Soviet society and politics. Unfortunately, this rarely seems to be the case. Even among Western graduate students and scholars who have spent extended periods of time living in the USSR, and whose careers are devoted to studying the country, there are typically bittersweet feelings. Warm memories of friends and colleagues, of vast expanses of natural beauty in the steppes and forests, and of ancient cities rebuilt after every war, are combined with outrage and disdain toward many of the characteristics of modern Soviet society. As one young American graduate student commented at the end of a year in the USSR: "As the train rolled away from Moscow toward the Polish border . . . both of us had a crazy sense of freedom; we felt released from a subtle and deadly confinement which, we only now realized, had sapped our spirits for ten months."[1]

This ambivalence toward life in the Soviet Union is not peculiar to foreigners; it is shared by many Russians as well. As one young Muscovite expressed it: "There is one man in me that loves this country strongly, very strongly. I am, after all, a Russian. But there is another part of me that wants to live and cannot do so here. Life is too hard. I can't go on being divided like this."[2] Such ambivalence is not unique to the Soviet Union, of course, but it is particularly striking in a country where the official and ubiquitously proclaimed truth is that the population is unwaveringly united behind the leadership of the Communist Party and is moving steadily toward the realization of a perfect society in which all needs will be satisfied and all legitimate desires fulfilled.

If increasing familiarity with the Soviet Union rarely overcomes this sort of ambivalence, it can nevertheless provide valuable insight into the sources of Soviet behavior and Soviet conceptions of the outside world. Without this understanding, the actions of Soviet leaders often seem simply arbitrary and motivated by hostility or indifference toward the reactions of the outside world.

1

Consider, for example, the plight of Yuri Balovlenkov, a Soviet citizen with a university degree in mathematics and physics. In 1979, Yuri married Elena Kusmenko from Baltimore, Maryland, in a Moscow ceremony. Shortly thereafter, Elena returned to the United States and Yuri applied to OVIR, the Soviet emigration agency, for permission to immigrate to the United States. After struggling with OVIR for three years without success, Yuri began a hunger strike, vowing to fast until he either died or his application was approved. The case got widespread publicity in the West especially after it was discovered that there were other Soviet citizens engaging in similar tactics.

The behavior of the Soviet government in this instance seems difficult to comprehend on either practical or moral grounds. Why risk the negative publicity of forcing a man to starve himself to death for the right to be with his wife? Why stimulate the various international human rights groups to protest further against "Soviet inhumanity"? Why provoke an American President and Congress, both of whom were in the midst of deciding whether to sell millions of dollars worth of badly needed grain to the USSR? And in the name of simple human decency, why not let the man be reunited with his wife?

There are no easy answers to these questions, but there is more than one point of view. The official reasons given by Soviet authorities for denial of the application involved two assertions: first, that Balovlenkov was in possession of state secrets as a result of his work (which had terminated eight years earlier) in a radio research institute and that therefore his immigration to the United States would constitute a threat to national security; and secondly, that Balovlenkov had engaged in illegal and antisocial acts in support of his application (such as the hunger strike and refusing to vote in local elections).

Beyond these official reasons, Soviet citizens and officials might well have raised other objections. Why did the young bride refuse to live in Moscow with her husband, since OVIR made it clear that she would be welcome? What about all of the people's money that was spent educating the man through the university level, which will have been wasted if he leaves the country? And what about the insult to both the Russian people and the nation from a man who would turn his back on his heritage for promises of an easy life in capitalist America? Or perhaps the whole incident was merely a plot by American intelligence agents to embarrass the Soviet government.

Are these reasonable objections, sufficient to justify OVIR's denial of an exit visa to Yuri Balovlenkov? Certainly in the context of Western legal principles and constitutional rights it is difficult to imagine refusing a citizen a passport on such grounds. But in the Soviet context, other forces, some historically generated, others intensively promoted by the Communist Party, are at work: a profound nationalism that ties Russians to their homeland no matter how great the difficulties and which tends to enshroud with a cloak of betrayal those who would forsake Russia; a tradition of subordinating legal regulations to more subjective considerations of social utility and individual merit; and a deeply rooted and constantly reinforced social conformism that evokes popular disapproval of rebellious individual conduct whatever the cause. Viewed in this light, the Soviet government's decision in the Balovlenkov case appears less an arbitrary injustice and more the consequence of some relatively fundamental characteristics of the Soviet state of mind.

Because this book is about how the Soviet government works, and especially how it makes major policy decisions, we will have to deal with these kinds of factors at length, just as Soviet leaders do. It is a central argument of this study that, despite the great personal power of the USSR's top leaders, they are increasingly obliged to work within a political culture and an institutional structure that limit their policy options and their ability to have decisions carried out. Ever since Stalin's death in 1953, a succession of leaders has struggled against these limitations in many different ways, but they have not, in my judgment, been winning. Throughout the comings and goings of the five post-Stalin General Secretaries, the underlying problems of the economy have remained much the same, and the government ministries have continued to resist all manner of reforms announced by the Party leadership.

The most serious challenge to this situation has been posed by the current leader of the Soviet Union, Mikhail Gorbachev. Assuming the post of General Secretary of the Communist Party in 1985 as the youngest Party leader since the 1930s, Gorbachev has openly condemned many of the characteristics of the Soviet system and purged most of the political elite that served under long-time General Secretary Leonid Brezhnev. Grobachev has launched a campaign of "restructuring" (*rekonstruktsia*) in all spheres of Soviet life and has decreed a policy of "openness" (*glasnost*) that has challenged the closed society that has for so long cramped Soviet development. Needless to say, he has in the process raised strenuous if discrete opposition. He has also unleashed forces for change that even he may not be able to control. Gorbachev is, therefore, beleaguered on both sides, from those who want greater changes than he is prepared to support and those who want no change at all. In the chapters that follow we shall trace the impact of the "Gorbachev era" on the major facets of Soviet government and society.

The range and extent of political authority vested in the Soviet General Secretary is probably unmatched anywhere in the world. Yet he must exercise that authority within the constraints of a number of forces that have developed and matured over the years ever since the revolution as well as some that carry over from much earlier periods. There are four such forces, or contexts, within which the exercise of political power takes place:

1. the historical circumstances of Russian and Soviet development: how Russia's past has influenced its present development and contributed to its present dilemma;
2. the ways in which both the government and the Communist Party are organized: how the structure of the political system affects its capacity to make and enforce political decisions;
3. the process of policy-making and administration: how groups and the mass public affect the policy-making process;
4. the attitudes and political behavior of the Soviet people: how the government attempts to shape public behavior and values and what success it has had.

Each of these contexts is the subject of a major section of this book. The main objective of the text is to highlight those elements of the political process that are most persistent and enduring and to examine the more immediate actions of the Soviet political elite in that overall context.

This approach raises a more speculative issue: If these kinds of forces are shaping the behavior of top political leaders, are they doing so in a routinized and perhaps even predictable way? That is, have these general forces begun to form rules or norms of political behavior to which even the top leaders must conform? If so, we may be seeing the development of an unwritten constitution in the Soviet Union, which would tell us more about how the system operates than the written one that now exists. It will take considerable time and a great deal more information about Soviet politics than we now have to resolve this issue. But in the chapters that follow, a search for the regularities of political behavior that may constitute unwritten rules will be part of our analysis.[3]

As an introduction to the politics of the USSR, it is useful to get a sense of the massiveness of its physical presence in the world and of the extraordinary variety of peoples who inhabit it. For the Soviet Union is less a country than an empire, extending across two continents and containing huge populations for whom Russian is a foreign language. The USSR conjoins religious communities and ethnic populations that in other parts of the world have been bitter enemies for centuries. And it has striven to create a modern nation-state out of all this diversity in a land whose climate and terrain, and location on the globe, have greatly complicated the attainment of this goal.

THE LAY OF THE LAND

It is difficult to imagine how vast the land mass of the Soviet Union is. Lacking only a few degrees of extending halfway around the world in the northern lattitudes, the USSR occupies eight and a half million square miles, a land area that would fit both China and the United States within its borders with room left for all of Western Europe. From east to west, it spreads over eleven time zones, so that the old saying—"The sun never sets on the British empire"—is almost literally true of the USSR. And it is so far north that that statement almost applies to a single location. Murmansk, situated on the Arctic Ocean, for example, gets only a few minutes of darkness a day during mid-summer.

Much of the Soviet Union is also flat, with broad plains, plateaus, and rolling hills stretching thousands of miles from the Baltic Sea into central Siberia, rarely reaching 3,000 feet of elevation. The main mountain ranges are in the distant east, near the Pacific Ocean and along the Mongolian border. Lesser ones—the Urals, Caucasus, and Carpathians—are aligned along the borders of the western, or European, part of the Soviet Union.

There are several ways to look at the natural and physical dimensions of the Soviet Union. Most geographers identify at least three major sectors: European

Russia, central Asia, and Siberia. They are very different from each other both in terms of climate, terrain, and vegetation and in terms of the sociocultural characteristics of the regions.

European Russia

Occupying a broad plain west of the Ural Mountains and north of the Black and Caspian seas, European Russia is the area most familiar to foreigners. It is the most highly developed area with a high concentration of the nation's industry and the bulk of its population. It also contains the best farmland, located in the *chernozem,* or "black earth," areas of the Ukraine.

Within European Russia are a number of subregions with an interesting diversity of climate, terrain, and economic activity. Bordering its eastern edge are the Ural Mountains, one of the richest sources of mineral resources in the USSR and the natural barrier that divides European Russia from Siberia. In the southernmost part of this area are the sunny resort towns of the southern Crimea, a peninsula jutting out into the Black Sea. Here much of the Soviet European population takes its vacations.

Further west lies the land adjacent to the Baltic Sea. Here are situated the three Baltic republics: Latvia, Lithuania, and Estonia. Like much of the land west of the Ukraine, the Baltic area is poor in resources and of marginal agricultural use. Inadequate drainage produces extensive marshes that keep agricultural yields low and force the population to import food from the Ukraine and elsewhere.

Central Asia

To the east of the Caspian Sea lies Soviet central Asia, a vast area of deserts and low hills that alternates between intense heat in the summers and chilling windy cold the rest of the year. Traditionally inhabited by nomads moving among widely separated oases, the lands of central Asia today are changing rapidly. Since World War II, Soviet leaders have been pouring large sums of developmental money into the area, attempting to exploit its meager agricultural potential and to establish an industrial and manufacturing base as well.

The area remains, however, less developed than most other areas of the country. It expends most of its economic activity providing raw materials and primary products to the more highly developed sectors of the country. The population is mostly Moslem and of Asian and Middle Eastern extraction.

Siberia

From the Ural Mountains eastward extends the largest and most forbidding region of the USSR. It reaches almost to the Pacific Ocean, separated from it only by a strip of land that Russians call the Far East. The term "Siberia" actually is only a colloquial designation of the area, not the formal name of a republic or region.

Siberia contains more than half of Soviet territory but only about one-tenth of its population.

Geographically, Siberia includes three broad areas, each bounded by a great river. Just east of the Ural Mountains begins the great West Siberian Lowland, a flat plain that drains gradually toward the Arctic Ocean by means of the Ob and Irtysh river systems. In the northern half of the Siberian Lowland there had traditionally been little economic activity except lumbering. But in the past decade, a vast development program has been under way to take advantage of newly discovered oil and gas reserves that may ultimately surpass those of the Urals.

Beyond the Yenisei River and on to the Lena River a thousand miles to the east extends the Mid-Siberian Plateau. Dissected by many rivers, the plateau is from 300 to 1,000 meters in elevation and divided into the vast coniferous forests of the taiga in the southern part and the severe Arctic plains of the north called the tundra, or "cold desert."

Beneath the surface of the land is the permafrost—earth frozen into solid ice to a depth in some places of nearly a mile. In the summer, a thin surface layer of ice melts, allowing what little vegetation there is to sprout briefly. But because the water from this melting cannot drain away, since all is frozen beneath it, it lies in vast swampy marshes until freezing over again in the fall.

The tundra covers the northern quarter of the country from the Urals east to the Pacific Ocean, capping both the Mid-Siberian Plateau and the more mountainous terrain of East Siberia and the Far East. From the Lena River eastward are the most remote and sparsely settled parts of the Soviet Union. In the northern reaches of this expanse some of the coldest temperatures in the world have been recorded. In Verkhoyansk, in northeast Siberia, for instance, the average January temperature is $-60°F$.[4] At that temperature, human breath forms dense, frosty clouds before one's face, and milk is sold in solid blocks like ice.

Much of the USSR beyond the Urals seems barely habitable because of both the terrain and the climate. Yet the whole area is being developed rapidly for its natural resources. Some of the labor involved is being extracted from prisoners and forced laborers, especially for the railroads and mines. But there is also an elaborate package of perquisites—much higher salaries, free housing, extended vacations and the like—available to any citizen willing to move eastward for even a brief period of time. Journalists report that spending a summer engaged in hard labor in Siberia has even become something of a fad in some intellectual circles in European Russia.[5]

RUSSIANS AND OTHER SOVIETS

In a formal sense, the country we are discussing is not "Russia" but the Union of Soviet Socialist Republics, or the Soviet Union for short. Likewise, the inhabitants of that land are not correctly identified as the "Russian people," or even as the "Soviet people." The proper term is the "Soviet peoples," a phrase coined to emphasize the multinational character of the population. If foreigners occasionally get the terms confused, there is consolation in the fact that Soviet leaders sometimes do also. On one recent occasion—a speech in Kiev carried over local television—the top leader of the country, Mikhail Gorbachev, put it this way:

> For all people who are striving for good, Russia—I mean the Soviet Union—I mean, that is what we call it now, and what it is in fact—for them it is a bulwark.[6]

In a Soviet population of about 280 million people, "Russians" (also known historically as "Great Russians") constitute only about half of this total. These, together with the Ukrainians and Belorussians, make up the Slavic peoples of the USSR, constituting about 72 percent of the population. The rest of the Soviet population is made up of more than a hundred nationalities and ethnic groups, who speak over eighty languages and write in five different alphabets. These groups range in size from the millions of Uzbeks, Tatars, Armenians, and Georgians down to communities of a few hundred people.

Many of the latter live in the northern and eastern lands away from European Russia's urban centers. The Soviet census report lists, among the "Peoples of the North," for example, twenty-three separate nationalities, none with more than 30,000 people. But the bulk of the population is urban, rather than rural. There are twenty-five cities with populations over one million residents, including even Novosibirsk, which is located in the remote reaches of eastern Siberia.[7]

The multinational character of the Soviet population is one of the USSR's most striking characteristics. In the thousand years of Russian and Soviet history, the nation's borders have changed many times, expanding to incorporate non-Slavs at one period then contracting later after defeat in a war or internal revolt. A number of the peoples now living within the Soviet Union have been conquerers of the Russian Slavs in earlier periods of history, and others have long traditions of national independence. Thus, relations between Russians and non-Russians in the Soviet Union have great significance for the integrity of the state as a whole.

Since earliest times, the Great Russians have occupied the central plains of European Russia while other ethnic groups have been arrayed along their borders. The modern distribution of peoples reflects this historic arrangement. The Great Russians are concentrated west of the Urals and well inland from both the Black Sea and the Baltic Sea, and from their traditional enemies in eastern and central Europe, the Middle East, and Asia. Only along the bleak tundra between Leningrad and Murmansk, where the USSR shares a border with Finland and Norway, do the inland Russians come in direct contact with the rest of Europe.

Between Great Russia and the powerful nations of Europe and Asia lie two territorial rings, one inside its borders and one outside. The outside ring includes, from west to east, the East European Communist countries (Poland, Czechoslovakia, Hungary, and Rumania), Afghanistan, Mongolia, and North Korea, leaving a long unprotected southern border with Turkey and Iran and an eastern stretch of China. The inside ring compensates for these gaps and further reinforces the core.

It is composed of fourteen Soviet republics, each containing a major non-Russian population group.

These republics provide a buffer, both militarily and culturally, between the Russian republic (Russian Soviet Federated Socialist Republic, or RSFSR) and the fourteen foreign countries that touch Soviet borders. In a contemporary political and legal sense, the fifteen republics that comprise the USSR constitute a single country, and Soviet leaders have made strenuous efforts over the years to integrate them into a harmonious social structure. But the differences among the peoples of those republics remain significant, and this presents the Soviet leadership with one of its most important challenges.

THE NON-RUSSIAN REPUBLICS

The Baltic Peoples

South of Leningrad on the Baltic Sea are the Soviet republics of Estonia, Latvia, and Lithuania. The cultural flavor of this part of the Soviet Union is distinctly Western European. The peoples in these republics were traditionally Protestant or Roman Catholic rather than Russian Orthodox, their languages use the Latin alphabet instead of Russian Cyrillic, and their attitude toward Russians is noticeably cool. In Estonia especially, an independence of mind and lifestyle is evident. Closely linked to the Finns by an almost identical language, Estonians watch Helsinki television and look westward for their cultural sustenance. Most of them have made little effort to master the Russian language, and they speak it ungrammatically and with a heavy accent. At its traditional song festival, where tens of thousands of voices join in singing folk songs, a young singer captured the feeling succinctly. "The first number," she said, "is dedicated to Lenin and the last song to the friendship of the Soviet peoples, but what is in between belongs to us."[8]

The Southern Slavs: Belorussia and the Ukraine

The Belorussians and Ukrainians are linked with Great Russia by race, a common religion, and Cyrillic-based languages, yet there are historic differences that distinguish them. Belorussia is largely assimilated into Russian culture and has, in fact, never enjoyed any extended period of national independence. Successively ruled by Lithuania, Poland, and Russia, the republic was fully absorbed by the Soviet Union after World War II.

The Ukraine, on the other hand, retains a cultural pride and uniqueness that have kept alive its differences from Great Russia, even though it has been a part of Russia and the Soviet Union since the seventeenth century. In 1917, the Ukrainians attempted to break free of Russia in the upheaval of the Revolution, but they were unsuccessful. As in Belorussia, the language of the Ukraine is similar to but not the same as Russian, and many Ukrainians prefer to use it. But in contrast, most Belorussian schools are taught in Russian, whereas a large (though declining) majority of Ukrainian schools are taught in the native language.[9]

Politically, the Ukraine has prospered since the Stalinist period. Numerous Ukrainian leaders have held positions on the Party Politburo, and two major national leaders, Nikita Khrushchev and Leonid Brezhnev (both Russians), spent years in the Ukraine on the way to the top. As they moved up, they brought Ukrainian colleagues along with them. In a political sense, therefore, the Ukrainian Republic is well integrated into the Soviet system.

The Moldavians

South of the Ukraine, lying along the Rumanian border, is the territory of Moldavia, the second smallest and yet most densely populated of the fifteen republics. Annexed by the USSR in 1940, Moldavia is the only area of the present-day Soviet Union that was not a part of the earlier czarist empire. It is an agricultural area known for its vineyards and tobacco fields.

The Transcaucasian Peoples

A traveler moving eastward from Slavic Russia into the Caucasus Mountains would be entering the territory of the Georgians, Armenians, and Azerbaijanis. The peoples in these republics are strikingly different from both the Baltic and Slavic populations of the western USSR and from each other as well. The Georgian people are Christian and of European descent, while the Armenians are Christian but have an Asiatic background. The Azerbaijanis are Moslem with a heritage of Mongolian and Persian cultures.

Georgia and Armenia are ancient civilizations with established roots that predate the Roman empire by a thousand years. Yet they are among the most modern and prosperous of Soviet peoples. Incorporated into Russia in the early nineteenth century, they have developed a way of living with their Soviet compatriots that allows them considerable freedom of economic and cultural activity.

The Azerbaijanis are an ancient but less affluent people, living mainly in the arid lowlands of the Eastern Caucasus. Their primary resource is oil; the capital city, Baku, sits atop one of the world's great oil reserves. Azerbaijanis are Shi'ite, rather than Sunni, Moslems, and are ethnically related to the people of Iran, with whom they share a national border.

The Central Asian Peoples

In czarist times, central Asia, like Siberia, was viewed simply as a remote outpost of the empire. The whole area was known as Russian Turkestan, and its present

Boundaries of Soviet Socialist Republics (S.S.R.)

Boundaries of Autonomous Soviet
Socialist Republics (A.S.S.R.)

Wrangel I.

BERING

SEA

OCEAN

SEVERNAYA
ZEMLYA

NEW SIBERIAN
ISLANDS

LAPTEV

SEA

SOCIALIST REPUBLICS

YAKUT A.S.S.R.

REPUBLIC

SOCIALIST

SEA

OF

OKHOTSK

Sakhalin I

Kuril Islands

BURYAT-MONGOL
A.S.S.R.

MONGOLIAN

REPUBLIC

CHINA

SEA

OF

JAPAN

NORTH
KOREA

SOUTH
KOREA

JAPAN

division into five separate republics did not occur until the 1920s and 1930s. The major ethnic groups in these republics—Kazakhs, Uzbeks, Turkmeni, Tadjiks, and Kirghizi—share a number of characteristics even though the Tadjiks are of Iranian descent while the others have Turkish and Mongolian roots. Their religion is Islam and they speak closely related languages. Living along the borders of Iran, Afghanistan, and China, which also include substantial numbers of these peoples, the central Asians have traditionally been nomadic, desert peoples, congregating in ancient oases that, in the late twentieth century, are rapidly expanding into medium-sized cities. Some of them—Bukhara and Samarkand in Uzbekistan, for example—are among the oldest cities in the world, dating back, in legend if not strictly in fact, to 3,000 years before the birth of Christ.

The central Asian population is increasing at a considerably faster rate than is the Slavic population. The people have also proved difficult to assimilate into Soviet culture. Many cling to Moslem values and social practices and to ways of life that defy the modernization that is underway throughout the country. Partly in an effort to counter this situation, the Soviet leaders have encouraged the migration of Slavic and Baltic people to central Asia. This has resulted in a substantial dilution of the indigenous populations, to the extent, for example, that Kazakhs account for only one-third of the total population of the Kazakh Republic. In the five republics together, only about two-thirds of the population are of the titular nationality,[10] and that proportion is declining despite the high birth rate.

THE SMALLER MINORITIES

The administrative division of the USSR into fifteen union-republics has afforded most of the larger ethnic groups a special identity as the constituent elements of the USSR. Each republic has its own constitution, Council of Ministers, and legislature, along with a number of formal rights granted by the constitution. In addition to the republics, designated territories of lesser political standing have been given to some of the smaller minorities. These include autonomous republics, autonomous regions, and national areas. All of these are contained within a union republic, most of them (twenty-one of twenty-eight) in the RSFSR.

These territories provide an important setting in which ethnic groups can preserve some degree of cultural uniqueness within the overall Soviet context. Major ethnic groups that have been denied territorial recognition, such as Germans, Poles, and Jews,[11] find it more difficult to retain their cultural identities.

The extent of land area and the diversity of peoples constitute both a resource and a challenge to Soviet leaders. They are an important part of the environment in which the political system operates, and we shall examine that connection in the chapters that follow.

NOTES

1. Andrea Lee, *Russian Journal* (New York: Random House, 1981).
2. Ibid., p. 146–47.
3. For an interesting discussion of this issue, see Graeme Gill, "Institutionalisation and Revolution: Rules and the Soviet Political System," *Soviet Studies* XXXVII:2, April 1985, pp. 212–26; and a brief discussion of this article by William Maley and Graeme Gill in the same journal, January 1986, pp. 103–108.
4. See Leslie Symons *The Soviet Union, A Systematic Geography* (Totowa, N.J.: Barnes & Noble, 1983), p. 39; and Dan Fisher, "Soviets Gold Rich 'Pole of Cold' has Relatively Easy Winter," *Los Angeles Times,* 4 April, 1979.
5. David Shipler, *Russia, Broken Idols, Solemn Dreams* (New York: Times Books, 1983), pp. 185–86.
6. *New York Times,* 11 August, 1985. One other term—"Soviet Russia"—is sometimes heard, presumably to distinguish the present, postrevolutionary system of government from "czarist Russia." This term, however, has no official standing and is better avoided.
7. *SSSR v Tsifrakh, 1983,* (Moscow: Financy i Statistika, 1984), pp. 11–12.
8. *The Soviet Union* (Alexandria, Va: Time-Life Books, 1985), p. 70.
9. See Helene Carrere d'Encausse, *Decline of an Empire* (New York: Harper & Row, 1978), p. 177.
10. Vadim Medish, *The Soviet Union,* 2d ed. (Englewood Cliffs, N.J.: Prentice-Hall, 1984), p. 50.
11. A Jewish Autonomous Region, Birobidjan, exists in the far east, but it is so far removed from the urban centers of European Soviet Union where most Jews live that no more than 1 percent of Soviet Jews have chosen to live there.

PART 1

The Creation of the Soviet Union

The Soviet Union of the 1980s bears little resemblance to Russia of a century ago. Today a modern, urbanized, Communist superpower stands in stark contrast to the backward, stagnant empire of the last Romanov czars. It is hard to imagine a modern country in which the changes of the twentieth century have been more dramatic.

And yet the USSR of today also bears little likeness to the postcapitalist utopia of Marx's imagination or even to the postrevolutionary society heralded in Lenin's early writings. The contemporary Soviet political system is far more the work of Joseph Stalin than of either Marx or Lenin. But even Stalin's system of government has been modified and superseded since his death.

Despite these incongruities, the Soviet political system of today bears the unmistakable imprint of all those influences. Beneath the patina of post-Stalinist Communism and world-power status, the USSR is still a country that endured centuries of czarist autocracy, a violent ideological revolution, and a quarter century of wrenching brutality and furious change during the Stalinist era. All have left their marks on the present political system. It is essential, therefore, that the student of Soviet politics attain a grasp of the impact of these three historic influences.

To emphasize the importance of the past is not to succumb to the fallacy of historicism. The contemporary Soviet Union is not the inevitable conse-quence of its past, either czarist or Bolshevik. Through the course of the past thousand years there were many critical periods in which the future development of Russia or the Soviet Union might have moved in any of several directions. That it took the road it did in each case was not inevitable, but it was significant. It demonstrated which social forces favoring or opposing change proved to be dominant at that time.

If the present is not the inevitable product of the past, therefore, it is at least consistent with that past. Nineteenth-century czarism might not have culminated in the 1917 Revolution, or Leninism in Stalinism, but in both cases they did. And the contemporary scholar is entitled to draw some conclusions from those facts. In the three chapters that follow in this section, the objective is not simply to review the history of the Soviet political system. Whatever the intrinsic fascination of Russian and Soviet history, our subject is contemporary Soviet politics. We shall examine briefly only those periods in the immediate and more distant past that seem to bear directly on the nature of the present political system. Our concern is particularly with the alternatives for future development that were available at different times and the choices that were made by those with the power to influence history. Whether other choices might have been made and whether, if so, the course of history might have been radically different, is something we are not given to know.

CHAPTER 2
The Origins of Soviet Autocracy

Shortly before midnight on July 16, 1918, Nicholas II, his wife, Alexandra, their son and four daughters, together with a doctor and three servants, were awakened by their Bolshevik guards and moved to a basement room of Ipatiev House with instructions to await transportation to a new location. Minutes later, a squad of soldiers burst into the room and opened fire with revolvers, killing all present. Thus in the small Siberian village of Ekaterinburg ended the lives of the last czar of all the Russias and his family, casualties of history and of powerful revolutionary forces that had risen up in Russia to end three centuries of rule by Romanov emperors and empresses.

Soviet historians invariably mark the 1917 Revolution as the end of one historic era and the beginning of a new one, conceived of by two German philosophers, Karl Marx and Friedrich Engels, and brilliantly carried out by Lenin and the Bolshevik faction of the Russian Social Democratic Party. Because history tends to be written by those on the winning side, this version of the meaning of the events of 1917 has become the conventional truth to generations of Soviet citizens. Even in the West, where the writing of history is a more disputatious vocation, few would deny the enormous importance of the cataclysmic events of 1917, not only for Russians but also for much of the rest of the world.

Consider the contrasts before and after the Russian Revolution. For hundreds of years prior to 1917, Russia's rulers were raised in splendor and privilege and assumed the throne as legitimate successors to the royal line, even where that legitimacy (as in the case of Catherine the Great, for example) had to be established through political intrigue, bribery, or murder. After the revolution, the acknowledged leader of the state was a middle-aged lawyer—Vladimir Ilyich Ulyanov, known as Lenin—who had spent most of his adult life in exile or hiding from the police. Lenin's colleagues in power included a potpourri of itinerant intellectuals, radical poets, labor organizers, and miscellaneous revolutionaries, all graduates of czarist labor camps and prisons.

Again, before the revolution, access to upper-class vocations and lifestyles was virtually closed to the 90 percent of the population who were peasants and laborers. After 1917, proof of a peasant or worker background was essential to opportunities for education, career advancement, and participation in the political process.

And in prerevolutionary Russia, the czar's power was virtually unchallenged, leaving to a single—sometimes brilliant, sometimes benevolent, sometimes demented—individual the fate of millions of silent Russians who looked upon the czar not only as ruler but also as God on earth. After the Revolution, the instruments of power passed, formally at least, to the great unwashed Russian lower class, whose membership in soviets (elected councils), village committees, mass organizations, and the Communist Party was declared to constitute a new form of mass democracy that had completely replaced the traditional autocracy.

As dramatic as the changes in Russian life and politics were during the first years after the Revolution, only fanatics and dreamers would argue that everything had changed; that the memories of wars and famines, of victory and devastation, of Mongols and Romanovs, of enslavement and emancipation, of obeisance to orthodox religion and veneration of the father/czar—all deeply embedded in the collective consciousness of the Russian people, celebrated in song and legend, and reflected in centuries of development of the national character—that all this was wiped out in a moment of revolution or even in a half-century of "reeducation."

It is, in fact, a central theme of this book that the Russian Revolution, despite its thorough destruction of the former ruling class and its replacement by a new elite and a new ideology, maintained the same absolutist and autocratic form of rule that had dominated Russia for over four centuries. For any other form or government to have arisen out of the 1917 uprising—liberal democracy, prole-tarian socialism, parliamentary monarchy, or whatever—would have required some foundation for it to rest upon: a parliament, at least, ready to assume real power; political parties that had already achieved the support of major elements of the population; an economic structure that stood to gain by radical change; a mass population receptive to the idea of self-government; and a set of ideas sufficiently persuasive to justify the changes to elites and masses alike. Most of the countries of Western Europe, for example, witnessed the building of such foundations over several centuries, foundations upon which were created institutions of parliamen-tary democracy, substantial degrees of individual freedom, tolerance for religious and ethnic differences (with some obvious exceptions), and economic systems characterized largely by private ownership and competitive market systems.

Was such a foundation being created in Russia in the centuries before the Revolution? Despite some gradual economic and political changes that were taking place in the period, the answer is clearly no. The foundations that were laid during the course of Russian history were invariably those that strengthened the autoc-racy and hampered the rise of new forces that might eventually have diminished and democratized the power of government.

The autocracy that governed Russia at the moment of revolution was the product of ten centuries of development, which produced, before and after the Revolution, a political system predicated on undivided and unlimited power, severe restrictions on individual freedom, a rigid orthodoxy of ideas, culture, and behavior, and a command economy based on state ownership and comprehensive planning. It is useful to view this long history in three periods, each of which marked a stage in the development of czarist absolutism and which provides a fruitful comparison with Western Europe during the same periods: (1) the period of *nation-building,* in which Moscow triumphed over other cities in melding together a nation and imposing on it a Muscovite style of rule (A.D. 900 to 1600); (2) the period of *monarchic absolutism,* during which rulers sought permanent economic and social bases for their power while competing forces struggled to limit that power (1600 to 1800); and (3) the period of *modernization and social change* (nineteenth century).

Throughout these periods, the diverging paths followed by Western Europe and Russia provide the clearest basis for understanding the profound political differences between them in the twentieth century. They will also help to explain why a Communist revolution, believed by Marx (and even by Lenin) to be far more likely to occur in Germany or England than in Russia, succeeded only in Russia and failed everywhere else in the aftermath of World War I.

CREATING A NATION (A.D. 900–1600)

The origins of the Slavic peoples who came to inhabit the ancient "Rus" are buried in the conjectures of medieval historians. Probably in the seventh century it was possible to distinguish among the three major groups that came to inhabit separate sections of eastern and northern Europe: the southern or Baltic Slavs (the present-day Bulgarians and Yugoslavians), the western Slavs (Czechs, Moravians, Poles), and the eastern Slavs, who came to be known much later as Russians.

Among these eastern Slavs were, by the ninth century, three distinguishable branches occupying adjacent territories. In the northeastern plains of the Volga and Oka rivers, where Slavs intermingled with Finns, the people later to be known as "Great Russians" were in the process of formation. In the southeast, the area where Kiev now lies amid the valleys of the Dnieper and Dniester rivers, were Slavs who had close contact with Byzantine civilization and with nomadic Turks and central Asians. These came in modern times to be known as "little Russians" or "Ukrainians" (which means "frontiersmen"). And in the northwest a third variation, later known as "White Russians," slowly developed from the absorption of Lithuanians by the Slavs in the western lands from Lake Ladoga south to the border of present-day Poland.

During the ninth century, the majority of Slavs were nomads dwelling in the forests and steppes of central Russia. As trade with European cities and with the Byzantine empire grew, settlements along the river plains expanded into towns and cities, both to promote trade and to protect the people from attacks by wandering nomads. In the north, Novgorod, Pskov, and Polotsk grew to control the territories around them; in the center, Smolensk and Rostov arose, while in the south, Chenigov, Pereaslavl, and Kiev dominated the countryside.

In all, there were over sixty Russian principalities of considerable importance and duration, as well as many more transient ones. The early development of Russia is concentrated in the story of three of them: Kiev, Novgorod, and Moscow. At different times, each was the dominant political, cultural, and commercial center of the eastern Slavic peoples. Each had its own character, which it imparted to the mosaic of Russian history. But in the end only one of them—Moscow—survived to create around itself and its rulers a unified, powerful, all-Russian state. It is intriguing, therefore, to consider the character of these three cities, for whichever of them had emerged as the dominant national center would have infused the whole of Russia with its unique nature.

Kiev

For three centuries, until its obliteration by the Russian armies of Andrei Bogolubsky in 1169, Kiev was the center of Russian civilization. Lying midway along the great inland water route between the Baltic Sea and Constantinople, Kiev was a natural trading and commercial center and accumulated great wealth from the endless caravans that plied the rivers and steppes of northeastern Europe. It was also a paragon of cultural achievement. "The Annals of this time," a British historian records,

> bear emphatic testimony to the learning of the Russian princes of the Great Kievan time, and to their zeal for culture—their knowledge of other tongues . . . , their wide reading, their book collections, their foundation of schools, their encourage-ment of Greek and Latin study, their reception of foreign scholars. Before the era of our Norman Conquest something of a Russian literature had been founded and there are Russian manuscripts of the twelth century which can almost be compared with really fine examples from the West.[1]

In many respects, Kievan Russia was more European than it was Russian. It never developed the extreme subordination of citizen to ruler that increasingly characterized the northern cities of Vladimir and, later, Moscow. In fact, the famous "Testament" (Pouchenie) of Kiev's Prince Vladimir, issued in 1113, stands as one of the most liberal statements of political rights to emerge from any part of Europe in that century. It not only granted the right of landowners and prominent citizens to share in the decision-making process and to be secure in their property and privileges, but it also made major concessions to the poor of Kiev who tended to be heavily in debt and badly treated. And this occurred a century before the Magna Carta was dragged out of a bitterly resistant King John of England.

Furthermore, political power was broadly decentralized in Kievan Russia, and the residents of the city-states had the right, through their city assemblies (vieches), to be consulted in the choice of a ruler. Occasionally, the people would reject a new ruler, complicating the succession process considerably.

The combination of a high level of culture, a relatively liberal economic and social orientation, and limited and decentralized political power seemed to offer to Kievan Russia, in its early years at least, the possibility of holding the northern Slavic peoples within the cultural framework of western and central Europe despite the influence of Byzantine civilization on Kiev.

Had Kievan Russia endured, the contemporary Soviet Union might have experienced a history far more closely linked to that of Europe, with its Reforma-tion and Renaissance, its Enlightenment in the eighteenth century, and its democratization in the nineteenth and twentieth centuries. But this was not to be.

For Kievan Russia existed at a time of mass migrations of Asian peoples toward Europe, of more or less continuous and unbelievably savage wars with these peoples, of the centuries-long struggle between the western and eastern branches of Christendom, and of gradually changing patterns of commerce and trade that eventually deprived Kiev of its central economic role in northern Europe. At another time, in another part of Europe, the basic values of Kievan Russia might have flourished. But in the steppes and forests of medieval Russia, they were no match for the powerful and violent forces that swept the country.

Lord Novgorod the Great

As Kiev declined, the northwestern city of Novgorod gradually became the center of north Slavic development. Situated on both banks of the Volkhov River, Novgorod was the chief link between the eastern Russian city-states and the trade routes of western Europe, and it was strongly influenced by the Scandinavian cultures of its closest neighbors. The striking thing about Novgorod (called "Lord Novgorod the Great" by its citizens) was its indominable spirit of independence as well as its commitment to a democratic form of government—to be sure, a thirteenth, not a twentieth, century form of democracy. Like other city-states, Novgorod was ruled by a prince, but unlike the others Novgorod's prince enjoyed only limited powers, which he shared with three other politicized groups: the permanent, landowning boyar class; the commercial class, which included many foreigners; and the mass citizenry organized into a popular assembly (*vieche*).

The principle of election as the proper way to chose leaders, which had begun to develop in the last decades of Kiev's existence, came to full flower in Novgorod in the twelth century. In 1126, the office of mayor (*posadnik*) was recognized as an elective office, followed shortly by that of the chief of the town militia. Within a generation, the bishop came to be elected, and before the end of the century even the position of prince was recognized as subject to the choice of the citizens of Novgorod.

As a democratic institution, the *vieche* was a crude but often decisive reflection of the popular will. It could be called into session by the prince or other official or, theoretically, by any citizen. Sometimes, rival *vieches* were convened by feuding officials each seeking vindication. As in other early democracies (the Puritan town meeting or the ecclesia of ancient Athens, for example), the *vieche* required unanimity for its decisions. When the mind of the gathering became clear, those who continued to protest were often "bludgeoned, ducked, drowned, put to the sword or expelled."[2]

Despite the frequent activities of the *vieche*, Novgorod was normally ruled by an elite of noblemen, wealthy landowners, merchants, and clergy. Where the prince was a dominant personality, such as Vladimir the Lawgiver in the eleventh century, or Alexander Nevsky in the thirteenth century, he ruled with a relatively free hand, although even Nevsky himself was briefly expelled from the city after an argument with the *vieche*. But the citizens of Novgorod were an ever-present threat to the rulers, and there is a long list of princes who were "shown the road" out of the city by an aroused citizenry. One historian called Novgorod "a fickle democracy, whose chief activity is commerce, and to whom the right of insurrection is sacred."[3] It was populated by citizens, not subjects, who demanded to be consulted on major decisions and whose ultimate approval was necessary to legitimize the authority of the prince.

During its ascendency, Novgorod commanded a great empire in northern Russia. But it was also seriously dependent on resources which it could not provide itself, chiefly goods received through trade with Europe and grain and other foodstuffs that the city was forced to import from the Moscow-Suzdal-Vladimir lands to the east. Ultimately, the independence of Novgorod was compromised by the weakness of its pluralist political system and its constant need for grain. As the power of Moscow increased, its princes were able to capitalize on both characteristics in bringing Novgorod under their control. Whether Novgorod could have protected her empire had Moscow's power not become so formidable is an unanswerable question. But like Kiev before her, Novgorod fell before Russian conditions that seemed to demand a more centralized, aggressive, and militaristic leadership than either city could provide. Ultimately, only Moscow proved capable of providing that leadership. But the price was very high.

Before considering the rise of Moscow, we must take account of one of the extraordinary conditions under which that rise took place. That was the Mongol occupation of Russia that began as Novgorod was declining and lasted until Moscow was securely established as the capital of the Russian nation.

The Mongol Invasion

"For our sins came unknown tribes. No one knows exactly who they are, nor whence they came out, nor what their faith is, but they call them Tatary. . . ."[4] Thus, the *Chronicle of Novgorod* describes the people who emerged out of the Gobi Desert in northern China to conquer much of the known world in the thirteenth century. Guided by the military genius of Genghis Khan, 300,000 mounted Asian horsemen moved westward across Siberia to the Ural Mountains and beyond into Russia, Hungary, and Galicia and southward to the Adriatic Sea.

In the spring of the year 1224, the first elements of an advance Mongol army were sighted on Russian territory and were met on the banks of the Kalka River by the hastily assembled forces of two great Russian princes, Mstislav the Daring and Daniel of Galicia. After a ferocious battle, the Mongols defeated the Russians and put the soldiers to the sword. As their war creed forbade the execution of military leaders, the Mongols built a great platform of wood on top of nearly a hundred Russian officers and princes and held a victory feast on the platform, crushing the Russians to death.

Disappearing as quickly as they had come, the Mongols did not appear again on Russian territory until 1236, this time under the command of Genghis Khan's nephew, Batu. And this time they were there to stay. In a relentless sweep across

European Russia, the Mongols descended like locusts upon city after city, destroying Ryazan, burning Moscow to the ground, turning aside before reaching Novgorod only because of impassable marshes but massing the full force of their armies for the drive on Kiev. That ancient capital of Russia was sacked so thoroughly that travelers five years later could find only a few scattered houses to mark where the city had once stood, and it was not until the nineteenth century that Kiev reemerged as a great and prosperous city. The barbaric cruelty of the Mongol undertaking was unsurpassed even by medieval standards. "They slew all," the *Chronicle of Novgorod* relates, "from the male sex even to the female, all the priests and the monks, and all, stripped and reviled, gave up their soul to the Lord in a bitter and a wretched death."[5]

The facts of the Mongol invasion and occupation of Russia are not in dispute, but a lively controversy surrounds the two and a half centuries (1236–1480) in which Russia lived under the "Tatar yoke." Some historians are convinced that the Mongol occupation is the primary source of absolutism in Russia. Thus, in a biography of the Romanovs, Virginia Cowles states that "although the Russians had been converted to Christianity at the end of the tenth century the Mongolian invasion two hundred and fifty years later had turned their piety into superstition, introduced autocracy in its most desperate form, and left behind a society both savage and perverse."[6] On the other hand, Jesse Clarkson contends that "the 'Tatar yoke,' catastrophic though the term sounds, made remarkably little difference to the history of Russia."[7]

In one sense, the issue is unresolvable, for we have no idea how Russia would have turned out had the Mongols never entered the scene. Further, there is little point in comparing Muscovite Russia after the Mongol occupation with Kievan Russia before. Moscow was different from Kiev in important ways long before the Mongol era began. Still, the Mongols ruled Russia for two and a half centuries. And the evidence, inferential though it may be, does lend itself to the conclusion that the Mongol influence in the development of early Russia was great and that it permanently strengthened the evolution of absolutism and autocracy in Russia.

The Mongols themselves were a people organized primarily for war. The political structure was strongly militaristic, and within the highest circles there was a ruthless pursuit of power that resulted in relentless intrigues, assassinations, purges, and a high degree of insecurity. The Khan ruled by divine right, and ruled absolutely over all aspects of the lives of his subjects. These qualities were symbolized by the title "czar," which the Russians first applied to the Byzantine emperor, then to the Mongol Khan, and only later, after the Mongol "Golden Horde" had disintegrated and their power had transferred to Moscow, to the Russian ruler Ivan III.

The most significant impact that the Mongol occupation had on Russia was in ensuring that Moscow, with its autocratic tendencies, would come to dominate and unite Russia, and in the process would undermine and eventually destroy the inchoate democratic and pluralist spirit of some of the other major cities. When the Mongol Khans commanded the payment of tribute, Muscovite rulers proved more than willing to cooperate in enforcing those commands. As the tribute was burdensome, the resistance of the Russian people was great. This pitted Moscow's rulers against their own people, and the princes often used Mongol troops to put down popular resistance.

As Moscow extended her dominance over Russia, the Khans supported the creation of a unified state in the interest of orderly collection of the tribute. When a city refused to pay or to provide recruits for the Khan's armies, the Mongols launched punitive expeditions, smashing towns and massacring the population. Michael Florinsky estimates that between 1240 and 1460, Mongol armies swept over Russian lands forty-eight times, an average of once every four years for over two centuries![8] And even after the empire of the Golden Horde broke up in the late fifteenth century, the Mongol states that continued to exist waged intermittent war on Russian cities for two more centuries.

What this demanded of Muscovite rulers was permanent military mobilization, sometimes against the Mongols, often against other Russians, and periodically against invading European armies. Under these circumstances, the centralization of power in Moscow and its harsh and absolutist application were inevitable and essential. Earlier tendencies toward citizen participation in government came to be viewed as unaffordable luxuries and were gradually eliminated. By the middle of the fourteenth century, the *vieche* had ceased to exist except in Novgorod and Pskov, and even there its significance declined sharply.

The legal and administrative systems of Moscow were also deeply penetrated by Mongol influence. The Code of the Great Yasa, given to the Mongol nation by Genghis Khan, was a primitive codification of customary law among the Mongols. This became part of the Russian code during the long Mongol occupation. Russian leaders were required to know the code and to abide by at least those parts that concerned their relations with the Mongols.

In one other way, perhaps the most important, early Russian development was profoundly affected by the Mongol occupation. This was in Russia's enforced isolation from Western Europe for two and a half centuries during which critical changes were taking place that would affect Europe's future for centuries to come. The Protestant Reformation brought a diverse and antiabsolutist quality to European society, while the Renaissance brought a civilizing influence at least to the upper classes. Literacy spread rapidly after the invention of movable type in the fifteenth century, and improvements in navigation and shipbuilding brought Europeans into contact with much of the rest of the world. By stark contrast, Russian civilization "had been completely thrown back, learning was almost lost, art in decline; and it is from this state of subjection, demoralization, and individual egotism that we must trace the beginnings of the power of Moscow."[9]

Moscow

As late as the twelfth century, when the mantle of Slavic leadership was passing from Kiev to Novgorod, Moscow was little more than a backwater outpost, avoided by ambitious princes and greatly overshadowed by the nearby towns of Vladimir and Suzdal. Yet within a century and a half, the few hundred square miles of Moscow's territory had expanded to well over fifteen thousand, incorporating within it many of the towns and settlements of the upper Volga and Oka river basins. Before another century had passed, Moscow had conquered and annexed Novgorod and other major city-states, ended the 250-year Mongol occupation, and unified the country for the first time into a strong political state with international ambitions.

In the process, the princes of Moscow extended to all of medieval Russia a form of rule that continues, in a modern version, to exist in the Soviet Union today. The essence of that form of rule is *absolutism,* the total monopolization of political power by the ruler. While in practice, no Russian or Soviet leader has succeeded in completely eliminating all other sources of potential power, the theory of absolutism as an ideology has dominated the minds of the ruling circles for centuries. It was, until the 1917 revolution, thoroughly supported by the Orthodox Russian church to the extent that religious excommunication was always a disciplinary weapon in the hands of the czar. It was deeply engrained in the psyche of the Russian peasant, who viewed the czar as a divine father and whose loyalty could be counted on in the long years of warfare, famine, and foreign occupation that periodically swept across Russia.

The rise of Moscow is reflected in the changing status of three major elements of medieval Russia: the boyar nobility, the peasantry, and the church. Through the Kievan and Novgorodian periods of development, the boyar class of major landowners and nobility constituted a political force that no prince could ignore. Exercising the "right of free service," boyars were able to shift their wealth and their peasant battalions from one prince to another in time of war so that their loyalty had to be purchased by a sharing of power. And their property was secure because their estates (called *votchina*) were privately owned and involved no obligation to the prince beyond the payment of taxes.

Through the fourteenth and fifteenth centuries, however, strong princes steadily diminished the independence of the boyars. The "right of free service" gradually disappeared as the boyars came to be severely punished for defections from one prince to another. To tighten the bonds even further. Muscovite rulers gradually transformed the *votchina* into *pomestie,* or estate ownership, tied to service to the state. By the sixteenth century, the difference between the two forms of estates had virtually disappeared, and all landowners were required to spend substantial periods of time in the service of the throne. This new status of the nobility was to play a crucial role in later centuries in preserving the autocratic position of the czar despite strong pressures for change.

The loss of independence and property rights suffered by the aristocracy was accompanied by an increasing yoke of servitude imposed on the peasantry. As agricultural productivity of the estates was usually the sole source of income for the landowners, they endeavored to tie the peasant ever more securely to an estate. For land was plentiful in early Russia, but labor was scarce. Peasants who ran away to avoid military service or high taxes could expect to homestead in more remote areas while often forcing former landlords into bankruptcy.

By the year 1500, national legislation had been enacted to restrict the movement of peasants and bind them to their landlords until their debts were paid off, which usually meant for life. Later the indebtedness was extended to the family of the serf, which locked successive generations into the bond of serfdom. As Alexander Yanov observes: "The free laborer gradually disappeared from the face of the Russian earth, and became a serf belonging either to other men or to the state. And this is how it would be for centuries to come."[10]

The institution of serfdom was profoundly debilitating to the Russian people and contributed directly to the strengthening of autocracy in modern Russia. Economically, serfdom prevented the development of a free labor force, which was essential for later industrial and manufacturing activities. Thus, it hindered the development of a bourgeoisie that could have challenged the power of the czar. Politically, it denied the peasants true citizenship, reducing them to the status of subjects who were never seen as legitimate participants in the political process. Socially, serfdom built a wall between the masses of peasants and the aristocracy, which prevented the kind of gradual accommodation of class interests that brought moderation and peaceful progress to most countries of Europe. In later centuries, the peasant/serf, having no legitimate channels through which to satisfy his needs and promote his interests, could either wait patiently until a conscience-stricken aristocracy threw a few crumbs his way, or rise up in violent revolt. For centuries the Russian peasant alternated between these two paths until the whole system collapsed in 1917.

The Orthodox Church suffered much the same fate as the nobility. After the 1441 unification of the Byzantine Church with Roman Catholicism, which the Russians vehemently opposed, the Russian church had lost its last link to an outside ecclesiastical authority that could challenge the Muscovite princes. Henceforth, the princes appointed and dismissed high Church leaders at will and the Church became an institution of the state. Thus was eliminated one other potential source of power with which to challenge the absolutism of the czar in later periods.

Despite the loss of independence suffered by the peasantry, the Church, and the nobility as the czars grew more powerful, it should not be concluded that this was solely the result of violence and coercion. Although brutal coercion was never far from the scene, it is also true that each of these classes found benefits as well as losses in their subordination to the czar. For the Church, Moscow represented a true center of Eastern Orthodoxy as well as a political force capable of protecting the Church's vast land holdings from warring princes.

The nobility gained protection from marauding tribes and European armies and retained many of its traditional privileges, indeed, many more than were retained by other European aristocracies in the late Middle Ages. And the peasantry often moved voluntarily into serfdom for the protection that a landed boyar could provide and the security of a communal existence that the large farm communities offered. If the peasant could never realistically expect to repay his debts to the landlord, and thus was probably indentured for life, at least his social standing was above that of slaves, and the rural village life he led had many compensations.

Furthermore, the country as a whole benefitted when the Muscovite czar could truly proclaim himself master over the entire country. By the sixteenth century, the success of Moscow's rulers in bringing order to the perennial conflicts among the lesser princes and in greatly expanding the kingdom of Moscow itself "contributed to the growth of a feeling of admiration for Moscow and its rulers, who inspired a sense of security and solidity in the people. . . . Moscow became the symbol of strength and unity."[11] The same mixture of resentment and pride has continued to characterize the attitude of many Russians toward their political system in the twentieth century.

To sum up, the formative period of Russian development (lasting until about 1600) produced a unified nation under the autocratic rule of a Muscovite czar, founded on a bitter history of war, hardship, and foreign domination, but also with a sense of nationhood and Slavic idealism that were destined to make Russia a formidable force in the evolving world of Europe and Asia. As one ponders the failure of modern Russia to conform to the broad changes in politics and culture that have liberalized and democratized the Western world during the past three centuries, there is no doubt that part of the explanation lies in the history of these formative years.

THE ERA OF MONARCHIC ABSOLUTISM: 1600–1800

The emergence of autocracy in Russia presaged a parallel development in Western Europe in the sixteenth and seventeenth centuries. The creation of nation-states out of feudal principalities greatly enhanced the power of the monarchs but also pitted them against the traditional nobility in a bitter struggle for power. European kings set out to destroy the power of the feudal nobility, and none attacked them more passionately than Louis XIV of France. He sold hundreds of noble patents to rich commoners, deprived the old nobility of their immunity to taxes, forced them to live at court if they wanted to hold on to their privileges, tore down the walls around their castles, and deprived them of their governmental positions. Louis also created his own national army, subjugated the Catholic Church, reduced the feudal parliaments to impotency, and built a strong national economy capable of making the state self-sufficient.

These changes were of enormous significance, for they meant the end of feudal constitutionalism and the emergence of monarchic absolutism. By the end of the seventeenth century, three great absolutist dynasties controlled most of continental Europe: the Bourbons in France, the Hohenzollerns in Prussia, and the Hapsburgs in Austria. At the same time, the Romanov dynasty was securely in power in Russia, and the czars ruled, as did the European monarchs, by virtue of the "divine right of kings." These apparently similar patterns of government concealed profound differences, however, reflected in the fact that within a century and a half, absolutism in Western Europe was in full retreat before a host of new challenges: the growing power of the bourgeoisie, the resurgence of parliamentary bodies, an aroused mass public, and the ideology of liberal democracy. In Russia, no such change took place, and at the time of the 1917 Revolution, czarist absolutism was still the dominant form of politics in that country. This dramatic difference resulted from three major factors.

The Nobility and the Bourgeoisie

The first difference involved the fate of the nobility in the two parts of Europe. In the west, kings destroyed the nobility as a significant class, whereas in Russia that was not necessary. Long before the seventeenth century, the nobility had been deprived of its independence and subordinated to the will of the czar. All property, titles, and privileges were tied to service to the state, which lasted a lifetime, either in the military or in the civil administration. The czar, therefore, had no need to destroy the nobility as a class, for they formed no threat to him. In fact, after Peter the Great's reign, subsequent czars increased the privileges of the nobility. The Charter of the Nobility, issued by Catherine the Great in 1785, gave to her favorite noblemen hundreds of thousands of peasant families and their land, which were formerly owned by the state. The charter also granted them the right to exercise governmental functions on their own properties.

The significance of preserving the nobility in Russia while destroying it in Western Europe can hardly be overemphasized. In Europe, the demise of the old aristocracy made way for a new class of wealthy and ambitious people to assume a leading role in the future development of the state. This was the bourgeoisie, composed of merchants, entrepreneurs, lawyers, bankers, and professional people. In the seventeenth and eighteenth centuries, they moved gradually into both the economic positions and political offices formerly monopolized by the nobility. They provided the financial income and the expertise that monarchs required to fight their wars, expand their economies, and maintain order in the cities and countryside. ". . . Even before the great revolutions of the seventeenth and eighteenth centuries," Jesse Clarkson writes, "this new class was able, by virtue of its economic independence, to set limits to the growth of the power of even the most absolute monarchs."[12]

In Russia, there was virtually no entrepreneurial class with independent financial resources, and given the dominant role of the landed aristocracy well into the nineteenth century, little possibility that a bourgeoisie would emerge. Overseas trade was carried on by English traders at St. Petersberg and most of Russia's goods sailed in British ships. Little support existed for industrial innovations or productivity; by 1800 Russian exports were still dominated by timber, hemp, pitch, and tallow, while iron dropped from 30 percent of exports fifty years earlier to 5 percent in 1800.

The absence of a bourgeoisie also affected the fate of the Russian peasantry, for the economic ambitions of a bourgeois class would have required a mobile and urbanized working class with technical skills, as was the case in Europe. In Russia in the seventeenth and eighteenth centuries, the peasantry sank ever deeper into serfdom as the nobility clung tightly to the land as its only means of producing wealth, and the czars abandoned the peasantry to the nobility.

Finally, the lack of a bourgeoisie in Russia protected the czars from mounting pressures for the development of political institutions sensitive to the interests of the new class. In Europe, in the confrontations between parliaments and monarchs that occurred with increasing intensity during these centuries, the new class invariably sided with parliament, more particularly with the lower houses of parliaments that were at the same time struggling against hereditary upper houses. In England, especially, the merchants and town leaders moved strongly to support the House of Commons in the confrontation that finally resulted in the civil war of 1642.

Modernizing Government

A second major factor was the development of bureaucratic and administrative agencies to govern the nation-states that were being formed out of feudal provinces in the seventeenth century. In most of Europe, these new agencies were staffed by commoners, usually lawyers and technically trained officials. Gradually, they formed a new sector of power in the political system, power that was based on expertise and the systematic administration of the laws rather than on high birth and private wealth. Efficient bureaucracies were created in Austria, Germany, and especially France, where the Napoleonic system, based on advancement by merit, the separation of political from administrative responsibilities, and a highly trained permanent civil service had been introduced. In Prussia, "the bureaucracy had worked itself free of the need for a continuing royal impulse."[13]

In Russia, despite the reforms of Peter the Great, the structures of government never developed that quality of professionalism and stability that characterized European bureaucracies. Peter established administrative agencies willy-nilly, then abolished them as his whims changed. In 1718, for example, he set up "colleges," or ministries, for foreign affairs, war, navy, revenue, justice, auditing, commerce, mines and manufacturing, and budget. Aside from those involved in making war, the colleges were highly temporary. They "underwent many changes in form and function, appearing and disappearing so rapidly in the decades following Peter's reign that keeping track of them would be an exercise in itself. A host of other offices, some collegial and some under a single head, emerged alongside them to serve this or that special purpose."[14] Peter also set up elaborate structures of local government, but soon abolished them.

Even at the highest level, this instability of institutions existed. Peter established a "Senate," as a kind of administrative cabinet, but never delegated it any significant power. His successors followed suit: Catherine I formed the Supreme

Privy Council; Ann created a *Kabinet;* Elizabeth had her *Konferentsia,* and Catherine the Great her *Soviet.* These bodies had little significance beyond the personal influence of their members.

The Nature of Monarchy

Finally, although European kings wielded autocratic power, as did the Russian czars, there was an important difference between the two in the nature of that power. From the sixteenth century to the eighteenth century, two different forms of absolutist rule succeeded one another in Europe. In the early period, theocratic absolutism was based squarely on the principle of divine right, namely, that the king was appointed by God and answerable only to Him. But this implied certain limitations on the ruler's power by virtue of "fundamental laws" to which the king was subject as was everyone else. In practice, the interpretation of those laws was pretty much the prerogative of the monarch, but the concept of limited power existed nonetheless. Monarchs were, in Jerome Blum's words, "limited if uncontrolled."[15]

In the eighteenth century, however, conceptions of monarchic rule were transformed during the Enlightenment by notions of reason and human well-being. The political tenets of the French *philosophes* produced a different justification for absolutism, whose most prominent spokesman was the English philosopher Thomas Hobbes. In his masterpiece, *Leviathan,* Hobbes argued that autocracy is justified not because it is divinely ordained but because it conforms to the dictates of reason. The alternative to autocracy was chaos, he said, and that was demonstrably in no one's interest. Reason also demanded that monarchs devote themselves to economic progress through modernization and innovation, raising the economic and legal status of peasants, reducing torture and brutality in society, and promoting public health and the welfare of children and other dependent citizens. In religious matters, "enlightened" monarchs were expected to be secular and tolerant of religious diversity.

In Russia, absolutism took a very different form. There, neither the limitation of fundamental or natural law nor the restraints of reason operated to limit the conception of the czar's role in the political system. Because the philosophies and morals of the Enlightenment failed to penetrate Muscovite society (despite the pretensions of Catherine the Great[16]), the idea of czarism based exclusively on the authority of God remained pristine and uncompromised until the monarchy itself collapsed in the ashes of World War I.

As the Romanovs and the nobility adhered tenaciously to the tenets of divine autocracy, the dismal circumstances of most peasants' lives failed to improve. Increasingly in the eighteenth century, the peasants were at the mercy of the nobility. All judicial and police processes outside the main cities were run by the landlords, and discipline was often arbitrary and harsh. Peasants on state lands fared considerably better than those on private estates, but czars and czarinas alike made lavish gifts of state land to generals, lovers, and even distinguished foreigners, and the peasants residing on such lands found their status even more depressed. Catherine the Great disposed of 800,000 state peasants in this manner, and her son, Paul, in the five brief years that he reigned, disposed of 530,000.[17] Further, by the end of the eighteenth century, serfdom had been extended to the Ukraine and other southern territories.

One of the most fateful legacies of Catherine's long reign was an intensifying of the alienation between the mass of peasants and the aristocracy. As the elite took up Western values, clothes styles, and culture, French became the language of the aristocracy and the number of Europeans who owned property in Russia increased. To many peasants, their landlords not only adopted European manners but often were in fact European and not Russian. While Western Europe was evolving into a complex hierarchy of social classes during this period, Russia remained rigidly divided between the mass peasantry and the aristocracy. There were merchants, military and clerical groups, townspeople, and other minor social strata, but they were small in number and sociologically insignificant. The separation between peasant and aristocracy was a major cause of the ultimate breakdown of the monarchy in 1917, for the absence of a more diversified social structure made it easier for the masses of Russians to unite in common opposition to the autocracy.[18]

The regime's failure to respond to the grievances of the peasantry led to periodic uprisings, the most serious of which was instigated by an illiterate Cossack named Emelian Pugachev in 1773. Leading a mass of runaway serfs, anticzarist Cossacks, non-Russian tribes from the Volga region, and Old-Believers protesting religious persecution, Pugachev threatened Catherine the Great's reign for over a year. In the end, the "vile comedy" was mercilessly crushed and Pugachev was brought to Moscow in an iron cage and publicly beheaded.

The reaction of the nobility was to turn the screws of repression ever tighter. As Lentin notes, "The [Pugachev] rebellion served to divide society more rigidly than ever into 'two nations.' At best, the peasant was regarded as a wayward and unruly child; at worst, as a mutinous savage. Either way, the moral was the same: he had to be kept firmly in his place. Reformist views took on an untimely and even subversive aspect, especially in the light of events in France [the revolution of 1789]."[19] Smaller uprisings were common throughout both the eighteenth and nineteenth centuries, but none lasted very long and all were met with brutal repression.

Catherine the Great died in 1796, and was succeeded briefly by her son, Paul, a neurotic tyrant whose assassination in 1801 was widely applauded within the aristocracy. The legacy that Catherine left to Russia was both splendid and tragic. Among her achievements was the expansion of the Russian empire to all parts of Europe that had ever been under Russian control, including Lithuania, a large slice of Poland, and the whole of the Crimea to the Black Sea. It was an era of "greatness" for Russia, an "outwardly brilliant reign," as one historian character- ized it.[20]

Inwardly, however, the "brilliance" was tarnished by Catherine's failure to deal with, or even understand, the profound malaise that had fastened itself on Russian society. On all sides, social conditions demanded change, but there was no mechanism for change. No constitution existed to mobilize mass protests against absolutism as occurred in Spain, Portugal, and Italy (1820); no parliament provided a stage on which to trumpet the liberal doctrines of the middle classes, as in England; no *Burschenschaften* (college student groups) paraded through the streets of Moscow demanding an end to tyranny, as they did in Berlin; no urban proletariat threw down their tools at the call of socialist union leaders, as they did all over Western Europe after mid-century; and no czar humbled himself before the rise of representative democracy, as did Queen Victoria in England, Frederick VII in Denmark, and monarchs in the Netherlands, Belgium, and Switzerland.

The attempts by Russian czars to deal with the problems of the next century clearly revealed the absence of any forces capable of reducing the power of the autocracy or of securing an effective voice for the Russian people in the councils of state.

THE NINETEENTH CENTURY: MODERNIZATION AND SOCIAL CHANGE

For Western Europe, the nineteenth century was one of those periods in history when everything changes. In that hundred years, nearly half the population moved from rural to urban environments and from farming to factories and offices; life expectancy nearly doubled; illiteracy was virtually eliminated; and governments changed from absolute monarchies to representative systems based on universal (male) suffrage. Large socialist parties were formed in almost all countries, and the idea that governments were responsible to the people was taking root throughout the European continent.

None of this occurred without struggle, and the old aristocracy vigorously resisted the changes. Revolts broke out repeatedly during the century, and monarchs did their best to put them down. But Europe was pregnant with change, and the forces for change had gathered strength and numbers and wealth, and they laid siege to absolutist monarchies until the latter could stand no longer.

These changes were the result primarily of three powerful forces that gathered momentum as the century wore on:

1. *Capitalism:* the accumulation of wealth for investment in private hands, which stimulated a phenomenal growth in industrial, manufacturing, and financial activities as well as in the political power of the bourgeoisie.
2. *Liberalism:* a fundamental commitment to the well-being and dignity of the individual, regardless of social class, and a positive duty of government to protect individual freedom and the exercise of individual rights. Health and welfare services were expanded greatly, free public education was introduced, and the rights of ordinary people were written into laws and constitutions.
3. *Democracy:* the rights of citizens to determine who shall govern them and to

ratify or reject basic governmental decisions. Gradually, the franchise was extended to the entire male population, and political parties came to reflect more closely the views of that population.

At the outset of the nineteenth century, these forces had tenuous footholds in Western Europe. But in the course of that century and the first years of the next, they would come to dominate Western Europe.

At the same point in time, none of these three forces had roots in the political culture of the Russian people. Although there were some wealthy families engaged in private enterprises, most investment funds were monopolized by the czar and those close to him. Aside from small-scale enterprises, all manufacturing and mining was funded and controlled by the state and was worked mainly by indentured serfs rather than free labor. The concept of the autonomous individual, so fundamental to liberalism, was not only not prevalent but was confuted by the deeply embedded notion of the commune, within which Russian peasants had lived for centuries and which historically took precedence over the individual. And democracy required forms of organization and resources that did not exist in Russia. Primarily they required political parties, which emerged in Europe as factions of the nobility and expanded to include the emergent bourgeois, intellectual, and professional classes. In Russia, these classes had relatively few members and even fewer resources with which to challenge the czar.

Nevertheless, the Russian aristocracy watched developments in Europe with great anxiety and did its best to shield the Russian people from their influence. Whatever reforms were necessary to resolve national problems in Russia, they would have to be consistent with the absolutist form of rule that remained strongly entrenched at the end of the eighteenth century. There was never, in the nineteenth century, any real prospect for liberal democracy or capitalism, for none of the social, economic, or political preconditions that were essential to such developments in Europe were present in Russia. Even among the most radical opponents of czarist autocracy, there was little support for Western liberal democracy.

The problems that Russia faced at this time were deeply troubling to many of the czar's advisers. The peasantry was chronically angry about its status; the economy was sinking ever lower in its capacity to compete with Europe or even to participate profitably in European trade; the state of education, medical care, communications, transportation, and urbanization was embarassingly inferior to that of even some of the lesser European states; and the need for money to run the empire was a constant problem for the czar. In a century when Western Europe was more or less at peace after the Napoleonic wars, Russia waged an almost continuous military campaign to expand the empire, and it lost a major confrontation with Britain, France, and Turkey in the Crimea (1854–1856).

The problems of Russia brought forth Russian solutions. Over and over, reforms were conceived by the autocracy only to be abandoned because of a czar's fear that the reactions to reform efforts constituted threats to his position, or because members of the aristocracy who served the czar worked to sabotage the reforms before they could take effect.

Reform and Reaction

In 1801, Alexander I began his twenty-five-year reign with considerable support from liberals. He initially abolished the harsh security practices that had existed since Peter the Great and established the "nonofficial committee" for the purpose of drafting a constitution for Russia. The committee met for two years before abandoning the effort, and in another two years the security apparatus was back in force. In 1809, Michael Speransky, a close adviser to Alexander I, was charged by the czar to begin drafting a constitution. This draft was completed and is generally held to have been even more liberal than those of Western European countries at the time, even including among its provisions the principle of separation of powers. Despite Alexander's interest in the document, reactionary circles around him persuaded him to reject the draft.

Alexander also made no secret of his repugnance toward the state of bondage in which most Russian peasants were held. Unfortunately, the proposals he had drafted, which looked toward the emancipation of the serfs, were forgotten after the 1820 mutiny of the Semenovsky regiment guards, which he took to be part of an international revolutionary movement directed against himself. At other times, those closest to the czar quietly refused to carry out his reform edicts. In the case of school reform, Alexander appointed Prince Alexander Golitsyn as administrator, a man Michael Florinsky called "a religious maniac and a fanatical reactionary."[21] Golitsyn destroyed the last vestiges of liberalism in the school system and purged it so thoroughly that at the end of Alexander's reign (1825) there were only 8,000 secondary schools for a population in excess of 50 million people.

Even Nicholas I, Alexander's brother and successor and generally considered to be the most conservative of the nineteenth-century czars, saw the need for some measure of reform. Nicholas came to power in the midst of the Decembrist Revolt, a futile attempt by high military officers to overthrow the autocracy and replace it with a constitutional republic. Deeply disturbed by the revolt, he nevertheless felt the need to alleviate the desperate plight of the peasantry. Over the years, Nicholas commissioned no fewer than nine secret committees to draft measures to improve the status of the peasants. In 1842 and 1844, laws were even passed that provided for the emancipation of serfs on a voluntary basis, but this rarely happened in practice.[22]

The czar who finally did emancipate the serfs was Alexander II, the "Czar Liberator" (ruled 1855–1881). As mass opposition to conditions in Russia increased and the Russians suffered a severe defeat in the Crimean War, Alexander II decided to move on a long list of public grievances. Beginning in 1855, a stream of decrees was issued by the czar's ministers aimed at modernizing various sectors of Russian society. The universities were opened to all who could pass the entrance exams, and formerly banned subjects were reintroduced. Restrictions on foreign travel were lifted and censorship was reduced (though not eliminated). But most significantly, on March 17, 1861, Alexander issued a proclamation abolishing serfdom throughout Russia. Unfortunately, the terms of the emancipation brought hardship to many peasants and failed in the long run to resolve the desperate conditions of their servitude. Emancipation did not mean individual freedom or legal equality for the peasants. It meant transfering control over the peasant from the landlord to the commune, a body of peasant farmers which had the authority to distribute land, set planting and harvesting decisions, and require labor of each peasant.

In a long run, the emancipation probably worsened the status of the peasants and increased their bitterness toward the system. From the time of the emancipation until the revolution a half-century later, the number and severity of violent peasant revolts increased markedly. And the harshness of czarist reaction kept pace.

In the mid-1860s, Alexander pressed for judicial reforms, striving to introduce into Russia such Western legal principles as trial by jury, an independent judiciary, and the presumption of innocence. But little came of it, and judges remained government officials under the arbitrary control of the minister of the interior. Later in his reign, Alexander formed the Supreme Executive Commission to respond to conditions of increased violence and terror in the countryside. The commission proposed reducing censorship, mitigating the security policy, forcing reactionary officials out of office, and creating local advisory bodies to communicate with Moscow on matters of concern. Alexander approved the commission's proposals on the morning of March 1, 1881. Two hours later he was assassinated, and his son, Alexander III, abandoned the reforms in favor of harsher measures of control, reducing the power of local government, and disenfranchising Jews and other "undesirables."

By the end of the nineteenth century, the sense of crisis in Russia had grown to epidemic proportions, culminating in the 1905 revolt of workers in St. Petersburg, which threatened to ignite the entire country in revolution. Under extreme pressure and with profound misgivings, Czar Nicholas II was persuaded to issue the "October Manifesto," which authorized the creation of the first national legislature, the Duma, and the expansion of civil liberties. True to form, however, at the first spark of legislative independence, Nicholas dissolved that Duma and the following one as well. After changing the election rules to ensure a more conservative body, Nicholas convened the third Duma in 1908.

If the first two Dumas were not a fair test of the potential of the constitutional system established in the October Manifesto, dominated as they were by radicals of various colors, the third Duma presented a different picture. "It was in this house," Geoffrey Hosking argues, "that the government had a genuine chance to achieve a stable working relationship with moderate public opinion." [23] That experiment failed, as did the attempt at parliamentary government instituted in 1917 after the last czar had been deposed. In neither case were the forces of moderate reform well enough established to fend off the extremism of either the czarist aristocracy or the parties of revolution. It is difficult not to accept Hosking's conclusion that "there are really no grounds for supposing that the Tsarist system could ever have made a constitutional order work or could have achieved the peaceful modernization of Russia."[24]

The tragic fact of efforts toward modernization and reform by all of the czars was that reforms invariably produced popular reactions that frightened the rulers, leading them to abrogate the reforms and install reactionary officials to return the country to orderly submission. But the fundamental reason for this was the absence in Russia of any economic or political forces capable of forcing the czar to introduce reforms in the first place, and to carry them out even at the cost of diminishing the czar's own power. Despite great pressures in that direction, the decision to institute a reform was always the czar's, and the option of calling off the reform if it seemed to threaten the position of the czar was always available.

As a consequence, pressures for reform in Russia rarely resulted in significant change. As in France under Louis-Philippe, Austria under Metternich, and Prussia under Frederick William IV, the absence of channels for change appeared to provide no course but revolution.[25]

The Intelligentsia and Radical Change

If there were few progressive forces for change in nineteenth-century Russia, there was nevertheless no dearth of schemes, philosophies, and ideologies describing what changes would be desirable. The political oppression of the times did not prevent an outpouring of political literature from writers of all degrees of talent, including some of Russia's greatest literary figures. It was the age of Pushkin, Turgenev, Tolstoi, and Dostoyevsky, and later of Chekhov and Gorky, not to mention Tchaikovsky, Rimsky-Korsakov, and Rachmaniov.

The significance of these personages, beyond their artistic greatness, was the role they came to play in Russian politics. In Western Europe the driving force behind the modernization of the states was the bourgeois middle class, those with a growing economic stake in ending autocracy and absolutism. Art and literature played a minor though useful role in condemning the inhumanity of industrialism, but on the whole European writers pursued artistic, not political, ends.

In Russia there was no bourgeois middle class to battle czarist absolutism, so the task fell to the intelligentsia—an amorphous "class" of writers, teachers, religious leaders, professional people, and military officers who were active in the life of the society, as well as dreamers, anarchists, revolutionaries, mystics, and a few whose grip on sanity was tenuous at best (the composer Scriabin, for example). The idea that art had a political function was incontestable in Russian circles by the middle of the century. This was exemplified in the works of great polemicists such as Herzen, Chernyshevksy, and, above all, Vissarion Belinsky. As Isaiah Berlin aptly states

> after [Belinsky] no Russian writer was wholly free from the belief that to write was,
> first and foremost, to bear witness to the truth; that the writer, of all men, had no

right to avert his gaze from the central issues of his day and his society. For an artist—and particularly a writer—to try to detach himself from the deepest concerns of his nation in order to devote himself to the creation of beautiful objects or the pursuit of personal ends was condemned as self-destructive egoism and frivolity; he would only be maimed and impoverished by such betrayal of his chosen calling.[26]

The intelligentsia, therefore, served Russian history in place of a middle class, but they had little stake in the wealth and property of the country or in its economic development and no direct influence on the politics of the autocracy. Lacking a clear social or economic base, they indulged in idealism, radicalism, reactionism, and other temptations of the mind to which the classless elements of society are attracted.

The alternatives to autocracy that were posed by the intelligentsia in the nineteenth century fell into three broad schools of thought: Slavophilism, Westernism, and Populism. The three concepts were not entirely separate. Both Slavophiles and Populists revered the peasant as a source of spiritual guidance for the nation, and all three opposed czarist autocracy. But they were also separated by profound differences in how each conceived the future of Russia.

Slavophilism. Adherents of Slavophilism indulged in an extreme nationalism that glorified everything Russian and condemned all foreign influences. European ideas introduced to Russia by Peter the Great were to be expunged, along with foreign tradesmen, scientists, and "rootless people" such as Scots, Jews, Armenians, and Gypsies.[27] Aware of the backwardness and suffering of the peasants, Slavophiles sought solutions not in the institutions and practices of Europe but in what they saw as the true traditions of Russia. From the communal spirit and profound religious commitment of the Russians, rather than from secular rationalism and individualism, would come the inspiration to lead humanity toward a better life. Politically, Slavophiles spoke for the nobility that had been humiliated by autocratic czars, and for the Zemsky Sobor[28] and other older forms of representative institutions. In a true sense, they were radical and conservative at the same time.

Westernism. Though sharing with Slavophiles a strong sense of the backwardness of Russia, Westernizers saw the remedies in the European model and in the efforts of Peter the Great to westernize Russia. They did not argue for the wholesale importation of European institutions into Russia, but believed that Russia and Europe had a common heritage and that Russia would benefit by pursuing that heritage in its own way. They strongly supported constitutionalism and freedom of expression as essential elements in the European culture.

Populism. The Populists took their inspiration from the mass peasantry—the *narodnichestvo*. In the 1870s, Populists disparaged so-called intellectual approaches to Russia's problems, arguing that those who would bring about change must "go to the people" themselves, work with them, struggle with them, and follow them as well as lead them. Unlike the Slavophiles, they welcomed the rationalism, individualism, and industrialization of the West, but envisioned a new form of peasant communalism adapted to those new concepts. Later in the century, the term Populism tended to be expanded to include revolutionary ideologies of peasant socialism and Marxism. However, Marxism in its various forms went far beyond earlier Populism in advocating revolution based on the urban proletariat rather than the peasantry.

What is important to understand is that none of these utopian conceptions of Russia's future had much relevance for the desperate social and political circumstances of the Russian nation. Slavophiles and Populists believed in the nobility of a peasantry, which in reality had no capacity for fulfilling the theoretical role assigned to it. Westernizers desired the establishment of political institutions and judicial practices for which there was no basis in experience in the entire history of Russia. Marxists wished to impose theoretical solutions of a kind that even Marx believed were probably not applicable to Russia.

The enduring reality of Russia was the centralized, absolutist, autocracy that it had always known. All of the institutions, legal traditions, social relations, and cultural imperatives were subservient to that reality. The example of Europe is highly instructive here. The only prospect for long-range change in the political system would have come from the gradual development of social and economic forces capable of challenging the autocracy—of an entrepreneurial class with independent wealth, a heterogeneous class structure with reasonable opportunity for upward mobility, a strong intellectual tradition of critical writing capable not only of uniting the intelligentsia but of moving the middle classes to action, political institutions—especially a parliament and bureaucracy—able to restrict and gradually diminish the independence of the monarch, and an educated public opinion that could articulate its demand for participation in the political system.

None of these conditions existed in prerevolutionary Russia; none of them exists today. This is not to argue that they could never exist or that some fundamental flaw in the Russian character condemns Russia to autocracy for all time. It is to argue only that the form of government that exists in the twentieth century in the USSR is consistent with the political foundations that existed for hundreds of years before the 1917 revolution. For the revolution to have produced either European parliamentarism, as appeared momentarily possible in the summer of 1917, or a true Marxist classless democracy, would have required a foundation of intellectual and institutional development that is simply not present in the history of the Soviet Union.

NOTES

1. C. Raymond Beazley, Nevill Forbes, and G. A. Birkett, *Russia from the Varangians to the Bolsheviks* (Oxford: Clarendon Press, 1918), p. 32.

2. Ibid., p. 46.
3. Ibid., p. 47.
4. Ibid., p. 51.
5. Ibid., p. 55.
6. Virginia Cowles, *The Romanovs* (New York: Harper & Row, 1971), p. 11.
7. Jesse Clarkson, *A History of Russia* (New York: Random House, 1961), p. 11.
8. Michael T. Florinsky, *Russia: A Short History,* 2d ed. (London: Macmillan, 1969), p. 45.
9. Nicholas L. Fr. Chirovsky, *A History of the Russian Empire* (New York: Philosophical Library, 1973), p. 182.
10. Alexander Yanov, *The Origins of Autocracy* (Berkeley: University of California Press, 1981), p. 6.
11. Beazley, *Russia,* p. 91.
12. Clarkson, *History of Russia,* p. 121.
13. Peter Gay and R. K. Webb, *Modern Europe* (New York: Harper & Row, 1973), p. 614.
14. George L. Yaney, *The Systematization of Russian Government* (Urbana: University of Illinois, 1973), p. 64.
15. Jerome Blum, *Lord and Peasant in Russia from the Ninth to the Nineteenth Century* (Princeton, N.J.: Princeton University Press, 1961), p. 227.
16. See Edward Crankshaw, *The Shadow of the Winter Palace* (New York: Viking, 1976), pp. 20–22.
17. Beazley, *Russia,* p. 350.
18. See Abbot Gleason, *Young Russia* (New York: Viking, 1980), pp. 2–4.
19. A. Lentin, *Russia in the Eighteenth Century* (New York: Harper & Row, 1973), p. 109.
20. Beazley, *Russia,* p. 344.
21. Florinsky, *Russia: A Short History,* p. 267.
22. Ibid., p. 278.
23. Geoffrey Hosking, *The Russian Constitutional Experiment* (Cambridge: Cambridge University Press, 1973), p. vii.
24. Ibid.
25. See Gay and Webb, *Modern Europe,* p. 710.
26. Isaiah Berlin, "Introduction," to Ivan Turgenev, *Fathers and Sons,* (New York: Penguin Books, 1978), pp. 13–14.
27. Clarkson, *History of Russia,* p. 180.
28. The Zemsky Sobor, or "assembly of the land," was a seventeenth-century form of local legislature, composed of nobility, gentry, intellectuals, and even some peasants.

CHAPTER 3
The Russian Revolution

THE BREAKUP OF THE OLD ORDER

The revolution that swept through Russia in 1917 ended the 300-year-old Romanov autocracy in a frenzy of violence and chaos. With the abdication of Nicholas II and the establishment of a provisional government, it seemed as if the past had been largely discarded and all roads to the future were open. Yet a scant decade later, a new autocracy even more powerful than the last had taken hold of Russia.

No one would argue that Lenin was Nicholas's inevitable successor, or that Stalin had to succeed Lenin. In the turmoil of the 1920s, Russia may well have been only an assassin's bullet away from a different course of development. Yet there is a connection between the political systems of the pre- and postrevolutionary eras that cannot be explained by the character of any individual leader. As argued in the previous chapter, czarist autocracy rested on socioeconomic and political foundations that obstructed the development of the pluralist institutions and popular involvement in government that had long been preparing Western Europe for modern parliamentary democracy. In this chapter we shall extend that argument by examining briefly the transition from czarism to bolshevism up to Lenin's death in 1924. In the next chapter we will examine the rise and nature of Stalinism in light of the same argument.

That Russia was undergoing a degree of change and modernization at the turn of the twentieth century is incontestable. Spearheaded by Nicholas II's brilliant finance minister, Count Sergei Witte, the development of a modern industrial economy had become a high priority. In the 1890s, the annual rate of economic growth was over 8 percent, the highest in the world, and it continued as the highest in Europe until the disaster of World War I.

In the Donetz Basin town of Yuzhovka, a colossal industrial complex was built and run by entrepreneurs from several countries, and it became the showplace of the era. It was at this enterprise, in 1909, that the young Nikita Khrushchev started work at the age of fifteen. The complex at Yuzhovka, like many similar installations, was managed by industrial combinations of Russian and foreign companies and much of the financing for the construction came from abroad. Foreign loans to Russia in 1914 amounted to some 6 billion rubles, which was about one-third of the total share of the capital invested in Russia in the first decade of the twentieth century. Clearly the major economic interests of Europe saw Russia as a prime area for rapid industrial development.

The demand for workers to man the new industrial plants was great, and the number of workers more than doubled between 1890 and 1912. Yet even at that, the three million urban workers constituted, at the outbreak of World War I, less than 3 percent of the total population, which included 97 million peasants and 10 million shopkeepers, tradesmen, and artisans. The absence of an urban industrial work force was accompanied by the virtual absence of an entrepreneural class with independent wealth, the class that had become such a dominant economic and political force in Europe. In Russia, the state was the principal source of investment funds and exercised general control over the process of industrial development. Given the absence of political power on the part of the aristocracy, decisions about development rested with a few government ministers, whose tenure in office was determined solely by the czar. As a result, the industrial development process was erratic and highly politicized.

Despite the shortcomings, Russian economic growth and modernization in the two decades before the revolution were impressive. And they were accompanied by positive developments in education, health, road building, and veterinary services. In 1912, both health and accident insurance were introduced for urban workers, and every factory employing 200 or more workers was provided with a "hospital fund." About this same time, four years of primary education were made mandatory for all children.

Even in that most intractable area—agriculture—an extraordinary movement toward reform was launched in the years following the end of the disastrous war with Japan (1904–1905). Under the guidance of Premier Peter Stolypin, the traditional communal form of rural living (the *mir*) was declared obsolete and most of the communes were abolished. Government banks assisted peasants in purchasing their own land and in obtaining the equipment to farm the land. By 1914, as a result, peasants in European Russia owned more than four times as much land as the nobility. By the time of the revolution in 1917 most of the Russian crop was farmed and owned by peasants.[1] Given a couple of generations of continued government support, the establishment of a differentiated social structure in rural Russia based upon private ownership of the land might have stabilized the countryside and permanently expanded agricultural productivity. That this might happen was one of Lenin's greatest fears, for it would surely dampen the revolutionary potential of the peasantry.

These rapid social changes heightened both the expectations and the frustrations of many Russians. The czarist government proved incapable of containing and directing the vibrant forces being loosed in the country, yet it still had sufficient power to prevent new political structures from taking over. Its incapacity to respond to the situation finally provoked a major crisis. On January 5, 1905—the day that came to be known as "Bloody Sunday"—200,000 unarmed St. Petersburg workers marched peacefully to the czar's Winter Palace, carrying pictures of Nicholas and requesting an audience with their "Little Father" to express their grievances. With the czar absent from the palace, government troops opened fire on the workers, killing and wounding many of them.

The outraged workers and students declared a general strike, which quickly spread to other cities. Within weeks, universities began to close down, revolts broke out in Polish Russia and in the Caucasus, high officials including the governor-general of Moscow were assassinated, peasant seizures of land increased rapidly, and a few military units mutinied against their officers. Confronting a situation clearly out of control, Nicholas finally consented to the issuance of the "October Manifesto," which authorized the formation of a national elected assembly, guaranteed protection for civil liberties, and granted universal (male) suffrage. Thus, Russia's first national legislature, the Duma, came into being in what much of Russia, and the world, believed was the Russian Revolution.

For the next dozen years, the moderate reform forces that dominated the Duma attempted to make constitutional government work in Russia. Throughout, the czar remained obstinately opposed to the idea of sharing power with the people. Without his support, the reforms continued with diminishing vigor through the early years of World War I, and they finally collapsed in the turmoil of military defeat and revolution. The principal players in this last act of the Romanov drama were the masses of Russian peasants and workers, the aristocracy, and the revolutionaries. The story of the Russian Revolution lies in the perceptions of these groups and in the interactions among them.

The Masses

Despite serious efforts toward national development and reform, the burden of poverty, cruelty, and violence that lay upon Russian society at the turn of the century remained largely unchanged. Undercutting the modest reform efforts was a peasant population growth that saw the number of peasants increase by 50 percent in the half-century before the Russian Revolution. And as their numbers increased their holdings diminished in size despite the Stolypin reforms. "Agricultural techniques were so primitive," Edward Crankshaw states, "and the climate so difficult, that the yield per acre had barely risen above the medieval level. . . . Only half the peasants had a horse to help them with cultivation."[2]

The individual peasant lived a life of acute poverty. When the crops were poor, peasant families subsisted on "famine bread" (*golodnye khleb*), which was made from goosefoot and other stringy weeds ground and mixed with diminishing amounts of flour as food shortages intensified. Bruce Lincoln reports that "in some regions the poorest peasants began to supplement their grain with famine bread as early as October; nearly all had to do so by Easter."[3] When the goosefoot was gone, peasants ate clay to keep alive. The physical results of this diet were predictable. It induced diarrhea, vomiting, and various other gastrointestinal disorders and resulted in long-term protein deficiencies that sapped the strength, and thus the productivity, of millions of Russian peasants.

Infant mortality rates were appalling. "Morning and evening, hungry peasant mothers took a few bits of precious black bread from their own ration, chewed it briefly, wrapped the mush in a bit of rag, and gave it to their infants to suck. Half of the children fed in that manner died in their first year."[4] In addition, the end of the nineteenth century brought a new disease to the Russian peasantry: syphilis—a common infection in developing urban environments but widespread among the rural peasantry as well. Medical science knew no cure at that time.

The lot of urban workers was little better. Although there was an elaborate set of government regulations in force protecting workers from harsh and irresponsible managers,[5] the administration of these rules varied widely from factory to factory. Most workers lived in barracks, some of which housed as many as 10,000 men and their families. Food supplies varied with the harvests, and in years of poor yields the city workers fared worse than the peasants. Most of the workers remained peasants at heart, tied to the land and retaining their status in the commune, to which they returned regularly.

The abysmal circumstances and the illiteracy of most peasants cut them off entirely from what Europeans (and upper-class Russians too) thought of as Russian culture. According to Russian-born historian Michael Florinsky,

> the complex and dazzling structure of that Russian culture, of which the educated classes were so justly proud, meant nothing to the peasant. The names of Tolstoi and Dostoevsky, of Tschaikovsky and Rimsky-Korsakov, were an empty sound to them. They had never heard of the Moscow Art Theater and the Imperial Ballet, which won the applause of the world; nor would they have been capable of enjoying or appreciating them if, by some extraordinary turn of fortune, they happened to be present at a performance.[6]

The Aristocracy

The Russian aristocracy, broadly conceived, consisted of a number of elements: the czar, his extended family, and close associates among the nobility; the landowning nobility (some 30,000 families) who owned estates in rural Russia; the military officer class; and the higher ranks of the clergy. The aristocracy was traditionally conservative and tended to oppose government plans for reform that surfaced in the early 1900s. This was especially true of the 30,000 noble families who, through their domination of local government institutions and the social and economic life of the peasantry, effectively dominated rural Russia.

In time they came to dominate the new national legislature—the Duma—as well. Through repeated rigging of the electoral system, the government ensured itself of a conservative majority in the Duma. The rural landed nobility used this majority to obstruct even those modest reform plans the government had been persuaded to adopt. Thus, the legislature, when it finally appeared in Russia, failed to offer an alternative source of political power to emerging economic and social interests. This greatly inhibited the pressures that might have forced the czar toward some degree of shared power.

In addition to the Duma, the 30,000 noble families also came to dominate the other two institutions through which Premier Stolypin attempted to bring about change: the State Council and the Local Economy Office of the Ministry of Internal Affairs. Thus, this minuscule element of Russian society found itself, according to

Leopold Haimson, "in a better position to resist the government's administrative and legislative initiatives in the last decade of the tsarist regime than it had been since the late eighteenth century."[7]

This dominant rural aristocracy displayed all of the negative characteristics that had destroyed the leading role of similar classes in Western Europe in the nineteenth century. It fought the industrial revolution bitterly and remained blindly ignorant of the changes that were taking place in Europe. It suffered a progressive loss of a sense of reality about Russian society and the desperate straits in which the vast majority of Russians found themselves in the first decade of the twentieth century. Ultimately, the aristocracy's sense of its own purpose and relationship to the problems Russia faced grew dim. A high court official and acute observer of St. Petersburg at the time, Count Paul Vassili (a pseudonym), summed up the aristocracy's state of mind:

> After a war [the Russo-Japanese War of 1904–1905] and a revolution [the 1905 uprisings] that should have awakened anew the attention of the public as to these important problems of the life of a nation it has entirely left off thinking about them. . . . Society, or what goes by that name, gives all its thought to ill-natured gossip. They read nothing except French novels of the worst kind; hardly glance at a newspaper; and their ideas about a journey abroad are summed up in a trip to Paris—where their whole interest centers in the music-halls and other places of the same light character. . . . [They do] not see, or perhaps do not want to see, the growing tide of revolution and anarchism that is gaining ground every day and preparing itself for the struggle out of which it knows it will emerge triumphant.[8]

The Liberal Intelligentsia

Russian liberalism was the practical manifestation of the Westernizer philosophy of the mid-nineteenth century. It emerged out of the constitutionalist movement of the 1880s and attached itself to the *zemstvo*, a rural assembly that administered programs of local welfare and relief, education, road building, and other social services. The *zemstvos* were created by law in 1864 as part of Alexander II's reform and were intended to provide a mechanism for political participation by the newly freed peasantry. Though thoroughly dominated by the landed nobility, the *zemstvos* were quite effective in alleviating some of the misery of the peasantry. During the great famine of 1891–1892, in fact, the *zemstvos* were far more successful in providing food to starving peasants than was the czarist bureaucracy.

In the desperate work of famine relief, many young professionals and technocrats, teachers, doctors, lawyers, and agronomists, as well as artists, musicians, writers, and clergymen, became dedicated to the cause of the peasants and intensely familiar with their suffering. These "*zemstvo* radicals" found like-minded educated people in all areas of Russia and pressed for the formation of organizations to express their common interests.

In 1904, the Union of Liberation was founded as an underground organization with *zemstvo* support. The Union published a program calling for representative government and for the formation of a national assembly of *zemstvo* deputies. A similar program was written by fourteen professional unions (those of university professors, teachers, doctors, pharmacists, and so on) in 1905 and a Union of Unions was founded to give voice to the program.

When the Duma was established in 1906, these liberals united in the Constitutional Democrat (Kadet) Party, under the leadership of Paul Miliukov. Unfortunately for the liberals, the weight of the Duma was in its extremities—the radical Left, which was determined to dominate or destroy the Duma, and the reactionary Right, which largely dominated the third and fourth Dumas. As with nineteenth-century Westernism, twentieth-century Russian liberalism had little ground to stand on. A limited constitutional monarchy dominated by a representative national legislature had little chance to survive in the turbulent conditions of Russian politics and culture.

The Revolutionary Intelligentsia

When revolution finally came to Russia, it was not the result of decisions made by revolutionary organizations, most of which were caught by surprise by the swift end of the Romanov dynasty in February 1917. The Romanov dynasty collapsed of its own weight in the winter of 1916/1917 in the face of a massive popular uprising involving both civilians and military units with the collaboration of large elements of the intelligentsia and major figures within the nobility itself. The role of the revolutionaries was an important but limited one prior to the revolution though of course they played a decisive role in the months that followed. There was little unity among them as well, despite their common opposition to czarism. There were two major forces: Socialist Revolutionaries and Social Democrats, the latter divided into Bolshevik and Menshevik factions.

Socialist Revolutionaries. The Socialist Revolutionaries (SRs) were heirs of the populist tradition of mid-nineteenth-century radicalism. They believed that the peasant commune (*mir*) was an ideal institution upon which to base a postczarist socialist system. Within the *mir,* peasants periodically reapportioned land that was collectively controlled, an act which engendered a spirit of communalism and equality. The peasant was, they argued, thus intrinsically more socialist than the proletariat who operated as individual and independent economic units. On the basis of the peasantry, Russia could move from a feudal society without going through a capitalist stage. Socialist Revolutionaries also recognized the importance of urban workers in the revolutionary movement and actively propagandized among them. But the peasant was the key to creating the new order.

Social Democrats. The Russian Social Democratic movement was based upon the ideas of Karl Marx and the application of Marxism to the Russian situation by an extraordinary group of intellectual revolutionaries that included Georgy Plekhanov, the founder of Russian Marxism, Julius Martov, Vera Zasulich, Paul Axelrod, Leon Trotsky, and, above all, Vladimir Ilyich Ulyanov, later known as Lenin.

Russia and Marxist theory were not an easy fit, and the theoretical difficulties involved in applying Marxism to Russian conditions caused deep rifts among the Social Democrats. At the second major conference of Social Democrats, held in Brussels in 1903, Lenin led a minority faction which, because of the temporary walkout of the Jewish Bund and several other delegates, found itself momentarily in the majority. With characteristic ingenuity, Lenin proposed a resolution that adopted for those present the name "Bolshevik" (majority), leaving for the other (larger) faction the name "Menshevik" (minority). Though Lenin's group was often in the minority in later years, the brilliant stroke of seizing the name "majority" paid handsome propaganda dividends.

The issues that divided the Mensheviks from the Bolsheviks were fundamental, at least on the theoretical level. They involved first of all the objectives that should be pursued by the revolutionary parties with regard to the proletariat. Mensheviks tended to believe that the desire of workers for better living conditions and gradual improvement in their political rights were legitimate goals and should be supported. They favored, therefore, efforts to legalize labor unions, ensure worker control over the unions, and represent workers in legislative bodies such as the Duma.

The Bolsheviks, on the other hand, argued against working for such immediate benefits, urging instead that the revolutionaries concentrate on overthrowing the czar and creating a socialist state. Lenin was convinced that urban workers would allow themselves to be bought off by minor increases in wages and benefits while the capitalists continued to exploit them for their own benefit.

The other major issue that divided the Mensheviks from the Bolsheviks was the organization and function of the Social Democratic Party. Mensheviks were temperamentally inclined to promote large public organizations for workers and to expand membership in the revolutionary organization as broadly as possible. Bolsheviks believed that open anti-government activity was merely an invitation to the police to arrest those involved. Lenin argued for a small, fiercely loyal, well-trained, and secret organization capable of functioning under the conditions of police repression that existed in Russia at the time.

These differences were clearer in theory than in practice, however. In confronting the changing conditions of Russia prior to the revolution, Bolsheviks and Mensheviks agreed on many matters, while ideological disputes often arose within each of the parties. Lenin occasionally sided with the Mensheviks, and Trotsky switched from menshevism to bolshevism only in June 1917, three months after the abdication of the czar. Some of the differences between the two factions were attributable merely to different states of mind and personalities of the leaders. Nevertheless, it is probable that had the Mensheviks taken power in late 1917, their regime might well have moved in somewhat different directions than that of Lenin.

THE TRANSITION

The Bolsheviks Come to Power

When revolution finally came, it was as a sudden explosion of pent-up social forces. There was no single cause, it followed no one's plan, and it even took many of those who most ardently desired it by surprise. If the Bolsheviks were not the cause, however, they were certainly the revolution's chief beneficiaries. Between February and October 1917, the Bolshevik Party emerged from its minority status in the Petrograd Soviet to become the dominant party in the national Congress of Soviets. Membership in the Party grew from 80,000 in April to over 200,000 by August. And in the Moscow city elections of 1917, the proportion of the popular vote received by Bolshevik candidates rose from 11 percent in July to 51 percent in October.[9]

The success of the Bolshevik faction of Social Democrats exhibits most clearly the failure of czarist Russia to develop the foundations of parliamentary democracy that eventually came to dominate Western Europe. As described in the previous chapter, the autocracy denied effective political participation to two elements of society that, in Western Europe, had fundamentally transformed the social and political orders: an independent bourgeois class of entrepreneurs, professionals and managers; and mass organizations such as labor unions and socialist parties.

When the czar was finally deposed, these two elements were left to form a new government grounded on a wholly new set of political principles. For each element a center of governance was quickly established: the Provisional Government, dominated by Constitutional Democrats and moderate elements of the old elites, as well as a substantial contingent of Socialist Revolutionaries; and the Petrograd Soviet, a raucous gathering of 3,000 workers, intellectuals, and radicals of all stripes.

With little experience in parliamentary government beyond the Dumas, the Provisional Government attempted both to serve the needs of its dominant elites and to placate the demands of the masses. Responding to liberal intellectual influences, it struggled to transform Russia into a new and freer social order. It granted equality and freedom of speech, press, assembly, and religion to all citizens. Minority rights were guaranteed and a national amnesty was decreed for political prisoners. Provincial governorships were abolished and political authority was delegated to local governmental organs, which henceforth were to be elected.

The assumption that enhanced political rights would satisfy the masses was a major miscalculation. Serious economic problems created large numbers of unemployed workers and millions of hungry peasants whose only objective was land. Yet Alexander Kerensky refused to instigate land reform for fear of alienating major allies in the Provisional Government and instead cracked down on radical leaders, arresting Trotsky and forcing Lenin to flee to Finland.

In the face of this, angry peasants instituted their own "reform" program. Landowners were murdered, houses burned, and land seized in a frenzy of violent expropriation. In the cities, workers became more desperate and short-tempered as food supplies dwindled and social services vanished. Soldiers deserting the front poured into Petrograd and Moscow, and local soviets were assuming power all over the western provinces.

With Bolshevik majorities emerging in many of the city soviets, Lenin, still in Finland, decided that the moment had come to seize power. As usual, he was a giant step ahead of his Party. His letter to the Petrograd Central Committee calling for a mass uprising so shocked the committee that it burned the letter and refused to discuss its contents. A week later (in October 1917) Lenin came to Petrograd in disguise to argue his case, which he did successfully. A week after that, he openly led the Bolsheviks and the people of Petrograd in a massive insurrection that took over the Tauride Palace and overthrew the Provisional Government. The Bolsheviks quickly took control in the major cities and established a government with Lenin as the President of the Council of People's Commissars, Trotsky as Foreign Commissar, and Stalin as Commissar of Nationalities.

The outcome represented the victory of neither the Provisional Government nor the Petrograd Soviet, but of a radical intellectual elite determined to shape society to its will. Once again, as in centuries past, the forces of absolutism had triumphed over those of compromise and diversity on the one hand and decentralized mass political power on the other. Still, there were many issues to be resolved for those who suddenly found themselves governing Russia. The final nature of the new political system was still some years from being established. The main issue, as in all autocracies, was the role of the autocrat. As Lenin moved into the Kremlin in the fall of 1917, his style and personality immediately began to shape the processes of government and to establish a model of leadership for those with whom he shared power and for his successors.

Lenin: Successor to an Emperor

Lenin's style as leader of the Bolshevik Party and the government underwent no radical change from that of his earlier revolutionary role. He still pursued single-minded goals with highly flexible tactics. He typically took a strong position on an issue and argued, often brilliantly, in favor of it. Opponents within and without the Party were attacked viciously and accused of counterrevolutionary sabotage, treason, and betrayal of the revolution, often accompanied with demands for expulsion from the Party. At the same time, Lenin often made tactical concessions to his opponents based upon his reading of the political climate. When his victory on an issue was assured, he frequently welcomed his opponents back into the Party and accepted their contrite affirmations of loyalty.

What was at stake for Lenin was both the substance of the issue and the unity and strength of the Party. He was prepared to live with a permanent split within the Bolshevik ranks rather than sacrifice his position on an important issue, but he endeavored to avoid splits if possible. Toward non-Bolsheviks, however, his attitude was unbending: They must be totally excluded from power because they represented ideological values and interests that were, in his mind, incompatible with bolshevism. How these groups were treated depended on the tactics they themselves adopted in resisting their elimination from the political scene.

Where those tactics involved actual armed insurrection, as in the case of the Left SRs in 1918, Lenin acted ruthlessly, arresting most of the SR delegates to the Fifth All-Russian Congress of Soviets and executing thirteen of them. Those leftist members of the Bolshevik Party who supported the Left SRs in the insurrection were, on the other hand, permitted to recant and accepted back into their posts in the Party. In dealing with other political parties, Lenin's tactics varied with the extent of the threat they represented to him.

Lenin's genius as a political leader rested both on his tactical sensitivity, especially his instinctive understanding of the strength of his opposition, and on the fierceness of his determination to have his way. In this there was never any room for true sharing of power or compromise of principle. The absolutism of his Bolshevik convictions mirrored the confidence with which Nicholas II and his predecessors convinced themselves of the rightness of their decisions and their roles. There could be but one source of truth; all opposition to that source was not only irrational but a betrayal of the legitimate government and the people.

At the same time, Lenin had a passion for change, for progress, for grappling with modern problems and moving forward. In his mind, there was little in Russia's past worth preserving; and in this he differed profoundly from his conservative predecessors. Lenin genuinely believed that the revolution had freed the Russian masses from the oppression and cruelty they had suffered under the previous ruling class. Grappling with the problem of how that freedom should be channeled in historically constructive directions was a problem that had never preoccupied the czars. Yet even here, there was a point of continuity: Both Nicholas and Lenin shared the assumption that the Russian masses had no capacity to make such decisions on their own, or even to understand their true situation. Unlike Nicholas, however, Lenin believed they could be educated and inspired to perceive their true interests and to act on them. But the responsibility for creating that capacity in the masses rested solely with the leadership, as did the decision as to when that historic moment had arrived.

In the four years during which Lenin actively led the new revolutionary government, his style and state of mind were applied to a range of fundamental issues facing the country. The ideology of "Leninism" emerged out of the resolution of these issues.

THE IDEOLOGY OF LENINISM

Dictatorship or Democracy

The most fundamental issue raised by the successful October Revolution was the nature of the revolution itself. Marxist theory envisaged a socialist revolution under advanced capitalist conditions in which the proletariat constituted the overwhelming majority of the population. The overthrow of the capitalist ruling class was to be followed by a brief "dictatorship of the proletariat," the chief functions of which were to stamp out the former ruling class and create the conditions in which the state apparatus itself could be abolished.

But the Russian Revolution did not fit the pattern. The proletariat was a small minority of the population, so a dictatorship of that proletariat would be rule by minority rather than by majority. Furthermore, it was obvious to most of the revolutionary leadership that the Russian proletariat, largely illiterate and politically naive, was in no position to assume direct power. That function would have to be performed in the name of the proletariat and the peasantry by the most advanced element of the revolutionary leadership.

The practical questions were who, exactly, would be involved in making governmental decisions and how could the Russian people be assured that their interests would be served by these decision-makers. To the first question, the Bolsheviks' answer was equivocal. Lenin himself never seriously contemplated sharing power with other revolutionary groups or with elected bodies operating independently of the Bolsheviks, but many members of his own party disagreed. The principal challenges to Bolshevik dominance came from two sources: the Constituent Assembly, which was scheduled to be elected in October 1917 and whose powers were unclear but potentially great, and the other revolutionary parties who tended to feel that they too had won a revolution.

In the elections to the Constituent Assembly, which the Bolsheviks had consistently demanded prior to coming to power in October, Lenin's own party received only one-quarter of the popular vote, which was far less than the Socialist Revolutionaries had received. Without hesitation, the Bolsheviks moved to close down the Constituent Assembly after its first day of meetings in January, 1918, and it never met again. In the absence of a massive reeducation of the public mind, the principle of popular election as a means of choosing leaders had no appeal at all for Lenin and most of his colleagues.

The problem of sharing power with the Mensheviks and SRs was more complex. On the very day that the Bolsheviks took power, the Second Congress of Soviets unanimously voted for a coalition government, and the position was supported by top-level Bolshevik leaders including Leon Kamenev and G.E. Zinoviev, both close colleagues of Lenin. To Lenin and Trotsky, however, the prospect was intolerable. In several party meetings, they argued vehemently against a coalition, accusing Zinoviev and Kamenev of treason and threatening them with expulsion from the Party. The Central Executive Committee ultimately bent to their will and rejected participation in government by the Mensheviks and SRs.

The problem of justifying the exercise of political power by a small group of nonelected leaders was a serious challenge to the Bolsheviks. The revolution, after all, had presumably been a *democratic* one waged by and for the masses of oppressed people—oppressed, that is, by a small group of nonelected leaders. If Lenin was not to be perceived as a new "czar," a revolutionary concept of democracy would have to be devised, one that combined the unlimited power of the Party leadership with democratic control by the masses.

The answer, for Lenin at least, lay in his conception of the "dictatorship of the proletariat and the peasantry," a conception that was more or less fully formed at the beginning of his revolutionary career. It presupposed a "single will" that expressed the totality of the interests of the proletariat and peasantry. This "single will" is democratic "precisely insofar as [the] revolution meets the needs and requirements of the whole people."[10]

Those needs and requirements are defined not by individual whims or interests but by the nature of the "revolutionary transformation from capitalism to socialism." This requires a carefully planned and highly disciplined course of action for which, under conditions of modern industry and society, the exercise of power by a single political party or even by single individuals is natural and essential. "There is absolutely no contradiction in principle," Lenin argued in 1918, "between Soviet . . . democracy and the exercise of dictatorial powers by individuals." The management of a large-scale industrial economy "calls for absolute and strict *unity of will,* which directs the joint labors of hundreds, thousands and tens of thousands of people. But how can strict unity of will be ensured? By thousands subordinating their will to the will of one."[11]

At the local level, the "dictatorship of the proletariat" was taken by many to mean direct worker control over all production and distribution facilities and a dominant majority in all institutions making economic decisions. With the Bolsheviks in power, factory committees formed spontaneously and moved to take control of factories from the former managers. The result was a drastic decline in production and chaos in the distribution of goods.

Nevertheless, the workers' actions were strongly defended by the left wing of the Party, who believed that worker control was the central purpose of a socialist revolution. Under Lenin's guidance, however, the predominant elements of the Party moved to curtail these actions. Trotsky proposed to form labor armies operating under military control and assigned to whatever segment of the economy needed manpower. Under this plan, the trade unions would function "not for a struggle for better conditions of labor . . . but to organize the working class for the ends of production, to educate, discipline, to exercise their authority hand in hand with the state in order to lead the workers into the framework of a single economic plan."[12]

On the issue of trade unions, Lenin preferred a more subtle formulation, conceiving them as a "transmission belt" by which the Party leadership could mobilize the proletariat for economic goals while retaining the facade of independence from the governmental bureaucracy. Either way, it was clear that the Party had no tolerance for independent trade unions or for the independent authority of workers over the operations of industrial plants.

Theoretically, then, the answer to the question, dictatorship or democracy, was, "both." It rested on the assumption that there was not, and could never be, a conflict between the true interests of the masses and the policies of the Party leaders. Hence, Western political phenomena such as competing political parties, popular elections of leaders, and limited terms of office were unnecessary in the unified, classless society that would be constructed in the new Russia. To oppose the single ruling party was to oppose the masses themselves, an act which could only be viewed as counterrevolutionary.

The operational term for this arrangement is "democratic centralism." This involves three phases: the widespread participation of the masses in discussion of all important policy issues; decision making by the top leadership; and the obedience of all to the decisions once made. The implication in this formula is that discussions should precede and form the basis for the decisions; but this implication is misleading. Decision making is an independent leadership function that may occur prior to, during, or following public discussion of an issue. "The principle of democratic centralism," Lenin explained,

> means specifically freedom of criticism . . . , as long as this does not disrupt the unity of action *already decided upon*—and the intolerability of any criticism undermining or obstructing the unity of action decided on by the party.[13]

The Party and the Government

The second major issue the Bolsheviks faced was the relationship of the Communist Party to the government. The 1918 Constitution, adopted in June of that year, established a hierarchy of soviets from the local level to the All-Russian Congress of Soviets. The latter was to exercise the supreme legislative authority and to constitute the highest organ of state power. However, it was to meet infrequently, and during the interim periods its authority would be exercised by the Central Executive Committee, which would appoint a cabinet, the Council of People's Commissars.

In reality, Lenin had no intention of using these agencies to set basic policies, despite the fact that they were dominated by Party leaders (Lenin himself was Chairman of the Council of People's Commissars). It was the Party apparatus that would guide the nation, using state institutions as well as mass public organizations to administer Party policies and to mobilize mass support for them. Thus, the 8th Party Congress, convened in March 1919, approved a resolution calling for the Communist Party to "master for itself undivided political supremacy in the soviets and practical supervision over all their work."[14]

To ensure rigid discipline in the Party itself, a small Political Bureau (Politburo) was created to supervise the work of the Party Central Committee, and elected local Party committees were to be replaced by appointed "political departments." Despite the storm of criticism that these further steps toward centralization of Party power evoked at the 9th Party Congress the following September (1920), Lenin supported them while tactically sympathizing with the charge of bureaucratic centralism raised by speaker after speaker.

The decision to establish the governmental decision-making function within the top Party organs rather than in the legislature or cabinet, despite the Bolsheviks' total control of those institutions, rested on two main arguments. First, the state was viewed by Marxists as an oppressive apparatus serving the interests of the ruling class. With the masses now in power, the state would be limited to seeing to the final destruction of the bourgeoisie and managing governmental administration during the transition to communism. This accomplished, the state was expected to "wither away" leaving a self-managed, free, and democratic society. What the function of the Communist Party would be under these circumstances was not addressed until years later, but in the immediate aftermath of the Revolution, the Party was clearly preferable to the state apparatus as the dominant political institution.

Secondly, reserving real political power for the Party leadership allowed Lenin to transform the other institutions of government, especially the soviets, into new forms of "democracy" that appeared to be vastly superior to similar institutions in capitalist countries. Large numbers of ordinary workers and peasants could be brought directly into the work of the legislature, the bureaucratic agencies, the courts, the police, the trade unions, and so on without intefering with the necessary work of government. For revolutionaries like Lenin, who had promised vast governmental powers and responsibilities to a population composed mostly of illiterate peasants, this arrangement had obvious attractions. It would become the pattern for all subsequent institutional developments in the USSR.

To support this idea of the place of the Party in the political structure, Lenin developed the ideological concepts of volunteerism, the primacy of political struggle, and *partiinost,* that defined and justified the active role he intended the Party to play. These were first developed in his early publication *What Is to Be Done?* (1902), and refined in later writings.

Volunteerism. Rather than subordinating revolution to the forces of history, Lenin defined a conscious, aggressive role for the Bolshevik Party that would take advantage of the opportunities that historical forces presented. It would be the Party's, not the government's or the people's, function to guide the development of the country in accordance with those opportunities.

The Primacy of Political Struggle. Lenin's fear that the proletariat might prove to be content with only minor economic gains reinforced his determination to keep the political struggle alive even after the proletariat had come to power through revolution. The dominance of the Party over the political system ensured that this would be the case.

Partiinost. This concept defines the requirement that all descriptions of reality as well as all expressions of opinion conform to the established positions of the Party. *Partiinost* requires a firm belief in the inevitable correctness of Party policies because they are based on its profound insight into the nature of historical development. Under Stalin, this perspective was extended to cover all scientific, technical, artistic, and sociological knowledge as well. In all areas of human endeavor, the Party's views were held to contain the exclusive truth.

The Police Power

At the core of every revolution is violence. "It would be extremely stupid and absurdly utopian," Lenin once wrote, "to assume that the transition from capitalism to socialism is possible without coercion . . . ."[15] But coercion against whom, and by whom, and for what purposes, and for how long—these were practical, not theoretical, questions and would be clearly answered during the first postrevolutionary decade.

It was clear that Lenin, like most of his czarist predecessors, was intent upon establishing a regime totally without effective or organized opposition. In addition, the nature of the revolution required a massive change in the traditional pattern of Russian life involving far higher degrees of personal discipline, willing subordination to authority, and capacity for change than most Russians were used to. These requirements, imposed upon Russia by the new Bolshevik leadership, were often met with hostility and resistance by workers and peasants whose appreciation of Marxist-Leninist theories of social change was rather limited.

To combat these "counterrevolutionary" forces, the Cheka (Extraordinary Commission to Fight the Counter-Revolution and Sabotage) was formed in December 1917, and by the end of the following year it had 30,000 members. At the same time, the Bolsheviks established penal camps to contain both political and ordinary criminals.[16] From the beginning, the Cheka had virtually unlimited criminal and political jurisdiction. The concept of "counterrevolution" extended not only to direct acts of sabotage and armed insurrection but also to membership in the Menshevik and SR parties, refusal to work where assigned, identification as an "intellectual," and economic speculation.

The measures used by the Cheka were as drastic as, in the minds of the leadership, the circumstances called for. Lenin himself advocated the summary execution of speculators during the Petersburg food shortage in early 1918. In a statement written in December 1917, but not published for twelve years, he urged that harsh measures be taken not only against the rich and the "rogues" but also against workers who failed to work hard enough. As an example to others, he advocated shooting one out of every ten idlers "on the spot."[17] In other contexts, Lenin called for reeducation, collective responsibility for individual behavior, and the use of persuasion and pressure to conform to Party dictates.

Lenin intended the Cheka to be subordinate to the Party leadership and, in the appointment of Felix Dzherzhinsky as its first chairman, promoted the policy that the Cheka would respect the Bolshevik Party and its leaders, refuse to lend itself to factional disputes within the Party, and devote its activities to external threats to the revolution. As long as Lenin lived, the Cheka abided by these principles, but as Stalin became more powerful, the use of the Cheka to enforce his will against other factions within the Party became more common. Finally, in the 1930s, the secret police organization became central to the administrative structure that Stalin created. But it had gained broad experience in methods of repression in dealing with the Russian masses from the very beginning of the Revolution.

That the Cheka was called an "Extraordinary" Commission implied that its tenure would be limited to the immediate postrevolutionary and civil war periods. Over the years, however, it and its successor agencies became a permanent part of the political structure of the Soviet government. Differences in the level, scope, and tactics of coercion engaged in by Soviet police agencies depend largely on the personalities and relationships of the top political leaders, as we shall see in a later chapter. As we shall also see, the Soviet regime has not relied exclusively or even primarily on physical coercion to maintain order in the state. It has in fact depended heavily on the inculcation of political loyalty through propaganda and agitation, formal education, political symbols, and widespread opportunities for popular participation in government.

Nevertheless, the concept of "counterrevolution" became a basic element of the Leninist ideology. Long after power was effectively concentrated in the hands of the Party elite, the specter of hostile forces within the country struggling to overthrow the government was kept menacingly alive. In this, Lenin shared the fears of the czars who maintained their own organizations of internal oppression dating back to Ivan the Terrible's establishment of the *Oprichnina* in the sixteenth century. Vigilance against the secret enemy remains to this day a preoccupation of the security forces of the USSR and an official justification for many of the constraints that restrict the activities of the Soviet people.

The Nationalities Problem and the Theory of Imperialism

For hundreds of years the Russian empire has been composed not only of Great Russians and other Slavic peoples (Ukrainians and White Russians) but also of millions of non-Slavic peoples who had enjoyed, in some cases, long histories as independent nations. In the revolutionary struggle against the czar, the Bolsheviks championed the desire of many of these peoples to secede from the Russian state and attain cultural and political independence, an advocacy that they believed would tend to weaken the czarist state. After coming to power, however, Lenin faced a more complex problem. He was determined to preserve as much of the czarist territory as possible; yet he was highly sensitive to the effect that the Russian Revolution would have on non-Western peoples in their struggles against European colonial powers. He did not want the revolution to be subject to the charge of imperialism.

In addressing the problem, Lenin argued that both the right of self-determination of non-Russian peoples and the revolutionary interests of the proletariat and peasantry must be respected, but the latter must take precedence. "Theoretically," he stated, "you cannot say in advance whether the bourgeois-democratic revolution will end in a given nation seceding from another nation, or in its equality with the latter; *in either case,* the important thing for the proletariat is to ensure the development of its class . . . . That is why the proletariat confines itself, so to speak, to the negative demand for recognition of the *right* to self-determination, without giving guarantees to any nation."[18]

Thus, the *right* to secede from the Soviet Union would be guaranteed to all non-Russian nationalities (as it is for the current Union Republics) but the question of whether such secession would be allowed in fact depended upon the interests of the class struggle. And there was no doubt in Lenin's mind that the interests of the Revolution would not be served by the disintegration of the czarist empire. "Firstly," he wrote in *The Question of Nationalities or Autonomisation,* "we must maintain and strengthen the *union* of socialist republics. Of this there can be no doubt."[19] The "invincible unity" of the Soviet peoples is an important ideological formula. We shall see in Chapter 12 how successful the Soviet leaders have been in implementing this formula.

To counter the potential charge of imperialism against the Soviet regime, Lenin also utilized a unique conception of international relations, his "theory of imperialism." By this conception, Western capitalist states had been able to forestall revolution in their own countries by exploiting the labor and raw materials of nonwhite peoples in the underdeveloped nations. The profits of this exploitation were used to bribe Western workers with higher wages and thus conceal the extent to which these workers themselves were being exploited. Thus, the onus of imperialism was shifted to the capitalist states.

System Principles and Goal Principles

Leninism is best understood if it is seen as serving two fundamental purposes: first, the legitimization of the Communist Party as the guiding and controlling force in Soviet society, and second, providing a vision of the good life in a society characterized by pure communism. The "system principles" associated with the first purpose are those that emerged from the coalescence of Lenin's pre-1917 theoretical views and his adaptation of those views to the real problems he faced once the Bolsheviks came to power. They include, as discussed above, the dictatorship of the proletariat, volunteerism, *partiinost,* the primacy of political struggle, counterrevolution, the unity of the Soviet nation, and the theory of imperialism.

The second purpose, "Communist construction," is served by a set of "goal principles." They define the quality of life that will be lived by the Soviet people under communism and the role of ordinary people in administering a Communist society. They include a number of radical formulas: a high level of material prosperity shared equally by all the people, popular participation in all activities of government and the judiciary, the elimination of differences between urban and rural life and between manual and intellectual labor, and the gradual "withering away" of the state apparatus and the transfer of governmental functions to public organizations. These idealistic values are rooted in Leninist thought and find continuous reflection in the current Soviet constitution (1977) and in the Program of the Communist Party of the Soviet Union (CPSU) (1986).

Both sets of principles are important to the Soviet system, but in different ways. The first set, establishing the Party's supreme position, is adhered to rigidly and uncompromisingly. Many aspects of its role in Soviet society are not even discussable in a public forum. The second set of principles evokes a contrasting flexibility and even ambivalence on the part of Soviet leaders. It is important to maintain the appearance of progress toward the goals of communism, but in practice the achievement of those goals is necessarily subordinate to the overall economic, military, and cultural development of the state. As the new Party Program states:

> The development of socialism into communism is determined by the objective laws of development of society, laws which cannot be ignored. Any attempts to go ahead too fast and to introduce communist principles without due account being taken of the level of material and spiritual maturity of society are, as experience has shown, doomed to failure and may cause losses of both an economic and political character.[20]

Thus, Leninism provides both a stable structure for organizing elite power and a useful degree of flexibility for governing the country. In later chapters we will explore the role of these ideological factors in a variety of governmental activities.

The Death of Lenin

Decisions on a host of major issues occupied Lenin and the Bolshevik leadership throughout the first three years of the revolutionary period. By the summer of 1921, the civil war was virtually over and the Bolsheviks had not only conquered the country but had also eliminated all potential political opposition to itself in the highest ranks of government and in the soviets. Lenin's triumph seemed complete, and yet he was experiencing increasing anxiety about the future. Late in the year (1921), the first symptoms of serious illness became apparent and he was forced to turn his mind to the troubling problem of a successor. In May of the following year, he suffered a mild stroke and retired from active work for several months. In December he was hit by a more serious stroke, which left him immobilized.

Though his mind remained clear and alert, his writings from the onset of his illness show a decreasing capacity for the trenchant common sense and realism that had characterized his life's work until then. Whether because of the illness or the developing political situation, he began to fear for the future of the revolution. He found increasing fault with his closest colleagues and disappointment with the political structure he had created.

He decried a growing ineffectiveness in the governmental institutions the Party had set up. "We have been bustling for five years," he wrote in March, 1923, trying to improve our state apparatus, but it has been mere bustle, which has proved useless in these five years, or even futile, or even harmful.[21]

He criticized the existence of bureaucrats "in our party offices as well as in Soviet offices,"[22] and demanded that these "rogues" be smoked out. For this purpose he proposed to upgrade the Workers' and Peasants' Inspection, giving them broad responsibilities for overseeing the conduct of state and Party officials. How a large inspectorate, composed mainly of ordinary workers and peasants could have carried out such a task is difficult to imagine.

His prescription for controlling the increasing factionalism among the top leaders of the Party was equally curious. His only concrete proposal was to enlarge the twenty-seven-member Party Central Committee, adding "a few dozen workers" who "can deal better than anybody else with checking, improving, and remodelling our state apparatus."[23] Lenin explicitly identified the source of greatest factionalism as coming from two of his closest associates: Trotsky and Stalin. "I think relations between them make up the greater part of the danger of a split, which could be avoided . . . by increasing the number of Central Committee members to 50 or 100."[24] The actual result of enlarging the membership of the Central Committee, which was done a month later, was to place even more power in the hands of the few leaders who comprised the Politburo and the Secretariat.

In prescribing remedies to long-term problems facing the new Soviet state, Lenin proposed idealistic and vague solutions quite uncharacteristic of his earlier writings. For example, in reflecting upon what he saw as the impending conflict with the capitalist bloc, he declared that Russia must become "civilized," the workers must retain the leadership and respect of the peasants, and the state must be run more economically. Stalin's ideas, involving rapid industrialization, strengthening the armed forces, and seeking beneficial alliances in the West, seem patently more practical and promising.

On the crucial issue of developing financial resources to fund the industrialization of the country, Lenin proposed to find the resources in "the greatest possible thrift in the economic life of our state. . . . We must banish from [the state apparatus] all traces of extravagance."[25] Again, Stalin had a more effective, albeit more draconian, response to the problem, as we shall see in the next chapter.

Finally, in reflecting upon a possible successor to himself, Lenin could find no one to recommend without reservations. In his famous "Testament," written in December and January, 1921/1922, he reviewed his immediate colleagues and found positive but also negative qualities in each. Trotsky displayed "excessive self-assurance" and evidenced "excessive preoccupation with the purely administrative side of the work"; Bukharin's notions of Marxism were deficient; Pyatakov showed "too much zeal for administrating"; and Kamenev and Zinoviev had already besmirched their records in their opposition to Lenin's call for armed uprising in October 1917. Lenin's harshest charges were leveled against Stalin who, he declared, should be removed from his position as General Secretary of the Party.

On January 21, 1924, Lenin died of cerebral sclerosis at the age of fifty-four.

Control of the Party was taken over by a triumvirate, or *troika,* composed of Zinoviev, Kamenev, and Stalin. Within five years Stalin had disposed of all serious rivals to power and had assumed the leadership of the Party and the state himself. Thereupon began the era of "Stalinism," which lasted for a quarter of a century and irrevocably transformed the new Soviet society.

Lenin's legacy to his country was a rich but mixed one, marked as much by the things he did not accomplish as by those he did. He played the leading role in the October Revolution, which brought the Bolsheviks to power, and he was instrumental in defining the principal organs of Party and government. He did not win every battle with his fellow rulers, but his intellect and personality made his views on all matters influential and, on many of them, decisive. Thus, he established effective *personal* authority over the political system.

At the time of his death, however, his most important work was left undone. He had not had time to establish the new forms of governance firmly enough to ensure that they would evolve in ways he would approve of. In particular, he had made no settled arrangement for choosing his successor, which made his own preferences largely irrelevant. He failed to imbue the Party Central Committee or any other collective organ with sufficient strength to avoid falling victim to a single leader. He created a powerful coercive apparatus but paid too little attention to controlling its abuses of power. And he failed even to ensure that the Party would continue to dominate the government, as indeed under Stalin it did not.

The long tradition of Russian politics made it likely that if these moderating and limiting features were not established by the highest levels of authority, they would never appear at all. For there were no effective pressures in the society at large for limitations on the rulers' political power; there were no independent economic or social interests powerful enough to make demands on the Bolsheviks; and there was no tradition supporting the people's right to be consulted about the choice of leaders or the policies of government.

With Lenin's death, therefore, as with the death of a czar, the future of the government depended heavily on the individual who would succeed him. The ascendance of Joseph Stalin was not Lenin's intention, but it was fully consistent with the nature of the governmental system that Lenin bequeathed to the Soviet people. We turn then to an examination of the towering figure of Joseph Stalin, who for twenty-five crucial years was the undisputed autocrat of the Soviet Union.

NOTES

1. David MacKenzie and Michael W. Curran, *A History of Russia and the Soviet Union,* rev. ed. (Homewood, Ill.: Dorsey Press, 1982), pp. 414–15.
2. Edward Crankshaw, *The Shadow of the Winter Palace* (New York, Viking, 1976), pp. 292–93.
3. W. Bruce Lincoln, *In War's Dark Shadow* (New York, Dial Press, 1983), pp. 49–50.
4. Ibid., p. 53.

5. See Bernard Pares, *Russia and Reform* (Westport, Conn.: Hyperion Press, 1907), pp. 452–59.
6. Michael T. Florinsky, *The End of the Russian Empire* (New York: Howard Fertig, 1973), p. 22.
7. Leopold H. Haimson, *The Politics of Rural Russia, 1905-1914* (Bloomington, Ind.: Indiana University Press, 1979), p. 9.
8. Paul Vassili, *Behind the Veil at the Russian Court* (London: Cassell, 1913), p. 388.
9. MacKenzie and Curran, *Russia and the Soviet Union,* pp. 468–71.
10. V. I. Lenin, "Two Tactics of Social-Democracy in the Democratic Revolution," in *Selected Works,* Vol. 1, (Moscow: Progress Publishers, 1967), p. 516.
11. V. I. Lenin, "The Immediate Tasks of The Soviet Government," in *Selected Works,* Vol. 2, pp. 672–73.
12. Quoted in Robert V. Daniels, *The Conscience of the Revolution* (Cambridge, Harvard University Press), 1960, p. 121.
13. Written in 1906, and quoted in Robert V. Daniels, *The Nature of Communism* (New York: Vintage Books, 1962), p. 88. Emphasis added.
14. Cited in Jerry F. Hough and Merle Fainsod, *How the Soviet Union Is Governed* (Cambridge: Harvard University Press, 1979), p. 82.
15. Lenin, "Two Tactics of Social Democracy," Vol. 1, p. 516.
16. Decree of the Central Executive Committee of September 5, 1918, cited in Helene Carrere D'Encausse, *Stalin* (London: Longman, 1981), p. 6.
17. Lenin, "How to Organize Competition?" Vol. 2, p. 518.
18. Lenin, "The Right of Nations to Self-Determination," Vol. 1, p. 614.
19. Lenin, "The Question of Nationalities on 'Autonomisation,' " Vol. 3, p. 751. Italics added.
20. *Draft Program of the Communist Party of the Soviet Union,* rev. ed. Published in *Reprints from the Soviet Press,* Vol. XLI, No. 9–10, November 15–30, 1985. Original in *Pravda,* 26 October, 1985.
21. Lenin, "Better Fewer But Better," Vol. 3, p. 776.
22. Ibid., p. 780.
23. Lenin, "Letter to The Congress," Vol. 3, pp. 737–40.
24. Ibid., p. 738.
25. Lenin, "Pages from a Diary," Vol. 3, p. 755.

CHAPTER 4
Stalinism

He was of very small stature and ungainly build. His torso was short and narrow, while his legs and arms were too long. His left arm and shoulder seemed rather stiff. He had a quite large paunch, and his hair was sparse, though his scalp was not completely bald. . . . His teeth were black and irregular, turned inward. Not even his mustache was thick or firm. Still the head was not a bad one; it had something of the folk, the peasantry, the paterfamilias about it—with those yellow eyes and a mixture of sternness and roguishness."[1]

This was Joseph Vissarionovich Djugashvili, alias Joseph Stalin. For a quarter of a century this man dominated the Soviet Union to an extent that would have been the envy of the most ambitious and tyrannical czar who ever lived. In the course of his rule, Stalin guided the newly formed Soviet Union to some of the most remarkable achievements in world history: the creation of a modern industrial giant out of a backward, rural society; a decisive military victory over the greatest war machine yet created; and the establishment of a political empire that encompassed eight formerly independent countries and a worldwide network of Communist parties willing to accept leadership from Moscow.

All this was accomplished, however, at an almost inconceivable cost in human suffering and social devastation. For these achievements, which ultimately became a source of great pride to most Soviet citizens, were imposed on a bitterly resistant population at a pace that defied imagination. To overcome this resistance, Stalin executed or consigned to the horrors of the Siberian forced labor camps thousands of governmental, military, and Party leaders, including all of Lenin's closest political comrades, and millions of ordinary citizens whose only crime was standing in the way of Stalin's will. In the course of World War II, Stalin uprooted and dispersed whole populations of non-Russian Soviet citizens on grounds of potential disloyalty, and he treated Soviet soldiers who were captured by the Germans as traitors subject to imprisonment upon their return home. The cost of establishing his postwar empire added additional millions to the toll of victims as non-Communist leaders of East European countries were purged and their lands occupied by the Red Army.

Both the extraordinary achievements and the inhuman barbarity of Stalin comprise his legacy to the USSR. The origins of that legacy lie in the personality of Joseph Stalin and in the chaotic decade following the 1917 Revolution when the future design of the new state was being hammered out by the leaders of the Communist Party. The principal consequence of that legacy is the Soviet Union of today. For the USSR of the 1980s was shaped far more fundamentally by Stalin than it was by Lenin or by the several leaders who came to power in the post-Stalin era.

It is therefore critical to understand the nature of Stalinism in order to make sense out of both the political system and the social environment of contemporary Russia. What follows is an analysis of Stalinism in terms, first, of the events of the 1920s out of which Stalin emerged as the dominant leader, and second the nature of the political and social system that Stalin created. Much of the rest of the book will explore the extent to which the USSR has evolved beyond Stalinism.

TRIAL AND ERROR: THE FIRST DECADE (1918–1928)

The Bolshevik takeover in 1917 launched a civil war that lasted for three years. During that period Lenin launched a program of "War Communism," a revolutionary reorganization of the economy that involved nationalization of all industries, massive requisition of grain to feed the army and city residents, the mobilization of labor cadres into military-style work batallions, and the instant creation of a huge bureaucracy to oversee the program. The result was a disaster, both economically and politically, even though it did not prevent the Red Army from triumphing in the civil war. After two years, industrial production had fallen off 80 percent from 1913 levels, agricultural production dropped by half, the army was forcibly confiscating peasant crops and paying for them with worthless paper rubles, and bread rationing had been instituted in the cities.[2]

As Lenin finally realized, the revolution could not merely be commanded to succeed. "Carried away by a wave of enthusiasm," he later admitted, ". . . we thought that by direct orders of the proletarian state, we could organize state production and distribution of products communistically in a land of petty peasants. Life showed us our mistake."[3] By the end of the civil war in 1921, the peasantry was in open rebellion; and at the Kronstadt Naval Base on the Baltic Sea, sailors who had been staunch revolutionaries three years earlier launched a full-scale revolt against Bolshevik rule.

To stave off the imminent collapse of the revolution, the government instituted a New Economic Policy (NEP) in the fall of 1921, which lasted for six years. The goal was to revitalize the agricultural sector and thereby provide resources and manpower to develop the industrial sector. In practice, this involved a Stolypin-like emphasis on providing material incentives to so-called middle peasants who would lead the mass peasantry toward a modernized agricultural sector. Gradually, the working class would "persuade" the peasantry to join cooperatives as socialism was extended into rural Russia. The process contemplated a gradual reeducation of the peasantry rather than state coercion. It also presumed a deferment of the goal of world revolution during the period necessary for internal Soviet development. It was even hoped that a period of international peace would generate a willingness of Western nations to provide some measure of economic assistance to the new Soviet state.

To implement the program, the government retreated rapidly from the revolutionary program of bolshevism, moving to decontrol small retail and wholesale trade and manufacturing operations while maintaining national control over the major industries. It freed producers to contract for raw materials rather than applying for them through planning agencies, and it permitted peasants to reestablish individual farms and to market their products at competitive prices.[4]

Within four years, the Soviet economy had undergone a dramatic improvement, but at the cost of what some leaders considered a basic threat to the revolution. A quasi-capitalist orientation was emerging in the countryside as more ambitious peasants (referred to as *kulaks*) began accumulating more and more land. In addition, a significant part of the economic system was slipping away from government control, and with it the people themselves. As peasants gained the power to decide to sell or withhold their grain, sections of the state planning mechanism became subordinate to market forces of supply and demand. This undermined the government's desire to fund industrial development through excess agricultural productivity.

Within the highest Communist party circles, debate over these issues became interwoven with the question of who was to succeed Lenin as head of the Party. A moderate element led by Bukharin argued that the NEP should continue indefinitely until the country had matured industrially, while a leftist element, led by Zinoviev and Kamenev, attacked the NEP agricultural policies as ideologically unacceptable and detrimental to the rapid buildup of the industrial sector.

Stalin's role in this struggle was calculated both to undermine his political competitors and to move the state in the direction of rapid industrial development. Although the political struggle sometimes required that he express a measure of support for the pro-NEP faction, his steady thrust was directed toward ending the NEP and renewing concentration on heavy industry.[5] Under his prodding, the leadership approved sharp increases in industrial-sector budgets through the mid-1920s. In 1928 alone, the Supreme Economic Council authorized a 50 percent increase in the industrial budget for the following year, a figure that the Party Politburo increased even further.[6]

Nevertheless, the Party leadership was not prepared to abandon the NEP at this point, and Stalin allied himself with Bukharin and the right-wing pro-NEP forces in 1927 and 1928 in order to destroy the left-wing faction. At the 15th Party Congress, held in December 1927 in Moscow, Stalin denounced the Trotsky-Kamenev-Zinoviev faction and persuaded the Congress to adopt resolutions that expelled seventy-five prominent left-wing Communists from the Party and exiled over thirty leaders, including Trotsky, Kamenev, and Radek, to remote parts of the country.

Crushing the "left-opposition" was a problem for Stalin, however, for the expulsion of the anti-NEP elements left the Party solidly committed to a continuation of NEP policies, which Stalin generally opposed. But circumstances in the countryside were changing and the negative aspects of the NEP policy were becoming clearer. In the spring of 1928, following the 15th Party Congress, the government's policy of charging the peasants high prices for manufactured goods while paying them low prices for their grain, in order to fund industrialization, produced increasing food shortages as peasants withheld large quantities of grain from the market in retaliation. Stalin was determined to move against the peasants as harshly as necessary in order to continue the industrialization plans contained in the Five-Year Plan adopted the previous year. He pressed the Party leadership to endorse confiscatory grain policies, "de-kulakization," and the use of military and police forces to enforce compliance.

Those "Rightist" leaders whom Stalin had supported in his struggle against the Left opposition now became his enemies in a new struggle for power and policies. The major figure on the Right was Nicolai Bukharin, a member of the Politburo and editor-in-chief of *Pravda,* the official party newspaper. Bukharin had substantial support in the highest levels of the Party, including the Moscow Party organization headed by Uglanov, the trade union organization of Tomsky, and among government administrators led by Premier Rykov. Stalin's strength lay mainly in the Party Secretariat and the organizational bureaus of the Party; in the Central Committee, which was strongly representative of rising younger Party cadres; and in the Party Control Commission with its powers of investigation and discipline.

In early 1929, a meeting of the Central Committee was convened to attempt to resolve these major policy differences. Amidst party officials largely supportive of Stalin, Bukharin and "Right Deviation" were decisively defeated, and Bukharin was expelled from the Politburo. At this moment, Stalin became Lenin's successor and the de facto leader of both the Soviet Communist Party and the Soviet state.

The process by which Stalin achieved this position established a pattern for the new Soviet system that has been maintained by all of his successors. In the 1920s there were no precedents for selecting a single Party leader. In fact, the assumption that there would be collective rather than individual leadership was generally held by the Party elite. There was no moment when a succession decision had to be made, no fixed term of office for any position, no specific office to be accorded whoever was chosen leader, and no clear scope of authority.

Lenin had gained and held his preeminent position largely because of his superior intellect, his seniority within the Social Democratic Party, and his charismatic personality. On all three counts, Stalin was overshadowed by one or another of his rivals for power, yet in the end he vanquished them all. He did so by demonstrating strength in three areas that proved to be decisive at that time, and are still decisive today:

1. *Personality.* In the midst of the often vehement and bitter debates on the course of the revolution, Stalin appeared to many lesser Party officials as a moderate who was determined to maintain the Party's power but flexible on major policy issues. His serious attention to his work, his willingness to take on detailed administrative tasks, and his modest demeanor among his colleagues attracted substantial support within the Party apparatus, and this compensated for his lack of charisma. Some, including Lenin in his last months, viewed the Georgian with misgivings, sensing those qualities of egocentricity and brutality that were to surface as Stalin's power increased. But for those Party officials whose contact with Stalin was infrequent these qualities were generally concealed.

2. *Issues.* Although, as we shall see below, Stalin was allied with both the Left and the Right at different times after Lenin's death, his basic orientation was quite clear. It was also more or less consistent with the long-term interests and values of the bulk of the Party apparatus. The positions he took on major issues— industrialization, the military buildup, the power of the Party over the government and the people, the use of coercion to enforce policies—all served to persuade important centers of influence within the Party elite that Stalin, rather than Trotsky or Kamenev or Bukharin, was the better choice for leader. The large majorities that supported Stalin at meetings of the Central Committee and the Party congresses held in the late 1920s were significantly those who agreed with him on the major issues.

3. *Organization.* Stalin's willingness to concentrate on administrative and organizational matters within the Party provided him with a powerful base of political support. As General Secretary, he had the authority to appoint, promote, transfer, and dismiss lower-level Party officials. As these officials became delegates to Party congresses and members of the central Party apparatus where major policy matters were decided, their indebtedness to Stalin was often repaid.

Thus, Stalin came to power, as have all of his successors, through a combination of personal qualities, positions on major issues, and organizational support within the Party. As his power increased after Lenin's death, he began to create the political machine that would ensure for him a level of dominance over the political system experienced by few rulers in world history. "Stalinism" became more than a period marked by one-man rule. It became a distinct system of government, a set of ambitious national policy objectives, and, perhaps most characteristically, a style of governance fashioned in the mind and the will of Stalin himself. We turn now to an examination of that phenomenon.

STALINISM AS A POLITICAL SYSTEM

For three decades after Stalin's death, there was no serious debate in the Soviet Union about the role of Stalin in Soviet history except in dissident literature.[7] Whatever interpretation served the interests of the current leadership was obligatory for all levels of Soviet society. Under General Secretary Gorbachev, however, the situation has changed radically. An increasingly critical attitude toward Stalin, including references to him as "dictator," "tyrant," and "criminal," have appeared in the public press in the mid-1980s. This is a result of Gorbachev's policy of *glasnost,* about which much more will be said in a later chapter.

In most of the rest of the world, the subject of Stalinism has long been a matter of lively interest among scholarly and political observers of Soviet politics. By raising critical questions about the current regime, an examination of Stalinism provides a crucial framework within which to assess political change in the Soviet Union. To what extent, for example, has the autocratic nature of Stalinism given way to more persuasive and participatory modes of political activity? To what extent have generational conflicts and changes in educational levels and social expectations come to operate as independent forces in the political system, limiting and shaping the policy perspectives of the Party leadership? And to what extent has the political system evolved beyond the need for and the possibility of another Stalin?

A consideration of these issues will occupy much of the rest of this book. To begin with, let us consider briefly the nature of the Stalinist political system in its original form as it was established in the second decade after the revolution (1927–1937). It consists of three sets of major institutions: those constituting the Communist Party organization, those that comprise the executive/administrative branch, and those that make up the legislative or elective branch. Of the three, the Party is the dominant political structure. Thus, how the Party is to be controlled has perennially been the central question.

By the time of the 14th Party Congress in 1925, less than two years after the death of Lenin, Stalin was clearly the dominant force in the Politburo, but his power rested on the support he had gathered in the leading Party organs that had been established in March 1919. At that time, the Party Central Committee had formed three new organs: a five-man Political Bureau (Politburo), which was to deal with policy matters; an Organizational Bureau (Orgburo) of the same size, which was to administer the Party organization; and a six-man Secretariat. The last agency was given no regular functions and was clearly subordinated to the other Party organs. By early 1922, Stalin had managed, in addition to his membership on the Politburo and the Orgburo (the only Party leader to serve on both bodies), to be appointed General Secretary of the Communist Party.[8] These moves were approved by Lenin and his senior colleagues, who were more interested in broad-scale policy-making than in the pedestrian administrative tasks of running the Party organization. In the following years, Stalin was to demonstrate the fateful consequences of this division of labor.

By acting discretely within the Secretariat, and supporting his actions through his allies in other organs, Stalin gradually encroached on the jurisdictions of the Orgburo and the Politburo regarding such vital matters as appointments to high positions in the Party and the government, the initiation of new policies, and the resolution of controversies among various leaders. Within a decade, Stalin's Secretariat was effectively in charge of appointing the heads of ministries, military leaders, high Party officials, and, most importantly, regional and local Party leaders all over the country. Gradually, he replaced supporters of his major opponents with his own people, thereby isolating his chief rivals in preparation for a final showdown. After 1928 there was hardly a local or regional Party secretary who had not been appointed by Stalin. As these officials were the main source of candidates for selection to the Central Committee, Stalin's control over that body was ensured.

As Stalin worked to concentrate Party power in those organs in which he had greatest influence, he also created a personal staff or cabinet to which the entire Communist Party structure would ultimately be subordinated. Later officially recognized as "Comrade Stalin's Secretariat," it consisted of little-known, younger proteges of Stalin who were not members of the Central Committee or other Party organs. When first appointed, their duties were largely technical and administrative, but as Stalin's grip on the Party machinery tightened, his personal secretariat came to replace both the Party Secretariat and the Politburo as the de facto executive agency of the Party. This small group of assistants gradually assumed responsibility for all high-level personnel appointments to Party, government, military, economic, and police agencies, and initiated or reviewed all policy proposals. Avtorkhanov reports that

> every single question concerning internal or external policy was examined and in practice predecided by Stalin's cabinet before being submitted to the principal organs of the Central Committee and then passed to the appropriate sections. The resolutions of these sections, which merely put the stamp of official approval on the recommendations of the technical experts in Stalin's cabinet, were then passed on for ratification by the Central Committee Secretariat, the Orgburo, and the Politburo.[9]

This network of control was extended outward from Moscow to regional and local Communist Party organizations through the appointment of "special sections" to each Party committee. Personnel in these sections answered only to Stalin's secretariat and functioned principally to observe the activities of the local Party committees and report on them regularly to Moscow. All communication between Moscow and the local Party organization was channeled through the Special Section. The Communist Party became essentially an administrative apparatus subordinate to the personal organization of the General Secretary.

Through these measures, Stalin succeeded in creating a personal political machine that permeated all levels of Soviet government and society. It rested on three pillars of power: the support of the major organs of the Party organization, the membership of which was largely under his control; the police apparatus that effectively terrorized the entire Soviet population including the senior leadership of the political system itself; and the enforced passivity of the population at large. It was the most completely dominating and relentlessly repressive political machine ever devised in a modern nation.

What Stalin gained in political efficiency through the effective silencing of all opposition, he lost to some extent in the bureaucratic inefficiencies attendant upon such extreme centralization. As Professor H. Montgomery Hyde remarks,

> the Soviet bureaucracy is a cumbersome and frequently unworkable machine. Initiative on the part of subordinate bureaucrats is stifled. Everyone seeks to avoid responsibility. Everyone looks to the top for a covering order. And since thousands of relatively unimportant, as well as all-important, problems must pass through Stalin's hands for final decision, the top is always jammed. Weeks are spent in waiting: commissars wait in Stalin's office; presidents of companies wait in the offices of the commissars; and so on down the line. . . . When Stalin got bored or

tired he would go off to one of his villas, giving orders that he was not to be disturbed; the top machinery would practically cease to function, and the whole thing was in a bottleneck.[10]

As we shall see below, the inefficiency of the administrative process did not prevent the remarkable transformation of Russia into a modern industrial and military giant. But it established a political process that imposed strong limitations on the further advancement of the Soviet system in the post-Stalin period.

STALINISM AS A SET OF NATIONAL OBJECTIVES

The system of government created by Stalin served primarily to ensure the continued dominance of the Communist Party and of Stalin himself as autocrat. But it also served as the political framework within which the major objectives of the postrevolutionary period would be pursued. And in that pursuit, the objectives as well as the methods used to attain them influenced the structure of government in important ways.

Pursuit of those objectives was also a major source of legitimation for the new regime. And the need for legitimacy was clearly present. For the Russian Revolution itself had not established the nature of the postrevolutionary era in the popular mind or authorized any particular faction to assume power. That was left to a struggle among contenders for power, and the winners were by no means assured of popular, or even elite, support. That support had to come in major part through the enlistment of the masses and the elite in the attainment of clearly desirable national goals. Stalinism epitomizes this relationship between political structure and national goals and the means used to achieve them.

The goals established by Stalin constituted nothing less than the total reconstruction of Soviet society. These goals were implicit in the Bolshevik ideology of the Revolution, as they were to some extent in the last years of czarism. But they were imbued by Stalin with a fanatical sense of urgency that arose not only out of revolutionary momentum but also out of a strong sense of international danger. In the shortest possible time, Stalin argued, the Soviet Union had to achieve four national objectives: the modernization of a backward society, industrialization, collectivization of agriculture, and the creation of a military establishment capable, for the first time in Russian history, of protecting the country and, of course, the Russian Revolution.

Modernization

Despite Marx's conclusion that socialist revolutions would normally occur only after capitalism had fully matured, no Communist revolution has ever succeeded in a capitalist state. Instead, Communist revolutions have invariably occurred in primarily agricultural states where industrial capitalism was at the earliest stage of development rather than the latest. For that reason, communism has come to be associated with social and economic modernization rather than with the collapse of mature capitalist systems.

In the Soviet case, modernization was an unspoken but powerful drive of the Stalinists who inherited the 1917 revolution. It was the antidote for "backwardness," a demeaning condition in which Russia was forever the victim of more advanced European nations. As Stalin once proclaimed, "We are fifty or a hundred years behind the advanced countries. We must make good this distance in ten years. Either we do it, or they crush us."[11]

Modernization as an antidote to backwardness had social, cultural, and emotional dimensions as well as military and economic implications. It involved a massive educational effort both to eliminate illiteracy and to provide the technical training required by industry and government. Urbanization developed rapidly as peasants were induced to move to cities with promises of jobs and a higher standard of living. As the control of the Party over the Soviet people spread to all parts of the country, the nationalization of social welfare kept pace. The government undertook to set up facilities for medical care, preschool education and child care, urban housing, recreation, and public works.

In the early 1930s, the spontaneity and experimentation of the NEP period gave way to the disciplined mass behavior required by the gigantic program of mobilization decreed by Stalin. To the extent that modernization involves the harnessing of mass populations to gigantic tasks of economic development and military defense, the Soviet Union undertook, and fulfilled, the goal in record time. However, the sociological and psychological attributes of modernization have been more elusive in Soviet development as we shall see in later discussions of contemporary Soviet culture.

Industrialization

The rapid industrialization of Russia was preordained regardless of who won the revolution or even if there had been no revolution. The old czarist leadership no less than the new Bolshevik leadership saw in industrialization both the necessary means to economic prosperity and the essential prerequisite to national security. "Without railways and mechanical industries," Alexander II's finance minister wrote, "Russia cannot be considered secure in her boundaries. Her influence in Europe will fall to a level inconsistent with her international power and her historic significance."[12]

For Marxist revolutionaries, industrialization was the inevitable fulfillment of an immutable historical process. A revolution for and by a proletariat could do nothing else but create a social system in which industrial labor was the most prevalent and the most morally superior form of human activity. That this caused the Bolsheviks problems, both theoretical and practical, with farmers, intellectuals, white-collar workers, the military, and women was true but, in the early years, largely irrelevant. The demand for industrialization was overwhelming; only the pace and the cost of the process were debated after the revolution, and that debate was resolved by Stalin's victory over his opponents.

The pace of industrialization depended on both the resources that could be amassed to finance it and the speed with which millions of Russian peasants could be mobilized and trained for industrial labor. Because Stalin anticipated, rightly as it turned out, receiving no significant financial assistance from abroad, there seemed no alternative but to squeeze the resources out of an already poor peasantry as well as from the emerging urban proletariat.

To accomplish this, the first Five-Year Plan, an economic program introduced in 1928, applied centralized control over the entire Soviet economy, set ambitious goals for heavy industrial production, directed 80 percent of the total investment funds to this purpose, and ordered the recruitment of millions of peasants as factory workers. To raise money, the state siphoned off "loans" from workers' wages, repeatedly raised taxes to new levels, bought foodstuffs from peasants at very low prices and sold them to workers at much higher prices, and intentionally depressed the general standard of living by some 40 percent between 1929 and 1932.[13] The government also exported large quantities of foodstuffs, despite desperate food shortages at home, to pay for the importing of machinery and raw materials.[14]

The economic goals of the first Five-Year Plan were highly unrealistic, yet the Party leadership decreed almost immediately that they would be fulfilled in four years rather than five. Within two years, the economic indicators were far below the expectations of the plan, yet at the 16th Party Congress in 1930 Stalin announced sharp increases in the goals, in some cases as much as 100 percent. In 1931 and 1932, as goal after goal failed to be met, Stalin kept increasing them and blaming "wreckers" and "saboteurs" for the country's failure to meet them. Finally, in January 1933, Stalin announced the successful fulfillment of the Five-Year Plan in only four years and three months![15]

Although the plan had hardly been fulfilled in any of the major economic categories, Stalin's proclamation of success was a source of widespread excitement and satisfaction. And indeed the four-year effort had produced impressive achievements. Some 1,500 large industrial enterprises were built during the period of the plan and whole new industries, such as machine-tool production, automobile and tractor manufacturing, chemicals, and aircraft production, were established. Overall, gross industrial output increased by 100 percent between 1928 and 1933, while heavy industrial production grew by 270 percent. Even the production of consumer goods climbed by 56 percent, although this was so far below the needs of the population that the standard of living of the Russian people declined substantially during those years.[16]

The Collectivization of Agriculture

Of all the obstacles that faced the new Bolshevik leadership, none was more of a problem than that most conservative of all Russian social classes, the peasantry. Illiterate, deeply religious, immersed in myths and superstitions, and consumer of voracious quantities of alcohol, the Russian peasant had little perception of the explosive and violent changes that the Bolshevik Revolution would impose on him.

In a theoretical (Marxist) sense, the peasant was almost irrelevant, for the engine of the Russian Revolution was the urban proletariat, not the rural peasant. Ironically, however, the rural nature of Russia quickly made the peasant the central figure in the brutal struggle to reshape the country in the Bolshevik image. The recruitment of an urban work force required hundreds of thousands of peasants to move to towns and cities and to adapt to the rigid discipline of the assembly line and the claustrophobic indignities of the urban ghetto. Those who stayed on the land had to meet vastly increased demands for food as the non-food-producing population swelled in number. Furthermore, the capital resources needed to fund industrialization had to come largely from the agricultural sector, which required extracting maximum productivity out of the peasantry while paying them as little as possible for what they produced. In a profound sense, the success of the economic revolution depended on the extent of sacrifice that could be exacted from the peasantry.

In comparison with American patterns of farming, Russian agriculture had always been a collective enterprise. In the nineteenth century, the abolition of serfdom had not created an independent peasant farmer but had replaced feudal estates with communes (the *mir*), in which villages had collective responsibility for the land owned by individual families and would redistribute strips of land periodically. The vast majority of the 16 million farms were smaller than twenty acres. As the population grew, productivity failed to increase significantly so the lot of the peasantry deteriorated and the demand for more land increased. Gradually, the czarist government grew disenchanted with the inefficiency of the *mir* and alarmed at the violent outbreaks that were occurring in the countryside with increasing frequency.

Following the violence of 1905, the czar's prime minister, P.A. Stolypin, launched a radical reform of the Russian countryside. The Decree of November 6, 1906, abolished the commune, provided for the consolidation of scattered strips into compact farms, and rescinded the laws that imposed joint family ownership of the land so that henceforth the eldest male member of the household was the legal owner.

The government's hope was that ambitious peasants would find individual ownership a powerful incentive to increase productivity and to exhibit greater loyalty to the monarchy. By the time of the 1917 Revolution, the number of large farms had increased dramatically to some 200,000, which controlled over a quarter of the arable land of Russia.

During and after the civil war (1918–1921) and through the period of the NEP, the peasants were encouraged to engage in individual farming. Unfortunately, overall food productivity declined, both because of the inefficiency of millions of small, primitive farms, and also because peasants tended to consume more food themselves and to withhold surplus products from the market in hopes of higher prices.

To Stalin, whose fanatic drive to industrialize the country was being frustrated by these factors, the need to end individual farming and to organize the peasantry for the massive task of industrialization was clear. By 1928, two forms of collectivized agriculture had been established: the "collective farm" (*kolkhoz*) and the "state farm" (*sovkhoz*). Collective farms were of three types: the *toz*, in which peasants retained their land but joined together to share tools and cooperate in the work; the *artel*, where all land was held collectively except for small plots retained by individual families; and the *commune*, where no private property was permitted and the peasants lived communally.[17] State farms, originally proposed by Lenin in 1919, were patterned after industrial establishments, with hourly pay, specialization of function, and hierarchical organization. Both forms of collectivized farming represented the end of the era of individual farming in the Soviet Union. By the end of 1928, there were over 33,000 *kolkhozy* in operation involving over 400,000 peasant households.[18] Yet this was only a modest increase compared to the avalanche that was about to begin. In December 1929, Stalin launched an all-out drive to "liquidate the kulaks[19] as a class" and to organize the entire hundred-million-strong peasantry into collectivized farm units.

It was clear also that the Party intended to adopt the *commune* type of collective by which peasants were totally disenfranchised and reduced to the status of serfs.[20] In fact, however, the *artel* remained the main form of collective farm throughout the Stalin era as the private plots provided a high proportion of the dairy and vegetable production of the country as well as a necessary cushion against the ever-present danger of famine.

In less than a year, over 70 percent of all peasant households had been collectivized.[21] Stalin ordered the physical removal of several million so-called kulaks and the forcible joining of collectives by tens of millions of other peasants. The resistance of the peasantry was ferocious, and villages became battlefields as Stalin ordered the military and secret police to enforce the Party's decree. Unable to resist such forces, peasants began to slaughter their livestock rather than see them confiscated by the state. The toll was appallingly high, including in 1929 alone the slaughter of 18 million horses (out of a total of 34 million). By 1933, 45 percent of the cattle and 67 percent of the sheep and goats had been slaughtered.[22] The poor harvests of 1931–1932 foreshadowed the famine of the following year, which cost several million Soviet lives.

The collectivization program was an economic disaster. The level of food production attained during the NEP period was not achieved again until 1939–1940, and the regeneration of stocks of cattle, pigs, sheep, and horses took even longer. Yet from the Party's standpoint, there were two overriding benefits that emerged. First, the collectivization of agriculture contributed substantially to the development of heavy industry by freeing tens of thousands of peasants, formerly occupied on private farms, for work in factories and mines, and by providing a far more effective way to tax agricultural productivity than was possible with 25 million private farms. These taxes, which greatly depressed the living standards of the peasantry, contributed substantially to the advancement of the industrial sector.

But the major achievement of the collectivization drive, from the standpoint of the Communist Party leadership, was the successful organization of the Russian peasantry into large organizational structures, the collective and state farms, through which the Party could dominate the countryside and begin the gigantic task of resocializing them to a modern (socialist) way of life and thinking. Henceforth, the dream of individual farm ownership, which had burned so long in the consciousness of the peasantry, was irrevocably dashed. The peasantry were permanently dependent upon the collective farm for their livelihood and survival, and the collective farm was solidly under the control of the Communist Party. In this sense, at least, the collectivization drive was a highly successful operation.

The Militarization of Soviet Society

The antipathy of the Western world toward the Bolshevik Revolution, combined with the historic insecurity of Russia's borders, generated an intense determination among the new leaders to strengthen the military power of the country. The weakness of the Russian army during World War I was painfully evident. Russia had had to import from abroad over three-fourths of the guns, ammunition, airplanes, and explosives used by its soldiers, and was even unable to supply all of them with uniforms and boots.

As early as 1927, the probability of attack from Western Europe had become a fixation with Soviet leaders,[23] and planning for the first Five-Year Plan focused significantly on the military needs of the country. The army was placed in a privileged position with respect to receiving the best-quality manufactured goods and the best-trained men. Massive emphasis was given to the development of metallurgy and of the internal combustion engine, which spurred the manufacture of tanks and airplanes. The building of new industrial plants was concentrated in the central and eastern areas of European Russia, a thousand miles away from the western borders so as to ensure their security during wartime. In agricultural areas, the formation of Machine-Tractor Stations (MTS) to mechanize the collective farms also provided a large reserve of men trained to operate and maintain heavy equipment and vehicles. These men later formed the core of the armored and motorized divisions of the Red Army.

Organizationally, the Party's military orientation was rapidly intensifying. By 1927, the Council of Labor and Defense had become a major policy-making organ headed by the Chairman of the Council of Peoples' Commissars. In every ministry, a department of military mobilization was created, and a special section of the State Planning Department (Gosplan) was created to deal with military needs.[24] At the same time, Soviet leaders undertook to provide some degree of military training for the whole Soviet population. A massive volunteer defense organization, named the Society for the Defense of the Soviet Union (*Osoaviakhim*), was formed to develop plans and facilities for the military training of civilians, and by 1932 there were 20 million members.

The Soviet emphasis on military power, both to maintain control over the country and the empire and to ensure the nation's security, has continued unabated to the present time. During Stalin's years in power, the military establishment was completely subordinate to the civilian Party leadership. In the past two decades, however, the weight of military priorities in Party decision making has increased and with it the political power of the Soviet military establishment. We shall look more closely at this development in a later chapter.

STALINISM: TACTICS AND STRATEGIES

Pursuit of these objectives by the Bolshevik leadership gave shape to the developing new Soviet nation. But the means adopted to promote the objectives came to characterize, even more than the objectives themselves, the essense of Stalinism. The underlying strategy called for the mobilization of the entire Soviet population in the shortest possible time. There was in Stalin's mind no possibility of awaiting the gradual transformation of the population and the system, one step at a time, throughout the rest of the century. Moved by fear of impending war, by the colossal scope of the goals he had set for the nation, and by his own relentless drive, Stalin created a political system organized for massive and rapid transformation in all areas of human activity.

The scope of Stalin's plan was historically unprecedented. By comparison, the efforts of Peter the Great or Kemal Ataturk or the Shah of Iran—reformers of no small ambition themselves—seem almost dilatory. To some extent the nature of the objectives dictated the means necessary to achieve them. But beyond that, Stalin's own personality must be considered a major determinant of the means used and of the intensity with which they were applied.

This "second revolution," begun in the late 1920s, involved two major tasks: the creation of a new elite, which was technically capable of carrying out the transformation of Soviet society and politically loyal to Stalin and obedient to his commands; and the mobilization of the mass population into a willing, enthusiastic, and dedicated force capable of overcoming centuries of backwardness and ignorance in the pursuit of modernization. To accomplish these tasks, Stalin relied both on harsh punitive measures and on financial and social rewards—the carrot and the stick. It was not enough for Stalin to destroy his enemies, real or imagined, and to eliminate all possible sources of resistance among the population. He demanded nothing less than total commitment to the new regime and its goals, and he employed a wide range of both aversive and constructive measures to achieve that end.

The Creation of a New Elite

By the time of the 14th Party Congress in 1925, Stalin had emerged as the most influential of the several remaining revolutionary leaders; and by the end of the decade the first Five-Year Plan was moving the country in the direction he desired.

Nevertheless, much of the debate in the leading Party organs retained its Leninist revolutionary flavor well into the 1930s. Arguments among the leaders about policy proposals drew heavily on different interpretations of the purposes of the revolution, the vague ideals of pure democratic communism, the theoretical propositions of Marxism-Leninism, the prestige of individual leaders who had been close comrades of Lenin, and assumptions about how Lenin himself would have handled a particular problem. Despite Stalin's dominant position, he was obliged to struggle with the Party elite, as Lenin had always done, over major policy questions. And his aversion to controversy over policies was, if anything, even more absolute than Lenin's.

As Stalin's own power increased, he moved to end this "government by debate" by removing from power all those who engaged in such debate, those who influenced others to engage in it, and those multitudes of middle-level officials who might assume that such debate was useful to progress. He also apparently intended to deal with several other elements of the existing elite whom he found intolerable. His chronic anti-Semitism expressed itself in a thorough purge of Jews from the Central Committee and Politburo,[25] while his antagonism toward the Leningrad faction of the Party leadership, headed by his old opponent Zinoviev, resulted ultimately in the destruction of that faction along with its leader.

The "purge" as an instrument of Stalin's rise to supreme power began as soon as Stalin was in a position to carry it out. After his defeat of Trotsky in 1927, arrests of "saboteurs" and "wreckers" began in earnest. In 1928, the first show trial was held at which forty-seven engineers from the Donets Basin were convicted of sabotage and, in some cases, executed.[26] Other such trials followed soon after, and in 1933 the Party Central Committee appointed a purge commission to oversee a thorough purge of the Party rank and file. As a result, well over a million Party members were expelled during the following two years, expulsions that increasingly resulted in loss of jobs, exile to the east, or imprisonment.

Using the 1934 assassination of a popular Bolshevik leader, Sergei Kirov, as an excuse, Stalin began to move against his colleagues in the highest positions of Party and state leadership. In August 1934, the first of three major show trials began with the arrest of Kamenev, Zinoviev, and other old Bolshevik leaders on charges of plotting to overthrow the government and murder Stalin. In 1937 and 1938, similar trials were staged for other leaders, and the charges were broadened to absurd dimensions. Long-time revolutionary colleagues of Lenin were convicted of being spies for Germany and Japan, of plotting to dismember the Soviet Union by detaching all of the non-Russian republics, of causing food shortages, train wrecks, and agricultural blight, and of having conspired *throughout their entire lives* for the defeat of communism in Russia. Through torture and threats against family members, as well as occasionally misplaced idealism and Party loyalty, most of the accused leaders were persuaded to confess to wildly improbable charges, thus giving a patina of legitimacy to the gruesome proceedings. The chief prosecutor, Andrei Vyshinsky, marked the conclusion of his case against some of the defendants with the triumphant demand, "Shoot the mad dogs!"[27]

The grand purge of Party and government officials finally ran its course by 1939 on the eve of World War II (though lesser purges continued to be instituted in subsequent years). In its wake lay a trail of destruction almost unimaginable to the modern mind. With the exception of Stalin himself, all active members of the Politburo who had served with Lenin were executed (save one who committed suicide), including the exiled Trotsky who was felled with an ax by a Stalinist agent in Mexico in 1940. Of the members of the Party Central Committee who were elected in 1934, at the "Congress of Victors" as it was ironically called, 70 percent were eliminated, mostly by firing squads. At the next Party congress, held in 1939, only 35 of the 1,827 delegates to the 1934 congress were present. In addition, according to Alec Nove, the purge claimed the lives of "almost every Party and state leader in every national republic within the USSR, on charges of treason, bourgeois nationalism, etc."[28]

Among the military officer corps, the most prominent victim was Marshal Tukhachevskii, one of the heroic figures in the civil war on the side of the Bolsheviks. In addition, the purge destroyed two of the other four marshals, fourteen of sixteen army generals, all full admirals, and about half the entire officer corps of the armed forces. The killing extended into the ranks of artists, writers, teachers, and scientists and left, in fact, no major area of the Soviet intellectual elite untouched.

Stalin's grand purge had two immediate consequences: It terrorized the Soviet elite into abject submission to Stalin's will, and it opened the door for the rapid career advancement of thousands of ambitious young men and women. There was suddenly a lot of room at the top, and at lower levels as well. Newly built higher institutes and universities filled with a new wave of students, many of whom were not recent high school graduates but workers and minor officials who were well beyond the conventional college age. Out of these student cohorts came a large percentage of high-level Soviet officials in the post-Stalin era. As Hough and Fainsod note, "in 1957 . . . some 45% of all USSR ministers had entered college at the beginning of the five-year plans, after working for some years in some relatively minor job or jobs."[29]

At lower levels equally dramatic changes occurred. From 1924 to 1933, membership in the Communist Party increased eightfold, and many of the new recruits were young people who were moving into higher-status occupations. By 1933, some 43 percent of party members were employed in white-collar jobs (as compared with 8 percent eight years earlier).[30] Hundreds of thousands of them were advancing into administrative and political work or into higher educational institutions in preparation for later career advancement.

From this perspective, the 1930s were an era of exciting opportunities for aggressive and ambitious young Soviets, some of whom ultimately reached the pinnacle of power. Leonid Brezhnev, for example, became a middle-level Party secretary in charge of a major industrial province at the age of thirty-three. Yuri Andropov was only twenty-six when, in 1940, he was appointed first secretary of the Communist Youth Organization in the Karelo-Finnish Republic. And Nikita

Khrushchev moved from relatively low-level Party work in 1929 (at the age of thirty-five) to the first secretaryship of the Moscow regional Party organization six years later. Even at the very peak of the political structure—the Politburo—the average age of its members in 1934 was only forty-eight (compared to sixty-eight in the 1984 Politburo).

To fuel the momentum of this upward surge, Stalin introduced a wide range of practical incentives. The most skilled factory workers were soon receiving ten to fifteen times what unskilled workers received. The salaries of military officers and Party officials also escalated in the early 1930s, but more important than monetary income were the privileges associated with different levels of occupational status. Housing, access to consumer goods, medical services, educational opportunities, and similar intangible benefits were allocated according to one's position in the hierarchy. Even food came to be distributed according to political and social status. Helene d'Encausse notes that, in the early 1930s, "foreign specialists had the right to 48 kilos [about 24 loaves] of bread a month, workers to only 24, and office workers and children to 12. For meat, the differences were even greater, the rations ranging from 14 kilos to 4.4 and 2.2."[31]

Whether these elite benefits were paid for by lower standards of living for the masses of Russian peasants and for low-skilled industrial and office workers is difficult to calculate.[32] Statistical data on this era are highly unreliable, and the calculation of the cost and worth of intangible benefits is rather subjective. Nationally, wages went up during the 1930s, but prices also went up, especially after the end of consumer rationing in 1935. In the latter half of the decade the economy as a whole made dramatic progress: Industrial productivity rose substantially above prerevolutionary levels, and agricultural yields, after the disastrous short-ages of the early 1930s, improved greatly. The grain yield in 1937 was, in fact, 50 percent higher than in 1913, the last prewar year. In any case, the sense of remarkable economic achievement was real and widespread, generating (in ironic juxtaposition to the terrifying fear of the purges) attitudes of optimism and commitment on the part of a broad stratum of upwardly mobile young careerists eager to share in the fruits of the revolution.

Mobilizing the Masses

The combination of repression and opportunity that Stalin applied to the Soviet elite was repeated on a much vaster scale among the population as a whole. The purge of the old elite was accompanied by a campaign of mass terror probably unparalleled in human history. Before it was over, MacKenzie and Curran state, "half the urban population of the USSR was on police lists and five percent had actually been arrested."[33] The categories of citizens subject to arrest defied all reason: friends and relatives of anyone already arrested; children of arrestees down to the age of twelve; fellow workers or friends involved in recreational activities (Nove reports that when the former commissar for justice, Krylenko, an avid mountain climber, was arrested, so were hundreds of others who also happened to be mountain climbers); people (even Communists) of foreign (especially German and Polish) extraction; and anyone who had traveled abroad or had contacts abroad. The "crimes" charged against such people included such ingenious inventions as "wrecking and diversionism," appeasement toward enemies of the state, secretly supporting the "Judas-Trotsky," failing to denounce someone later arrested, and on and on.

The absurdity and the tragedy of the mass purges are devastatingly portrayed in several of Alexander Solzhenitsyn's novels, such as this passage from *The First Circle:*

At the beginning of the war they jailed him for "anti-Soviet agitation"—some neighbors who hankered after his apartment denounced him (and then got it). True, it turned out that he hadn't done any agitating, but he *could* have done it, because he listened to the German radio. True, he didn't listen to the German radio, but he *could* have listened, since he had a forbidden radio receiver at home. True, he didn't have such a receiver, but he *could* have had one, since he was a radio engineer by profession, and when he was denounced they did find two radio tubes in a box at his place.[34]

Stalin's suspicion of the West, even Russia's allies during the war, brought more suffering on the people. In his memoirs, the composer Dmitri Shostakovich relates how Stalin's hatred of the West was transferred to Russians who had had any contact with Westerners. "A man received a letter from America and was shot. And the naive former Allies kept sending letters and every letter was a death sentence. Every gift, every souvenir—the end. Doom."[35] Stalin's personal reaction to a person or event often had tragic consequences. "Sometimes," Shostakovich recalls, "it took only a trifle to make Stalin angry, a careless word. A man talked too much, or was, in Stalin's opinion, too educated, or carried out Stalin's orders too well. That was enough. He perished."[36]

It is difficult to be sure how many Soviet citizens fell victim to the Stalinist purges. Western estimates range from a "low" of "tens of thousands"[37] to a high in the tens of millions. Stalin himself was alleged, by Winston Churchill, to have put the number of victims at 10 million, but that apparently included the collectivization campaign and the famine of the early 1930s as well as the purges.

For those who survived the terror, the conditions of life became both more oppressive and, at the same time, more ripe with opportunities for improvements in one's status. On the negative side, a harsh labor discipline was imposed with the introduction of "labor books," which every worker was required to maintain. Tardiness or absenteeism at work was subject to reprimands and loss of pay, the right to leave a job was severely curtailed, and, after the European war broke out in 1939, quitting a job without authorization became a criminal offense. In 1932, the death penalty was imposed for stealing socialist property.

On the positive side, many ordinary Soviet citizens improved their personal situations during this period. Many of them joined the Communist Party, the proportion of them holding white-collar jobs increased from 8 percent to 43 percent during the 1924 to 1932 period, and millions of peasants improved their status and income by moving to urban centers to work in industry.[38]

Thus, with the mass citizenry as with the elite, the Stalinist transformation combined a high degree of fear and brutality with extraordinary opportunities for social and economic advancement. It is not surprising therefore that contemporary Soviet reflections on the Stalinist period involve mixed and conflicting emotions.

Building Authority

The importance of both fear and opportunity in establishing the new Soviet regime was undoubtedly very great. Yet these alone would probably have produced little more than alienation and opportunism among the Soviet people. For that reason, Communist governments have never settled for mere obedience from their subjects. They have invariably attempted to generate loyalty and enthusiasm among the masses, creativity and altruistic devotion to the Party among the elite, and the respect of the outside world.

The Soviet approach to these objectives formed a unique and successful program of revolutionary legitimation, one that has provided a model for all other Communist systems. Beginning in the early 1930s, when terror and brutality were intensifying throughout Soviet society, Stalin endeavored to convince the Soviet people that not only was the Communist Party all-powerful but that it was also infallibly correct in its decisions and morally justified in its exercise of power. This required of the people, elite and masses together, an extraordinary psychological adjustment, what David Shipler has called a "willing suspension of disbelief,"[39] an act of faith that rendered them oblivious to much of the reality that surrounded them.

To bring this about, Stalin moved in four complementary directions: the creation of a "cult of personality" around the top Party leader, the adoption of a "liberal constitution," the identification of bolshevism with Russian patriotism, and the control of all public and most private information.

The Cult of Personality. In the twentieth year of Stalin's power (1949), his future successor, Nikita Khrushchev, referred to the General Secretary in this manner:

> Millions of people nurture feelings of deepest love and devotion for Stalin who, together with Lenin, created the Bolshevik party and our socialist state, who enriched the theory of Marxism-Leninism and raised it to a new and higher level. This is why all the peoples inhabiting our land so warmly and with such filial love refer to the great Stalin as their father, great leader, and teacher of genius. . . . Comrade Stalin like a loving gardener tends and cares for all the men and women.[40]

By then, the adoring panegyrics expressed by Khrushchev were so routine as to seem commonplace. Stalin had become, through the artful use of a massive propaganda machine, the Great Genius in All Fields of Human Endeavor. Besides his universally acknowledged political mastery, Stalin was portrayed as the guiding inspiration for all art, music, literature, and science. He made madly acclaimed statements in the fields of biology, history, engineering, and genetics and imposed his personal tastes even where it led to absurd inconsistencies. The plays of Mikail Bulgakov, for example, were all suppressed by Stalin except for one, *Dni Turbinykh,* which he went to see fourteen times.[41]

As the years in power accumulated, the real Stalin receded more and more from public view. After 1935, he rarely left the Kremlin except to visit one of his dachas in the countryside. In his place emerged a mythical Stalin, the delineation of whom required the rewriting of the whole history of the revolution making it clear that next to Lenin (to whom Stalin always deferred in public), Stalin was the real hero and father of the revolution.

This mythical Stalin touched a profound chord in the Russian psyche. Inculcated into children in the earliest grades in school, promulgated by all forms of communications media, and written into all ceremonial and ritualistic expressions, the greatness of Stalin inspired soldiers to shout, "Long Live Stalin" as they went to battle and moved purged leaders to praise him as they went to the gallows on his orders.

That this worshipful effusion was genuine for most Russians is beyond question. A dissident Soviet author attests that

> throughout his one-man rule [Stalin] was popular. The longer this tyrant ruled the USSR, cold-bloodedly destroying millions of people, the greater seems to have been the dedication to him, even the love, of the majority of people. These sentiments reached their peak in the last years of his life. When he died in March, 1953, the grief of hundreds of millions, both in the Soviet Union and around the world, was quite sincere.[42]

How Stalin succeeded in creating the cult around himself is a complex matter. The glorification of successful revolutionary leaders is of course a common occurrence. And the dramatic changes wrought by the revolution may have imbued the population with a sense of mystery and wonder at the work of the national leaders. The low level of literacy and cultural development and the deeply religious nature of the Russian people also provided a climate receptive to claims of omniscience and moral rectitude. Russians had for centuries viewed the czars as godlike mortals exercising the authority of a divine being.

Further, the exercise of reason and common sense served not to generate skepticism about the claims of the all-knowing Stalin but to entrap people even more deeply in the rhetoric of the cult of personality. To believe that Stalin deserved credit for all of the achievements while exonerating him of blame for all of the horrors came to seem the only rational point of view. Consider these plaintive words of the writer Pis'mennyi regarding Stalin's responsibility for the terror:

In those years it was impossible to understand what was happening. You could become an informer, go mad, commit suicide, but if you wanted to live, the most convenient way for an unhappy, distraught, but honorable person clinging with his last ounce of strength to his place in society—I repeat and will go on repeating a thousand times—was to *believe*. To believe without reasoning, without second thoughts, without proofs, as people believe in omens, in God, in the devil, in life beyond the grave. The thought that all social actions could be prompted by the criminal designs of a single man who had appropriated the full plenitude of power, and that this man was Stalin, was blasphemous, was unbelievable.[43]

The psychological impact of a political structure exhibiting both infallibility and omnipotence had a profound effect on the Russian people, both the elite and the masses alike. It ended the experimental heterogeneity of the NEP period and created a centrally proclaimed orthodoxy over all phases of Soviet life that was enforced by belief in its verity, by fear of arrest, and by the countless more subtle mechanisms of social control. As Pis'mennyi avowed, for most Russians there was, psychologically, no alternative but to believe.

Constitutionalism. As the purges and show trials moved relentlessly forward in the mid-1930s, Stalin made a dramatic move to persuade his own people as well as opinion-leaders in Europe and the United States that the Soviet system was evolving toward a liberal democracy. In February 1935 he authorized the drafting of a new national constitution that would mark the end of the revolutionary period in the USSR and the beginning of a new era of class harmony, democratic government, and individual freedom. The "Stalin" Constitution was adopted in 1936 after intensive discussion at 527,000 meetings attended by 36.5 million people, which produced 154,000 proposed amendments. Ultimately forty-three changes, mostly in wording, were made in the document following the public discussion.

The new Constitution established a national bicameral legislature that was to have "supreme legislative power," regular secret elections based on universal suffrage, direct representation of ethnic minorities in the national parliament, the right of republics to secede from the USSR, and the rule of law adjudicated by an independent judiciary. At a time of growing threat to individual rights in Germany, Spain, and elsewhere, the new Soviet Constitution guaranteed the broadest array of civil and personal rights of any existing constitution. In addition to the usual rights to free speech, press, and assembly, Soviet citizens were guaranteed access to "printing presses, stocks of paper, public buildings, the streets, communications facilities, and other material requisites for the exercise of these rights" (Article 125); women were accorded equal rights with men in all spheres of life; all races and ethnic minorities were to be treated equally; and freedom of conscience, religious and secular, was guaranteed.

In a period in which economic depression gripped the Western world, the new Soviet Constitution also promised every citizen the right to an education, a job, a seven-hour workday, annual vacations with full pay, maintenance in old age and during illness or disability. No constitutions in the Western world came even close to this range of guarantees.

At the same time, the new Soviet Constitution described the Communist Party as the "vanguard of the working people in their struggle to build communist society and . . . the leading core of all organizations of the working people, both government and non-government" (Article 126). Lest there be any misunderstanding about the importance of this provision, the official newspaper of the Communist Party, *Pravda,* launched a campaign of clarification. "The introduction of the Stalin Constitution," it stated on November 3, 1936,

> undoubtedly augments the guiding role of the Bolshevist Party. Only a hopeless idiot or a conscious foe of socialism can talk about weakening or diminishing in the new setting the vanguard role of the party.[44]

The guarantees of individual freedom were also strictly subordinated to the "good of society" as determined by the Party leadership. As *Pravda* stated on June 2 of the same year,

> he who makes it his task to unsettle the socialist structure, to undermine socialist ownership, who would mediate an attempt on the inviolability of our native country—he is an enemy of the people. He gets not a scrap of paper, he does not set foot over the threshold of the printing press, to realize his base designs. He gets no hall, no room, no cover to inject poison by word of mouth.[45]

The next year, the leadership found it necessary to remind lower-level Party officials that the "free and secret elections" described in the Constitution should not be taken to imply that the people were actually going to select representatives of their own choice, either in legislative elections or in Party elections:

> As is well-known, at the time of the electoral assemblies in the primary organizations many Party leaders refrained from guiding the elections and left matters to take their own course. . . . Instead of recommending and actively defending Communists worthy of being elected to Party organs, many Party leaders prefer to preserve at conferences a cowardly neutrality. Such conduct has nothing in common with Bolshevism. Such conduct attests misunderstanding of Party democracy. Abstention from leadership in elections may result in accidental, untested people getting into the Party organs. The task of the Party leader is to assist the assembly or conference to select and to elect by secret ballot the most worthy Communists, those most devoted to the Central Committee.[46]

As a condition for enjoying the rights and privileges granted by the Constitution, the document itself imposed serious obligations on citizens. They were obliged to "respect the rules of socialist society," to engage in productive labor "as a duty and a matter of honor," to "maintain labor discipline," and to protect public property "as the sacred and inviolable foundation of the Soviet system" (Articles 130 and 131). Those who committed crimes against public property became "enemies of the people" (Article 131).

Adoption of the 1936 Constitution occurred at the height of the purge trials and the mass police arrests that were terrorizing the country. It is difficult to avoid the conclusion that Stalin's "liberal" Constitution was a transparent attempt to distract attention from the horror at home ("a syrup designed for those who were just about to swallow the bitter pill of the Great Terror," as Ronald Hingley described it[47]) and to generate support from the Western democracies against the growing threat of Nazi Germany. While these were undoubtedly calculated advantages to the Party leaders, the reception of the new Constitution by the Soviet people involved other factors as well.

The Soviet Constitution proclaimed a new era in the development of the Revolution: the end of the class struggle in Russia, the establishment of representative political institutions, and the extension of political rights and social benefits to all the people. It demanded no less than total loyalty to the new regime as the price of enjoying those privileges, and the Soviet people were on the whole willing to pay that price. Only those "enemies of the people" who continued to subvert the national effort to move forward were excluded, and there was little sympathy wasted on them among the citizenry.

In addition, with the publication of the Stalin Constitution, the USSR appeared to be rejoining the community of democratic nations after two decades of revolutionary violence. The creation of Western-style political institutions and a liberal "bill of rights" offered the possibility that the Russian Revolution was finally evolving toward the democratic principles that had always been claimed for it. That this was not to be was not nearly as clear in the 1930s as it became in the 1950s and 1960s.

In 1977, a new Constitution was adopted (see Appendix A) after extensive national discussion. Its principal features are similar to those of its predecessor, although the role of the Communist Party has been given much more prominence, and the duties of citizens have been relatively more emphasized than their rights and privileges.[48] The sections of the Constitution that continue to have significance in the contemporary life of the Soviet people are those that establish the dominant role of the Communist Party and those that guarantee social benefits to the people. Provisions dealing with freedom of speech, press, religion, and so on are inoperative, even in the limited sense in which they were originally granted. The printing presses and assembly halls have not been opened even to loyal citizens except as the Party deems permissible. Nor have any other provisions ever been allowed to stand in the way of "the Revolution."

The USSR is not, therefore, a constitutional political system in the Western sense. The establishment of democratic political institutions and guarantees was never intended to alter the seat of power or to divest the leadership of its historic right to determine the national interest. Legislatures, elections, civil rights guarantees—all were understood within the Leninist tradition, and are still understood, to be available only in conformance with, and in support of, the conception of the national interest that the current leadership adheres to.

Patriotism. The victory of bolshevism in 1917 brought with it a fierce determination to abandon the past and to transform Russian society into a modern, secular, socialist nation. The new rulers set about reinterpreting Russian history in terms of Marxist theory, in which the moving forces were not great czars, generals, and military conquests, but social classes motivated by material interests. In the voluminous writings of the preeminent Bolshevik historian M.N. Pokrovsky, prerevolutionary history became a record of impersonal historical forces, reflected in the struggles of the Russian masses, which eventually led to the democratic Revolution of 1917. Little significance was accorded to the likes of Ivan the Terrible or Peter the Great or to such dramatic events as the Decembrist revolt or the emancipation of the serfs. The Orthodox Church in particular was viciously attacked as an institution of czarist oppression and atavistic superstition.

Through the NEP period and the years of the first Five-Year Plan, this attitude persisted, but then in 1934 it changed abruptly. In that year Stalin decreed an end to the campaign against Russia's past, attacking the now-deceased Pokrovsky and moving on several fronts to restore popular respect for at least some aspects of prerevolutionary Russia. New works of history were commissioned in which the heroic feats of the great czars and military leaders became subjects once more for veneration. A plethora of historical novels on patriotic themes issued forth, national monuments and historic battlefields were restored and opened to Russian tourists, and the great literary and artistic achievements of Russian culture were reintroduced to the public. The Pushkin Festival held in 1937 was turned into a major national celebration of Russian literature, and as the danger of war with Germany increased the emphasis of the Bolshevik leadership on traditional cultural values also expanded. After the outbreak of war in 1941, as Dunlop notes, the Stalinist regime "granted official amnesty to Dostoevski and summoned him to do battle with the Germans."[49]

Stalin's attitude toward the Orthodox Church changed more slowly and to a much more limited extent. By 1939, the Party's principal antichurch organization, the League of Militant Godless, counted over 5 million members, and the Orthodox Church itself had been reduced from 40,000 prerevolutionary parishes to a few hundred administered by only four remaining bishops.

It was not until the attack on Russia by the German armies that Stalin was moved to reconsider the possible usefulness of the Orthodox Church in mobilizing the Soviet people for war. The Church leadership itself facilitated the change by declaring total support for the Soviet state in the war effort and demonstrating its ability to generate popular support for the government and raise massive amounts of money. The government responded positively by discontinuing publication of atheist journals and closing all antireligious museums.[50] Before the end of the war, Stalin had also permitted the election of Metropolitan Sergei to the position of patriarch of the Church, a position that had been left vacant since 1925, and the formation of a new Holy Synod to administer Church affairs.

The immediate causes for Stalin's about-face on official attitudes toward the Russian past were the critical need for public support in the upcoming struggle with the capitalist West and the domestic need to rebuild national morale after the period of terror. Patriotism could serve both purposes, and Stalin successfully tapped a deep reservoir of devotion to the ancient motherland. Perhaps one of Stalin's most successful tactics was his ability to link the Communist Revolution with the Russian nation. We shall deal in a later chapter with the effects of this linkage on the behavior and values of the Soviet people after the Stalinist era.

The Control of Information. In the system of "Stalinism," controlling information is not limited to ensuring that negative information does not become public. Its larger purpose is to create a "reality" for the Soviet people in which the Party and its leader are infallible and omniscient and in which the overwhelming masses support Party policies. To this end all forms of communications media, including expressive media such as films, plays, operas, symphonies, folk songs, architecture, and modes of dress and hair styles, were turned in the most intensive propaganda campaign in history.

To ensure its success, the Party leadership took monopolistic control of all newspapers, publishing houses, performance halls, and meeting places. It created a vast network of censors who operated under direct Party control to ensure that only approved points of view were communicated. And it established numerous channels of secret communication so that officials on different levels would learn only what the leadership considered it necessary for them to know. All government and Party activities and personnel at the upper levels were secured from public criticism, except where Stalin decreed otherwise. For the populace itself, a regime of silence was imposed over vast areas of ordinary life. The intent was constantly to reinforce the belief that the Soviet Union was successfully overcoming all obstacles and moving toward the achievement of the world's most affluent, peaceful, and just society. That belief was an important source for the legitimacy of rule by the Communist Party and its leaders.

In one sense, the effort was eminently successful. During Stalin's lifetime, and for decades thereafter, the habit of expressing only views clearly consistent with the Party line has been deeply ingrained in the public mind. On the other hand, the control of information has clearly failed in its more important purpose: to create a genuine public belief in the version of reality presented by the Party. The sharp divergence between the approved image of Soviet life and the actual conditions of that life has generated a mass cynicism and disregard for the truth that deeply infuses Soviet society. It is only with the advent of Mikhail Gorbachev's policy of *glasnost* (openness) and the revival of serious studies of public opinion in the mid-1980s that the scope of that divergence is gradually being revealed. Its consequences will be evident as we examine the workings of the Soviet political system in the following chapters.

CONCLUSION

The chief architect of contemporary Soviet society was Stalin, not Lenin or Marx or any more recent leader. The organizational and personal tactics that Stalin used to come to power have set the pattern for subsequent rulers. The extreme concentration of power, the glorification of the leader, and the intolerance of opposition all characterize Soviet politics today. The myth of "Soviet democracy," symbolized by parliamentary institutions and popular elections, was also Stalin's creation. And the subordination of the individual to the Party's goals, enforced by a massive web of surveillance and supervision, which ultimately rests on coercion without the protection of law—this too was the legacy of Stalin.

In the 1980s, the issue of Stalinism is being raised in a new context. As General Secretary Gorbachev moves to impose his own radical vision of Soviet development on the nation, the issues of power, public responsibility, individual rights and interests, and the role of coercion in social change are increasingly intruding on the deliberations of Soviet leaders and, more importantly, on the reflections of prominent intellectuals. There is renewed and urgent talk of "democratization," of truth and objectivity in public life, and of the importance of the individual in a Communist society.

In all of this, the specter of Stalinism remains an important factor. Respect for strong leadership and for an orderly, controlled society is a longstanding characteristic of the Russian mind. In the turmoil that accompanies the Gorbachev reform movement, calls for a return to order and discipline are likely to find an attentive audience. This possibility is one of the key elements in the analysis of the Soviet political system that follows.

NOTES

1. Milovan Djilas, *Conversations with Stalin* (New York, Harcourt, Brace & World, 1962), p. 61.
2. David MacKenzie and Michael W. Curran, *A History of Russia and the Soviet Union,* rev. ed. (Homewood, Ill.: Dorsey Press, 1982), p. 488.
3. Ibid.
4. See Robert C. Tucker, *Stalin as Revolutionary* (New York: W. W. Norton & Co., 1973), pp. 372ff.
5. For a useful discussion of this point, see Jerry F. Hough and Merle Fainsod, *How the Soviet Union Is Governed* (Cambridge: Harvard University Press, 1979), pp. 139ff.

6. Ibid., p. 142.
7. For an excellent collection of such writings on the significance of Stalinism, see Stephen F. Cohen, *An End to Silence,* New York: W. W. Norton & Co., 1982.
8. For a brief discussion of these developments, see Hough and Fainsod, *How the Soviet Union Is Governed,* pp. 124ff.
9. Abdurakhman Avtorkhanov, *Stalin and the Soviet Communist Party* (New York: Praeger, 1959), p. 104.
10. H. Montgomery Hyde, *Stalin: the History of a Dictator* (New York: Farrar, Straus & Giroux, 1972), p. 237.
11. Quoted in George F. Kennan, *Russia and the West Under Lenin and Stalin* (Boston: Little, Brown, 1961), p. 288.
12. Mackenzie and Curran, *Russia and the Soviet Union,* p. 352.
13. Helene Carrere d'Encausse, *Stalin* (New York: Longman, 1981), p. 23.
14. There was nothing new in this policy. It had been done by czarist officials in the past. As Alexander III's Finance Minister Vyshnegradskii remarked in 1891, "We must export though we undereat." Quoted in Mackenzie and Curran, *Russia and the Soviet Union,* p. 355.
15. See Roy Medvedev, *Let History Judge* (New York: Random House, 1971), pp. 102ff.
16. Ibid., p. 107.
17. Adam Ulam, *A History of Soviet Russia* (New York: Holt, Rinehart & Winston, 1976), p. 94.
18. Ian Grey, *The First Fifty Years, Soviet Russia 1917–67* (New York: Coward, McCann, 1967), p. 236.
19. *Kulak* means "fist" in Russian; it was used derogatively to refer to small landowners who made profits on agriculture through the employment of peasant laborers.
20. Adam Ulam cites the January 1930 Central Committee directive, which ordered "the Commissariat of Agriculture . . . to work out in the shortest possible time a Model Charter of the artel form of the collective farm as a *transitional stage toward a full commune.*" See Ulam, *History of Soviet Russia,* p. 96.
21. Grey, *The First Fifty Years,* p. 237.
22. Ibid., p. 238.
23. D. Fedotoff White, *The Growth of the Red Army* (Princeton, N.J.: Princeton University Press, 1944), p. 279.
24. Ibid., p. 279.
25. Boris Bazhanov, Stalin's secretary for several years, states that "at the Fourteenth Congress [1925] . . . Stalin not only removed the Jewish Party leaders from the centers of power but also took an important step toward the complete elimination of the Jewish part of the party leadership from all of the higher councils. Only Trotsky, Zinoviev, and Kamenev still remained in the Central Committee." From "I Was Stalin's Secretary," in George Baily, ed., *Kontinent 4,* (New York, Avon: 1982), p. 463.
26. Michael T. Florinsky, *Russia: A Short History,* 2d ed. (London: Macmillan, 1969), p. 490.
27. Mackenzie & Curran, *Russia and the Soviet Union,* p. 503.
28. Alec Nove, *Stalinism and After* (London: George Allen & Unwin, 1975), p. 54.
29. Hough and Fainsod, *How the Soviet Union Is Governed,* p. 169.
30. Ibid., p. 168.
31. d'Encausse, *Stalin,* p. 30.
32. d'Encausse argues that "the working class . . . was the great victim of the policy of income differentiation which was then rapidly developing." See Ibid., p. 29. But Jesse

Clarkson and others have argued that no reliable data exist to prove the point either way. See Jesse D. Clarkson, *A History of Russia* (New York: Random House, 1961), p. 612.

33. MacKenzie and Curran, *History of Russia and the Soviet Union,* p. 505.
34. Alexander I. Solzhenitsyn, *The First Circle* (New York: Harper & Row, 1968), p. 248.
35. Solomon Volkov, ed., *Testimony: The Memoirs of Dmitri Shostakovich* (New York: Harper & Row, 1979), p. 138.
36. Ibid.
37. George Kennan, *Soviet Foreign Policy, 1917–1941* (Princeton, N.J.: D. Van Nostrand Company, 1960), p. 89. And see the interesting analysis in Hough and Fainsod, *How the Soviet Union Is Governed,* p. 176ff.
38. See Hough and Fainsod, *How the Soviet Union Is Governed,* pp. 169–170.
39. David K. Shipler, *Russia: Broken Idols, Solemn Dreams* (New York, Times Books, 1983), p. 94.
40. Quoted in Avtorkhanov, *Stalin and the Soviet Communist Party,* p. 250.
41. Alec Nove, *Stalinism and After,* p. 66.
42. Medvedev, *Let History Judge,* p. 362.
43. Quoted in Ibid., p. 366.
44. Quoted in Clarkson, *History of Russia,* p. 631.
45. Ibid., p. 630.
46. Ibid., p. 631.
47. Ronald Hingley, *Joseph Stalin, Man and Legend* (New York: McGraw-Hill, 1974), p. 243.
48. For an extensive discussion of the 1977 Constitution, see Robert Sharlet, *The New Soviet Constitution of 1977* (London: Kings Court, 1978).
49. John B. Dunlop, *The Faces of Contemporary Russian Nationalism* (Princeton, N.J.: Princeton University Press, 1983), p. 18.
50. Ibid., p. 19.

PART 2

The Organization of Power

Since the moment the Bolsheviks came to power in October 1917, supreme political power has always been effectively exercised by a small elite of senior Communist Party leaders. Yet over the years the official description of the nature of Soviet government has changed significantly. In the first months after the October Revolution, the first Soviet Constitution granted supreme governmental authority to the All-Russian Congress of Soviets, a popularly elected body. When the 1936 Constitution was adopted, supreme governmental authority shifted to the newly created Supreme Soviet, a national legislature elected by direct and universal suffrage. The role of the Communist Party was briefly mentioned in two sections of the Constitution, but there was no hint of its real role in the political system.

By the time the present Soviet Constitution was adopted in 1977, a major change had occurred in the official description of the political system. The popularly elected legislative organs were featured prominently, but the Constitution made explicit the overwhelming dominance of the state by the Communist Party. It continued to describe the Party in democratic terms, as if the leadership were elected by the mass membership and responsible to it. But aside from this obvious malapropism, the Constitution accurately identified the Party as the heart of the system.

As a matter of fact, there had never been any doubt of the Party's political role even among those most ardently proclaiming the democratic nature of the system. Official Party publications as well as directives to Party officials had always stressed the necessity of ensuring that whatever democratic forms were utilized in a given period the Party organizations must control and manage the process to achieve the leadership's goals. And this has always been the case.

We need to examine, therefore, the Communist Party above all, as the supreme political force in the USSR. In addition, however, various governmental organs as well as the national legislature play important roles in the system. Indeed, as I will argue in the following chapters, both institutions share the power of the Party in managing the political system as a whole. It is this sharing of power, and what it demonstrates for the real role of the Party leadership, that exhibits the true nature of Soviet politics.

In the following three chapters we will examine not only the Communist Party but also the government, including the military and the police apparatus, and the national legislature. We shall be concerned with several key questions: Who has political power? How did they get it and how do they keep it? How is power distributed among the various parts of the political system?

CHAPTER 5
The Communist Party

To call the Communist Party of the Soviet Union (CPSU) a "political party" is to begin with a misnomer. If by that term, one imagines a mass organization of shifting membership periodically mobilized to conduct election campaigns, one can have no conception of the Soviet Communist party at all. For the CPSU is a very different sort of organization.

It is a permanent, bureaucratized, executive organization whose top leaders exercise supreme political power in the USSR. Its full-time employees are trained for their jobs in special schools and are found wherever Soviet citizens work, play, study, and live. Party members are expected to be models for all citizens, and their behavior is constantly scrutinized by Party officials. As a whole, they are alleged to have a special insight into the working out of the "laws of history" that guide the development of the Soviet Union.

In the current Soviet Constitution (Article 6), the Communist Party is described as

> the leading and guiding force of Soviet society and the nucleus of its political system, of all state and public organizations. . . . The Communist Party determines the general perspectives of the development of society and the line of domestic and foreign policy of the USSR, directs the great constructive work of the Soviet people, and imparts a planned, systematic, and theoretically substantiated character to their struggle for the victory of socialism.

In this respect, at least, the Soviet Constitution provides an accurate description of the political system. The Communist Party exercises political power at the core of every governmental agency, economic enterprise, educational institution, army unit, and youth group in the Soviet Union. Its chief function is not to administer these organizations directly but to see to it that the policies and objectives of the Party leadership are carried out in all spheres of Soviet life. The line between "guiding" and "governing" is, to be sure, a fine one, and it is often transgressed in the give-and-take of practical politics. But it is a useful distinction to maintain as we assess the political power and role of both Party and non-Party governmental organs.

WHO BELONGS TO THE PARTY?

From the small, clandestine revolutionary organization founded by Lenin in 1898, the Soviet Communist Party has grown into a mass organization of 17,480,000 full and candidate members, or about 6.5 percent of the Soviet population. To

91

understand the importance of this army of Party members we need to consider who they are and how they function to support the dominant role of the Party leadership in the political system. The question before us is: To what extent and in what ways is the Party as a whole different from the general population, and what is the significance of those differences? We shall look at the membership in terms of six characteristics: social position, occupation, education, age, sex, and ethnicity.

Characteristics of Membership

Social Position and Occupation. Soviet sources typically categorize citizens in one of three social groupings: workers, peasants, and "employees and others" (the latter including white-collar workers, creative artists and scholars, officials, military officers, and so on). In characterizing Party membership, however, these categories are used to indicate the *social origin* of members rather than their present occupations. Because many Party members whose parents were workers or peasants, or who themselves started their careers as such, have moved to white-collar occupations, such data greatly exaggerate the "worker/peasant" composition of the Party.

Hence we can only estimate the actual distribution of members in terms of their social position. Based on data from republic rather than national sources, Bohdan Harasymiw estimates that the Party consisted, in the mid-1970s, of 30 percent manual workers, 20 percent peasants, and 50 percent employees and others.[1] Among manual workers, the occupations most highly represented in the Party are industrial (factory), construction, and transportation workers. In white-collar occupations, those in the fields of science, education, health, and culture are most represented.[2]

Ever since Stalin's death in 1953, there has been a continuing emphasis on increasing the proportion of working people in the Party. By 1981, admission of new members to the CPSU had shifted heavily in favor of industrial workers (60 percent of new members, up from 42 percent in 1961) and against agricultural workers (10 percent, down from 22 percent in 1961). Among the other 30 percent of new members (employees and others) in 1981, there was also an important trend: Those in more highly specialized and technical professions were being recruited at an increasing rate while office workers and functionaries were being recruited in far smaller numbers (just over 3 percent of new members in 1981, down from 13 percent in 1961).[3]

These trends reflect both Party policy and the normal development of the Soviet work force. The proportion of Soviet citizens who leave farming and take up urban occupations continues to increase, while the overall educational and skill level of urban workers and professionals also increases. The Party has attempted both to accommodate these changes and to continue its emphasis on recruiting new members from among the urban proletariat.

Education. Over time, the proportion of Party members with a higher education is increasing, both because the Party actively recruits such people and because already enrolled Party members are encouraged to raise their educational qualifications. But the educational level of the general population is also increasing, and, surprisingly, it is doing so at a faster rate than that of the Party membership. Thus the gap between the Party and the society regarding educational levels, which traditionally favored the Party, appears to be diminishing.[4]

Age. Both the Soviet population and the CPSU membership have, naturally, aged over the years since the October Revolution. But in contrast to educational levels, the aging factor finds the society and the Party moving in opposite directions. During the Brezhnev years, restrictions on Party recruitment increased the average age of Party members because fewer young people were being admitted. At the same time the proportion of younger people in the general population was increasing.[5] The possibility of a growing generation gap is at least intimated by this fact.

Sex. Women have traditionally been underrepresented in managerial and administrative positions in the USSR and in the ranks of industrial workers, from which the Party recruits a large proportion of its members. Therefore it is not surprising to find them underrepresented in the Party as well. Although the number of women in the Party has been increasing in recent decades, they still constitute only about one-quarter of the membership.[6] The situation is strongly affected by resistance in Muslim areas to women actively engaging in public affairs, and by the pressures on all Soviet women simultaneously to hold down jobs and to take care of housekeeping and childrearing. There is little time left for political involvement.

Ethnicity. The distribution of Party members among the various national republics follows the pattern of economic development rather closely. Thus, one finds most Party members residing in the RSFSR (62 percent in 1981) and concentrated in urban areas, with the highly developed Baltic republics running a close second.[7] The lowest proportion of Party members is found in the central Asian republics, despite the fact that these have been areas of greatest population growth in the past decade.

Within each republic, the distribution of members reflects educational achievement rather than ethnic differences. The titular nationality in each republic is better represented in the CPSU only where it is better-educated than outsiders who live in the republic (who are mainly Russians and Ukrainians). Thus, in Georgia and Kazakhstan, for example, the native ethnic group is better represented, but in the other central Asian republics this is not the case. Lesser nationalities, those without Union Republic status, tend to be much less well represented in the CPSU, with the exception of Jews, whose proportion of membership is nearly three times that of the country as a whole.[8]

The Saturation Factor

As all this indicates, the 6.5 percent of the Soviet population who belong to the Communist Party are found in all sectors of the society and in all organizations. But that percentage suggests that Party members are a very small minority of the organizations in which they function and of the society as a whole. In fact, this is misleading, and for two reasons. First, as a proportion of the *politically significant* sector of society, rather than of the society as a whole, the number of Party members takes on far greater importance.[9] If we exclude, for example, everyone under age eighteen (the minimum age for admission to the Party), the percentage of Party members rises to 8.6 percent. And as few people actually join the Party before their mid-twenties (the average age at admission in 1975 was twenty-seven), the percentage of Party members relative to those actually eligible for membership is even higher: about 10.5 percent.

There are qualitative adjustments to be made as well. We are interested not only in numbers of members but also in the relative importance of people selected for membership in the Party. To the extent that the Party recruits *influential* citizens, its authority is enhanced. It does so, for example, by recruiting men in far greater numbers than women, the more highly educated over the less well educated, older rather than younger people, and urban over rural residents (because of the importance of urbanization in the industrial and managerial sector). Among this element of the population (well-educated urban males over the age of thirty), the proportion of Party members may be as high as one-third to one-half. And through such "influential" members, the Party magnifies its influence in families, work environments, and social settings throughout the society.

The other reason why the 6.5 percent Party membership figure is misleading is that it conceals a wide discrepancy in the proportion of Party members found in different occupations. Some occupations are clearly more important to the maintenance of Party power than others. Thus, we should expect to find a higher proportion of Party members in those occupations, and in fact we do. T.H. Rigby has proposed three categories of Party membership as it relates to occupation:[10]

- *Party-restricted Occupations.* These include occupations in which all or nearly all (95 to 100 percent) of those engaged are members of the CPSU. Party officials are naturally included, along with leading government officials at every level from national to local, directors of factories and collective farms, military officers, judges, and police officials.
- *High-saturation Occupations.* Occupations in which 20 to 50 percent of those employed are Party members include government officials and economic managers at secondary positions on every level, academics (especially social scientists), directors of schools and institutes, and a broad range of lesser bureaucratic officials.
- *Low-saturation Occupations.* In this group are occupations whose proportions of Party members are at or below the national percentage and who

are therefore underrepresented, at least statistically. They include workers in industry and construction, farm workers, and vast numbers of retail and service personnel.

The importance of over- or underrepresentation of different segments of the Soviet population lies in the fact that the Communist Party is the primary avenue along which Soviet citizens can advance to positions of prominence and affluence in society. The more important the position, the more difficult it is to attain without membership in the Party, and for a wide range of high-level positions, Party membership is mandatory. The Party is, in this sense, clearly an elite organization, and there is constant and growing pressure on the Party leadership to admit ambitious and well-educated professional and technical people to membership.

While sensitive to the importance of such people to the future development of the country, the Party leadership, especially during the Brezhnev years, was insistent on maintaining the proletarian character of the Party and protecting it from being overwhelmed by "careerists" and economic opportunists. The rate of admission of working people to the Party increased under Brezhnev while the overall rate of growth in the size of the Party decreased sharply.[11] This has meant fewer opportunities for the better-educated elements of society to achieve Party membership and a consequent narrowing of career opportunities. There is no doubt that this development has been a continuing source of stress within the post-Brezhnev Soviet elite.

JOINING THE PARTY

Although the Communist Party rules the Soviet Union, membership in the Party does not necessarily endow the individual with significant political power. In fact, the vast majority of Party members are fully employed at some non-Party job, spend much of their time carrying out routine tasks assigned by Party committees and leaders, and receive little if any compensation for their trouble.

Nor does Party membership guarantee every member a more privileged existence in Soviet society. It does not necessarily mean an earlier promotion or a better apartment or more frequent vacations. While Party membership is useful and often mandatory in a wide range of upper-level careers, reaching those levels depends more on the individual's ability and ambition than on his political connections. A career in the Party itself, of course, requires Party membership from the beginning, and for many ambitious young Soviets this is the surest road to power and privilege.

Joining the Party also makes personal demands on members, which nonmembers can largely ignore. There is a large time commitment involved in attending mandatory meetings, mobilizing the citizenry for mass activities such as voting, absorbing Party doctrines and policy positions so that they can be conveyed to fellow citizens, and a host of similar activities. In addition, Party members are expected to live an exemplary life, to serve as moral examples to their community. A member who falls into heavy drinking or absenteeism from work tends to be treated more severely than a nonmember, and this person risks expulsion from the Party. This would place him or her in a state of disgrace, which can have negative consequences both professionally and personally.

The decision to join the Communist Party is a serious one. Why Soviet citizens join is difficult to know with any precision, for Soviet academics have not yet been allowed to probe subjects as politically sensitive as this.[12] But it would seem to involve elements of careerist ambition, genuine patriotism, ego gratification, and an interest in being "on the inside" of the political structure with access to information and prominent local officials that is not available to nonmembers.

Typically, the young Soviet citizen joins the Party in his or her late-twenties, having spent ten years or so in the Young Communist League (Komsomol) and his or her childhood as a member of the Little Oktobrists (ages six to nine) and the Young Pioneers (ages ten to fourteen).[13]

The procedures for gaining admission to the Party are complex and exacting. An applicant must be sponsored by three persons who have been members for at least five years and will agree to be responsible for the new member during his or her probationary period. After submitting various documents, the applicant is interviewed at an open meeting of the local Party organization. A favorable decision (normally made in advance of the interview by the local Party leadership, but formally voted upon at this meeting) sends the application to the next higher Party level where it must also be approved. Upon admission, new members pay a small initial membership fee and begin to pay monthly dues of around 2 to 3 percent of their earnings.

After all this, the individual is still only a probationary member, required to wait for a year before being judged again for full membership. During this trial year, he or she will be observed closely by Party officials to be sure the member's behavior is consistent with the standards expected of Party members. He or she will carry out minor Party assignments, work diligently at one's job, and attend courses on Marxism/Leninism and contemporary Party policy to deepen one's understanding of Soviet ideology. In the end, the probationary member will almost surely be approved for full membership unless he or she has a change of mind in the course of the year.[14] If this happens, or if the person is denied membership by the Party leadership, the individual's application is terminated, usually without prejudice. (An expulsion or a personal decision to leave the Party *after* attaining full membership is more serious and may have significant and negative personal consequences.)

ROLES OF PARTY MEMBERS

Once in the Communist Party, an individual has several long-term choices to make regarding the extent of his or her involvement in Party affairs. There are four categories of membership:

1. *Rank-and-File Members.* For the vast majority of members (about 97 percent), Party membership is a part-time activity carried out where they work and live and in their free time. Among these members, however, there are varying levels of commitment and responsibility. About 70 percent of the members carry on minimal duties involving attending meetings, helping to get out the vote during elections, generating attendance at mass Party functions, and carrying out a wide variety of individual tasks assigned by Party leaders. Rank-and-file members hold no formal offices in the Party, receive no pay, and are not involved in decision making.
2. *The Aktiv.* Those who hold formal positions in the Party hierarchy are referred to as the *aktiv,* and they make up about one-quarter of the Party membership. They are volunteers and conduct Party business in addition to maintaining full-time employment, but they are actively engaged in directing the affairs of the Party on each administrative level. They include people involved in propaganda activities, "instructors" who lecture and conduct classes on ideology and Party policy, secretaries of primary Party organizations in cities and the countryside, and members of Party committees and special commissions. The *aktiv* serves as the primary source of recruitment to full-time Party positions and is therefore a normal step for anyone considering a career in Party work.
3. *Reserve for Promotion.* Members of the *aktiv* who demonstrate effectiveness and loyalty in subordinate positions in the apparatus or as members of various committees may be identified by local leaders as desirable candidates for future appointment to full-time Party positions. Appointment to the Reserve for Promotion, therefore, is a crucial step up the ladder for a young *aktiv.* As such it often confronts the person with a difficult choice: whether to continue on one's current career path or give it up in favor of a career in the Party. The opportunities in the latter are substantial, of course, and appointment as a Party official tends to be highly competitive.
4. *Career Party Officials.* Of the more than 17 million Party members, only about 200,000 to 250,000 are employed full-time in the Party apparatus.[15] These are employed as leading officials at every level of the national and local administration, but are concentrated heavily in the major cities, especially Moscow. Their primary function is to manage Party operations at all levels from the small rural cell up to the Politburo itself.

THE STRUCTURE OF THE PARTY

The organizational structure of the Communist Party reflects its primary function in the political system. It is not organized to represent interest groups or to win popular elections, as Western political parties typically are. It is organized to direct the activities of all other political structures. It has, therefore, both a vertical (hierarchical) dimension to its structure and a horizontal one.

Vertically, it is composed of Party organizations at every level of administration, from the national organs in Moscow, to republic and regional levels, to large and small cities, and down to the most remote village and collective farm. The organization at each level is subordinate to the one above it, from which it must receive approval on all major decisions. Leaders of lower organs are normally promoted to higher-level organs or demoted back to lower ones. Policy directives and decisions are made "above" and passed down the ladder for administration below. Input from the lower levels moves languidly upward, but the structure is far more effective in processing orders downward.

Horizontally, the Party organization at each level interacts with all other governmental agencies at that level and has some levers of control that it can exercise. Thus the Party organization of a city such as Leningrad is set up to interact continuously with the Leningrad city government, the city branches of all the national government ministries, and the city representatives of trade unions, military units, and police detachments.

In many and complex ways, the vertical and horizontal dimensions of Party activities conflict with each other, as we shall see when we examine the policy-making process in the Soviet system. But let us look first at the organization itself.

The Primary Party Organization (PPO)

Every member of the Party, including Gorbachev himself, belongs to a primary party organization, of which there are over 400,000 in the country. PPOs may be formed wherever there are at least three Party members employed or housed, and most PPOs have fewer than twenty members. However, some are far larger, especially those that exist in large industrial complexes and educational institutions. Here there may be thousands of members, organized into subgroups within shops and departments. The Moscow University PPO, for example, has over 7,000 Party members among the students and faculty organized into several hundred subgroups.

Each PPO is headed by a secretary and, in the larger organizations, operates through a Party Committee as well. Except in the largest PPOs, the secretary is a part-time official whose regular job is with the enterprise where the PPO is located. The general membership of a PPO is required to meet at least once a month, although criticisms in the press make it clear that many local organs follow a less rigorous schedule of meetings. The PPOs have broad responsibilities, including the admission of new members, mobilizing fellow workers in Party-sponsored activities, and carrying out various tasks delegated to them by higher organs of the Party.

Regional Party Organizations

Above the primary level, the Party is organized along the lines of the state administrative structure. Clusters of PPOs come under the jurisdiction of district (*raion*) or city (*gorod*) Party committees, and these in turn answer to regional (*oblast*), territorial (*krai*), and Union Republic Party organs. On each level, the internal features of the Party organizations are similar. Each has a general membership, which meets regularly to hear reports and vote on proposals of the leadership, an executive committee that conducts business between general meetings, various administrative bureaus charged with investigative and managerial responsibilities, and a first and second secretary and other officials depending on the size of the organization.

While each Party organization is directed by an executive committee or council, the chief political leader is the first secretary. On the regional and union-republic levels, and in the major cities of Moscow and Leningrad, the first secretary has wide powers over all other party and governmental organs operating in his or her territory. Many secretaries on this level also have all-union responsibilities as members of the national Central Committee and, in the case of a few powerful figures, on the national Secretariat, or Politburo. In any case, recruitment to this highest level of Party power draws heavily from among the regional and union-republic secretaries. Their importance is also indicated by the efforts national Party leaders make to have their supporters named to these positions and to cultivate political support within their ranks.

At the union-republic level, where Party organizations are large and complex, the administrative structures are similar to those at the All-Union level. Republics have central committees, politburos, and secretariats that operate similarly to their counterparts on the higher level. Therefore we will examine these organs as they function for the country as a whole.

NATIONAL PARTY ORGANS

As a general rule, organizational charts of Soviet institutions should be read upside down, especially where elections are involved. Large, popularly elected bodies that are normally shown as superior to smaller executive and steering committees are, in fact, invariably dominated by those committees and completely subordinate to them. Thus, we begin looking at the Party structure by examining the Party Congress, which, according to Communist lore, is the source of all party authority. And we conclude with an analysis of the Politburo, which is, of course, where the real power lies.

The Party Congress

Within the Party structure, the ultimate authority is attributed to the Party Congress, an assemblage of about 5,000 Party members who gather in the Palace of Congresses in the Kremlin once every five years (or so) for a week. Official statements proclaim that every congress is a milestone, a new stage on the path of progress. Important policy-making and organizational principles of the Party, its political strategy and tactics are worked out at these congresses, which also chart the general political course for the immediate future and for a long time ahead.[16]

In fact, all such matters are worked out well ahead of the opening of a congress.

A Party Congress is an international event, drawing delegations from Communist parties and governments all over the world and receiving massive press coverage including live television. The principal event on the agenda is the "State of the Party" address always presented by the General Secretary, in which past accomplishments and future plans are elaborately set forth, shortfalls are criticized, and the membership is encouraged to "continue the advance toward the construction of full communism."

The General Secretary's report, which may last several hours, is followed by a lengthy economic report by the Chairman of the Council of Ministers and a financial report. Subsequent days are absorbed with "debate" on the reports of the leadership, during which scores of speakers outdo each other in expressing their approval of the reports and heartfelt gratitude to the leaders. Culminating the economic debate is the vote to approve the next five-year economic plan (ignoring the fact that the new plan will have been in effect for months by the time the congress convenes). No negative voices are heard throughout the proceedings, although minor criticisms may be levied against a government ministry or lower-level organization.

During the Brezhnev era (1964–1982), Party congresses settled into a routine pattern that seemed to emphasize even more than usually their dignified, rather than effective, role in the political system. All votes were reported as unanimous, speeches contained unrestrained praise of Brezhnev as leader,[17] and an aura of satisfaction with the progress of the nation pervaded the proceedings.

Nevertheless, some characteristics of the congresses suggest that there is more going on than is evident on the surface. A congress is, after all, a gathering of some very important people, along with many who are not so important. Consider the following distribution of delegates to the 27th Party Congress (1986) by occupation:

Delegates to the 27th Party Congress (1986)[18]

	Percent, rounded to nearest tenth
Party officials (full-time)	21.5
Soviet, trade union, and Komsomol officials	13.6
Industrial and urban workers	34.1
Agricultural workers	13.9
Economic managers	11.0
Intelligentsia, including artists, writers, scientists, physicians, teachers, and performing artists	5.4

As the list indicates, of the 5,000 delegates to the 27th Congress, more than a thousand were Party officials, half of them holding positions at regional and district levels. These are men (and a very few women) who occupy powerful positions in the Party hierarchy and who, collectively, constitute the most important constituency of those relatively few who command from Moscow. From their ranks, members of the Party Central Committee are selected, and they carry primary responsibility for fulfilling Party goals throughout the country.

Accordingly, the leadership is highly sensitive to the views of this collectivity of middle-level officials. Arkady Shevchenko reveals, for example, that at the 24th Party Congress (1971) Nikolai Podgorny, then Chairman of the Presidium of the Supreme Soviet and locked in a struggle with Leonid Brezhnev for dominance in the Politburo, received 270 negative votes from congress delegates for reelection to the Central Committee, thus clearly exposing his unpopularity in the Party.[19] Several years later, he was removed from his position, which was then assumed by Brezhnev himself.

Zhores Medvedev, in his biography of Yuri Andropov, describes a similar dynamic at work in the 23rd Party Congress (1966). Mikhail Suslov was in charge of organizing the congress for the Politburo and "this enabled him to influence the composition of the new Central Committee," which is voted on by the congress but nominated by the Politburo. Medvedev concludes that

> By the time the Congress came to an end Shelepin's chances of becoming leader had diminished and Suslov had become the second most important man in the Party.[20]

A Party Congress is not a decision-making forum, but it provides a focal point for assessing the mood of the broad leadership structure of the Party, for exposing both established and aspiring national leaders to the scrutiny of the regional cadres, and, in subtle ways, for calculating the political strength of individuals and factions within the top Party leadership. This is especially true, and critical, during periods of leadership instability such as the one instigated by the death of Leonid Brezhnev in 1982.

The Central Committee

On a smaller scale, and at a higher political level, the Central Committee of the CPSU is similar to the Party Congress. Its membership is formally elected by each Party Congress and consists (as of the 27th Congress in 1986) of 307 full members and 170 nonvoting candidate members. As in the congress itself, the membership is primarily Russian and male and contains all of the top Party leadership. In addition, there are leaders of various other activities including the government ministries, the military, the diplomatic corps, and distinguished academicians and artists. Distribution of membership is shown below.

Membership in the Central Committee, 1986[21]

	Percent, Rounded to nearest tenth
National Party apparatus	13.7
Republic and regional Party apparatus	30.0
National government administrators	25.1
Republic and regional government	5.2
Military	8.1
Diplomatic personnel	3.9
Police	0.9
Writers, artists and editors	1.3
Academic administrators	2.0
Scientists	0.3
Trade union leaders	1.3
Workers and peasants	7.2
Miscellaneous	1.6

The Central Committee is clearly far too large to conduct Party business and, in any case, consists mostly of people who are not Party officials and whose only contact with the committee is at the semiannual meeting. Nevertheless, the committee also contains most of the highest-level Party and government leaders on the national and regional scene. It has the potential, therefore, of offering a setting in which important, even dramatic, events may occur. In the Khrushchev years, Central Committee meetings hosted several important debates on major policy issues and, in fact, once rescued Khrushchev's career as Party leader when the Politburo (in 1957) voted to remove him.

During the Brezhnev era, the Central Committee, like the Party congresses, evolved into a more routine gathering of the leadership of various Party and governmental hierarchies.[22] Meetings are held just prior to each semiannual meeting of the national legislature (the Supreme Soviet), and members hear a series of set speeches that rarely absorb more than a day of their time. If a cursory reader of the Soviet press gains the impression that the Central Committee is more important than this description suggests, it is because a steady stream of directives and policy decisions are issued in its name, most of them at times when the committee is not in session and has had no opportunity to vote on them.

The serious work of the Communist Party is carried on by two Party organs that, though formally subordinate to the Central Committee, are in fact the seat of real power in the Soviet Union. These are the Politburo and the Secretariat, to which we now turn.

The Politburo

The Soviet Politburo (an abbreviation of "Political Bureau") is a small group of political leaders who normally meet each Thursday morning in a spacious, wood-paneled room adjacent to the General Secretary's office in the Kremlin. The meetings are chaired by the General Secretary or, in his absence, by another member, the identity of whom is sometimes an important clue to the distribution of power in the Politburo. What the members talk about at their weekly meetings is largely a matter of speculation despite the fact that a summary of some of their agenda items has regularly been published in the past few years. Clearly not all matters discussed appear on the published agenda, and real differences of opinion and the outcomes of votes where taken are among the most closely guarded secrets in the Soviet Union.

The Politburo acts as a board of directors for the USSR. In its hands is concentrated the supreme governing power not only over the Communist Party but also over all matters of public interest. By the mid-1980s, the Politburo had become one of the most stable power structures in the world, rivaled perhaps only by the United States Supreme Court in the longevity of its members and the deliberateness of its actions. At the time of Leonid Brezhnev's death in 1982, the average age of full Politburo members was just over seventy years. Brezhnev himself had been the leader of the Politburo and the country for eighteen years and was only the third person to have held the post of General Secretary in the sixty years since the position was created.[23]

There are normally a dozen members of the Politburo, although the number is not fixed and has been as high as twenty-five for a brief period. There are also six to ten candidate members who participate in deliberations but do not exercise the vote. The members represent a diversity of power centers within the overall political system. In recent years, there have been three major clusters of members, arranged as shown in Table 5.1.

This grouping of Politburo members is not necessarily fixed or permanent. The inclusion of government ministers is a fairly recent innovation, dating only to the mid-1970s when Brezhnev added three positions (the heads of defense, foreign affairs, and the KGB) to the Chairman of the Council of Ministers as full members. In earlier years, nearly all Politburo members had been Party officials, rising typically from positions as republic or regional Party secretaries. In some cases they were promoted to national positions along with appointment to the Politburo. But since Khrushchev's time, several Politburo seats have been occupied by regional officials who have continued in those positions.

The flexible nature of Politburo membership is illustrated by the changes that often follow the death or the firing of a member. Among the ministers, only the Council Chairman appears to have a designated seat. When Minister of Defense Ustinov died in 1984, his replacement as minister, Marshal Sokolov, was only given candidate membership on the Politburo. And the same happened with the ouster of Victor Grishin in 1986. The presence of the Minister of Culture as a candidate

TABLE 5.1. MEMBERSHIP IN THE POLITBURO (FEBRUARY, 1988)

National Party Officials	
Gorbachev	General Secretary, Central Committee
Ligachev	Central Committee Secretary
Nikonov	Central Committee Secretary
Yakovlev	Central Committee Secretary
Zikov	Central Committee Secretary
Solomentsev	Chairman, Party Control Commission
Candidate Members	
Dolgikh	Central Committee Secretary
Razumovsky	Central Committee Secretary

Regional Party Officials	
Scherbitsky	First Secretary, Ukrainian Republic
Slyunkov	First Secretary, Byelorussian Republic
Candidate Member	
Solovev	First Secretary, Leningrad

Government Officials	
Chebrikov	Chairman, Committee for State Security (KGB)
Gromyko	Chairman, Supreme Soviet Presidium
Shevardnadze	Minister of Foreign Affairs
Ryzhkov	Chairman, USSR Council of Ministers
Vorotnikov	Chairman, Council of Ministers, RSFSR
Candidate Members	
Demichev	First Deputy Chairman, Supreme Soviet Presidium
Maslyukov	Chairman Gosplan
Talyzin	First Deputy Premier
Yazov	Minister of Defense

member is unusual and appears to be related more to the standing of the incumbent than to the importance of the position.

Among the regional Party leaders, there is also no clear pattern. When Tikhon Kiselev died in 1983, his successor as first secretary of the Belorussian Party organization was not given Kiselev's candidate membership on the Politburo. Likewise, Grigori Romanov was made a full member of the Politburo while he was first secretary of the Leningrad Party organization, but after his promotion to the Secretariat his successor in Leningrad did not immediately join the Politburo.

The fact is, membership on the Politburo comes about through co-optation by the sitting members in a process that is totally hidden from public view. No doubt official position counts heavily in the decision, but other factors are also important: relationship with the General Secretary and with other senior Politburo members, a personal evaluation of the abilities of a prospective candidate, and a perception of the probable reaction of the broader Party elite to a particular appointment.

With the naming of Mikhail Gorbachev as General Secretary in 1985, and in view of the advanced age of several of the members, the composition of the Politburo began to change almost immediately, and more changes are likely in the future. Still, it is worth examining briefly the careers of the present leaders (full members as of February, 1988), for they tend to exhibit typical patterns by which aspiring politicians arrive at the top.

As is evident from the biographies of the Soviet leadership, the membership of the Politburo includes only men and, with one exception,[24] this has always been the case. Normally, they are also a largely Russian group, although in the early Stalin years both Georgians (Stalin's nationality) and Jews were strongly overrepresented relative to their strength in the population. The new Politburo formed by Gorbachev includes three non-Russians out of thirteen full members. On the other hand, in the whole period since the October Revolution only eight of the fifteen republics have ever been represented by a full member on the Politburo (RSFSR, Ukraine, Belorussia, Latvia, Georgia, Armenia, Azerbaidjan, and Kazakhstan).[25]

In terms of geographic origin and social class, the Soviet Politburo is probably unique among the executive organs of modern industrialized nations. It contains an unusually high proportion of members who were born and raised in towns or villages rather than cities and whose parents were manual laborers or peasants. Since 1925, there has never been more than one member of the Politburo at a time who was born in Moscow or Leningrad.[26] This is in sharp contrast to prerevolutionary Bolshevik leaders who tended to be urban intellectuals of the middle class.

The "social origins" listed for Soviet leaders have a certain ideological bias, which is perhaps natural in a country ostensibly run by the working class. Nevertheless, for whatever credit is due their fathers, at least eleven members of the 1980 Politburo had worker or peasant backgrounds. This fact is counterbalanced by the fact that all of them moved into the white-collar ranks early in life as Party careers beckoned them. Before or during the transition, moreover, nearly all managed to earn degrees at higher institutes even though a number of current members did so in night schools while fully employed.[27]

The Secretariat

If the Politburo can be referred to as the executive arm of the Central Committee, then the Secretariat might be viewed as its administrative arm. Composed of ten to twelve Secretaries, the Party Secretariat has primary responsibility for managing the affairs of the Party both domestically and internationally. Because the Party's responsibilities extend to all aspects of Soviet government, the Secretariat is also a kind of super governmental bureaucracy. But as there is already a formal governmental structure—the Council of Ministers—whose chief responsibility is also the management of the Soviet government, the role of the Secretariat is clearly a complex one. Understanding the relationship between the Party bureaucracy, managed by the Secretariat, and the ministerial structure managed by the Council of Ministers is the key to fathoming the real locus of power and decision making in the Soviet system. We shall examine this relationship in the following chapter.

Organizationally, the work of the Secretariat is apportioned among the individual secretaries. Although they meet once a week as a body to discuss matters of common concern, each secretary works with considerable autonomy in

Mikhail S. Gorbachev (b. 1931, Russian). Appointed General Secretary of the Party in March 1985 following the death of Konstantin Chernenko. At the time he was the Politburo's youngest member and has been widely regarded as the first of a new generation of leaders. The son of a peasant family, he holds degrees in law from Moscow University and in agriculture from Stavropol, where he subsequently served as regional Party secretary (1970–1978). Appointed to the CPSU Central Committee in 1971, he became a Central Committee Secretary, with responsibility for the nation's agriculture in 1978. A year later he was made candidate member of the Politburo and in 1980 a full member.

Victor Chebrikov (b. 1923, Russian). A metalurgist by training, Chebrikov became a district Party secretary at the age of twenty-eight, later promoted to the city and regional Party levels. In 1967, he moved to employment with the Committee on State Security (KGB) where he has spent his subsequent years, rising from department head to deputy chairman and finally to chairman of the KGB in 1982. He also holds the rank of general in the army. An alternate member of the Politburo since 1983, he was promoted to full membership in April 1985.

Andrei Gromyko (b. 1909, Russian). Although only appointed to the Party Politburo in 1976, Gromyko is perhaps the most senior member by virtue of his long tenure as foreign minister, a position he held for twenty-nine years. Prior to that he was ambassador to the United States, Great Britain, and Cuba and represented the Soviet Union on the U.N. Security Council. Only recently (1983), he was given the additional position of First Vice-Chairman of the USSR Council of Ministers. Since Gorbachev came to power, Gromyko has been moved aside, presently occupying the position of Chairman of the Presidium of the USSR Supreme Soviet. His control over foreign affairs appears to have passed to Foreign Minister Eduard Shevardnadze and to Anatoly Dobrynin, long-time ambassador to the United States, who was recently appointed to the Party Secretariat.

Yegor Ligachev (b. 1920, Russian). Graduate of the Ordzhonikidze Aviation Institute and the CPSU Higher Party School, Ligachev has spent his entire career in Party offices. Starting as first secretary of the Novosibirsk regional Komsomol, he held Party posts at the city and regional levels, spending eighteen years as first secretary of the Tomsk regional Party committee. From there he moved to Moscow in 1983, appointed by Andropov as a department head in the Central Committee and, later that year, as a secretary of the Central Committee with responsibility for Party appointments and personnel matters. In March 1985, the newly designated General Secretary Gorbachev promoted Ligachev to full membership on the Politburo, thereby skipping the candidate membership stage that normally precedes full membership.

Viktor P. Nikonov (b. 1929, Russian). Nikonov's career has been in the field of agriculture, for which he was educated at the Azov-Black Sea Agricultural Institute. He has worked mainly in Party positions dealing with agriculture, first as deputy head and then head of the agricultural department of the Krasnoyarsk Party Committee. He spent eighteen years as Second Secretary and First Secretary of province Party committees before moving to the central government administration of the RSFSR. There he served as Minister of Agriculture from 1983 to 1985, when he became Party secretary for agriculture. Although lacking candidate member status, he was appointed a full member of the Politburo in June 1987.

Nikolai Ryzhkov (b. 1929, Russian). His early career was in industrial management, starting as a worker then as shift foreman, workshop superintendent, and chief engineer in a heavy engineering plant in the Ural Mountains. In the 1970s, Ryzhkov advanced to First Deputy Minister of Heavy and Transport Engineering and then First Deputy Chairman of the USSR State Planning Committee. In 1982 he was named to the Party Secretariat with overall responsibility for economic affairs. He was made a full member of the Politburo in March 1985, and six months later succeeded Tikhonov as Chairman of the USSR Council of Ministers.

Vladimir Scherbitsky (1918, Ukrainian). By profession a chemical engineer, Scherbitsky came to the attention of Leonid Brezhnev in Dnepropetrovsk and was made Party secretary of a chemical factory at the age of twenty-seven. Within twelve years (1957), he rose to become a secretary of the Ukrainian Party Central Committee and a member of its Presidium. Four years later he became Premier of the Ukraine and a candidate member of the CPSU Politburo, but a serious falling out with Khruskchev resulted in his demotion to the provincial level in 1963. With Khrushchev's ouster in 1964, Scherbitsky was restored to his positions by Leonid Brezhnev and promoted to full membership in the Politburo in 1971. Recent relations between Scherbitsky and Gorbachev seem strained, leading to speculation that Scherbitsky may not last long in the new Politburo.

Eduard Shevardnadze (1928, Georgian). A graduate of a state teachers' institute, Shevardnadze has spent his career in Party work. He held successively higher positions both in the Komsomol and in city and regional Party offices in Georgia. In 1965 he became Minister of Internal Affairs for the republic and in 1972 was made Republic First Secretary. In a surprising move in July 1985, Gorbachev announced Shevardnadze's appointment as Foreign Minister, replacing Andrei Gromyko, who had held the post for nearly thirty years. At the same time, Shevardnadze was promoted from candidate membership on the Politburo (held since 1978) to full membership.

Nikolai Slyunkov (1929, Belorussian). A graduate of the Belorussian Institute of Agricultural Mechanization, Slyunkov spent twenty years working in factories producing farm machinery, rising by 1972 to the position of general director of the Minsk Tractor Production Association. In that year he shifted briefly to full-time Party work as First Secretary of the Minsk City Party Committee. Then he spent a decade as vice-chairman of Gosplan. Later as Secretary of the Belorussian Republic Party organization, he was promoted to candidate membership on the CPSU Politburo in 1986 and, the following year, was named a Secretary of the Central Committee, and full member of the Politburo.

Mikhail Solomentsev (1913, Russian). Educated at Leningrad Polytechnic Institute, his early career led through positions as foreman and chief engineer to the directorship of a large factory after World War II. He moved into governmental administration as chairman of a regional economic council, head of the Central Committee Department of Heavy Industry, and for twelve years (1971–1983) as Chairman of the Russian Republic Council of Ministers and a candidate member of the Party Politburo. In 1983 he transferred to Party work as chairman of the Party Control Commission and achieved full membership in the Politburo.

Vitaly Vorotnikov (1926, Russian). After taking a degree in aviation technology, Vorotnikov alternated between Party positions and the leadership of the district legislature in Kuibyshev. Promoted to the first secretaryship of Voronezh district and membership in the CPSU Central Committee, he was advanced further to the position of First Deputy Chairman of the Russian Republic Council of Ministers (1975–1976). At that point, in an apparent clash with Brezhnev over corruption in the Party and government, he suffered a serious reversal of fortunes, being exiled to the chairmanship of the Soviet-Angolan Friendship Society for three years followed by two as ambassador to Cuba. After Brezhnev's death, Vorotnikov was brought back to Moscow as a candidate member of the Politburo in June 1983, and six months later was promoted to full membership. At this time he also assumed the chairmanship of the RSFSR Council of Ministers.

Alexander N. Yakovlev (1923, Russian). Despite a doctoral degree in history, Yakovlev never pursued an academic career. Instead, he entered full-time Party work at an early age, first in Yaroslavsky Province then in the *apparat* of the Party Secretariat in Moscow. He specialized in agitprop activities, becoming deputy head of the propaganda department of the Central Committee in 1973. Shortly thereafter, he fell out of favor with Brezhnev and was dispatched for ten years to Canada as ambassador. After Brezhnev's death, Gorbachev brought him back to Moscow as his chief adviser in matters of propaganda, the press, and the arts. There he rose rapidly to positions as Party secretary (March 1986), Candidate Member of the Politburo (January 1987), and full Politburo member (June 1987). Yakovlev is credited with much of the stimulus for Gorbachev's *glasnost* campaign.

Lev N. Zaikov (1923, Russian). With a background and educational degree in engineering, Zaikov spent two decades in industrial management, becoming the director of a scientific-productive trust in the 1960s. He moved into political administration in 1973 when he was appointed chairman of the Leningrad City Soviet executive committee. In 1983 he succeeded Grigory Romanov as first secretary of the Leningrad Oblast Party organization. The following year, he became a member of the Supreme Soviet Presidium, and in July 1985 was named a secretary of the Central Committee, apparently in charge of military-industrial affairs for the Party. Following the 27th Party Congress in March 1986, Zaikov achieved full membership in the Party Politburo.

those administrative areas assigned to him or her. There is also a recognizable hierarchy of secretaries, in which some have greater power and responsibilities than others. The unquestioned leader is the General Secretary, who has overall responsibility not only for the Secretariat but also for the Politburo and government. This individual also has a personal secretariat that, in Brezhnev's time, included assistants for internal affairs, foreign relations, foreign Communist parties, and so on.

Next in rank are the five or six secretaries who are also members of the Politburo. They clearly outrank those who are not on the Politburo, a difference that Michael Vozlensky argues justifies distinguishing between secretaries and undersecretaries.[28] Sometimes a senior secretary other than the General Secretary will accumulate vast personal responsibilities. Mikhail Suslov, for example, supervised, until his death in 1982, the whole field of ideology including culture, science, and education, the international Communist movement, and Soviet foreign relations. In doing so, he supervised the work of at least two other secretaries and, indirectly, the department heads who worked under them and the ministers and department heads who carried similar responsibilities in the Council of Ministers and the Supreme Soviet. Secretaries who are candidate members of the Politburo fall somewhere between the full members and the nonmembers in the status hierarchy.

The specific responsibilities of the secretaries are not publicized, but press reports and indirect evidence have afforded a reasonably reliable picture of the organization. The Secretariat contains some twenty-four departments, which have responsibilities for all facets of Party and government activity, including the following:[29]

- *Party Affairs:* Departments supervise Party organs at all levels, Party membership, local soviets, trade unions, the Komsomol;
- *Industry:* Heavy and light industries, defense industry, transportation and communication, machine-building;
- *Agriculture:* Machinery, the food industry;
- *Ideology and Information:* Writers and artists, propaganda, the press, educational institutions, science;
- *Foreign Affairs:* Relations with foreign countries and with foreign Communist parties, foreign trade, international organizations;
- *Financial Planning:* State planning agencies, the state bank, price controls, statistical information;
- *Law and Security:* Ministry of Justice, KGB, Supreme Court, civil defense.

The officials who staff the twenty-four Central Committee departments constitute the apparatus of the Central Committee. They include only a few members of the Central Committee itself, as department heads and deputy heads, and number only about 1,500 altogether.[30] Thus, reference to the "Central Committee" as a major Party organ may have any of several meanings: the full Committee gathered twice a year in plenary session, the much smaller number of full-time members and candidate members who hold positions in the *apparat*, or the entire *apparat* including both the full-time Central Committee members and all of the nonmembers who staff the *apparat* departments.

SUBORDINATE PARTY ORGANS

In addition to the major organs of Party power, there are several important but subordinate organs that carry out essential functions in support of the Party leadership. These include the Party Control Commission, the Central Auditing Commission, and the Komsomol (Leninist Young Communist League).

Party Control Commission

The "control" function of the Party was conceived by Lenin as the means by which the Party leadership could ensure that members were following the prescribed rules and conforming to the demands of personal behavior required by the Communist Party. In 1919 Lenin had set up the Commissariat of Workers and Peasants Inspection (Rabkrin) to watch over government officials, and this eventually merged into the Party Control Commission. It serves the Party leadership as a disciplinary organ deeply involved in purges of Party members, rooting out corruption among officials, and maintaining constant surveillance over the bureaucracy.

Although Lenin anticipated preserving a measure of independence for the Party Control Commission, forbidding its chairman to hold membership on other Party committees, Stalin quickly subordinated it to his own apparatus. Thus, the Commission has never exercised any independent authority, and it operates at all levels of the political structure under the direction of regular Party officials. It was, in fact, abolished for a time by Leonid Brezhnev in 1967, and its functions were taken over formally by the regular Party organizations. Its present chairman, Mikhail Solomentsev, is, like all previous chairmen (since Lenin) a full member of the Politburo.

The work of the Party Control Commission is relatively public, by Soviet standards. It frequently publishes results of its investigations in the press and criticizes both government and Party officials for errors and malfeasance. The commission invites communications from Party members and receives a wide range of complaints and suggestions, which it is charged with investigating and resolving. It often acts as a kind of Party judiciary in adjudicating charges against Party members and hearing appeals from members expelled by lower Party organizations.

Central Inspection Commission

At each Party Congress, the membership of the Central Inspection Commission is approved for another five years. The commission is subordinate to the Central Committee, and its members take a relatively active part in the deliberations of the departments of the Secretariat. A major function of the commission is to ensure that the central Party apparatus is working according to Politburo expectations. It periodically reports on the handling of citizen letters that pour into the Central Committee offices (some 700,000 per year), on the use of budgeted funds by Party agencies, and on the payment of dues by Party members, and it seeks to expose abuses in any of these areas.

The commission also regularly audits the books of Party organs, such as the various publishing houses, including *Pravda*. It watches for financial irregularies as well as deficiencies in the management of these enterprises, which provide the second largest source of income for the CPSU (membership dues provide the bulk of the Party's income). To carry out these extremely broad responsibilities, the commission has branch commissions at all levels of the Party bureaucracy, employing over 50,000 people in the task.[31]

The Komsomol

As membership in the Communist Party has become increasingly important for upward social mobility, it has become more selective in its recruiting. In the past ten years, the vast majority of new members (some 70 percent) have been recruited through the Komsomol (formally, the Leninist Communist Youth League). It is in fact difficult for a young adult to attain Party membership without having been a member of the Komsomol.

With over 38 million members, the Komsomol is the largest single youth organization in the USSR, perhaps in the world. Virtually all Soviet youths join at the age of fourteen and remain members through their secondary-school years. After that, however, the dropout rate is high. Although the maximum age for membership is twenty-eight, relatively few members last anywhere near that long. Remaining in the Komsomol depends largely on personal circumstances after graduation from secondary school. Those who enroll in colleges or technical institutes retain membership in large numbers in order not to jeopardize the privilege of advanced study and the high expectations for desirable jobs afterwards. Young people who go to work after secondary school have less incentive to devote time to organizational activity that has little bearing on their income or advancement. In addition, factory and farm directors have far less interest in encouraging Komsomol membership—because of the time it takes away from production—than do teachers and school administrators.

Komsomol is involved in a surprising variety of activities. In addition to administering its mass membership, it publishes the widely read national daily newspaper, *Komsomolskaya Pravda,* and over 230 other newspapers and magazines for young people. It manages three publishing houses, which produce over 75 million books annually. It has local organizations in virtually every factory, farm, upper-level school, and office complex in the country, and it carries out political education, mobilizes youths for special campaigns, and plays a major role in recruiting young people for admission to the Communist Party itself. As the official Soviet representative of worldwide youth, Komsomol also maintains relations with similar organizations in most countries of the world, sponsoring international conferences and distributing financial support to sympathetic organizations.

Komsomol is organized much like the Communist Party. It has executive committees on every level from rural villages to the all-union level. Republic and national congresses are held regularly, and the organization is managed by a national First Secretary and Central Committee. Control over the organization by the Party is carried out through several provisions in the Komsomol rules. Whereas ordinary members must give up membership after the age of twenty-eight, this does not apply to Komsomol leaders. They are regularly admitted to Party membership but continue as Komsomol leaders. The delegates to national Komsomol congresses are, in fact, primarily members of the Communist Party, not the Komsomol (except as leaders).[32]

It is difficult to assess the success of Komsomol in instilling in young people loyalty and dedication to Communist authorities. Much testimony in recent years portrays Soviet youth as indifferent to politics and ideology, skeptical about the benefits of self-sacrifice, and eager to maximize the chances for elevating their standard of living. A recent reflection by a young Soviet woman seems to capture the mood:

> I enrolled in the Komsomol at the earliest possible age, 14. And I was very pleased about it. We belonged to the first generation that looked on these matters in a cynical way. We understood that this step, which we could take on our own, would allow us to live better later on. I understood this. But belonging to the Komsomol was also a form of socializing, as we young people saw it. We'd get together, talk about interesting things. But, mainly, people joined the Komsomol so as not to be different, so as to avoid complications later on. Only a few didn't join. I was in no way different from the other students. I was a Komsomol member like everyone else, but political views neither united nor divided us. There simply were no political views.[33]

Whatever the ideological attraction, or lack of it, membership in the Komsomol appears at least to have been widely accepted as a normal and unavoidable stage in the growing-up process. It provides a pleasant social setting for young adolescents and even serves as a small milestone in the lives of its new members—a modern coming of age for Soviet youth. And it is an act of social conformity that ensures a smooth relationship with the "authorities."

Prior to joining the Komsomol, young Soviets have all had years of socialization in two other Party-sponsored youth organizations: the Little Oktobrists and the Pioneers. Both organizations include virtually every Soviet child of the appropriate age, and they are administered by the Komsomol. These are not specifically Party organs but mass organizations that serve to introduce young people to the social structure within which they will conduct their lives. They teach them the values of the society, serve as sources of public discipline, and organize most of their free time.

THE DYNAMICS OF PARTY RULE

What is intriguing about the exercise of power at the highest levels of the CPSU is the extent to which it depends on flexible arrangements among the leaders. A person's official position in the hierarchy may or may not clearly indicate his or her real standing in the power structure. Much depends on individual personalities, on networks of relationships with other leaders, on seniority, and on the subtle calculations that identify some leaders as rising and some as declining. It is not necessarily the case, for example, that a department head in the Secretariat ranks higher than a minister, or that full members of the Central Committee are always more influential than candidate members. Even within the Politburo, the tides of power are constantly in motion. Every so often they produce a visible change in the political landscape: Someone's resignation is announced, or another is granted additional responsibilities, or a third makes a key speech to a Party Congress. But such developments are rarely sudden. They normally result, instead, from gradual realignments that shift the levers of power toward some leaders and away from others.

This subtle peregrination of political influence results from several basic characteristics of the relationship among the top Party leaders. First, there are no fixed terms of office for any member of the ruling elite. Stalin was General Secretary for thirty-one years, Khrushchev for eleven, Brezhnev for eighteen, Andropov for two, and Chernenko for one. In all cases except that of Khrushchev, who was purged, the terms would no doubt have been longer had death not intervened. In elite positions below the level of the Politburo/Secretariat, death remains a common reason for changing incumbents, but promotions, demotions, transfers, and retirements are even more important.

Second, at the highest level of Party leadership, there are no clearly defined areas of responsibility for most individual leaders, including the General Secretary. At times, a General Secretary has also assumed the position of Chairman of the Council of Ministers (Stalin, Khrushchev), while at other times this has not been the case. It appears, in fact, that there has been, since Khrushchev's ouster, an unwritten understanding among Politburo members that no single individual should hold the top position in both the government and the Party.[34] Similarly, the position of Chairman of the Presidium of the Supreme Soviet (the titular head of state) was assumed by Brezhnev only in the last five years of his leadership, but was assumed almost immediately by Andropov and Chernenko and then declined by Gorbachev when he came to power.

Those members of the Politburo who are ministers of state (such as Foreign Minister Shevardnadze and KGB chief Chebrikov) have relatively clear governmental responsibilities, but as members of the Politburo they necessarily get involved in a much wider range of issues and may develop substantial influence in other policy areas. Positions in the Secretariat tend to have less well defined jurisdictions. From time to time policy areas are added or taken away from individual secretaries, usually indicating a rise or decline in the political standing of the individual. And the death or resignation of a secretary often results in a redistribution of responsibilities among two or more of the remaining secretaries.[35]

Third, the formal members of the Politburo are not equally involved in policy-making. This is to some extent a function of residence. Those Politburo members who do not live in Moscow work under a disadvantage. They often do not receive, or receive only after a delay, some of the documents and information distributed to the Moscow group. Furthermore, ad hoc meetings are sometimes called on short notice and there is considerable informal discussion among members in the course of the week—most of which the nonresidents miss out on. Arkady Shevchenko, in fact, talks of a "Politburo within the Politburo," referring to the Moscow members.[36]

Nonmembers also play an important role in Politburo deliberations. The heads of Central Committee departments, the editors of *Pravda* and *Izvestia*, the President of the Academy of Sciences, and the First Secretary of the Communist Youth Organization are often, in some cases regularly, invited to attend the Thursday meetings.[37] And since conclusions are normally reached not by voting (which only members may do) but by consensus, nonmembers can often be quite influential.

These three characteristics of the top leadership—their unlimited terms of office, the uncertainty of their policy responsibilities, and their uneven involvement in decision making—combine to create a political environment in which the relative standing of the top leaders is always open to question. It is true that only a majority of the Politburo can formally deprive a member of his (or her) position, and this is an infrequent event except in the first year or so of a new General Secretary's term.[38] Nevertheless, the danger of losing ground to other members of the Politburo and the possibility of eventual loss of membership is a constant concern. It can happen because of poor performance in one's policy area (the demotion of Dmitri Polyanski in 1977 because of agricultural failures, for example), disagreement over basic Politburo policy (as in the purge of Voronov in 1972 over foreign policy issues), personal corruption (as in the cases of Madame Furtseva and V. P. Mzhavanadze), or the fall from grace of a member's patron on the Politburo (as with the fall of Grishin after the death of Brezhnev).

The natural response to this perpetual danger is to utilize the very substantial resources of Politburo membership to protect one's position. This requires a member to draw upon a "structure of support" from outside the Politburo. Such a structure consists mainly of Party and governmental officials in key positions whose alliance with a Politburo member not only protects the member's position but also enhances the officials' own career opportunities.

The formation of a political support group is crucial to a politial career in the Soviet Union. It normally begins early in a person's life when he or she latches on to a "patron" who is on the rise. As the patron advances, this individual seeks opportunities for one's "clients" to advance as well, and they in turn begin to identify clients of their own. By the time an official reaches Moscow and a top position, this person will have developed a broad network of clients upon whose support he or she can count in one's own struggle to advance up the ladder. When Yuri Andropov became General Secretary in 1982, for example, he quickly moved a group of new leaders into the Politburo, all of whom (including Gorbachev) had been associated with him in earlier positions. Gorbachev, in turn, brought a number of regional Party officials such as Shevardnadze and Yeltsin to Moscow when he succeeded to the top post.[39]

Within the Party apparatus, the critical sources of support lie in the ranks of republic and regional Party secretaries, especially first secretaries. These officials play three important roles in the political processes of the Party: (1) They are the chief administrators in their regions and responsible for making the programs and policies of the top leadership succeed; (2) they are the principal source of appointments as delegates to the Party congresses and members of the Central Committee; and (3) they are the main source for the recruitment of new national leaders when vacancies occur.

With respect to policy areas, it is also important for a Politburo member to have support within the appropriate ministries and state committees.[40] Officials in these agencies are major sources of policy initiatives; they provide data and information necessary to the successful implementation of policies, and, if antagonized, can place formidable bureaucratic obstacles in the path of even the most senior leaders. But governmental support is less important than Party support, and in this competition, Politburo members who also serve on the Secretariat have a decided advantage over members whose primary home is in the ministries or the regional Party apparatus. This is a major reason why the top Soviet leader is always chosen from among the secretaries on the Politburo rather than from among other Party officials or government ministers.

In summary, it is important to understand that, although there is great political power concentrated in the highest agencies of the Communist Party, the effective use of that power to achieve the goals of the Soviet leadership requires cooperation and support from key officials throughout the structure and from the rank-and-file members as well. More than one leader has fallen because of his inability to develop and maintain that support.

NOTES

1. Bohdan Harasymiw, *Political Recruitment in the Soviet Union* (London: Macmillian Press, 1984), p. 97.
2. T.H. Rigby, "Soviet Communist Party Membership Under Brezhnev," *Soviet Studies* XXVII, No. 3, July 1976, p. 333.
3. Harasymiw, *Political Recruitment,* p. 62.
4. Harasymiw reports the annual rate of growth of persons with higher education in the Party was 5.1 percent between 1977 and 1981, while for the general population it was 6.9 percent. See Ibid., Table 5.10, p. 112.
5. Between 1959 and 1973, the proportion of the population that was under forty years of age increased from 43 percent to 55 percent, while the proportion of that age group in the Party declined between 1965 and 1977 from 56 percent to 43 percent. Figures from Harasymiw, *Political Recruitment,* p. 126.
6. Ronald J. Hill and Peter Frank, *The Soviet Communist Party* (London: George Allen and Unwin, 1981), p. 38.
7. Harasymiw, *Political Recruitment,* p. 117.
8. Harasymiw estimates from Soviet sources that in 1976, 15.4 percent of Soviet Jews belonged to the Communist Party. The percentage is declining however, no doubt partly due to emigration. See Ibid., p. 119.
9. The statistics used here are from Jerry Hough, *The Soviet Union and Social Science Theory* (Cambridge, Mass.: Harvard University Press, 1977), pp. 125–33.
10. T.H. Rigby, *Communist Party membership in the U.S.S.R., 1917–1967* (Princeton, N.J.: Princeton University Press, 1968), p. 449–53.
11. Between 1976 and 1981, the last years of Brezhnev's rule, an average of 360,000 people joined the Party each year, compared with an annual average of 762,000 during the last Khrushchev years (1962–1965). Figures are from Basile Kerblay, *Modern Soviet Society* (New York: Pantheon, 1983), p. 248.
12. For a Soviet assessment of some of the disapproved reasons for joining the Party, see *Pravda,* 3 February, 1985, p. 2.
13. These three organizations provide early socialization and political education to all Soviet youth and will be discussed later in the context of political socialization.
14. Hill and Frank estimate that the failure rate of applicants for full membership is about 3.5 to 4 percent. See Hill and Frank, *Soviet Communist Party.*
15. The exact number of full-time officials is not known, and estimates among Western scholars range from 100,000 to about 400,000. See Helene d'Encausse, *Confiscated Power* (New York: Harper & Row, 1980), p. 123.
16. *The CPSU, Stages of History* (Moscow: Novosty Press Agency, 1975), p. 7.
17. For what it is worth, it was reported that Brezhnev received 42 seconds of applause at the 25th Party Congress (1976), up from 28 seconds at the previous congress (1971) and 25 seconds at the one before that (1966). Other Politburo members averaged only 2.7 seconds of applause at the 25th Party Congress. *Radio Liberty Bulletin,* 128/76 (March 6, 1976), p. 16. Cited in Robert G. Wesson, *Lenin's Legacy: The Story of the CPSU* (Stanford, Calif.: Hoover Institution Press, 1978), p. 252n.
18. *Pravda,* 28 February, 1986, p. 5.
19. Arkady N. Shevchenko, *Breaking with Moscow* (New York: Alfred A. Knopf, 1985), p. 179.
20. Zhores A. Medvedev, *Andropov* (New York: W. W. Norton & Co., 1983), p. 52.

21. Occupations culled from the brief biographies of Central Committee members given in John L. Scherer, *USSR, Facts and Figures,* Vol. 11 (Gulf Breeze, Fla: Academic International Press, 1987), pp. 50–63.

22. Daniels points out that membership on the Central Committee is mainly determined by the office a person holds, rather than vice versa. See "Officeholding and Elite Status: The Central Committee of the CPSU," in Paul Cocks, Robert Daniels, and Nancy Whittier Heer, *The Dynamics of Soviet Politics* (Cambridge, Mass.: Harvard University Press, 1976), p. 91.

23. Stalin was the first General Secretary, appointed in 1922. Lenin had been the Party leader and member of the Politburo until his death in 1924 but his principal position was Chairman of the Council of Peoples Commissars, a governmental position.

24. Khrushchev appointed Ekaterina Furtseva, then Minister of Culture, to the Politburo (called Presidium at the time) in 1957 and removed her in 1961.

25. John Loewenhardt, *The Soviet Politburo* (New York: St. Martin's Press, 1978), p. 58ff.

26. Ibid., p. 58, Table 6.

27. Ibid., p. 59, Table 8. Also see Hough and Fainsod, *How The Soviet Union Is Governed,* pp. 469–70.

28. Michael Vozlensky, *Nomenklatura: The Soviet Ruling Class* (Garden City, N.J.: Doubleday, 1984), p. 266.

29. The list contained here is not one of departments by title, but a description of policy areas covered by the departments. The deletion and merging of departments, as well as the creation of new departments, is a frequent occurrence, and these changes are often made without public announcement. For a recently published list of all Central Committee departments, see John L. Scherer, *USSR, Facts and Figures Annual* (Gulf Breeze, Fla: Academic International Press, 1984). p. 29. Also see Hough and Fainsod, *How The Soviet Union Is Governed,* pp. 412–17 for a list of the responsibilities of each department.

30. The exact number is not known and is subject to widely varying estimates. The number given here was calculated by Jerry Hough and seems a reasonable estimate. See Hough and Fainsod, *How The Soviet Union Is Governed,* p. 423–24.

31. For the report of the Commission Chairman, G. F. Sizov, to the 27th Party Congress, see *Pravda,* 26 February, 1986, p. 11.

32. At both the 1958 and 1962 Komsomol congresses, 59 percent of the delegates were full or candidate members of the Party. See Allen Kassof, *The Soviet Youth Program* (Cambridge, Mass.: Harvard University Press, 1965), p. 53.

33. Quoted in Kevin Klose, *Russia and the Russians* (New York: W. W. Norton & Co., 1984), p. 233–34.

34. Nevertheless, there is evidence that Brezhnev attempted, unsuccessfully, to add the premiership to his General Secretaryship in 1970, and there is no assurance that a future leader will not make the same attempt. See John Dornberg, *Brezhnev: The Masks of Power* (New York: Basic Books, 1974), pp. 244–45.

35. At the death of Mikhail Suslov in 1982, for example, the vast jurisdiction he had accumulated, encompassing ideology, cultural institutions, international communism, and relations with China among others, was not inherited by a single successor but distributed within the Secretariat and Politburo. Gromyko's standing as the most authoritative voice in foreign policy-making was no doubt enhanced, as was Demichev's in the area of Soviet culture.

36. Shevchenko, *Breaking with Moscow,* p. 176, is the basic source for the information in this paragraph.

37. Ned Temko, "Soviet Insiders: How Power Flows in Moscow," *The Christian Science Monitor,* 23 February, 1982.
38. Of the twenty-nine men who served as full members of the Politburo during Brezhnev's rule (1964–1982), only seven were removed against their will. And, as Helene d'Encausse points out, in each case there appeared to be justifiable reasons for the action. See d'Encausse, *Confiscated Power,* pp. 165–66.
39. For further discussion, see John P. Willerton, Jr., "Clientelism in the Soviet Union: An Initial Examination," *Studies in Comparative Communism,* XII:2,3, Summer-Autumn 1979, pp. 159–211; and Gyula Jozsa, "Politishe Seilschaften in der Sowjetunion," *Berichte des Bundesinstituts fur Ostwissenschaftliche und Internationale Studien,* #31, 1981.
40. For an analysis of clusters of support among Politburo members on foreign-policy issues, see Philip D. Stewart, James W. Warhola, and Roger A. Blough, "Issues Salience and Foreign Policy Role Specialization in the Soviet Politburo of the 1970s," *American Journal of Political Science,* 28:1, February 1984, pp. 1–22.

CHAPTER 6
The Governmental Structure

In some ways, describing what the government of the Soviet Union does is easier than defining what it is. The dominance of the Communist Party over the entire political system suggests that we might call *it* the government. Yet in the USSR, a clear distinction is made between the Party and the government, and there is a full structure of executive and administrative organs outside the Party organization, headed by the All-Union Council of Ministers, that carries out governmental functions. There is also an elaborate system of legislatures capped at the national level by the USSR Supreme Soviet. In common parlance, the executive branch is called the government while the legislative branch comprises the system of soviets. The functions of the two branches are quite dissimilar, and we shall deal with them separately in this chapter and the next.

The government of the USSR is a vast edifice of ministries, councils, boards, departments, and agencies and is probably the largest and most complex governmental structure in the world. Its size alone, compared with other modern states, is gargantuan, for it has responsibility not only for normal governmental functions but for vast areas of human activity that, in non-Soviet-type states, are managed by private organizations or by individuals themselves. Thus, the Soviet government manages every factory and farm in the country, every restaurant, gasoline station, and barbershop, every newspaper and magazine, every sports team, youth organization, social club, and vacation resort. Virtually every citizen is employed by the state, shops in state-owned stores, and is born, married, and buried in state-owned facilities.

Needless to say, an administrative bureaucracy large enough to encompass all of these activities is not likely to be a model of efficiency and frugality. The Soviet press publishes a continual barrage of criticism that exposes bureaucratic bungling, insensitivity to human problems, and corruption. It is, in fact, always open season on governmental bureaucrats as long as the criticism does not touch the top leadership or the major policies of the Communist Party.

It is not size alone, however, that complicates the administrative apparatus. Two other factors play a critical role in the problem. First is the federal nature of the Soviet Union. Because all levels of territorial administration have rule-making authority, the question as to which level should make which decisions is a complicated one, especially in the many administrative areas where no clear jurisdictional boundaries have been drawn.

The other complicating factor derives from the role of the Communist Party apparatus in the rule-making process. In principle, the governmental and Party roles are clearly distinguished: The Party sets national goals and mobilizes the people toward accomplishing those goals while the government directs the actual work of the society. In practice, this distinction constantly breaks down and poses one of the most serious unresolved dilemmas of the Soviet political system.

In the following pages we shall examine these problems and assess their significance for the political process. Our concern will be with three questions: How is the governmental apparatus organized? How much power and authority does it have in relation to the Communist Party apparatus? And what are its intrinsic strengths and weaknesses in addressing the needs and interests of the Soviet people?

THE USSR COUNCIL OF MINISTERS

The structure of Soviet government is in a constant state of flux, reflecting changing ideas as how best to organize the bureaucracy to carry out the will of the Communist Party leadership. The development of the governmental structure reflects the classic management dilemma: the need on the one hand for specialized agencies to concentrate on specific aspects of an overall task and on the other the need to coordinate the separate agencies to ensure they are contributing to common objectives.

In the Soviet case, there have long been two types of governmental agencies to correspond to these two needs: *ministries* that manage specific sectors of the economy and society such as industry, health, and education, and *state committees,* like the State Planning Committee, whose main purpose is to coordinate the activities of groups of ministries that are engaged in related activities or in matters common to all ministries. In the post-Stalin years, the ratio of ministries to state committees has shifted back and forth, reflecting the changing views of successive leaders. In the late 1950s, Nikita Khrushchev instigated a radical alteration of the governmental structure, abolishing all twenty-five economic ministries and decentralizing their functions to "regional economic councils" (*sovnarkhozy*) while more than doubling the number of state committees at the national level.

After Khrushchev was purged in 1964, his reform was scrapped. The ministries were reestablished in Moscow and most of the state committees were abolished. In addition, a rapid expansion of the number of ministries took place as the management of the economy grew increasingly complex. But with the addition of forty-six new specialized ministries in just twelve years (1962–1974), the need to coordinate their activities became increasingly pressing. Gradually the emergence of new state committees responded to that need. (See Table 6-1.)

In fact, the differences between ministries and state committees are less clear than these data suggest. In some cases, there seems to be no clear distinction between the two. There is, for example, both a ministry of construction and a state committee for construction. In the case of education, a ministry manages higher and secondary education while a state committee is in charge of vocational and technical education.

TABLE 6.1. EXPANSION OF THE COUNCIL OF MINISTERS, 1962–1984[1]

	1962	1974	1984
Ministries	15	61	63
State Committees	20	12	22

The same looseness characterizes the level of authority exercised by these agencies. There are three levels of ministries and state committees: *all-union* bodies that administer national policy matters and exercise jurisdiction over all lower branches throughout the country; *union-republic* bodies that administer matters of joint concern to the nation as a whole and to the individual republics; and *republic* ministries that handle matters of regional or local importance, such as highway construction. Again, these distinctions appear rather eccentric: The production of natural gas and petroleum are managed by all-union ministries while the coal and petrochemical industries are administered by union-republic ministries. Furthermore, republics differ considerably in the number and type of ministries and state committees they create and what responsibilities they assign to them.[2]

The USSR Council of Ministers is the collective body that encompasses all of these state organs, and others besides. It is composed (in 1984) of 118 members, distributed as follows:

Positions on the USSR Council of Ministers (1984)[3]

- Chairman
- First Vice-Chairmen (3)
- Vice-Chairmen (11)
- Ministers (63)
- Chairmen of State Committees (22)
- Chairman of the Board of the USSR State Bank
- Director of the USSR Central Statistical Administration
- Chairman of the USSR People's Control Committee
- Chairmen of the Republic Councils of Ministers (15)

The full Council of Ministers meets about once a month. But given its size, it seems unlikely that it does more than hear speeches and reports from government and Party officials. To conduct most of its real business, the Council operates through its fifteen-member Presidium, an executive committee composed of the chairman, first vice-chairmen, and vice-chairmen. During Stalin's rule, the existence of the Presidium was never publicized, and was in fact superseded by an even smaller "bureau" of close advisers to the then General Secretary. In the new Constitution of 1977, however, the Presidium has been clearly identified as a "standing body of the Council of Ministers to deal with questions relating to guidance of the economy, and with other matters of state administration" (Article 132). The Presidium meets regularly on a weekly basis in the Council of Ministers building in the Kremlin.

As a small executive body of the larger Council of Ministers, and headed by a senior member of the Politburo (the Premier), the Presidium appears to be similar to cabinets that dominate European parliamentary systems, but the impression is misleading. The Presidium is not, for example, a collection of all of the most important ministers. The 1984 Presidium included the foreign affairs minister (Gromyko) but not the defense minister or the chairman of the KGB even though both men are members of the larger body and head vital ministries. The fact is, both police and defense matters are handled directly by the Party organs, not by the Council of Ministers. With occasional exceptions, the foreign minister is also not a member of the Presidium. In practice, the Presidium is limited essentially to economic and cultural administration and is not, therefore, the general governing body that Western cabinets normally are.

PARTY CONTROL OVER THE GOVERNMENT

In reflecting on the power of Joseph Stalin, T.H. Rigby once remarked that the key to that power was not "that Stalin personally decided everything, which would have been physically impossible, but that he personally decided anything he wanted to. . . .[4] It would not be an exaggeration to say the same thing about the present-day Party Politburo. There is no political organ capable of overruling a decision of the Politburo, unless the Politburo itself is so divided as to precipitate a national crisis. But meeting once or twice a week for a few hours, the Politburo is physically incapable of considering more than a fraction of the stream of studies, reports, policy proposals, and draft laws that call for political decisions.

The measure of its power therefore lies not only in the decisions it makes and enforces but also in the decisions it causes others to make, without its direct involvement. To do so, it relies on organizational structures like the Supreme Soviet, the Council of Ministers, the Central Committee, the KGB, the trade unions, the lower party organizations, the voluntary associations, and many others. To ensure that these organizations are capable of carrying out its political will, the Party leadership must share power with them. Just as the Politburo exercises its power over the leaders of those organizations, so those leaders must have power to exercise over their own subordinates and all those citizens whose work they supervise. The real power of the Party leadership, therefore, rests not in the political power it has concentrated in its own hands but in the effectiveness with which it is able to *distribute* power so to expand, rather than reduce, its own capacity to rule.

Accordingly, there are power structures operating throughout the Soviet political system. They provide individual officials with the capacity to impose direction and discipline on the work of others and, equally important, to protect themselves from the reactions of those they command. The Politburo's main goal is not, as is sometimes argued, to diminish the political power of other organizations, but to maximize their power along "constructive" lines, that is, in ways that intensify the party leadership's capacity to govern. "The political life of Soviet society," a party document states,

> is characterized on the one hand by an intensive expansion of the leading role of the Communist Party, and on the other by a strengthening of the authority of governmental and social organizations, of all links in the political system.

The Party's task is

> not to take upon itself the functions of governmental and social organizations or to turn them into mechanical implementers of its policies . . . but to elevate their role and significance in all spheres of the life of socialist society.[5]

The Party leadership utilizes the vast political structure of government for two purposes: to assist the leadership in developing sound policies and programs and to ensure that those policies, once approved by the leadership, are effectively carried out. To do this successfully is an enormous task. To meet it, the Party leadership has developed a number of control mechanisms that operate throughout the system.

The first mechanism functions to ensure that all government officials who are elevated to positions of power are loyal to the Party leadership and effective in their jobs. This mechanism is called *nomenklatura*: the process by which the Party controls appointments to all important political offices. The second, managed through *Party committees* (*partkoms*), attempts to ensure that all levels of the bureaucracy are obedient to Party policy and procedures. The third, which is directed by the Secretariat and departments of the Central Committee, carries out continuous control of the government through Party agencies that parallel the major components of the governmental structure. The combination of these mechanisms constitutes the core of the Soviet governmental process.

There is a fourth mechanism, or task, that is equally if not more important than the other three in maintaining a stable system of government. That is the creation in the country as a whole of a mass willingness to be governed in this manner, to support the goals and policies of the leadership, and to cooperate with the subordinate agencies established to carry them out. This broad aspect of the political process will be examined in the next section of the book. In the present chapter we are concerned with the first three tasks of the Party leadership, with the ways in which a small group of Party leaders attempts to control the vast mechanism of government, and with the degree of success they have had in doing so.

Creating the Political Elite: The Nomenklatura

To maintain control over the vast structure of government, the Party leadership oversees the promotion of men and women to all important leadership positions in all parts of the system. But given the huge number of such positions, the process of appointment, transfer, promotion and demotion, and firing of officials is itself a vast and complex one.

The key instrument by which this is accomplished is the *nomenklatura,* which is simply a list of politically important positions or jobs to be filled. Before a person can be appointed or elected to one of these positions, the candidate must be approved by whatever agency has that position on its *nomenklatura* (including the Party in most cases). The scope of positions included in the *nomenklatura* system is very broad. Party officials at all levels as well as officials of all economic enterprises, soviets, trade unions, military units, government bureaus, and the like hold positions that are included on the *nomenklatura* of a higher-level Party committee. This allows the party leadership to set standards and criteria for the appointment of officials, to guard against the rise of power structures outside the Party, and to recruit promising leaders into the party ranks themselves.

Nomenklatura are maintained not only by Party organs but also by non-Party agencies that have administrative or executive responsibilities in the system. These include, for example, government ministries, military command bureaus, soviets at all levels, and trade unions. There are also two types of *nomenklatura:* primary (*osnovaia*) *nomenklatura,* which carries the power of appointment to such positions, and consultative (*uchetnaia*) *nomenklatura.* The latter lists positions concerning which Party committees must be consulted but over which they do not have formal authority. It enables Party leaders at each level to be aware of personnel changes occurring in their jurisdiction and to raise objections if they wish.

Given the Party leadership's determination to dominate the political system, it is not surprising to find all significant administrative positions on one or another of the Party's *nomenklatura.* The general rule is that a position on one administrative level is listed on the *nomenklatura* of the Party organ on the next higher level. For example, the chairmanship of a city soviet or the directorship of a local factory would be listed on the *nomenklatura* of the regional Party committee. But the factory director would also be listed on the *nomenklatura* of the ministry to which his factory is subordinated, as well as being on the *consultative nomenklatura* of the local (city) Party committee.

Furthermore, because the importance of various officials in a factory differs according to their position, the level of their *nomenklatura* will also differ. It is not unusual, for example, for a factory director to be on the republic-level Party committee's *nomenklatura,* his chief assistant on the regional-level list, and his chief engineer on the local level. On the other hand, if the engineer's position should be considered especially important, as in the development of a new weapons system, his position might be on a higher level than that of the factory director.

Actual control over the appointment, promotion, and firing of officials outside the Party apparatus is often the result of struggles among various Party and government organs to secure their own power bases. The established policy regarding personnel decisions reserves a role for both Party and non-Party organizations, but in this policy, as in many others, the Party leadership attempts to delegate authority while retaining the ultimate right to overrule that authority. Here is how the policy is stated in a recent publication issued by the Central Committee's Academy of Social Sciences:

> The Communist Party directs the recruitment and assignment of leading cadres not only of Party organizations but also of governmental, economic and social organizations. . . . [But] Party organizations and their leading organs directly decide questions of selection, assignment and relieving only of Party officials. As far as governmental, economic and social organizations are concerned, the Party exercises its influence on the selection of leading cadres through political and moral authority, by means of persuasion.

This is understood to exclude *nomenklatura* positions, however, which are (theoretically) under the exclusive control of Party leaders:

> Not a single official whose position belongs to the *nomenklatura* of a Party committee . . . may be appointed or relieved without the prior agreement or decision of the appropriate Party committee.

Furthermore, even where non-Party organizations have authority to appoint, promote, and fire officials, the Party must be consulted in each case and its views seriously considered. If Party officials disagree with a personnel decision, they may demand a change. Moreover,

> if an official rejects the demand (*trebovanie*) of the Party, made on the basis of the political or professional quality of a candidate, that Party organization has the right to correct the official or to appeal to higher [Party] organs about him.[6]

Thus the personnel process for officials is highly complex and politically sensitive. It is complicated even further by the very size of the operation. The number of *nomenklaturists* (those holding positions on any *nomenklatura*) is not known exactly because the Soviet Union never publishes the lists, but careful analysis by Western scholars allows us to make an estimate that some 2 million Soviet officials are on one *nomenklatura* or another.[7] The Party Central Committee alone is reported to have over 40,000 positions on its *nomenklatura*.[8]

The *nomenklatura* process has also become more complex as a result of the decentralization in Communist Party personnel practices since the death of Joseph Stalin. Both the number of positions needing to be filled and the increasing need for specialized training and expertise in many of them required that recommendations from the level at which the appointment was to be made had to be given greater weight. Approval by higher-level Party committees has come to follow more closely the recommendations from below, and non-Party bodies, such as ministerial agencies and local soviets, have developed additional *nomenklatura* of their own. Technically, higher-Party committees have the right of approval for these non-Party *nomenklatura,* but in large numbers of cases that approval tends to be pro forma.

To illustrate the difficulties all this creates in practical terms, consider the dilemma of the director of a truck manufacturing plant who wishes to appoint a new chief engineer. Needing to work closely with the new man, the director will naturally wish to have some personal input into the choice. The chief engineer's position will probably be on the *nomenklatura* both of the regional Party committee and the republic-level Ministry of Transport Construction. The city Party committee will need to be consulted and perhaps the executive committee of the local soviet as well.

In such a case, the final decision does not necessarily rest with the regional Party committee. If the republic minister had a strong preference that differed from that of the regional Party secretary, the minister might well prevail, given his professional concern with the qualifications of the candidate. And the fact that the minister, who is undoubtedly a Communist Party member and probably a member of the republic Central Committee, would himself be on a higher *nomenklatura* than the regional Party leader would give him considerable political advantage in the disagreement. If the matter could not be resolved on that level, either office might seek to involve its own higher-level officials in an attempt to override the preference of the other. At the top, one can imagine the all-union Minister of Transport Construction persuading the Chairman of the USSR Council of Ministers to take up the matter with his colleagues on the Politburo. If he does so, he may have to confront a powerful Party Secretary whose authority may appear to be challenged by the dispute over the appointment.

This is a way of pointing out that the formal dominance of the Communist Party over all other institutional structures does not necessarily mean, in practice, that Party committees and secretaries always prevail over governmental officials at the same, or even lower, administrative levels. Much depends on the political standing of the individuals involved, their connections with higher-level officials, and the reasonableness of their respective sides of the dispute.

There is one further dimension to the *nomenklatura* that has an important bearing on the political process. With rare exceptions, the appointment of an individual to a *nomenklatura* position carries with it a permanent tenure in the *nomenklatura.* Short of conviction for a criminal act or defeat in a high-level power struggle, a *nomenklaturist* may expect to retain his position, or be transferred or promoted to another *nomenklatura* position of no lower status, for the rest of his life.[9] In this sense, the *nomenklatura* creates a stable political, economic, and social elite, composed (mostly) of Communist Party members who occupy leading administrative positions in all formal institutions in the country. The authority of the highest Party leadership over this group, as well as the privileges and benefits that are granted to them, serve as a major control mechanism by which the Party organization manages the governmental structures of the system.

Controlling the Government from Within: The Partkoms

The Communist party leadership's control over *nomenklatura* is supplemented by its control over all members of the Party who hold positions in non-Party organizations. Thus, in addition to the personal loyalty each Party member owes to the Party, in each ministry or other government agency all Party members form a Party committee, or *partkom*. Although the *partkom* includes the minister, deputy ministers, and other important officials, all of whom are necessarily Party members, the *partkom* is headed by a secretary who is often not one of the major officials.

Partkoms are established by and directly subordinate to the regular Communist Party committee on each territorial level.[10] This gives a city Party committee, for example, direct authority over all of the *partkoms* in the city, and thus over the agencies and organizations in which the *partkoms* are functioning. But remember that control over the *nomenklatura* of these same agencies is held at a higher (regional) level. Thus the Party's two chief instruments for controlling the work of non-Party organizations—*nomenklatura* and *partkoms*—are not exercised by a single Party organization on any level (except at the very top where the Central Committee combines both powers). This diffuses somewhat the authority of any given Party committee over the non-Party agencies in its territory.

The *partkom* is theoretically a strong channel through which the Party leadership can exert its will on the whole structure of Soviet government and society. As one official stated,

> The Party carries out its policies on governmental issues primarily through communists . . . working in governmental organs.[11]

Party members are expected to give their first loyalty to the Party regardless of where they are professionally employed. Party committees on every territorial level are supposed to run seminars and training sessions for members of *partkoms* to increase their effectiveness and their willingness to keep watch over their employing organization. However, the inevitable conflict of loyalties involved in this dual role for Party members employed in non-Party organizations sharply reduces the overall effectiveness of the *partkoms*. The Party press carries frequent admonishments to *partkoms* to increase their initiative and their effectiveness.

Overseeing the Work of Government: The Secretariat and the Ministries

Probably the most direct and effective means of Communist Party control over the government is through the departments of the Party Secretariat. As explained in the previous chapter, the Secretariat is organized into twenty-four departments, corresponding in large part to the major administrative responsibilities of the Council of Ministers. Thus, both the Minister of Agriculture and the Chairman of the Secretariat's Department of Agriculture have a major responsibility for Soviet agriculture.

The relationship between these two administrators is crucial but difficult to discern because Soviet scholars never explore such political questions and because the relationship tends to rest heavily on personality factors and on the political connections of the two individuals. Either person may be of greater or lesser prominence within one's own organization. The minister, for example, may also be a member of the Presidium of the Council of Ministers or even a member of the Party Politburo. The department head could be, and generally is, subordinate to a Party secretary, but in some cases a secretary may serve as head of a major department.[12]

Without ignoring these complications, it is possible, in a crude sort of way, to identify an overall hierarchy of authority in the Soviet political system, at least as it concerns the Party and the government (leaving out the police, military, regional authorities, etc.). Figure 6.1 presents such a hierarchy.

The complicated relationships that characterize these individual interactions make it very difficult to draw any firm conclusions about the relative power of the collectivities to which they belong. Is the Council of Ministers more or less powerful than the Central Committee Secretariat and its departments? Part of the answer lies in the functional distinction that the Party leadership tries to maintain between

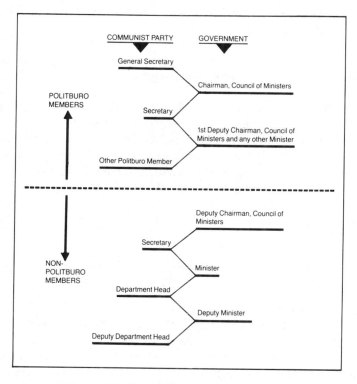

Figure 6.1 Hierarchy of Political Authority[13]

them. As stated above, the Central Committee's role is not to administer the country but to ensure that the government does so in accordance with Communist Party policy. There is a real sense in which the Party and the government *share* objectives, and this is reflected in the fusion of leadership that characterizes the two. Four leading ministers are full members of the Politburo, while virtually all ministers are members or candidate members of the Central Committee. Many of the major figures in the Secretariat departments have spent substantial parts of their lives working for government ministries, and some will do so again before they retire.

POWER STRUCTURES IN THE GOVERNMENTAL BRANCH

There can be no doubt that the Communist Party leadership, concentrated in the Politburo, is politically superior to any combination of government, police, or military officials outside the Politburo. Nevertheless, the actual governance of the country is carried on by the government, not the Party, and for that the Party leadership has delegated to a broad array of governmental agencies the right to make binding decisions.

This necessary sharing of power creates a permanent source of tension and potential conflict between Party and governmental officials at every level. Organizational structures set up to manage important sectors of the national enterprise strive to maximize their power and to protect themselves from outside interference. For both these reasons, the Party leadership is forced to deal with power structures external to its own organization. That the Soviet Party leadership does so effectively is not to say that such power structures do not exist or that they are incapable of challenging Party supremacy. To retain its dominant position, the Party leadership must constantly attend to the management of these power structures, ensuring that they do not exceed their delegated authority.

The government is, therefore, a set of powerful institutional structures facing an even more powerful Party organization in a dynamic and constantly evolving relationship. There are three such power structures with which the Party leadership shares its power: the domestic economic apparatus, the police establishment, and the military. All three are, of course, organizationally contained within the Council of Ministers, each being headed by a minister or chairman who is technically subordinate to the Chairman of the Council of Ministers and the Presidium. In fact, however, each is a separate structure of power whose primary political relationship is with the Politburo and the Secretariat rather than the Presidium of the Council of Ministers. This splintering of governmental authority is in fact one of the major sources of Party power.

Let us examine then these three major governmental power structures. We shall be interested primarily in the means by which they express and protect their policy interests and the nature of their relationship with the Party leadership.

The Economic Apparatus

A large majority of the national ministries and state committees (sixty-three out of eighty-five) are directly involved in administering some facet of the national economy. They are at the heart of the economic development of the Soviet Union, which has been a prime objective of the Party leadership ever since the October Revolution. As the economy has grown more complex and the economic growth rate has declined in recent years, the leadership's determination to modernize the economic administrative apparatus has increased. The task is a difficult and frustrating one, however. Success depends heavily on the effectiveness of the ministries and state committees in carrying out Party directives.

The problem is that the ministries seem constantly to be falling short in this task. Over the years they have been prime targets for accusations of bureaucratism, redundancy, failure to understand the problems, resistance to innovation, and outright corruption. The ministerial apparatus seems as often to be portrayed as an obstacle to economic progress as it is a means. As a consequence, it has been subjected to one "reform" after another as successive leaders struggled with the problem. As Khrushchev gathered political power in his hands in the late 1950s, he attacked the ministries head on. In early 1957, he carried through the Presidium (as the Politburo was then called) a drastic proposal for abolishing most of the central ministries and establishing regional economic councils (*sovnarkhozy*) in their place. The councils would be closer to production and easier for regional and local Party agencies to supervise.

This reform was abandoned by Khrushchev's successors immediately after they purged him in late 1964, but the problems remained. As Brezhnev moved into the leadership of the Politburo, he pressed for reduction in staffing levels in the ministries, some "deconcentration" in administration, and a sharp increase in the role of Party committees in administrative agencies. Brezhnev reconciled himself to a highly centralized structure, as Khrushchev had never done, but he struggled to loosen the structure and modernize its operation. His support of the creation of regionally based "production associations," which combined various factories, research institutes, and administrative offices into single economic units, was intended to rationalize economic production without doing away with the ministries. And he increased the number of Party-trained generalists who were assigned to high positions in the ministries in order to intensify the Party's influence in ministerial activities.[14]

Despite the Party's efforts to control the government, the economic ministries are able to preserve a significant measure of authority for several reasons:

1. They are massive bureaucracies with layer upon layer of officials and staff personnel who enjoy a high degree of job security. However determined a Party leader, or a minister for that matter, may be to initiate reforms, the weight of the ministerial bureaucracy makes it difficult for it to change directions.
2. The ministries contain vast amounts of experience and knowledge essential to the fulfillment of Party-determined policies. Many of them have established

research institutes that provide long-term expertise and academic respectability to the operations of the ministries. Many ministries have also set up teaching institutes for upgrading the training of their own employees, often over the resistance of Party officials who see them as competitors of the higher Party schools that have traditionally trained government administrators.[15]

3. The ministerial apparatus is strengthened by the established practice of leaving to ministerial leaders control over the internal structure of the ministries.[16] The Party leadership maintains the *nomenklatura* for all top positions, but below that level the ministries themselves are more or less in control of personnel and organizational matters. *Partkoms* operate on every level of the bureaucracy, but their task is a difficult one. Their obligations to the Party committee may conflict with their responsibilities to the agency that employs them, especially in matters involving inefficiency and corruption where the Party's interest in exposure confronts the agency's inclination toward concealment.

   Official criticism of *partkom* inefficiency suggests that they tend to subordinate themselves to the leadership of the ministry or state committee in which they operate. Gorbachev himself has publicly criticized the Party committees of some ministries for having "abandoned the supervisory function to which they have an obligation under the statutes of the CPSU."[17] The problem is borne out by a high-level Soviet defector who revealed that in the Foreign Ministry the *partkom* was never involved in substantive policy-making at all. Instead it occupied itself with matters of personal behavior and obedience to routine instructions. "I cannot count," he stated,

> the hours I spent in Party organization meetings in the ministry, listening to or delivering dull reports on doctrinal matters or on the foibles and failings of other "comrades." As a rule, the pettier the subject, the longer the discussion of it.[18]

4. The ability of a ministry to specialize on a relatively narrow sector of the economy is an additional source of strength relative to that of the Party organization. On the national level, the Party is elaborately organized, through departments of the Secretariat, to pay close attention to the activities of the major ministries. But on the regional and city levels, Party leaders are necessarily generalists rather than specialists. An *oblast* (regional) Party secretary has dozens of branch ministries to be concerned with, in addition to all other organizations in his or her region. This individual rarely has the time or the expertise to delve into any one organization in any depth.

   For a variety of complex reasons, then, the Party leadership finds the ministerial apparatus a formidable, and often resistant, structure through which to direct the economic development of the state. In matters of high national policy, the Politburo and Secretariat clearly have the upper hand over the ministries and planning agencies. But in carrying out the goals and policies of the Party leadership, the economic ministries have their own resources of power, which are potentially directed in pursuit of their own purposes and sometimes even in defiance of those of the Party leadership.[19]

Nevertheless, since the death of Brezhnev in 1982, the new leaders have renewed their attempt to get control of the ministerial establishment. Under General Secretaries Andropov and Chernenko, a purge of ministers and chairmen of state committees began and has picked up steam in the first years of Gorbachev's rule.[20] These changes are part of Gorbachev's oft-stated determination to effect real reform in the economic sector. In a later chapter we shall examine the nature of that reform.

The Police Establishment

When Lenin set up the Cheka (the All-Russian Extraordinary Commission for Combatting Counterrevolution and Sabotage) shortly after the October Revolution, he was continuing a tradition of secret police that dated back to Ivan the Terrible in the sixteenth century. The czarist Okhrana organization that hounded Lenin and his fellow revolutionaries was born again in 1918 in the service of the new leaders of the Soviet state. It has functioned ever since as the largest domestic police establishment in the world with political responsibilities for state security that far transcend its law enforcement duties.

As we have seen, Stalin developed his secret police forces into one of the major instruments of his rule. Their overall charge was to ensure the loyalty and obedience of the Party, the government, and the society. To ensure the loyalty of the secret police to himself, he periodically purged its leaders and replaced them with new appointees.

By the time of Stalin's death in 1953, the secret police had accumulated vast experience in the methods of terror, mass suppression, and counterespionage, and they operated without constraint throughout Soviet society as well as abroad. Lavrentia Beria, Stalin's last appointment as head of the state security forces, attempted to consolidate the various police organizations into a single force strong enough to bring him to power as head of the Communist Party. To forestall that possibility, the Politburo conspired to arrest and execute Beria within months of Stalin's death and to take steps to reduce the political power of the security forces in the future.

Since then, the KGB (Committee for State Security) has operated as an independent police agency controlled directly by the Politburo through a chief who is normally a member of the Politburo. Since Beria's purge, its chiefs have included Alexander Shelepin (1958–1961), who was a Party secretary as well as a member of the Politburo, and Yuri Andropov (1967–1982), who later became General Secretary of the Communist Party. During his brief year as head of the Party, Andropov appointed former high KGB officials to the directorship of the Ministry of Internal Affairs (Vitaly Fedorchuk) and to the Vice-Chairmanship of the Council of Ministers (Geidar Aliev, also elevated to full membership on the Politburo). While this may not have constituted "turn[ing] over the Soviet dictatorship to men from the KGB," as John Barron argues,[21] it demonstrates at least that association with the state security forces is no hindrance to a political career in the USSR.

The enforcement of state security is divided between two organizations: the KGB and the MVD (Ministry of Internal Affairs). The latter, backed by a 250,000-man army, is responsible for putting down popular disturbances, riots, or insurrection wherever they might occur in the country, and for regular police functions. (The MVD will be discussed in Chapter 12.) The KGB's authority exists wherever such events might be connected with foreign agents or influences. Because Soviet suspicion of outside agitation almost invariably arises in internal events, the boundary between KGB and MVD jurisdictions is obscure at best.

The KGB is organized into a number of functional directorates that carry out specific responsibilities:[22]

1. *First Chief Directorate.* This directorate conducts KGB operations abroad, managing networks of agents and illegals in virtually every country in the world. It gathers information, assesses world conditions for the Politburo, recruits operatives, disseminates disinformation, and carries out active measures of intelligence operations.
2. *Second Chief Directorate.* Responsible for internal security, this directorate has offices and agents throughout the Soviet Union. Its primary targets are political and economic corruption, espionage, the behavior of citizens who travel abroad or have contact with foreigners in the country, and the surveillance of foreign journalists, students, and tourists.
3. *Border Guards Directorate.* This directorate comprises some 300,000 to 400,000 military troops who patrol Soviet borders to prevent Soviet citizens from defecting and outsiders from entering the country illegally. This army, equipped with artillery, armor, and patrol ships, affords the Party leadership a military force outside the regular armed forces for use in case the latter should prove unreliable.
4. *Third Directorate.* This comprises a large number of agents and informants who operate in the Soviet armed forces to ensure the loyalty and obedience of the military.
5. *Fifth Chief Directorate.* Established during Yuri Andropov's term as KGB chief, this directorate focuses on dissidents, religious believers, and nonconformists in Soviet society. It engages in surveillance, arrest and interrogation, and "relocation."

In addition, other directorates carry out such diverse duties as providing security for top Party leaders, surveillance of foreign embassies, and cryptography.

The Communist Party's control over the security forces is ensured only at the top of the power structure. The appointment and activities of the KGB chief are controlled by the Politburo, and this individual is normally a member of that elite group. Below that level, KGB units are formally subordinate to Party organs at each level, but in practice they operate with considerable independence, and one of their objects of control is the Party organization itself. KGB offices are organized in every factory, enterprise, college, and military unit in the country, and there is a branch office in every Soviet city and town. In addition to salaried employees, a vast army of paid and nonpaid informers keeps tabs on the citizenry and reports any transgressions to authorities. Collectively, they constitute a major power center in the governing structure of the Soviet political system.

Politically, the KGB presents no serious challenge to the Party leadership. Since the death of Stalin, the leadership has moved firmly and collectively to subordinate the police apparatus to the Party structure. It is subject to continuous supervision by the Administrative Organs Department of the Central Committee and works closely with Party committees at all levels. Unlike the military, the secret police enjoy little public respect and would find the popular climate decidedly hostile in the face of any attempt to replace the Party as the dominant power structure.

The Soviet Military

The military forces of any country present the civilian political leadership with a permanent challenge. From the politicians' point of view, the military needs to be powerful enough to ensure the security of the country from outside enemies and, when necessary, from internal unrest, and at the same time not so strong as to threaten the dominance of the civilian leadership. The effectiveness of the military rests heavily on the professionalism and specialized training of the officers and their ability to command obedience among their own uniformed personnel—qualities that tend to insulate them from civilian control. In the Soviet case there is an additional factor: the high standing of the armed forces among the population because of the victory in the "great patriotic war" (World War II) and because of the popular perception of the USSR as a superpower able to compete militarily with the United States.

Despite these advantages, the Soviet military has always been subordinate to the political leadership. Over the years important disputes have arisen between military and political leaders, often resulting in compromises in policy or in funding levels. But no general or admiral has ever won in a showdown with a General Secretary; on the other hand, many military leaders have been purged from their positions after such disputes. In the long run, of course, governments rarely experience showdowns among senior officials. In the normal course of politics, relations among Soviet political and military leaders are complex and dynamic, yielding advantages to one side or the other depending on the issues, the personalities, and the times.

The relationship between the military and the Communist Party leadership rests on three interrelated foundations, each of which contributes to the pre-eminence of the Party over the military. The first is the long tradition of civilian leadership that has existed in the Soviet system since the October Revolution. The Soviet Constitution, as well as all other basic documents of the political system, make clear the supreme responsibility of the Party for the governance and development of the nation. While the military is given great credit for its heroic struggle in World War II, the true responsibility for the victory is always attributed to the Communist Party. For the military to attempt to replace the Party as rulers of the USSR would constitute a rejection of the whole history of Soviet communism. That, of course, does not mean it could never happen, but the well-established subordination of the military to the Communist Party is a substantial obstacle to it ever occurring.

The second foundation of Party/military relations arises from the unquestioned importance of the military to the survival of the Soviet Union. The idea that war is inevitable, though no longer a part of Soviet military doctrine, is deeply embedded in the Bolshevik mentality. Lenin always expected a Communist Soviet Union to be involved in wars with Western "bourgeois" countries. "The victory of socialism," he wrote in 1916, "does not at one stroke eliminate all war in general. On the contrary, its presupposes wars."[23] This fixation on war and defense had ensured that the military would occupy a privileged position in the councils of the Party leadership. The satisfaction of military needs for weapons and equipment has always had top priority in the Soviet economic system, and the need for manpower takes precedence over civilian labor needs. In the post-Stalin era, the determination of the Party leaders to make the USSR a world superpower with a military force equal to that of the United States and NATO has intensified their willingness to provide the military with virtually a blank check.

As a result, the military is bound to the Party leadership through the strongest of all institutional interests: a steady supply of resources and a constant reaffirmation of the importance of military power to the survival of the state. Under these circumstances there has been little incentive for the military leadership to challenge the Party's monopoly of political power. They share essentially the same interests; hence, the division of labor between them serves both their interests. The Party is left unchallenged to rule the political system, and the military is able to concentrate its attention in its field of greatest interest and expertise.

The third foundation of Party/military relations is the control structure which the Party leadership maintains to ensure its dominance over the military establishment. However strongly the factors of national tradition and self-interest may persuade the military to accept a subordinate position, the Communist Party leadership never relies wholly on such intangibles. In the case of the military, as with the Supreme Soviet and the Council of Ministers, an elaborate set of controls is maintained by the Party leadership to ensure obedience to the Party will. And as with the other institutions, the controls work with something less than 100 percent efficiency. To assess this dimension of the Party/military relationship, we must look first at the organization of Soviet military forces.

The Organization of Soviet Armed Forces. In many respects outsiders can only guess at the nature of the Soviet military establishment, for the level of secrecy surrounding it is traditionally very high. Furthermore, in the past several years, evidence has accumulated that both military doctrine and the organization of the armed forces are changing in response to changing world conditions. Thus we can only give an approximate description of the Soviet military and its relationship to the Communist Party.

Defense Council. As in all fields of policy-making, decisions about military affairs and organization are ultimately in the hands of the Politburo of the CPSU. The highest command posts are on the Politburo *nomenklatura,* and strategic policy matters are discussed at Politburo meetings. But within the membership of the Politburo there is a core group that exercises supreme authority over the military forces. This is the Defense Council, known to exist since at least 1964 and headed by the General Secretary. The Defense Council is responsible for the national security in the largest sense, including military strategy, the administration of the armed forces, defense production, civil defense, and those aspects of foreign policy that bear on national security. Although the actual membership is never publicized, it is likely that the Defense Council was composed, during the last year of Brezhnev's rule, of the following leaders:[24]

Brezhnev:	General Secretary of the CPSU and Chairman of the Defense Council
Tikhonov:	Chairman of the Council of Ministers
Ustinov:	Defense Minister
Gromyko:	Foreign Minister
Andropov:	Chairman of the KGB
Chernenko:	Central Committee Secretary

All of these men were members of the Party Politburo at the time and probably would have been identified as its leading members. There is, however, no reason to believe that the positions represented by the members of the Defense Council are fixed, or that whoever occupies them would automatically have membership on the Defense Council. As we have seen with the Politburo itself, effectiveness on the highest political level often depends more on the individual than on his official position. It is important to note, however, that no professional military officers have been given membership on the Defense Council.[25]

The Supreme High Command: The Headquarters (SHC Stavka). Even less well publicized than the Defense Council, the Supreme High Command Headquarters (SHC Stavka) is primarily a wartime command structure that was headed by Stalin during World War II. It has apparently continued to exist since then under a succession of titles, and it carries responsibility for the direct command of the armed forces in the field. This includes preparing missions and directing their fulfillment, forming and deploying joint military forces on various fronts, and the training and supplying of the armed forces.

This command agency is also chaired by the General Secretary of the CPSU. However, it is a joint Party/military body that probably includes several other members of the Politburo along with the chairman of the military General Staff and the military heads of the different military services. It may be that the SHC Stavka is essentially the Defense Council with the addition of the top military leaders. In any case, it is clear that the civilian Party leadership exercises exclusive authority over the armed forces, both through the Defense Council and through the Politburo as a whole, allowing the military leadership into the decision-making process only at the third level.

The Supreme High Command: The General Staff. At this level, the chiefs of the various military services form a high command similar in its responsibilities to the United States' Joint Chiefs of Staff. They coordinate the activities, in war and in peacetime, of the different branches of service and carry out the policies of the civilian and military leaders on the SHC Stavka. The chairman of the General Staff, currently Marshal Sergei Akhromeyev, is the number-two man in the defense establishment, ranking right after the Minister of Defense.

Collegium of the Defense Ministry. Within the Defense Ministry itself, as in all ministries, the minister and deputy ministers, the chief of the Main Political Administration (about which more below), and some other high officials of the ministry constitute the Collegium. This agency deals with matters of logistics, training, political indoctrination, combat readiness, and the selection of cadres. The Defense Minister has usually been a civilian and, in the case of Dmitri Ustinov (Defense Minister from 1976 until his death in 1984), a member of the Party Politburo.

Political Controls over the Military. Typically, the Soviet Party leadership exercises several levels of control over non-Party institutions, as we have seen in the cases of the Supreme Soviet and the Council of Ministers. The same is true of the armed forces. We can identify four different forms of control in the contemporary Soviet Union. The first is the hierarchical decision-making structure that lodges highest authority over military affairs in two Party organs (the Defense Council and the Politburo) *above* the level of the highest military council. With two brief exceptions, Marshals Zhukov (June-October 1957) and Grechko (1973–1976), no professional military leader has ever sat on the Party Politburo, and none has had membership in the Central Committee Secretariat or the Presidium of the Council of Ministers.[26]

The second layer of control arises through the normal control that the Party hierarchy exercises over its own members. In the case of the military, this includes virtually all higher-level military officers (colonel and above) and many of the younger officers and noncommissioned officers. Overall, about 20 percent of all military personnel are members of the Communist Party and therefore subject to its discipline.[27] Party committees exist at all levels of military organization. The military is often referred to as the "Party in uniform" to emphasize the close connection between civilian and military objectives.

The third and fourth forms of control are exercised by two organizations that operate directly under the control of the top Party leadership: the Main Political Administration (MPA) and the Committee on State Security (KGB). Both deserve closer attention as their importance to the stability of Party rule over the military is especially great.

The Main Political Administration (MPA). This agency, responsible directly to the Party hierarchy rather than to the military high command, is charged with ensuring that Party policies are understood and carried out by the military services. To do so, it operates an elaborate network of uniformed officers at every level of the military establishment who share the authority of the military commanders. The MPA was originally established before the October Revolution in 1917 and was called the Military Organization of the Central Committee. Since then it has undergone numerous name changes but has remained the Party's most direct line of control over the military establishment, operating directly out of the Secretariat.

At the top level, the MPA is headed by a chief who works through a bureau. Because this is a Party rather than a government (military) position, the chief is responsible to the Secretariat rather than the Defense Minister or the Presidium of the Council of Ministers. The organization of the MPA is elaborately structured for its wide range of responsibilities. Figure 6.2 depicts this structure.

The real strength of the MPA lies in its hierarchy of political officers who are assigned to every military unit in the country and abroad. These officers carry military rank but are appointed by the Party leadership and are not accountable to

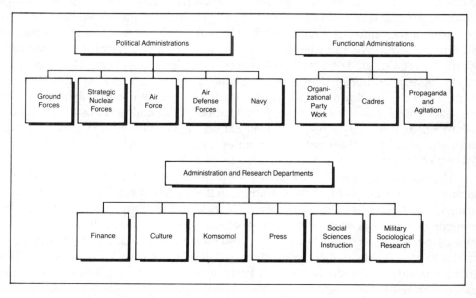

Figure 6.2 MAIN POLITICAL ADMINISTRATION[28]

the military commanders with whom they work. Originally called "military commissars," they were first appointed to supervise the czarist army officers who were recruited immediately after the October Revolution to lead the Red Army. To prevent conspiracies against the new Bolshevik regime, a commissar's signature was required to approve all orders of a military commander.

The role of the commissars was complicated in 1924, when the Central Committee adopted the principle of "unity of command." According to this formula, the military commander was to be in sole command of the unit and the commissar subordinate to him, although still responsible for the political behavior of the unit. In the years that followed, both in wartime and peacetime, these two principles, and the commissars and commanders who were required to follow them, triggered incessant conflict.[29] The military officers often resented the commissars' interference with their command function, and the commissars constantly battled for equal or dominant status for the Party hierarchy. The formal status of the commissar alternated between Deputy Commander (Zampolit) and Political Commander (Politrug) depending on whether the political officer was viewed as subordinate to the military commander or his equal.

The "unity of command" principle is further diminished by the existence, since the 1930s, of *military councils.* These are a form of collective leadership of military units at the higher levels. They are typically composed of the military commander and his deputy and chief of staff, the political commander or "comrade", the Party secretary in the district, and several other leading officers. The council is responsible to the Party Central Committee, to the Defense Ministry, and to the higher military command. Decisions in the councils are by majority vote. However, there is a proviso that if the political commander disagrees with a decision, he may appeal over the head of the military commander to a higher Party authority.

The existence of the military councils obviously represents a retreat from the "unity of command" principle. Over the years, the professional military corps has resisted this diffusion of command while Party officials, including Party "generals" and "marshals," have sought to strengthen it. During Khrushchev's rule, the grounds for ousting Marshal Zhukov from the Politburo were, in part at least, his attempts to reduce the power of the Main Political Administration and increase that of the military commanders. After his forced retirement in late 1957, his successor, Marshal Malinowski, carried out the Politbuoro's determination to alter the balance again in favor of the political comrades.[30]

By the 1980s, the roles of the military and political agents had evolved in a number of directions. Military councils exist at the higher levels (headquarters of the branches of service, military districts and fronts, and special border and foreign military commands), while at the lower operational levels, the principle of unity of command is more fully exercised. Political officers at the higher levels have substantial staffs of deputies, functional departments, and instructors who oversee the Party's interests in the lower levels of command. In addition, the MPA controls the publication of all military journals, books, and newspapers including *Krasnaia Zvezda,* the chief military publication whose editor is a member of the executive bureau of the MPA.[31]

How effective is the MPA as an element of control over the Soviet military?[32] The answer lies in the conflicting forces that operate on MPA officers in carrying out their duties. On the one hand, they are primarily subordinate to higher-level MPA officers while also required to accept the leadership of their immediate military commander. On the higher levels especially, military disagreement with Party policies or decisions creates potentially serious conflict between the political and military commanders. Where this happens, the MPA provides an important check on the attitudes of individual commanders, thus making it difficult for factions among military officers to be formed.

On the other hand, a continuous process of co-optation goes on between the military and political officer corps. The tendency of the two officers in any military unit to share similar values and perspectives and to cooperate rather than struggle against each other is continuous and pervasive. MPA officers are career officers who are often recruited from among military personnel. They are trained in MPA academies both for their political duties and for effective work in a military unit. In recent years, up to one-third of their training has been devoted to operational and technical military subjects, and they are expected "to assist the 'line' officers in the maintenance of military discipline, high levels of professional competence, and the combat readiness of the unit. . . ."[33] In addition, the political officers benefit from the general respect and privileges that are accorded to the military officer corps. This provides an additional motivation for MPA officers to seek a respected place among the regular military officers.

As a result of these influences, it is probable that the Communist Party's control over the military through MPA officers is compromised by the divided loyalties that seem inherent in the position. Fritz Ermarth has concluded that

> the political officer has been assimilated into the military establishment so thoroughly that the question of his loyalty, whether it is first to the Armed Forces or first to the Party apparatus, now stands open.[34]

The KGB and the Military. KGB units and agents infiltrated throughout the armed forces constitute the fourth, and ultimate, Party control over the military. Through its "third directorate," special units (*osobie otdely* or "OO") conduct permanent surveillance, indoctrination, and information gathering on all branches of the armed services, reporting directly to their own superiors rather than to military commanders. Agents monitor correspondence and telephone conversations on military posts and investigate all instances of suspected espionage or rule violations.

The KGB also maintains its own troops along the borders of the country and has a contingent stationed in Moscow that serves to guard the Kremlin and the Party leadership from any armed threat. While the chief purpose of the KGB's military activities is to conduct counterintelligence operations, its separate existence within the military clearly gives the Party leadership an important lever of control over the armed forces.

In summary, we return to our initial judgment: The several power structures operating in the Soviet governmental system have significant resources for exercising power in a system dominated by the Communist Party leadership. Their power comes from an unavoidable delegation of decision-making authority by the Party leadership. The limitations on that power likewise come from the Party leadership through a variety of both intangible and administrative controls that operate throughout the system.

NOTES

1. Data from 1962 and 1974 are from Robert Siegler, *The Standing Commissions of the Supreme Soviet* (New York: Praeger, 1982), p. 31. For 1984, see *Pravda,* 13 April 1984, p. 1.
2. For a detailed analysis of this diversity, see A.P. Proskurin, "Cistema ministerstv, gosudarstvennikh komitetov i bedomstv soyuznoi respubliki: Faktory, obuslovlivayushchie ee postroenie," in V. I. Semenkov and V. I. Shabailov, eds., *Ministerstva, Gosudarstvennie Komitety i Vedomstva Soiuznoi Respubliki* (Minsk: Nauka i Tekhnika, 1984), pp. 22–26.
3. *Pravda,* 12 April 1984.
4. T.H. Rigby, "Stalinism and the Mono-organizational Society," in Robert C. Tucker, ed., *Stalinism: Essays in Historical Interpretation* (New York: Norton & Co., 1977), p. 60.
5. *Partiinoe Stroitelstvo, nauchnie osnovy partiinoi raboty, Vol. 2* (Moscow: Mysl, 1985), pp. 132 and 128.
6. This and the previous two quotations are from A.M. Korolev, V.N. Shestakovsky, and S.K. Chykin, *Kadry: Reshayushchaya Sila Partinovo Rukovodstva* (Moscow: Mysl, 1984), pp. 14.15.
7. See T.H. Rigby and Bohdan Harasymiw, eds., *Leadership Selection and Patron-Client Relations in the USSR and Yugoslavia* (London: George Allen & Unwin, 1983), p. 3. A much lower figure—750,000—was suggested by Michael Voslensky in his *Nomenklatura: The Soviet Union Ruling Class An Insider's Report* (Garden City, N.Y.: Doubleday, 1984), pp. 92–96, but most Western scholars accept the higher figure.
8. Basile Kerblay, *Les Marches Paysans en U.R.S.S.* (Paris: Librairie Armand Colin, 1968), p. 258.
9. See Voslensky, *Nomenklatura,* p. 81ff.
10. *Partkoms* themselves have no authority over lower-level *partkoms* of the same organization. The *partkom* of a regional soviet, thus, has no authority over the *partkom* of a city soviet. See S. I. Surnichenko, A.M. Mysaev, and Ye. N. Tarasov, *Partiinoe Stroitelstvo, Nauchnie Osnovy Partiinoi Raboty, Chast II* (Moscow: Mysl, 1985), p. 157.
11. M.S. Smirtyukov, *Sovetskii Gosudarstvenny Apparat Upravleniya* (Moscow: Izd. Politicheskoi Literatury, 1982), p. 54.
12. Agriculture offers a clear example of this general phenomenon. In the 1960s, the government's chief of agriculture, Dmitri Poliansky, was also Deputy Chairman, then First Deputy Chairman, of the Council of Ministers and a full member of the Party Politburo. Clearly, no agricultural administrator in the Secretariat could match his authority. As Poliansky fell from favor in the 1970s, he was replaced in the government by a new minister of agriculture who held no higher position. About the same time (1978), the

Secretariat's Department of Agriculture was taken over by a new secretary, Mikhail Gorbachev, a man clearly on the rise. As a result, authority over agriculture shifted significantly from the Council of Ministers to the Party Secretariat.

13. The information for Figure 6.1 has been gleaned from various sources, including the perceptive analysis of the issue by Jerry Hough in Jerry F. Hough and Merle Fainsod, *How the Soviet Union Is Governed* (Cambridge, Mass.: Harvard University Press, 1979), pp. 438–43.

14. T.H. Rigby, "Der Sowjetische Ministerrat Unter Kosygin," Bundesinstitute fur Ostwissenschaftliche und Internationale Studien, Report #21, 1977, p. 38.

15. From interviews with Moscow officials by Carol W. Lewis and Stephen Sternheimer in their *Soviet Urban Management: With Comparisons to the United States* (New York: Praeger, 1979), p. 163.

16. Smirtyukov, *Sovetskii,* p. 176.

17. *Pravda,* 12 June 1981, p. 1.

18. Arkady N. Shevchenko, *Breaking With Moscow* (New York: Alfred A. Knopf, 1985), p. 86.

19. In a detailed study of the power of the economic ministries, Alice Gorlin concludes that "Soviet ministries have extraordinary power" and that "attempts to curb this power have failed." See "The Power of Soviet Industrial Ministries in the 1980's," *Soviet Studies,* XXXVII:3, July 1985, p. 361.

20. Andropov and Chernenko replaced 50 percent of the chairmen of state committees, 28 percent of the ministers, 28 percent of the members of the Presidium of the Council of Ministers, and 33 percent of the chairman of the presidia of Union-Republic Councils of Ministers. Source: Eberhard Schneider, "Der Ministerrat der UdSSR unter Andropow und Tschernenko," *Bericht des Bundesinstituts fur Ostwissenschaftliche und Internationale Studien,* No. 16, 1985, pp. 5–10. In his first years, Gorbachev purged at least thirty ministers and chairmen of state committees. Source: *U. S. News and World Report,* January 20, 1986, p. 33.

21. John Barron, *KGB Today: The Hidden Hand* (New York: Reader's Digest Press, 1983), p. 17.

22. The information comes from Barron, *The Hidden Hand,* Appendix B.

23. V.I. Lenin, "The Military Programme of the Proletarian Revolution," *Lenin, Selected Works,* Vol. 1 (Moscow: Progress Publishers, 1967), p. 779.

24. This list of probable members of the Defense Council comes from Michael J. Deane, Ilana Kass, and Andrew G. Porth, "The Soviet High Command Structure in Transformation," *Strategic Review,* Spring 1984, p. 58.

25. It is possible that, as an exception to this rule, General of the Army V.M. Chebrikov attained membership on the Defense Council as a result of his assuming chairmanship of the KGB after Brezhnev's death.

26. There are, of course, numerous "political generals" among the Party leaders, men who have been awarded military rank because of their political, rather than their military, accomplishments. Brezhnev, for example, was made a marshal in 1976.

27. Estimated in John L. Scherer, *USSR: Facts and Figures Annual,* Vol. 8 (Gulf Breeze, Fla: Academic International Press, 1984), p. 94.

28. From M.G. Sobolev, *Partiino-Politicheskaya Rabota v Sovetskoi Armii i Flote,* rev. ed. (Moscow: Voennoe Izdatelstvo, 1984), p. 53.

29. For an interesting history of this conflict, see Yosef Avidar, *The Party and the Army in the Soviet Union* (University Park: Pennsylvania State University Press, 1983), chapter 1.

30. See Timothy J. Colton, *Commissars, Commanders, and Civilian Authority: The Structure*

of Soviet Military Politics (Cambridge, Mass.: Harvard University Press, 1979), chapter 8 for a full discussion of the Zhukov affair.

31. See Edward L. Warner, *The Military in Contemporary Soviet Politics* (New York: Praeger, 1977), p. 72–73.
32. For a useful summary of conflicting Western views on this question see Amy W. Knight, "The KGB's Special Departments in the Soviet Armed Forces," *Orbis,* Summer 1984, pp. 257–58.
33. Warner, *Military in Soviet Politics,* p. 74.
34. "Soviet Military Politics," *Military Review* (61:1), January 1968, p. 34. Quoted in Warner, *Military in Soviet Politics.*

CHAPTER 7
The Soviet Parliament

In the chaotic spring and summer months of 1917, the political center of the Russian Revolution was the Petrograd (now Leningrad) Soviet. Arising almost spontaneously out of the violence of the 1905 uprising, the Petrograd Soviet, like similar institutions in other cities, expressed the growing consciousness and political power of the urban work force. It counted about 2,500 members who were elected in factories and military barracks throughout the city. As the provisional government floundered in the summer of 1917, the Petrograd Soviet gained a measure of raw power based mainly on its potential to call out thousands of workers into the streets in opposition to the government.

The uniqueness of the soviet lay in its rejection of conventional parliamentary forms of deliberation and decision making. It disdained the slow processes of debate and compromise of "bourgeois parliaments," demanding instead quick decisions and immediate execution of its will. It maintained a mass rather than a representative character with close and continuous ties to the urban workers for whom it spoke. Its members were nonprofessional politicians who received no pay for their work, a matter of great pride to the membership. Of course, under these conditions, deputies were able to convene only occasionally when time off from their regular jobs could be arranged. In the interim periods, a smaller executive body was empowered to carry on the responsibilities of the soviet. Above all, the soviet sought to express the direct power of the proletariat (and later the peasantry) in the revolutionary changes that were engulfing Russia. All of these antiparliamentary characteristics of the early soviets were to become the traditional bases of the modern system of soviets in the USSR.

In addition to expressing the will of the proletariat through elected deputies, the soviet had an even broader mission: the training and preparation of citizens for self-government. Arguing that the state would eventually "wither away" after a successful socialist revolution, Lenin looked upon the soviets as a mechanism for drawing citizens into the administration of government at the local level and for socializing them to the new Soviet order. They would also serve to collect and pass on to the leaders a broad sampling of public opinion arising from their close contact with the citizenry.[1]

As the Bolsheviks consolidated their victory, the Communist Party leadership began to develop the hierarchy of governing institutions that came to mark the mature Soviet state. The basic principle was to designate small executive bodies within larger assemblies and to shift real power to the smaller body. In the case of the soviets, the All-Russian Congress of Soviets came to be described as the source of supreme governmental power in the new state. But in view of its infrequent meetings and its unwieldly size, an All-Russian Central Executive Committee (CEC) of about 200 members was appointed to carry out its governing functions. Within a month of the October Revolution, an even smaller executive body consisting of about eight Party leaders, the Presidium of the CEC, had been formed to govern between sessions of the CEC, and the latter gradually lost power. By the time Stalin was in control, the CEC, like the Congress of Soviets before it, had become locked into that pattern of unanimous voting that marked the end of its serious role in policy-making.

THE STALINIST LEGISLATURE

With the adoption of the "Stalin Constitution" in 1936, the modern structure of soviets came into being. By then, Stalin wanted not only to give the system of soviets a firmer constitutional base for domestic political purposes but also to demonstrate to the outside world the higher form of democracy that had supposedly been achieved by the Soviet revolution. He created, therefore, as the central institution of the political system, a legislature that was far more closely tied to the masses of citizens than any European legislature and one that had, on paper at least, supreme authority over all aspects of Soviet government. At the same time, Stalin moved to ensure that the legislature would have absolutely no capacity to interfere with the real power structure which he himself controlled.

Until Stalin's death, the Supreme Soviet remained largely moribund as a political institution. Elections were held regularly and the legislature convened to approve resolutions and pass laws, but the extreme concentration of power in Stalin's hands left little room for legislative involvement in the process of government.

The post-Stalin period, on the contrary, has witnessed a gradual change in the role of the Supreme Soviet. While overwhelming political power continues to reside with the Party leadership, evolving economic and social conditions in the country have brought in their wake new demands on the political process. The Party leadership has gradually found uses for the legislature and has permitted a subtle but significant evolution in its political role.

This is separate from, and should not be confused with, the role of the Supreme Soviet as described in the Constitution and repeated endlessly in the effusions of Soviet ideological propaganda. Here the old myth of popular rule that dates from the October Revolution remains unblemished by time and as empty in substance as it is elaborate in form. It is expressed most clearly in the 1977 Constitution, which defines the Supreme Soviet as "the highest body of state authority of the USSR . . . [which is] empowered to deal with all matters within the jurisdiction of the Union of Soviet Socialist Republics . . ." (Article 108). In the words of a recent Soviet publication:

Being the highest representative body of the Soviet people and wielding supreme state authority, the Supreme Soviet of the USSR is the pinnacle of the system of

Soviets. As such, it commands attention; whatever it says is carefully studied and every major decision it takes often evokes wide response both at home and abroad. All the threads of top-level management of the Soviet state lead back to the USSR Supreme Soviet. All other higher bodies are responsible and accountable to it; only it has the right to pass national laws."[2]

At every level, the soviets "direct all sectors of the state, economic, and social and cultural development, either directly or through bodies instituted by them, take decisions and ensure their execution, and verify their implication" (Article 93).

The Supreme Soviet is also authorized to appoint members to and supervise the work of all other state bodies, including the Council of Ministers, the Supreme Court of the USSR, the Procurator General, the Committee of Peoples Control, and the Presidium of the Supreme Soviet. In addition, only the Supreme Soviet has the authority to adopt and amend the Constitution, admit new republics to the USSR, and approve the budget and economic plans of the country. Regarding all such matters, the Supreme Soviet functions "on the basis of collective, free, constructive discussion and decision making" (Article 94). All members have an equal right to speak on pending issues and decision making is by majority rule.

Thus states the Soviet Constitution. In the real world of Soviet government, however, it is no exaggeration to say that the Supreme Soviet does none of these things on its own initiative. The things it does do are of another order and we shall examine them presently. First, let us consider briefly the organization of the Supreme Soviet and the nature of its activities. Then we will take up the central political issue: how the Party leadership manages, decade after decade, to control the legislature so completely that no challenge to the Party's authority from that quarter is even conceivable. The mechanism of control is worth examining in detail, for it reveals a great deal about the inner workings of the Soviet political process.

ORGANIZATION AND MEMBERSHIP OF THE SUPREME SOVIET

The Supreme Soviet is composed of two chambers, the Soviet of the Union and the Soviet of Nationalities. Each chamber has 750 elected deputies who serve five-year terms and are eligible for reelection. And each chamber elects its own officers, which include a chairman and four vice-chairman. The legislature normally meets twice a year in Moscow in formal sessions that last two or three days. On the regional and local levels, soviets are unicameral (one chamber) and of a size appropriate to the level at which they function, and they meet more frequently.

The membership of the Supreme Soviet clearly distinguishes it from western European legislatures. Many of its elected members are people who would stand no chance of serving in the national legislature in Britain, France, or the United States, as Table 7.1 shows.

TABLE 7.1 CHARACTERISTICS OF USSR SUPREME SOVIET DEPUTIES ELECTED IN 1984[3]

Occupations		
Workers and peasants	769	(51.3%)
Economic managers and specialists	68	(4.5%)
Scientists, professionals, artists, teachers	134	(8.9%)
Communist Party officials	250	(16.7%)
Government and Soviet officials	198	(13.2%)
Trade Union and Komsomol officials	19	(1.3%)
Military personnel	55	(3.7%)
Age groups		
21–30	331	(22.0%)
31–40	186	(12.4%)
41–50	334	(22.3%)
51–60	414	(27.6%)
Over 60	235	(15.7%)
Educational levels		
Complete higher education	789	(52.6%)
Incomplete higher education	24	(1.6%)
Secondary only	644	(43.0%)
Less than secondary	41	(2.7%)

Unquestionably, as Soviet spokespeople proudly assert, this is a legislature that in demographic terms is highly representative of the Soviet people. Over half of the deputies are workers and peasants, more than a third are under forty years of age, and nearly half have no more than a secondary education. In addition, a third of the members are women, and the general membership contains citizens of sixty-three different nationalities. As we shall see later in this chapter, however, the political makeup of the legislature reflects a different set of criteria for selecting deputies, one that ensures effective control by the Party leadership.

The Presidium of the Supreme Soviet

When the full Supreme Soviet is not in session, a thirty-nine-person executive committee called the Presidium carries out most of the legislative functions of the government. The membership of the Presidium includes a chairman or president and a first vice-chairman, fifteen vice-chairmen who are also chairmen of their respective Union Republic Supreme Soviets, a secretary, and twenty-one additional members designated by the leadership from among the deputies to the Supreme Soviet. Typically, the latter group includes six to eight members of the Party Politburo and Secretariat.[4]

Since 1977, the Presidium has normally been chaired by the General Secretary of the Communist Party who thereby attains a position as chief of state in addition to being head of the Party. This is not yet a settled pattern, however. Prior to

Brezhnev's assumption of the chairmanship, no General Secretary had held that position. After Brezhnev's death, his successors did not automatically or immediately succeed to the position. Gorbachev, for example, appointed Andrei Gromyko to the chairmanship of the Presidium, rather than assuming the position itself. But he may decide to do so at some future time.

The Presidium is legally responsible and subordinate to the Supreme Soviet, but considering the infrequency and brevity of the latter's sessions, the Presidium has been endowed with an unusually broad range of powers. The Soviet Constitution authorizes it to interpret the laws of the country, ratify treaties, appoint and recall diplomatic representatives of the USSR, appoint and dismiss the military high command, declare war, and proclaim martial law. To do all these things, it has specific authority (Article 123) to promulgate edicts and decrees without the need for subsequent legislative approval. On only four matters does the Constitution specifically require that acts of the Presidium be ratified by the Supreme Soviet (Article 122): amending existing legislative acts, approving changes in the boundaries between Union Republics, forming and abolishing ministries and state committees, and appointing and firing ministers of state. In none of these matters, of course, would the Presidium act on its own initiative or without clear directions from the Party leadership.

Formal meetings of the entire Presidium occur irregularly about every two months, but the leadership and the staff function continuously throughout the year. They carry on the normal functions of the Presidium; they also plan for upcoming sessions of the Supreme Soviet, prepare the agenda for the sessions, and coordinate the work of the Supreme Soviet and its standing commissions during sessions.

Standing Commissions

Like most legislatures, the Supreme Soviet conducts some of its business in committees, or standing commissions as they are called in the USSR. During Stalin's time, and for more than a decade after his death, the four existing commissions in each chamber had little more to do than the Supreme Soviet itself. They consisted of a Legislative Proposals Commission, a Budget Commission, a Foreign Affairs Commission, and a Credentials Commission, and each had about ten members.

In the 1950s and early 1960s, there was no substantial change in the prominence of the standing commissions system on the national level, but on the republic and regional levels, the number of commissions began to proliferate. Specialized commissions were being formed for such economic sectors as heavy industry, transportation, agriculture, and construction, and for social concerns such as education, culture, health, and so forth.[5]

By the mid-1960s, pressures to extend this expansion to the national level produced a new statute that sharply increased the number of commissions in the USSR Supreme Soviet and tripled the number of deputies appointed to commissions.[6] In addition, the statute broadened the functions of the commissions, granting them the legal authority to initiate legislation, to oversee the activities of specific government ministries, to institute investigations into the fulfillment of laws (referred to as the *kontrol* function in Soviet terminology), and to have access to all information and government officials necessary to the performance of their duties.

The number of commissions has been periodically increased since the 1967 reform. In the Eleventh Convocation of the USSR Supreme Soviet (elected in 1984), there are seventeen commissions in each chamber.

Standing Commissions of the Supreme Soviet, 1985[7]

General Subject Commissions

- Credentials
- Legislative Proposals
- Foreign Affairs
- Science and Technology
- Conservation and the Use of Natural Resources

Economic Sector Commissions

- Planning and Budget
- Industry
- Energy
- Transport and Communication
- Construction and Construction Materials
- Agro-industrial Complexes

Public Welfare Commissions

- Consumer Goods and Public Services
- Health and Social Security
- Public Education and Culture
- Women's Labor and Living Conditions, Protection of Motherhood and Children
- Youth Affairs
- Communal Living and the Urban Economy

Standing commissions normally convene in the last few weeks before a semiannual convocation of the Supreme Soviet itself. They consider draft legislative proposals that have been presented to the Supreme Soviet and prepare them for consideration by the whole chamber. Specialists and interested parties often participate in the deliberations of the commissions, although only commission members (deputies to the Supreme Soviet) are permitted to vote. In fact, not even all elected deputies are eligible to serve on standing commissions. To avoid possible conflicts of interest, the 1967 statute on the Supreme Soviet prohibits a number of categories of deputies from sitting on commissions: members of the

Supreme Soviet Presidium, officers of the two chambers, ministers of the government, members of the Supreme Court, and the Procurator General.

Council of Elders

Each chamber has a Council of Elders, but this body is only occasionally referred to in Soviet writing and little is known of its functions. The councils are authorized "to agree on what questions have to be included in the agenda, on the sessional order for discussion of these questions, and on the composition of the bodies elected by the Supreme Soviet and its chambers."[8] Presumably the officers of the two chambers are included as members of the Council of Elders. Beyond that, the seats on the council are distributed according to electoral regions, with a fixed number of seats going to each republic, autonomous republic, autonomous region, and national area. This produces about 150 members of the Council of Elders in each chamber,[9] obviously too large a group to deal directly with the matters charged to it. Decisions on the legislative agenda and similar matters are made by the Party leadership and presented for unanimous approval to the Council of Elders just before each session of the Supreme Soviet.

THE SUPREME SOVIET AND THE PARTY LEADERSHIP

It has always been difficult for Western observers to take the USSR Supreme Soviet seriously. In the half century since the institution was formalized in the Stalin Constitution, no Supreme Soviet has ever rejected a legislative proposal of the leadership or failed to approve a Party nominee for government office. In no instance, in fact, has a deputy ever voted against a proposal of the Party leadership.[10] As everyone understands, when an elected deputy raises his or her hand to "vote" on a legislative proposal, that person is merely signifying his or her understanding that a bill is at that moment becoming a law. And as we shall see below, many bills become laws without anyone raising a hand.

This sort of political institution raises two intriguing questions. First, how does the Party leadership exercise such apparently perfect control over an institution so formidable in size and lofty in constitutional standing as the national parliament? And secondly, given the effectiveness of the control mechanisms, is the Supreme Soviet able to perform any significant services to the political process and the nation beyond what the Party could provide by itself? In other words, if the Communist Party has as much control over the the political system as it appears, why bother with institutions like the Supreme Soviet?

We shall examine first the control mechanisms themselves. In this there are two basic objectives for the Party leadership: control over who gets elected to the Supreme Soviet (and all the other soviets) and control over their behavior once elected. In the following pages we shall try to clarify just how these controls function, how successful they are, and how the Soviet people have reacted to them. Both the controls and the reactions are crucial to the continuing stability of the Soviet system.

CONTROLLING WHO GETS ELECTED

The Electoral Process

The day after the 1984 national elections, the Soviet press announced routinely that 99.99 percent of eligible voters had actually voted.[11] That is within a fraction of a percentage of the announced turnout at *every* election in the past half century. And this remarkable response occurs in a country where voting is not required by law. Even if one accepts (1) that Soviet citizens come under considerable local pressure to show up at the polls on election day even though not required to do so by law, and (2) that a sizable number of citizens who are recorded as voting have not actually done so (both of which we shall consider below), the institution of Soviet popular elections is impressive.

Elections to the Supreme Soviets (national and republic) are held every five years and to the local soviets every two and a half years. Deputies are elected in a process that the Constitution refers to as "universal, equal, and direct suffrage by secret ballot" (Article 95). Excluding the certified insane and the criminally incarcerated, every citizen eighteen years and older is eligible to vote.

As the principal monument to Soviet democracy, elections are elaborately organized and widely publicized throughout the country. In anticipation of an upcoming election, various official organizations, such as the Communist Party, the Komsomol, trade unions, major economic enterprises, and military units, are authorized to nominate candidates for seats at all levels of soviets. In practice, the single candidate who is to be nominated for each seat is determined by the appropriate Party executive committee after consultation with the other organizations. But it is common to solicit public reactions to prospective nominees, as the leadership would prefer, other factors aside, to present a genuinely popular and respected candidate to the electorate. Soviet writers frequently allude to instances in which constituents have caused the withdrawal of a candidate through their negative reactions, but the actual number of such cases is difficult to determine.[12]

Several months before election day, an army of "agitators" is mobilized to contact all voters, inform them about the official "issues" of the campaign, and secure their commitment to vote in the election. Each agitator is responsible for fifteen to twenty voters, while groups of agitators work under the supervision of the local Party organizations. In addition to the 11 million or so agitators, an equal number of citizens are involved in the election as appointed members of election commissions, which are responsible for overseeing the election and counting the ballots. Thus, some 15 percent of the electorate have official roles to play in the election.

On election day, always a national holiday, polling stations are set up virtually everywhere there are people. In addition to the usual locations in cities and towns, they are established, according to Professor Krutogolov,

> at nomadic encampments of the shepherds and cowherds in the Central Asian and Caucasian republics and the reindeer-breeders in the Far North, at wintering stations, at airports and on long-distance trains and ships that are at sea on the day of the elections . . . [and] at hospitals, sanatoria and invalid homes.[13]

Casting a ballot is a simple process. Voters merely appear at their poling places, receive a ballot and, assuming they intend to vote in favor of the official candidate, fold and drop the ballet into the ballot box. If one decides to vote against the candidate (by crossing out the candidate's name), he or she may enter a polling booth provided by law at each polling station. While this makes it easy for authorities to identify negative voters, and thus obviates the constitutional guarantee of a secret ballot, the political significance of using a polling booth is probably small. Estimates of the number of voters who do so tend to be far higher than the number of reported negative voters, which suggests that there are other reasons for using the booths as well. Soviet sources report that some voters, in fact, just write their names on the ballot to confirm that they voted; others write patriotic slogans while still others write obscenities. Some voters apparently write nothing at all but enter the booth merely to exert their right to do so or to register a mild protest at the absence of real choice in the election. The risks involved in such behavior in the post-Stalinist Russa appear to be minimal.[14]

This electoral process produces over 2 million elected deputies at every election and demonstrates, at least, both the effectiveness of the Party's electoral organization and the acceptance of the process by the Soviet population. Despite the option of voting against the Party's candidate, official reports indicate that this rarely happens: in the 1985 national elections, of the 2.3 million candidates for republic, regional and local soviets, only 90 were defeated by failing to receive a majority of the votes cast.[15] Most Western observers have argued that, because the election has no role in deciding who the country's leaders shall be, the only real function they serve is to legitimize the Communist Party's dominant role in governing the country.

The spectacle of 160 million adult Soviet citizens voluntarily trooping to the polls to vote for the Party's single preselected candidate clearly allows the Party leadership to claim the legitimacy of widespread popular support. But recent evidence suggests that many citizens view elections quite negatively. Theodore Friedgut, for example, talked with Soviet emigrants in Israel and reported that

> none has as yet expressed any positive opinion of the electoral system, and more than any other participatory institution it appears to evoke sentiments ranging from skepticism to contempt.[16]

Increasingly, Soviet citizens are also finding ways to avoid voting altogether. Absentee ballots are available to people who expect to be away from home on election day, and in recent years no proof of absence has had to be presented. Many citizens obtain such ballots and simply dispose of them. Local electoral commissions attempt to compensate for the shortage of ballots this produces by various unauthorized practices, such as returning names of absentee voters to the voting lists and stuffing enough ballots in the box to account for them, or by allowing one family member to vote for several others who hold absentee ballots. How many citizens avoid voting through the use of absentee ballots is not known, but it appears to involve 15 to 20 percent of the electorate, mainly residents of large cities.[17]

This creates an unpleasant situation for local election commission heads and party officials, for a full turnout at the polls is an important indication of their organizational effectiveness. On the other hand, it also produces a little leverage for people willing to push the authorities a bit by trading their vote for a small service or favor. A typical case is the resident who insists that repairs to his street or to the plumbing in his apartment be made before election day as the price of his vote. A short story by dissident Alexander Zinoviev, "Elections" (*"Vybory"*), tells of a group of peasants who refused to vote unless a church was reopened that had been closed by the government. When the tale was described to a group of Soviet emigrants,

> all respondents agreed that this was a perfectly plausible incident; many gave examples of election bargaining from their own experience and assured us that such actions have become increasingly common in recent years, particularly on the part of workers.[18]

All of these developments suggest that public respect for the electoral process has been waning in the post-Stalin era. Refusal to participate in meaningless elections has become, according to one former Soviet defense attorney,[19] one of the major causes of expulsion of university students. In the mind of the average citizen, the probable result is a growing cynicism and disrespect for the pseudo-democratic nature of the electoral process. "He cannot," dissident Andrei Sakharov has written,

> be unaware of the political degradation to which he is subjected by these "elections without choice"; he cannot fail to realize the insult to commonsense and human dignity inherent in this pompous ceremony.[20]

In contemporary journals and books, arguments in favor of introducing competitive elections have frequently been expressed.[21] During his first year in power, Gorbachev began publicly to support the idea, and by mid-1987 it had become Party policy. Prior to the June 21, 1987, local elections for Soviet deputies, the Supreme Soviet Presidiums in each of the union-republics approved resolutions introducing multicandidate elections on an experimental basis.[22] In the election, voters in some districts were offered more candidates than seats to be filled and permitted to cross out the names of candidates they disapproved of. A simple majority of votes was needed to be elected. Where more candidates than needed won election, those with fewer votes became alternate deputies.

The Party leadership's current intention is to extend multicandidate elections not only to the entire country in elections to soviets, but also to the election of Party officials and economic managers. Such elections took place at a few locations during 1987, and more are expected in the next few years. A great deal of uncertainty exists over the possible consequences of competitive elections. Where they have taken place, especially in factories, there has been evidence of official interference with the process and tampering with the results.[23]

The move toward competitive elections has also produced new procedures to ensure that Party officials continue to be satisfied with the outcomes. In the nomination process, where multiple candidates are put forth, electoral commissions formed by the local Party committees have been give the authority to "discuss the nominations, take decisions for or against them and, if necessary, make changes in the list of candidates. . . ."[24] As a further control, the Party instituted in 1987 a "certification procedure" for all officials elected to soviets and other public bodies. After each election, certification commissions meet to evaluate the fitness of officials for their positions and report their findings to "the appropriate higher authority." This authority is empowered to remove the elected official from office if he or she proves unsatisfactory.[25]

The intention of General Secretary Gorbachev in promoting competitive elections seems clear. He is anxious to strengthen public confidence in elected officials by subjecting them to periodic reviews by their constituents. There is no indication, however, that he plans to abolish or even weaken the *nomenklatura* system that has maintained Communist Party power over the bureaucracy so successfully for so long. In order to fuse the two processes, the Party is promoting both a greater voice in the choice among candidates by the general public and tighter controls over the selection of candidates by the Party. Whether this will be perceived by the Soviet people as a move toward democracy remains to be seen.

Who Gets Elected to the Soviets

The characteristics of deputies who are chosen for election to the Supreme Soviet, as well as to other soviets, are carefully tailored to the interests and policies of the Communist Party leadership. The raw membership data presented above suggest that a majority of deputies are ordinary citizens, as distinguished from prominent officials or professionals. The problem of control, however, makes it desirable to ensure that a preponderance of the most reliable citizens, such as Party members and leaders, government officials, and recipients of state awards, dominate the legislature. And such is the case.

This becomes clear if we take a closer look at the deputies and their relationships to the Supreme Soviet. First, the membership may be divided into those who are elected to only one five-year term (freshmen) and then replaced by others, and those who are elected to two or more terms (veterans). It is true, as official spokespersons state, that more than half of the membership of the Supreme Soviet is replaced after each election (58.4 percent in the 1984 election), but the impression this offers of a constantly evolving membership is deceptive. In truth, not all deputies are subject to this rotation. A large group of deputies has been reelected time and again, and these veterans turn out to be substantially different from the freshmen members. In the 1984 Supreme Soviet elections, for instance, the 1500 elected deputies included 875 first-time (freshman) deputies and 625 reelected incumbents (veterans).[26] Many of the veterans have already enjoyed long tenure in the Supreme Soviet, as indicated in Table 7.2.

Thus, nearly half (41.7 percent) of the deputies in the Supreme Soviet will have served for ten years (two terms) by the end of the present term, and 239 deputies (16 percent of the total membership) will have served for eighteen years (four terms) or more. Two members, in fact, will mark the completion of forty-six consecutive years in the Supreme Soviet.[27]

This bloc of veteran deputies provides stability and continuity to the Soviet parliament. Veterans maintain the procedures and traditions of the Supreme Soviet and serve as models for the behavior of new members. Because reelection is itself an honor and a mark of Party favor, veterans are no doubt strongly inclined to subordinate their personal interests to those of the leadership. And because they tend to be of higher political and professional standing than are freshmen deputies, as Table 7.3 indicates, their influence over the behavior of the legislature as a whole is correspondingly great.

As we see, the more influential Supreme Soviet deputies—members of the Party and, especially, members and candidate members of the Central Committee—are heavily concentrated among the veteran deputies. On the other hand, the types of deputies who are generally of least influence in a political system—young people, women, workers, and peasants—are overwhelmingly concentrated among the freshman deputies.

The point is emphasized by an additional revelation from these data: The categories of less influential members are significantly overlapping, thus increasing the political impotence of the deputies involved. For example, most of the deputies who are members of the Komsomol, and therefore among the youngest members,

TABLE 7.2 TENURE IN THE SUPREME SOVIET[28]

	Years served by those reelected in 1984 (assuming all serve to the end of their present terms in 1989):									
Years:	10	14	18	22	26	30	34	38	42	46
Number of Deputies:	269	117	72	73	46	21	10	2	3	2

TABLE 7.3 POLITICAL CHARACTERISTICS OF FRESHMEN AND VETERANS

	Freshmen (in Percent)	Veterans (in Percent)
Members of the Communist Party	57.4	93.4
Members or Candidate Members of the Central Committee	1.6	44.6
Members of Komsomol (rather than the Party)	22.3	0.3
Women	47.3	12.3
Workers and Peasants	75.7	17.1

are also women (82.2 percent). And women make up most of the non-Party element as well (71.7 percent).

In one other way—the prevalence of Great Russians over other nationalities—the Party leadership has stacked the membership of the Supreme Soviet. According to the Constitution (Article 110), the seats in the Soviet of Nationalities are apportioned according to ethnic groups in the country as follows:

Union Republics (15)	32 seats each	=	480 deputies
Autonomous Republic (20)	11 seats each	=	220 deputies
Autonomous Regions (8)	5 seats each	=	40 deputies
Autonomous Areas (10)	1 seat each	=	10 deputies
	Total:		750 deputies

Technically, this should produce a Soviet of Nationalities containing 32 ethnic Great Russians, or 4.5 percent of the Soviet (all elected from the RSFSR) and 718 of other nationalities. In fact, the Soviet of Nationalities has 226 Russian deputies (30.1 percent), most of whom were elected from non-Russian areas of the country. The Uzbek Republic, for example, counts among its 32 deputies only 21 Uzbeks along with 7 Russians and 4 others. In the Soviet of the Union, where Uzbekistan is allocated 39 deputies according to its population, its elected deputies include only 25 Uzbeks along with 11 Russians.

As a whole, nearly half of the deputies to the Supreme Soviet (45.4 percent) are Great Russians, whereas strict adherence to the Constitution would produce only 28.1 percent Russians. Thus, Russians are substantially overrepresented in the national legislature, and this constitutes another sort of control exercised by the top leadership, which is also overwhelmingly Russian.

The assignment of elected deputies to membership in the standing committees, where (as will be discussed below) most of the work of the legislature is carried on, exhibits another form of leadership control. About four-fifths of all deputies are assigned to committees, but the proportion of Party and government officials among committee members is higher than for the Supreme Soviet as a whole and the proportion of workers and peasants is lower.[29]

Furthermore, although only 6.5 percent of the Soviet population belongs to the Communist Party, fully 71.5 percent (in 1984) of the deputies to the Supreme Soviet are Party members, and another 15 percent are members of the Young Communist League, the Party's youth organization. The proportion of Party members among those who hold positions of responsibility in the legislature, as members of the Presidium or the standing commissions, for example, is well above the 90 percent mark.[30]

The chairmen of the standing commissions exhibit the same characteristics. In the 1966–1970 Supreme Soviet, nineteen of the twenty-six chairmen were Party officials, and most (twenty out of twenty-six) were members or candidate members of the Party Central Committee. Thus, the control of the Party leadership is enhanced by the fact that the closer one gets to the core of authority in the legislature, the greater the predominance of Party and government officials and others of unquestioned political reliability.

CONTROLLING THE SUPREME SOVIET

The Soviet electoral process is designed to produce a body of deputies who are loyal, compliant, deferential, and respected by their constituents. As far as we know, the process succeeds and should ensure the Party leadership's control over the legislature itself. But the effectiveness of the Soviet control process depends upon establishing multiple layers of control, each one reinforcing the others. Thus, in addition to the electoral process, there is another major control system in operation that acts to enforce strict limitations on the functioning of the Supreme Soviet as an institution.

The most obvious limitation is the infrequency and brevity of its sessions. Convening only twice a year for three to four days, the Supreme Soviet has little opportunity to delve deeply into legislative matters. To be sure, the standing commissions afford additional opportunity for members to consider draft proposals, but even they normally convene only in the two to three weeks prior to the semiannual convocation of the legislature. And there is a further control operating in those meetings as well. Deputies from all over the country are brought to Moscow for the formal convocation of the Supreme Soviet but not necessarily for the additional weeks required for commission meetings. This is especially true for the ordinary worker and peasant members of commissions, whose absence from their jobs is often difficult to arrange. Consequently, when standing commissions meet in advance of Supreme Soviet sessions, those members who attend are primarily the more prominent Party and government officials who live in Moscow or have the means to come to Moscow for the meetings. And because a voting quorum for the commissions is a simple majority of the membership, the absence of the worker and peasant members is no hindrance to conducting business. The added control over the standing commissions that this affords the Party leadership is obvious.

Finally, the way in which the Presidium of the Supreme Soviet functions offers an additional and very effective mechanism of control over the legislature. The Presidium is authorized to act for the Supreme Soviet in the months between its formal sessions, with the understanding that such actions will be submitted for approval to the legislature when it next convenes.

The actual record of Presidium actions presents a different picture. Much of the legislative activity it carries on between sessions involves no urgency at all. In one year, the Presidium issued edicts detailing the dimensions of the Russian continental shelf, changing the name of a government ministry, and altering a previous law dealing with labor disputes. All were subsequently submitted to the Supreme Soviet for approval, but it is hard to see any special urgency in these matters.[31]

Furthermore, the timing of Presidium actions bears little relationship to the meeting schedule of the Supreme Soviet. Edicts covering complex national problems are sometimes issued by the Presidium only days before the convening of the full Supreme Soviet. If, in fact, a real emergency arose requiring legislative action, the Presidium is empowered (Article 121 of the Constitution) to convene a special session of the Supreme Soviet at any time.

The Presidium also enjoys constitutional authority to carry on a wide scope of other activities without subsequent legislative approval (Article 121). As mentioned earlier, it may interpret laws of the USSR, ratify treaties, appoint and recall diplomatic representatives of the USSR, appoint and dismiss military leaders, declare war, and proclaim martial law. Clearly the Presidium does none of these things on its own initiative but acts under the direction of the Party leadership. Thus, the Presidium is a small but powerful executive committee that is effectively used by the Party leadership to minimize the need for a more active legislature. Controlling a thirty-nine-member executive organ is obviously simpler than controlling a 1,500-member legislature, especially as the Presidium chairman is always a full member of the Politburo.

POLITICAL FUNCTIONS OF THE SUPREME SOVIET

If one focused only on the issue of political power, reflected in the total domination of the legislature by the Party leadership, one would miss an important feature of the Soviet political system. As we have argued before, the top leaders need far more than control over their subordinates to manage the USSR successfully. They need institutions that can mobilize popular support for national policies, help identify national problems and contribute ideas toward their solution, convey the attitudes and anxieties of the masses of citizens to the leaders, and legitimize the decisions of the leaders through formal approval in accordance with a recognized constitutional process.

The fact is, once the issue of power is settled, there are a number of services an elected legislature can perform that promote the overall goals of the Party leadership. They fall generally into three categories: legitimization, policy-making, and *kontrol.*

Legitimization

One of the Supreme Soviet's roles is to legitimize Party rule by formalizing important policy decisions into the "laws of the land." Changing a policy into a law (*zakon*) by vote of the Supreme Soviet grants it a kind of special authority that is recognized in the judicial and legal processes of the nation. Beyond that, the very existence of an elected legislature symbolizes "socialist democracy" by expressing such ideological values as the equality of citizens and of nationalities, the presence of workers and peasants in the highest deliberative bodies of the state (never possible in a "capitalist" country), the participation of the masses in the governance of the country through direct elections, and the accountability of the government to the people's legislature. Election to a soviet honors the person elected and generates feelings of self-respect, pride, and gratitude, feelings that are radiated to family, friends, and co-workers.

How deeply these legitimizing influences are absorbed by the Soviet people is impossible to know. Certainly, the extent to which the real powerbrokers get involved with and give their time to the soviets at all levels suggests that they *think* there is benefit to the system as a whole and to their own dominant positions.[32]

Policy-making

Although the Supreme Soviet has no independent power to amend or overrule decisions of the Communist Party leadership, many elected deputies are successful practitioners of their professions outside the legislature and therefore may have expertise to lend to the solution of policy problems that confront the national leadership. Because the Supreme Soviet poses no political challenge to the leaders, they are relatively free to consult with the deputies on a broad range of matters without any real risk to their decision-making power. This consultation occurs in the standing commissions and special commissions of the Supreme Soviet and in recent years it has expanded significantly.

There are mainly two practical functions that the standing commissions perform: reviewing draft legislative proposals received from other agencies and *kontrolling* or monitoring the performance of government agencies in administering legislative enactments. The review process involves detailed consideration of proposed laws that are handed down from ministries, departments of the Central Committee, or combinations of Party and government agencies.

Commissions are authorized to obtain whatever documents, reports, statistics, and so on they require from all levels of government in order to analyze the proposed law effectively. They may consult with outside specialists from academic institutes, with government officials, with managers and employees of enterprises affected by the legislation, and with other members of the Supreme Soviet.

Commissions in each chamber often work with other commissions interested in the legislation and with their counterpart commissions in the other chamber.

Because many of the legislative proposals submitted to the Supreme Soviet are complex, multifaceted bills, such as the Five-Year Plan, standing committees regularly form *preparatory commissions* and consultative groups to deal with specific sections of proposed bills.[33] A *preparatory commission* (*podkomissiia*) consists of twenty to sixty members among whom are experts in various fields, many of whom are not elected deputies to the Soviet. This provides an opportunity for a standing commission to bring outside specialists from academic institutes, government agencies, republic- and regional-level organizations, and elsewhere into the discussion of a bill.

The number of preparatory commissions formed to deal with specific legislation can be quite large. Peter Vanneman reports that for consideration of the 1970–1975 Five-Year Plan, the Supreme Soviet formed thirty-two subcommissions, each of which held a hundred sessions.[34] Where highly detailed or specialized questions of this kind arise, standing commissions may also form working groups (*rabochie gruppy*). These groups are used widely by the Legislative Proposals Commission and the Foreign Affairs Commission.

What the standing commissions provide is an opening up of the legislative process to a broad array of academic and administrative specialists who are not formal members of the Supreme Soviet or the government. This preserves a delicate political balance between the Party leadership's need for expert opinion on the solution of social problems and its determination to preclude the Supreme Soviet from attaining significant political power. The policy input comes heavily from nondeputies, who therefore cannot vote in the legislature, while decisions on how that input shall affect the proposed legislation are reserved for deputies voting in commissions, which are tightly controlled by the Party. The leadership, therefore, can accept or reject the viewpoints of its co-opted specialists without according them any significant political power.

The *Kontrol* Function

The other major involvement of the Supreme Soviet in the governmental process is through the process of *kontrol,* which means, in the Soviet context, the authority to investigate and monitor the fulfillment of laws passed by the Supreme Soviet. *Kontrol* is exercised by standing commissions, usually through the appointment of preparatory commissions. These commissions have the right to demand reports from governmental agencies or other organizations whose activities are relevant to the jurisdiction of the commission. Members of these commissions may also make on-site inspections to ensure the accuracy of their information about a sitution.

Kontrol involves a very broad spectrum of activities. The energy commissions of the Supreme Soviet, for example, may require periodic reports of ministries dealing with energy on both the national and regional level, oil and gas production enterprises, regional and local soviets, as well as individual officials. They may also subpoena records for their perusal and the administrators themselves for personal testimony. Agricultural commissions monitor such matters as the fulfillment of the annual grain production plan or the activities of a single collective farm.

A decision to monitor a ministry or an industrial plant is no doubt made by Party authorities, but the instigation for the decision may come from an individual deputy, a standing commission, or the Presidium, or from a complaint from a citizen or outside organization. Under some circumstances, the monitoring may involve only a single inquiry, which is satisfied by an examination of documents or the testimony of an official. In other cases, however, especially in key sectors of the economy, monitoring may be a permanent activity, requiring periodic reports from enterprises or organizations on the fulfillment of economic planning goals.

The *kontrol* function is essentially an investigative, not an executive, function as the standing commissions have no authority to order changes or to discipline malefactors. Their recommendations may be sent to the agency involved or to the Council of Ministers, but there is no legal obligation for either to accept the recommendation. In the case of the Council of Ministers, the law does not even require a response to the commission. If a response is made but is unsatisfactory, the commission can submit its recommendation to the Supreme Soviet Presidium, which does have the authority to issue binding directives (*ukazy*). Given the political weight that resides in the Presidium, often including the Secretary General of the Party, a decision to issue such a directive mobilizes considerable political force behind it.

Carrying out the *kontrol* function, rather than policy-making activities, dominates the schedule of the standing commissions.[35] Although we know relatively little about these activities, there are some facets of the *kontrol* process that suggest at least a potential for making an impact. The preparatory commissions that carry out *kontrol* for standing commissions are small in size, usually three to six members, and heavily weighted with high-level Party and government officials. For example, a recent preparatory commission formed by the Commission for Trade and Everyday Services to study shortages of consumer goods included the following members:

- Chairman, autonomous republican council of ministers;
- Chairman, regional soviet executive committee;
- Chairman, city soviet executive committee;
- First secretary, regional Party committee;
- Chairman, republican Trade Union Congress.

At times, preparatory groups have even been chaired by heads of Central Committee departments, which is reaching very high in the Party hierarchy. The involvement of important Party and government officials in the Supreme Soviet *kontrol* process makes it probable that when questions are asked or documents requested, responses will be forthcoming. On the other hand, the lack of staff personnel attached to the preparatory commissions makes it unlikely that in-depth systematic studies of the agencies being monitored can be carried out. *Kontrol,* thus, tends often to be an exchange of personal viewpoints among the participants, the results of which go into reports submitted by them to the standing commissions.

We do not really know how effective these *kontrol* processes are. They rest largely on the influence that can be exerted through the exposure of organizational deficiencies and individual malfeasance. When this is carried on by upper-level Party and government officials, as in the standing commission *kontrol* process, such exposure can carry considerable weight. Decisions to act on the basis of this information are clearly reserved for decision-making organs of the system, which the Supreme Soviet is not. But in a system organized to allow the Party leadership to direct virtually all of the economic, social, and political activities of 270 million people, the Party leadership is heavily dependent on sources of accurate information about the functioning of all aspects of the country. The elaborate activities of the standing commissions in gathering such information, activities that have expanded considerably in recent years,[36] provide the Party leadership with a valuable source of information and evaluation.

There is, of course, constant resistance to these investigative activities by those being investigated. Complaints are frequently voiced in the news media concerning the failure of various agencies to respond to requests for information or suggestions for change offered by the standing commissions. But as the number of commissions and subcommissions increases along with the number of government and Party officials who are members, the ability of the commissions to affect government by publicizing administrative shortcomings and generating support for new legislation should also increase.

The Supreme Soviet as a whole faces the same dilemma as that of the commissions and subcommissions. To the extent that it presents no political challenge to the Party leadership, it can be permitted to contribute to the governing process in a variety of ways. But by the same token, its powerlessness minimizes those contributions, for government and Party officials are more or less free to ignore the actions of the Soviet. Nevertheless, it seems clear that the involvement of the Supreme Soviet in both policy-making and *kontrol* has increased considerably in the past decade and may well continue to do so in the future.

LOCAL SOVIETS

Below the national level is an elaborate network of soviets, each with jurisdiction over its own geographic area. The national and republic levels have Supreme Soviets, with presidia and councils of ministers. All levels below that are referred to as "local soviets," each of which is directed by an executive committee whose chairman is roughly comparable to a mayor in the United States.

Local soviets are consistently portrayed in Soviet political literature as the essense of Soviet democracy. There are over 50,000 of them nationwide, to which well over 2 million deputies are elected every two and a half years. In addition, the standing commissions of the local soviets recruit some two and a half million volunteer activists who contribute their time to the work of the soviets. Because the proportion of new deputies elected each time is close to 50 percent, and the turnover of volunteers is at least as great, the number of Soviet adults who are involved with the work of the soviets in the course of a decade is probably in excess of 8 million.

Deputies to soviets at all levels are required to maintain close contact with their constituents through regular visitation hours, attendance at meetings, and carrying complaints and suggestions to higher authorities. In practice, some deputies work diligently at these tasks while others pay scant attention to them. Still, the position of deputy to a soviet is an honorable one, attainable only by approval of a Party committee and formal election by one's neighbors, fellow workers, and constituents. The millions of citizens who serve, or have served, as deputies to soviets, provide a huge reservoir of people who have found favor and honor in the eyes of the political leadership. The relationship between such feelings and loyalty to the regime is bound to be close.

NOTES

1. For a fuller account of the origins of the soviets, see Peter Vanneman, *The Supreme Soviet: Politics and the Legislative Process in the Soviet Political System* (Durham, N.C.: Duke University Press, 1977), chapter 1; and Adam B. Ulam, *A History of Soviet Russia* (New York: Holt, Rinehart & Winston, 1976), chapter 1.
2. V.M. Chkhikvadze, *The Soviet Form of Popular Government* (Moscow: Progress Publishers, 1972), p. 95.
3. These data are from *Deputaty Verkhovnovo Soveta SSSR, Odinnadtsaty Soziv* (Moscow: Izvestia, 1984), p. 3–4.
4. For the full membership of the Presidium following the 1984 elections, see John L. Scherer, *USSR: Facts and Figures Annual*, Vol. 9 (Gulf Breeze, Fla: Academic International Press, 1985), pp. 13–14.
5. Robert S. Siegler, *The Standing Commissions of the Supreme Soviet* (New York: Praeger, 1982), p. 35.
6. The text of the law appears in *Pravda*, 13 October 1967.
7. Source: *Ezhegodnik, Bolshoi Sovetskoi Entsiklopedii* (Moscow: Sovetskaya Entsiklopediya, 1984), p. 11.
8. V.M. Chkhikvadze, *Soviet Form of Popular Government*, p. 110.
9. This figure is calculated for the Soviet of Nationalities from the specific number of seats allocated to each territorial division as presented in Ibid., p. 110. For the Soviet of the Union, Chkhikvadze states that the Council "comprises representatives of groups of deputies elected from each region" without specifying what he means by region. But there is no reason to believe the Councils would be of greatly different size in the two chambers.
10. Peter Vanneman cites one instance in which a deputy proposed some amendments to a draft law on marriage and the family just as the final vote was to be taken. Because the

amendments seemed to have considerable support, the chairman recessed the session until the next day to allow time for considering the amendments. The amendments were approved the following day and a possible first (and only) negative vote in the Supreme Soviet was avoided. See Vanneman, *The Supreme Soviet*, p. 87.

11. *Ezhegodnik*, p. 9.

12. One Soviet author stated that there were 2,000 such cases (of some 2 million candidates) in the 1965 elections, but there is no way to verify it. Cited in Vanneman, *The Supreme Soviet*, p. 86.

13. M.A. Krutogolov, *Talks on Soviet Democracy* (Moscow: Progress Publishers, 1980), p. 92.

14. For the sources and further discussion on this point, see Vanneman, *The Supreme Soviet*, pp. 112–13.

15. Lev Tulkunov, *How the USSR Supreme Soviet Functions* (Moscow: Novosti Publishing Agency, 1987), pp. 21 and 37.

16. Theodore H. Friedgut, *Political Participation in the USSR* (Princeton, N.J.: Princeton University Press, 1979), p. 75; also see Zvi Gitelman, "Values, Opinions and Attitudes of Soviet Jewish Emigres," paper presented to the American Association for the Advancement of Slavic Studies, Atlanta, Georgia, October 9–11, 1975, cited in Friedgut, idem.

17. Varying estimates are discussed in Victor Zaslavsky and Robert J. Brym, "The Structure of Power and the Functions of Soviet Local Elections," in Everett M. Jacobs, ed., *Soviet Local Politics and Government* (London: George Allen & Unwin, 1983), pp. 70–71.

18. The Zinoviev story appears in *Grani*, No. 102, 1976, pp. 97–103. Cited in Zaslavsky and Brym, "Structure of Power," p. 367, where this quotation also appears.

19. Ibid., p. 368.

20. Quoted in ibid., p. 70.

21. See Ronald J. Hill, "Soviet Literature on Electoral Reform: A Review," *Government and Opposition* (Vol. 11, No. 4), Autumn 1976, pp. 483–86.

22. *Pravda*, 29 April 1987, p. 1.

23. See, for example, the account of an election in Moscow for the directorship of the transport Construction Research Institute in early 1987 in the *New York Times*, 29 May 1987, p. 3. A contested election for the first secretaryship of a district Party committee in Siberia is reported in the *Los Angeles Times*, 11 February 1987, p. 12.

24. *Pravda*, 29 April 1987.

25. The enabling legislation was published in *Vedomosti Verkhovnovo Soveta SSSR*, No. 12 (2398), March 25, 1987, Item 153, pp. 147–49; translated in *Current Digest of the Soviet Press*, 39:15, May 13, 1987, p. 18.

26. The proportion of freshmen is in fact somewhat exaggerated here, as a few of them will likely be reelected in 1989, and thus are potential veterans rather than true freshmen. This gives even greater weight to the role of veterans, although of course some veterans will retire as well.

27. These two deputies are Nikolai Patolichev, who has been USSR Minister of Foreign Trade for nearly thirty years, and Alexei Federov, who was Ukrainian Minister of Social Welfare for twenty-two years and is currently Chairman of the Commission for Former Partisans.

28. The data in Table 7.2, and all other statistics regarding the Supreme Soviet deputies elected in 1984, come from the biographical data published in *Deputaty Verkhovnovo Soveta SSSR*, except where otherwise indicated.

29. A study of four standing committees in the Soviet of the Union between 1966 and 1970 revealed the following percentages: proportion of Party officials in the Soviet as a whole:

21 percent; in the four committees: 44 percent. The proportion of workers and peasants in the Soviet was 38 percent; in the four commissions, 10 percent. See D. Richard Little, "Soviet Parliamentary Committees After Khrushchev," *Soviet Studies,* July 1972, p. 47.

30. Little found that Party members on the four standing commissions constituted 92 percent of the membership. Ibid., p. 49.

31. See D. Richard Little, "Legislative Authority in the Soviet Political System," *Slavic Review,* 30:1, March 1971, p. 66.

32. The legitimacy of the Soviet regime has intrigued most students of Soviet politics over the years. For some interesting and contrasting views on the issue see Severyn Bialer, *Stalin's Successors* (Cambridge: Cambridge University Press, 1980), pp. 183–205; and Stephen White, "The USSR: Patterns of Autocracy and Industrialism," in Archie Brown and Jack Gray, eds., *Political Culture and Political Change in Communist States* (New York: Holmes and Meier, 1979), pp. 46–56.

33. The most extensive discussion of these organs is in Siegler, *Standing Commissions,* pp. 66–72. Much of the information in this paragraph comes from Siegler's excellent study.

34. Vanneman, *The Supreme Soviet,* p. 124.

35. See Siegler, *Standing Commissions,* p. 108, note 66; and Shugo Minagawa, *Supreme Soviet Organs* (Tokyo: The University of Nagoya Press, 1985), p. 221.

36. Siegler, *Standing Commissions,* offers this conclusion (p. 104), as does Vanneman, *The Supreme Soviet,* pp. 168–69.

PART 3

The Policy Process

The extreme concentration of political power in the Politburo suggests that policy-making ought to be a simpler and more efficient process in the USSR than it is in pluralist democratic societies. A decision by the Politburo, after all, does not have to be approved by a parliament or adjudicated by a supreme court or tested with the voters in the next election. Some policy decisions are indeed taken by the leadership with little or no consultation with any of those agencies. This is especially true of personnel decisions, such as those involving membership in the Politburo or Secretariat, and of some aspects of defense policy.

The typical policy-making process, however, is far more complex. Many social and economic problems, in the USSR as elsewhere, stubbornly resist the efforts of even the most powerful leaders to resolve them. As First Deputy Prime Minister Aliev asked at the 27th Party Congress in 1986, "Why is it that from congress to congress we raise the same problems? . . . Why is it over so many years we have been unable to pull out the roots of bureaucracy, social injustice and abuses?"[1] The fact is, the leadership is frequently divided on how to proceed and makes decisions that are always in danger of being sabotaged by bureaucrats or overruled by the facts of Soviet life.

To generate successful policies, therefore, requires not only political power but also information and experience in dealing with the problems of contemporary Soviet society. The need to solve problems, not just make decisions, opens the policy-making process to various combinations of individuals, institutions, and opinion groups that have useful contributions to make and whose cooperation is necessary for carrying out the Party's will. And it creates a limited but significant role in policy-making for the masses of citizens as well. In the following three chapters, we shall examine the policy process in a variety of settings, focusing on the nature of the policy process and the roles of diverse participants in that process.

CHAPTER 8
How National Policies are Made

In many respects, *how* national policies are made in a political system distinguishes that system from others more clearly than who holds power or how they got it. Political systems that look almost identical in form—Italy and West Germany, for example, or China and the Soviet Union—nevertheless address problems in quite different ways and often come out with radically different solutions.

In none of these countries is there a standard or fixed process by which all policies are made. Yet in each of them there are established patterns of interaction and behavior that are adapted to the problem of the moment. In this chapter we shall focus on the policy-making patterns that we can observe in the Soviet Union. We present three case studies so that significant variations in the policy process can be clearly illustrated. Then a number of general conclusions about Soviet policy-making will be discussed.

IDEOLOGY AND POLICY-MAKING

Why some policies are adopted and not others is of central importance. Soviet propagandists insist that all national decisions serve to fulfill an overall plan contained in the ideological formulations of Lenin and his successors. We should start, therefore, by examining this proposition.

The ideology of Soviet communism was described earlier (Chapter 3) as consisting of two major elements: "system principles" that define the fundamental nature of the political system and the Party's supreme role in it, and "goal principles" that describe the development of the country as it moves gradually toward the final goal of pure communism. System principles are essentially fixed and uncontroversial, as they generally are in stable political systems. They are rarely subject to policy debates, even though there is a certain amount of tension in the relationships between various institutional actors, such as the Party, the military, the ministries, and the republic governments. Short of a real crisis, all national policies will be consistent with the established character of the political system.

Goal principles, on the other hand, are inevitably subject to change and redefinition as the society develops. The official designation of the Soviet Union in its present stage is "developed socialism," presumably an advance over the "all people's state" that existed during the Khrushchev era. Beyond the fact that one slogan characterized Khrushchev's policy priorities and methods while the other characterized those of Brezhnev, there is no evidence to suggest that national policies in either era were *deduced* from these ideological formulations. Many of Khrushchev's policy innovations were scrapped after he left office, so a new formula had to be devised to account for the Brezhnev approach. More recently, the new Soviet Constitution adopted in 1977 revives the concept of the "all people's state" once again.[2]

In the mundane task of devising solutions to pressing problems, ideological formulas are as often a hindrance as they are an inspiration. Of far greater importance to the fate of specific policy proposals are factors of cost, potential effectiveness, political acceptability, and popular approval. In this respect, the USSR is scarcely different from other nations at comparable stages of economic and social development.

THE ACTORS IN THE POLICY-MAKING PROCESS

Because the Party leadership must be seen to be in control of the policy process at all times, the ways in which nonleaders can articulate problems, raise issues, argue for policy changes, and challenge the status quo are limited and often difficult for outsiders to observe. Nevertheless, within those limits a great deal of activity takes place. Problems are pressed onto the public agenda by individuals, groups of like-minded citizens, government and Party agencies, and various combinations of all of these.

Individuals

In setting national policy, a General Secretary is, of course, in a unique position. As each General Secretary has demonstrated, his own will is an important factor in the development of the USSR. This was especially true of Stalin and Khrushchev, both of whom sometimes instituted major changes in policy without first seeking consensual support even among the rest of the Politburo. Khrushchev's initiation of the Virgin Lands agriculture program in central Asia and his abolition of the Machine Tractor Stations serving collective farms are notable examples of this. Typically, the succession of a new General Secretary generates a flurry of new priorities and budgetary allocations, which then become the established parameters for further development.[3] Sometimes, as in the cases of Khrushchev and Gorbachev, the inauguration of a new leader creates an aura of serious reform that pervades the whole system. Policy initiatives also come from all of the other major leaders in their areas of jurisdiction.

Outside of the leadership circles, the influence of individuals on national policy is very limited. Nevertheless, some outsiders manage to have a substantial impact. Most often these are illustrious academics and intellectuals whose advocacy of a particular point of view strikes a favorable chord. Yevsei Liberman, an economist from Kharkov, had a major impact on the subject of economic reform in the early

1960s. As is usually the case, Liberman's close association with General Secretary Khrushchev greatly enhanced his influence.

Since Gorbachev came to power in 1985, an even more important role has been assumed by economist Abel G. Aganbegyan, who was attached to the Siberian branch of the Academy of Sciences in Novosibirsk before Gorbachev brought him to Moscow in 1985. For years, Aganbegyan had advocated radical changes in the economic system, which, finally, have come to have a major effect on the thinking of Gorbachev and the new Politburo. Prominent academics work closely with ministries and Party organs and often promote their own ideas for reforming the system. The key to such influence is the high professional standing of the individual, which may even outweigh the influence of important political leaders.[4]

Groups

The question of group influence in Soviet policy-making has been widely debated among Western scholars in recent years.[5] There is no doubt that in the USSR some people who hold a common view of a policy issue have opportunities to express that view to the political authorities. The argument is over whether such an aggregate constitutes an "interest group" in the Western sense of that term; and if so whether the existence of such interest groups entitles us to describe the Soviet political system as "pluralist."

Interest groups in Western democratic systems generally exhibit a number of characteristics: a commitment to a common set of beliefs and values, the opportunity to interact regularly with each other to formulate and discuss those interests, the conscious determination to influence government policy in favor of those interests, and channels of uncensored communication through which to generate professional and public support. To be considered components of a Western-style pluralist system, such groups would have to be voluntary, competitive, nonhierarchical, and free of state control.

As recent case studies of a number of policy decisions have revealed, some of these conditions appear to have been met:

- In drafting a law to punish vagrants and "social parasites" in the 1950s, the concerted opposition of many lawyers and judges caused the leadership to withdraw an initial draft and reconsider some of its provisions;[6]
- In the 1960s a "veritable reform movement" developed to lobby the government for changes in the wartime Law on the Family, which had encouraged illegitimacy and made divorce difficult and costly;[7]
- In a long-term attempt, begun in the 1970s, to prevent the environmental destruction of the Lake Baikal area (see Case Study 2, later in this chapter), a number of academic research institutes, journal editorial boards, and concerned individuals joined forces to oppose further industrial development by the paper and pulp industries.[8]

Increasingly, established academic institutes and professional associations are coming to participate regularly in policy-making in their fields. The formation of the All-Union Institute for the Study and Prevention of Crime in 1963, for example, gave criminologists and lawyers direct access to the USSR Supreme Court and the Procuracy (Attorney General's office) in revising the criminal law.[9] In the area of foreign affairs, Soviet think tanks such as the Institute of the United States and Canada, the Institute of Oriental Studies, and the Institute of the International Labor Movement offer policy analyses to the Central Committee and to relevant government ministries.

Some Western scholars believe that, as institutes of this type proliferate, they are developing a degree of semiautonomous influence over policy-making.[10] If so, they are nevertheless operating under a special and highly restrictive set of circumstances. Whether they are composed of journalists, scholars, or local administrators, they are all employed by organizations that are subject to Party control through *nomenklatura* and the *partkoms*. The kinds of policy arguments they are able to make are subject to normal press censorship, and the Party leaders can, and often do, step in at any moment and silence public comment on any given problem. None of these restrictions work perfectly, of course, but they are effective enough to ensure that at any given time the Party leadership is in control of the deliberative processes to the extent that it wishes to be.

It is, therefore, an exaggeration to speak of a Western-style "interest group structure" or "pluralist" political system in the Soviet Union. Interest aggregates are unable to offer significant political support to politicians in exchange for favorable legislation. The ultimate power of the Communist Party leadership to override the interests of any institution or group without risking its dominant position is the essential difference between authoritarian and pluralist systems. Yet there is unquestionably a broad diversity of views within the Soviet population. Lawyers, factory managers, academics, and farmers all have distinct sets of interests and values that they share with others in their professions or organizations. And they have regular opportunities, through personal interaction, conferences, professional journals, and prominent spokesmen, to forge their views into specific policy positions.

When such people become linked to a common issue through personal contact or organizational relationships, they may form what can be called "opinion groups." These are normally contained within a single organization, such as an academic institute or government ministry. They have no independent authority, but within their respective organizations they can often exert considerable influence on their own officials and, through them, on the political leadership as well.

When opinion groups in various agencies and institutes make common cause over an issue, they may form "policy coalitions" in support of their objectives.[11] If they have access to journals or newspapers, because they themselves publish them or have attracted sympathetic editorial boards, they have the means to promote their own views and to mobilize wider support. We shall see in the case studies that follow how important this opportunity has been.

What these opinion groups or policy coalitions do not have is the independence to continue to press their views against a firm decision by a high Party or governmental body. In every case study reviewed, there were junctures at which the leadership acted to end debate on particular issues and to insist on general conformance with its decision.

What exists for these participants in the policy process are what Thane Gustafson has aptly called "windows of opportunity" through which some of the force of public opinion, especially that emanating from prominent specialists, can influence the thinking of decision-makers. But it is a limited and temporary opportunity. "As the window threatens to close," Gustafson points out,

> we observe the increasingly constrained position of the experts, for they have no independent bases of power or means of publicity once the political leadership commits itself and is no longer receptive to debate on every side of the question.[12]

There is no doubt that government and Party officials lean heavily on professionals and experts in reaching many kinds of policy decisions. But these advisers in turn are even more dependent on the willingness of decision-makers to pay attention to them. The personal preferences of leaders count heavily in the Soviet system, and the need to accommodate those preferences is one of the facts of life for all who would seek their goals through the political process.

Outside of this established pattern, on the fringes of the political process, a new phenomenon is emerging in the Gorbachev era: A network of unofficial lobbying groups is attempting to affect government policies. At a conference of such groups held in Leningrad in August 1987, an extraordinary range of interests was represented. A coalition of environmental groups calling themselves Epicenter criticized a number of government policies and even attempted to run one of their leaders for a seat on the local soviet, albeit without success. Other groups included Delta, another environmental lobby whose major purpose is to block construction of a large flood-control dam near Leningrad, Spasenye (Salvation), dedicated to the preservation of historic buildings, and the Association for Experimental Fine Arts, which presses for uncensored publishing and art exhibitions.

Party officials have shown mixed reactions to this development. While not prohibiting the August conference, and even providing meeting rooms, officials required all participants to register their names with local authorities and banned all foreign reporters. Nevertheless, a prominent Soviet cultural magazine, *Ogonyok*, welcomed the conference as "one of the first serious experiments in the sphere of practical democracy."[13] No doubt a great many potential interest groups exist in Soviet society, desirous of operating independently and in most cases in opposition to government policies. Whether the Gorbachev regime will move toward legitimizing them and accepting their participation in the policy-making process remains a matter of speculation.

Institutions

"Institutions" are official government and Party agencies that have formal responsibilities for administering policies and programs in their areas of jurisdiction. They are naturally involved in the policy process but in ways that are peculiar to the Soviet system. Institutions vary widely in their importance to the process. Some, such as the Supreme Soviet, the full Council of Ministers, and the Party Central Committee, have vast formal authority but little actual involvement with the making of policy. Their meetings are infrequent and involve more people than could effectively establish policies.

At the other extreme are the true policy-making collectives, headed by the Politburo, of course, but including also the Presidium of the Council of Ministers, the Secretariat, the Defense Council, similar agencies on the republic level, and so on. Each is a small executive organ of a larger collective, and each has broad policy responsibilities. When there is a determined consensus within any of these agencies, especially the Politburo, the opposition of lower bodies is unlikely to make much difference.

A common form of institutional involvement with policy-making is the competition among government ministries in the shaping of an important policy. In the field of energy policy, for example, there has been a high-level struggle over the past decade among a number of national ministries. The main issue is whether principal reliance for energy should be placed on coal, oil, gas, or nuclear power. Since the 1960s, the Party leadership has emphasized each of these in turn largely in response to the effectiveness of the relevant ministry in making its case. With nuclear power operating under a serious cloud in the 1980s, mainly because of the Chernobyl disaster, the Ministry of Gas seems to have prevailed over its competitors for a lion's share of developmental and capital resources for energy.[14]

Similar competition exists among many agencies of government. It exists because these ministries have basically different, and competitive, interests and because the Politburo has been unable to arrive at a collective decision on a policy matter. There are times, in fact, such as the 26th Party Congress (1981), at which, as Thane Gustafson notes, the Party leadership accepts "a postponement of hard choices on *all* of the major issues facing the Kremlin."[15]

That genuine debates take place in the Politburo is certain, and the quality of debate is no doubt enhanced by the regular presence at Politburo meetings of nonmember specialists, officials, and trusted advisers, as well as candidate members of the Politburo. If one could imagine such a debate on any given Thursday morning, one would probably find one or two members strongly supporting a particular course of action, several others relatively uninformed on the specific problem and indifferent to the choice of options, two or three who see potential trouble for their own operations in the future and who would prefer not moving ahead at this time, and one or two others who may be well-informed and strongly opposed to the option.

The view of the General Secretary is critical, of course, but not necessarily decisive. Factions that form in the Politburo are also of great importance. They may be temporary alliances around a particular policy option or semipermanent commitments to one course of action or another. During the Brezhnev years, for example, some Western scholars argued that the Politburo was divided into factions that supported, respectively, detente with the West, an intensification of the worldwide class struggle, and rapid expansion of the Soviet military forces.[16] The unfortunate fact is that we know very little about the factionalism that may affect Soviet policy-making. The shroud of secrecy that surrounds top-level Soviet politics is very effective.

The vast institutional structure of Soviet government—the ministries, agencies, boards, and bureaus—are deeply involved in attempting to promote their own versions of policy choices, and the decision-makers are inevitably affected by this activity. This accounts in part for the fact that, despite the unchallenged authority of the Politburo, decisions are often so long in coming. As we shall see below, it has sometimes taken years to achieve a consensus among the top policy-makers on a complex national problem.

THE PROBLEMS OF SOVIET SOCIETY

In the simplest terms, a social "problem" is any situation that a significant element of society finds unsatisfactory: lack of adequate housing, transportation, or jobs; environmental pollution, unpopular leaders, excessive crime. The extent to which people are aware of such problems depends both on their personal circumstances and on the communications media. In the United States, for example, the media, especially television, focus heavily on the deficiencies of contemporary life, causing, according to some critics, a high level of anxiety about public safety and well-being. The constant outpouring of problems that "demand action" tends to outstrip the government's capacity to deal with them, leaving the impression that in many social areas government is either ineffective or indifferent, or both.

In the Soviet Union, bad news from official sources has traditionally been a commodity in relatively short supply. Such matters as crime rates, airplane crashes, drug abuse, or casualty figures from the Afghan war have rarely been mentioned in the Soviet media. A dramatic example of this was the refusal of the government to provide detailed information on the explosion and meltdown of the Chernobyl nuclear reactor station in 1986, despite clouds of radiation that reached into Scandinavia and Western Europe. This silence creates a widespread impression among the people, routinely encouraged by the media, that the murders, robberies, swindles, and disasters of modern life are features of capitalist rather than socialist society. Until a problem is officially recognized by the authorities, it does not formally exist as a subject for public discussion. There are no Ralph Naders or Howard Jarvis's in the USSR mobilizing citizens to compel government to change its ways.

The Communist Party's control of the communications media ensures that, for the most part, *its* perceptions of society's problems are the controlling ones. The organs of censorship are not perfect, however, and Party policy is not always clear. Sometimes, reform proposals that run contrary to the views of the leadership surface briefly in the press. Just prior to the 27th Party Congress in 1986, for example, a number of letters appeared in *Pravda* sharply criticizing the corrupt behavior of some officials that had been detailed in earlier issues of *Pravda*. Some of the letters condemned the "special canteens, special shops and special hospitals" available to higher officials,[17] a condemnation that was subsequently criticized in the same publication as being excessive and improper.

A more direct confrontation broke out in 1984 on the sensitive issue of expanding the role of private enterprise in the USSR. An article by Evgeny Ambartsumov in *Voprosi Istorii (Questions of History)* arguing in favor of the idea was criticized several months later in *Kommunist*, the main theoretical organ of the CPSU. *Kommunist* charged Ambartsumov with adopting "a shallow approach to Leninist theory" and criticized the editorial board of *Voprosi Istorii* for failing to exercise proper editorial vigilance. The editors of the offending journal publicly admitted their error and undertook to correct it.[18]

In the mid-1980s, General Secretary Gorbachev has strongly encouraged a more open policy for the press (*glasnost*). In response, many social problems have been given publicity in the mass media and have aroused official concern. We shall deal more fully with the impact of *glasnost* in Chapter 11.

The problem then is how to get one's concern adopted by the leadership as a legitimate issue. How this is done is vital to all political systems and is one of the principal bases upon which political scientists differentiate among types of political systems.

How Problems Become Issues

In any political system, the time and the interests of politicians are limited. Some problems will be taken up by the political leadership and dealt with one way or another; others will be ignored. Still others lie in restricted areas where they cannot be raised in a public way. In the USSR, for example, the selection of Mikhail Gorbachev as General Secretary or the desirability of a military draft may be problems for some citizens, but they do not enter the realm of public debate because they call into question basic commitments of the political leadership. The government's agenda, therefore, does not contain all the problems of society, but only those that have become "issues" by virtue of having been recognized by the leadership as suitable for action.

The right and duty of the General Secretary to place problems on the national agenda is obvious, and that right is shared by all other major leaders. Gorbachev, for example, indicated in his address to the 27th Party Congress in 1986 that the Politburo would be considering an increase in rents and food prices in the near future, a matter that had not been publicly debated for many years.[19] Brezhnev initiated similar changes in his campaign for greater assistance to the private sector in agriculture in 1976 and in his later proposal to substitute oil for coal as the major source of energy.

Many items crop up on the public agenda even without this sort of top-level initiative. An unlawful strike or demonstration, the death of a leader, or an upcoming Party Congress necessarily require a range of decisions. Routinely, in a society based so heavily on economic planning as the USSR, monitoring the plan and dealing with shortfalls are permanent agenda items. Often one negative situation will trigger a concern for other problems. Declining productivity in industrial plants, for example, has been an important cause of the current concern for drunkenness among workers and for deficiencies in urban housing and transportation. In fact, of the items on the regularly published Politburo agenda, the vast majority are ongoing issues that have been receiving regular attention from the leadership.

Many issues are initially raised by lower-level Party and government agencies without prior approval from above. Local officials cannot always know just how the top leadership will react to their raising a particular problem. If the reaction is negative, the problem tends to be shunted aside at a higher level.[20]

Issues sometimes emerge from yet another channel: the anger or frustration of individuals or groups of citizens who begin to speak out for change. In 1956, for example, a conference of collective farm chairmen erupted into loud calls for an end to the machine-tractor stations that had monopolized control over heavy farm machinery for two decades.[21] In the Brezhnev era, demands for reforming the Family Law statutes emanated from an enterprising journalist supported by a number of academics at conferences and in professional journals.[22] In recent years, the struggle to protect the environmental health of Lake Baikal got on the public agenda through the persistent efforts of a policy coalition of academics, local officials, journalists, and concerned citizens. We will explore this matter more fully in the case study at the end of the chapter.

Why Some Problems Do Not Become Issues

The top leadership's ability to keep issues *off* the national agenda is at least as important, and as clear an indication of its power, as its ability to place issues *on* the agenda. The prevailing orientation of the leadership is officially to encourage broad participation in articulating problems whose solution would improve Soviet life. The newspapers give elaborate coverage to letters from citizens, and there are mandatory procedures for following up on complaints.

As a consequence, the administrative organs at all levels are swamped with citizens' problems, many of them highly individualistic. The matter is complicated by the fact that many problems—inadequate housing, for example, or shortages of consumer goods—are the results of general budgetary and planning decisions over which harassed local officials have no control. Naturally, officials bump these problems up to higher levels of the bureaucracy if they can. Some problems raised by citizens fall outside the boundaries of acceptable complaint and become the responsibility of Party or police agencies.

There are two ways in which the Party leadership deals with the problem of preventing unacceptable issues from arising. One is its maintainance of "exclusion rules," which operate to distinguish between acceptable and nonacceptable subjects. These rules inhere in the institutions and conventional practices of Soviet communism and are enforced through ideological and procedural fomulas and through threats of repression by the police and the courts.[23] A general understanding of these rules by the public acts as an automatic filtering device to screen out issues that the leadership considers dangerous or objectionable.

To deal with the problem on a more practical level, the state and Party bureaucracies have procedures and officials for screening the issues before they get on an agenda. These "gatekeepers," as they have been called, are administrative officials who see that potential agenda items are approved by all agencies that may have an interest in the matter. In many cases, an objection from a Party committee or a ministry will keep the item off the agenda or kill it altogether. This exercise of "negative power" keeps a reasonably tight lid on the number and types of issues that can be formally raised for discussion.

The secrecy that surrounds the whole process of deciding which issues to take up is another tool in the hands of the leadership. Secrecy about certain issues applies not only to outsiders but also to high officials who are deemed by yet higher officials not to have a "need to know." Thane Gustafson relates the surprise experienced by U.S. negotiators in the Strategic Arms Limitations Talks in the early 1970s when they discovered that their civilian counterparts on the Soviet side were not cleared to have some types of information about their own armament levels.[24]

In cases where the leadership feels compelled to take up an issue that had previously been prohibited, its exercise of negative power may be suspended for a time. In recent years, in fact, "zones of suspended negative power"[25] have broadened as the need for solutions to economic and social problems has intensified. Secrecy also seems to be diminishing, although it remains at a very high level. In accord with *glasnost,* professional journals and even the national press have published sharp criticisms of technological deficiencies (in computers, for example), agricultural failures, and other sensitive matters.[26]

An even more sensitive area has opened up since Gorbachev came to power in 1985: the Afghan war. The Soviet press began to deal more frankly with some of the unpleasant realities of that war, including reference to increasing Soviet casualties.[27] Until then, the war had been described as a minimal Soviet action being waged to assist a friendly people to preserve their independence from imperialist forces. As the casualities mounted, however, the number of families affected by the loss or injury of young men also increased. The point finally came when the disastrous nature of that involvement could no longer be concealed, and official recognition in the press began to give a more realistic view of the conflict.

In the same manner, the excessive consumption of alcohol by Soviet citizens has long been a problem strongly affecting labor discipline and economic productivity. It became one of the most pressing national issues when Gorbachev launched a campaign in his first few months in power to reduce the sale and consumption of alcohol. Thus, the national agenda is expanding, but the authority to let this happen continues to reside with the Party's top leadership.

DRAFTING PROPOSALS

Issues normally appear on the agendas of decision-making agencies in two forms: items for initial discussion, and draft proposals. Any issue that would normally end up as a law, decree, or policy statement is formulated into a draft proposal early in the deliberative process. There are usually so many agencies that have to be consulted on major issues that a formal document is the only practicable form in which to solicit reactions.

The process of getting up a draft proposal adheres to two operational principles: the obligation of consulting widely among potentially interested parties before a decision is made, and the desirability of achieving consensual agreement on the issue *before* it comes up for a final decision. This contributes to delays in the policy-making process because of the time it takes to circulate the draft proposal.

The consultative procedure is a complex one. The ministry responsible for the general policy area normally drafts the proposal, then circulates it to all agencies, governmental and Party, which have an interest in the issue. Where disagreements arise, ad hoc committees are usually established to iron out the differences before the document goes further. These committees are formed at all levels, including, frequently, that of the Politburo. Sometimes they work well and efficiently, while at other times they give only a cursory look at a proposal or pass the buck to a higher level.[28] If an agency persists in opposing some part of the proposal, it drafts an objection that circulates to all other agencies along with the original draft. If the resisting agency is important enough, or if the Politburo itself is divided on the issue, a decision on the policy may be very long in coming.

In the case of the Family Law Reform, for example, a draft that had completed the long consultative process was presented in the Supreme Soviet in 1962, requiring only Party approval to become law. Yet no such action was forthcoming, and two years later a new draft was readied for national publication. Again silence descended on the issue. A further draft appeared in the Supreme Soviet in 1968, and was this time published for nationwide discussion and subsequently enacted into law.

The revising of the Civil Law on Tort Liability during Khrushchev's tenure was similarly slow. At least five successive versions of the law were circulated over a five-year period before approval was obtained.[29] Similarly, the 1983 Law on Labor Collectives took three years to write in a way that satisfied the Politburo and the various ministries involved.[30]

DECISION MAKING

The ultimate decision-maker in the Soviet Union is the General Secretary of the Communist Party. Although Stalin, Khrushchev, and Brezhnev differed considerably in their relations with their colleagues on the Politburo, each endeavored to impose his own priorities on the political system, and each eventually succeeded in doing so. Without the use of terror, the task for Khrushchev and Brezhnev was more complex. This was especially true for Brezhnev, whose style was to strive for consensus rather than confrontation, and who therefore was inclined to concede more of his policy preferences than was Khrushchev, and was more frequently confronted with opposition. Nevertheless, in important matters, as George Breslauer concludes, "Brezhnev almost always won."[31]

But the matter is, of course, not that simple. The General Secretary gets his way not merely because he holds the post but because in achieving it he has demonstrated that he has the Politburo's support, and because having the position allows him to increase that support through careful appointments to high Party and government positions. He also increases his political authority by promoting policies that offer effective solutions to national problems. Thus, the decisions made by the General Secretary necessarily rest upon the whole elaborate policy-making process we have been describing.

At the level of the government ministries and Central Committee departments, collective decision making has always been a kind of ideal in the Soviet conception of government. In the early years of Soviet power, it was considered a revolutionary advancement over the czarist system of autocratic rule, and an advisory committee was formed in each ministry to broaden participation in decision making. The process proved inefficient, however, encouraging ministers to defer to the collective in order to avoid personal responsibility for failures. To counter this, the power of the advisory committees was reduced in the 1930s in favor of the single executives. In the post-Stalin period, however, the authority of the collective has increased again, reinforcing the principle of broad participation in decision making.

Typically, a government ministry has two collective bodies that play important roles in the decision process:

1. *Agency Committees:* Representatives of the various agencies and departments of a national ministry form a permanent committee to review all draft proposals and other matters for the benefit of the minister who must make the decisions. Agency Committees are "in-house" bodies, composed of officials subordinate to the minister and thus part of his "team."

2. *Interagency Committees:* To ensure representation of all agencies that have similar policy concerns, ministries also have collectives that bring such representatives together on a regular basis. Because it is common for a major policy area to be the responsibility of numerous government agencies, such committees help coordinate matters of general policy. The administration of urban transit systems, for instance, involves a wide range of agencies. Each form of transportation—underground railways, taxis, buses, and streetcars—is run by a separate ministry. Spare parts, paint and metal for repairs, electricity, and ticket-issuing machines are all supplied by separate government agencies whose work must be coordinated.[32]

Where a policy matter has become of critical importance to the leadership, a special interministerial coordinating commission may be established to handle it. There are a number of such committees currently attached to the Council of Ministers, including the Military-Industrial Commission, which is responsible for the defense industry, and the Commission for Economic Ties with Foreign Countries.[33] Because natural gas came to be so heavily emphasized at the 26th Party Congress (1981), a special commission of the USSR Council of Ministers was created to manage that area.[34] Representatives of all ministries with any responsibility for gas production and utilization are represented on the commission.

This emphasis on participation and coordination in decision making has several effects. Attempts to reach consensus prior to a decision tend to make for conservative decisions, purged of any provision that was objected to by any party. By the same token, the process tends to produce decisions that administrative agencies can live with and will conscientiously implement. Participation also gives any interested agency not only a chance to influence the final policy but also time to mobilize support at higher levels if its interests may be harmed by the policy. This often pushes decisions to higher levels, where competition for the attention of decision-makers is even more intense.

The right of interested agencies to participate in policy-making is not independently guaranteed. It depends in each case on the willingness of the Politburo or other top-level faction of the leadership to allow it to occur. At any point, the Politburo can short-circuit the process, either by placing the matter on its own agenda for a decision or by ordering that the matter be dropped from the agendas of other organizations.

GOING PUBLIC

The policy-making process in the USSR is conducted largely on a "need to know" basis. One Western specialist estimates that some 85 percent of the decrees of the Council of Ministers are never published but are only circulated among agencies involved in the matters.[35] Nevertheless, as a growing number of policy case studies have shown, many major policy issues are put forth for public consideration. When, and for what purpose, this is done depends on the nature of the issue and the attitudes of the top leadership.

When an issue goes public, it involves one, or both, of two separate publics: a *specialist public* and a *general public*. The specialist public includes academics, professional experts, writers, and government and Party administrators who are not directly involved in the decision-making process but who have a strong interest in the issue. In the area of urban housing, for example, the proposals initiated by Khrushchev in the 1950s were widely discussed by organizations of professional architects, academics in the Academy of Architecture in Moscow, city administrators, and economic managers. Initially, articles appeared in professional journals and conference reports but not in the general press, as the leadership wished to avoid generating high public expectations for better housing.[36]

In his move to abolish the machine-tractor stations, Khrushchev again attempted to confine the discussion to professional economists and agricultural administrators. He made several important speeches on the subject that were not published until after the issue had been decided.[37] Brezhnev did the same in preparation for the 1983 Law on Labor Collectives, permitting considerable controversy to surface in the limited confines of professional conferences and journals.[38]

Where major social and economic policies are involved, opening up the discussion on draft proposals to specialized professionals has become almost routine. A major reason for this is the fact that the government's failure to do so in some important cases has produced ineffective or even unenforceable policies. The education reform of the late 1950s and the development of an environmental policy in the 1970s and 1980s are examples of the failure of Party policies because of the absence of consensus among specialists and administrators.

Opening up discussion of draft policies to the general public is another matter. The "need to know" principle combined with the Party's control of the national press means that the initiation of a public discussion is a deliberate act of the leadership. It is done for any of several purposes: to publicize an important policy change, to build popular support for the new policy, to manifest the exercise of popular democracy called for by the Constitution, and, in some cases, to assist one faction of the Party leadership to create a broad climate of acceptance for a policy in order to strengthen its position against an opposing faction.

At what point in the policy process a general public discussion is undertaken is also a political decision. With some policies, it occurs before the top leadership has reached consensus on the issue. In such cases, the discussion can be a factor in that decision. Khrushchev was particularly inclined to use public discussions to overcome resistance to change, as he did in the case of local Party opposition to his plan to cultivate vast new areas of land in Kazakhstan (the Virgin Lands Program). In most cases, however, the opening of an issue to the general public *follows* the real decision-making process. The draft proposals that are the basis for the discussion are usually altered in minor ways as a result of the discussion, either because some reasonable changes were proposed or merely to lend credibility to the process itself.

When an issue finally does enter the public arena, the scope of the discussion process can be remarkably broad. The adoption of the Law on Labour Collectives in 1983 was a typical performance. Soviet sources report that over 110 million citizens attended meetings called to discuss the draft law. All major Soviet newspapers organized discussions of the draft and countless citizens wrote letters commenting on its proposals. Over 130,000 proposals were processed by the press and the Presidium of the Supreme Soviet.[39] In the end, some seventy-five changes in the draft were incorporated in the final statute. None of them involved major alterations in the basic thrust of the law, but neither were they mere editorial changes.[40]

IMPLEMENTING POLICY DECISIONS

The real test of a policy is its effectiveness in solving a problem, and this depends partly on the aptness of the policy and partly on the willingness and ability of those to whom it is directed to carry it out. Policies, after all, are made at the top by relatively few officials, but they must be implemented at the bottom by an army of local administrators whose enthusiasm for the policy may be somewhat less than that of the leaders.

In a stable society such as the Soviet Union, government policies are normally carried out with some degree of success. But there are examples of spectacular policy failures resulting from the unrelenting opposition of individuals, organizations, and, sometimes, the general public as well. In the Khrushchev era, this happened to the General Secretary at least twice: in the 1958 reform of the school system, where a coalition of academic administrators, journalists, school teachers, and some high Party officials brought about its defeat six years after it was introduced, and in his "antiparasite" (criminal law) reform, which attempted to give public gatherings broad powers to discipline neighbors and co-workers. In the latter case, the failures of the reform were widely publicized in the press and criticized by the Supreme Court before the reform was finally abandoned.

In the case of the 1983 Law on Labor Collectives, the statute required additional legislation to implement specific provisions. After passage, the law continued to generate intense opposition in some administrative quarters, where "opponents of reform apparently remained in a position to veto policies which could threaten entrenched interests."[41] In other major policy goals that have been pursued over several decades—curbing the influx of people into the major cities, reducing alcoholic consumption, or encouraging respect for manual labor— widespread public opposition has prevented much progress.

Implementing Party policies often encounters difficulties for two basic reasons. First, the authoritarian nature of the political system precludes more than a modest and occasional input from the administrative apparatus or the general public. Claiming sole responsibility for the development of the nation, the Communist Party leadership often pursues goals that conflict with the real interests of the population. Furthermore, it often has little to offer in return for compliance with its decisions. The system places primary reliance on exhortation, publicity campaigns, and calls for self-sacrifice in the interest of "building communism" rather than more tangible incentives. Policies that demand higher individual productivity or less drunkenness are rarely accompanied by more consumer goods on the shelves or more money in the pay envelope.

The second problem arises from the internal conflicts that often emerge from the policy-making process. In the struggle over pollution at Lake Baikal, for example (see below), the policy demand that factories reduce the amount of chemicals they pour into the lake ran smack into the equally pressing need to bring the factories up to full production as soon as possible. In the industrial sphere, the demand that factory managers get more productivity out of their workers is contradicted by the guarantee of full employment, which ensures a person a job regardless of one's effort. And even with the best of intentions, Soviet administrators are often unable to carry out the policy of the state. Consider the report of a Siberian journalist on the problem of enforcing an antipoaching law:

> Poachers, who today are equipped not only with rapid-fire guns but also with cross-country vehicles, hydrofoils and even helicopters, frequently operate with impunity. Furthermore, the fish inspectors are under the Ministry of the Fish Industry, the game wardens under the Ministry of Agriculture, and the forest inspectors under the Ministry of Forestry. Their efforts are uncoordinated. . . .[42]

CASE STUDIES IN POLICY-MAKING

In order to see the policy-making and implementation process in greater detail, we shall examine three case studies that trace the development of specific national policies adopted in the post-Stalin years. At the end of the chapter, we will offer some general conclusions on the nature of policy-making in the USSR.

The three case studies exemplify different styles of policy-making during the 1960s and 1970s. The first two present almost opposite patterns as regards the role of the Party leadership and that of non-Party groups and individuals. In the case involving the adoption of the 1977 Constitution, the Party leadership acted with a high degree of secrecy and relatively little input from professional groups or the general public. The Lake Baikal case, on the other hand, emerged out of popular concern over rising pollution levels in the Baikal area. That concern was eventually translated into new government policies, but the impetus for change clearly rested with the concerned public rather than the government or the Party.

The adoption of most policies follows a process that lies somewhere between these extremes. The third case study, relating the struggle against "hooliganism" over three decades, illustrates a more typical pattern in which leadership authority interacts with group and public interests to create new policy.

Case 1: The Adoption of the 1977 Constitution

The sudden announcement in May 1977 that a draft of a new constitution would soon be published no doubt took most Soviet citizens by surprise. The first commission established to draft a new constitution had been appointed fifteen years earlier by Nikita Khrushchev, but no document had appeared in all that time. Following Khrushchev's removal from power in 1964, his successor, Leonid

Brezhnev, was designated the new chairman of the Constitutional Commission. In 1970, Soviet officials again began talking publicly about work on the document, but as late as the 25th Party Congress in 1976, only passing reference was made to the matter.

The need for a new constitution emerged as a natural complement to the new policies and methods of governance that were introduced, mainly by Nikita Khrushchev, after Stalin's death in 1953. The existing Constitution, adopted in 1936 and widely referred to as the "Stalin Constitution," was seen as a reflection of an earlier "stage of development" in the USSR as well as a tribute to a man and a style of rule that were no longer acceptable to most of the new leaders. It had, in fact, been amended over 250 times before a new constitution was finally adopted. After Khrushchev's startling denunciation of Stalin at the 20th Party Congress in 1956, and his own emergence as both General Secretary of the Party and Chairman of the Council of Ministers, the beginning of a new political era seemed imminent. It required, along with new leaders, a new set of basic documents defining and justifying the nature of "post-Stalinism," which officially has come to be called "developed socialism."

Khrushchev set about providing those documents, starting first with a new Communist Party Program, which was approved at the 22nd Party Congress (1961). By then, work on the new constitution was already under way. The following April, the Supreme Soviet formed a commission to draft the document, with the General Secretary as its chairman. The commission formed itself into nine subcommissions, each directed to deal with a major aspect of the new constitution.

From that point, which was the last significant public discussion of the new constitution for fourteen years, a series of high-level political controversies repeatedly delayed the completion of the draft document. The first was Khrushchev's rapid loss of political power during 1962 and 1963, owing to increasing top-level opposition to his Party and government reforms, his unorthodox economic and military policies, and his generally erratic style of leadership.[43] Secondly, Brezhnev's own ambitions led him to attempt a restructuring of the relations among the major political institutions after he consolidated his power as General Secretary.[44] This further delayed drafting a new constitution, for that document would have to incorporate the resolution of all major political issues.

Finally, there was the difficult issue of the "liberal" nature of the Stalin Constitution. In an effort to generate Western support and distract attention from the horrors of collectivization and the purges that were in full swing, the 1936 Constitution emphasized a broad array of individual rights and democratic procedures while almost ignoring the role of the Communist Party. After Stalin's death, the new leaders had to decide on the degree of realism that would be introduced into the new constitution, and on this there were no doubt strong differences of opinion. In the end, substantial changes were made in highlighting the role of the Communist Party, emphasizing the duties of citizens more than their rights, and more clearly defining the dominant role of the state in the political system.

Until these issues had been resolved, the new constitution could not be written, and in the post-Stalin era that took the better part of two decades. For the Soviet Constitution is widely viewed, both at home and abroad, as a settled statement of the position of the leadership on a whole range of issues. Even though it is not binding on the party leadership, it is an important source of legitimacy for the leaders and must not be subject to charges of obvious falsehoods.

The drafting of the new constitution was shrouded in secrecy during the years before it was unveiled in 1977. There is little that is publicly known about the debate over the issues within the government and Party or about the identity of the specific agencies and individuals who were involved. However, the general issue of constitutionalism did generate, during this period of time, a lively debate among legal scholars and academics. The main issue was whether "constitutional law" constituted a field of study distinct from "state law," with the implication that if it did then the Constitution itself should be regarded as legally superior to ordinary law. The orthodox response was to deny the existence of "constitutional law" and to stick rigidly to the subject of "state law."

In the early 1970s, a number of books and articles were published that argued the opposite view. The argument was advanced by a group of faculty members at the University of Leningrad School of Law in a collection of articles published in 1975.[45] Robert Sharlet reports that informal communications at the time the new Soviet Constitution was published indicated that the "constitutional law" proponents appeared to have prevailed. There are faint reflections of the argument in the general tenor of the new document, but it is difficult to pin the content of specific sections to this debate.[46]

What is more important is the range of constitutional issues that were omitted from the debate. Although the issue was the difference between constitutional and ordinary law, nothing was said about how conflicts between laws and the Constitution should be resolved, or about the even more delicate question of the status of Party decrees in relation to the national Constitution. These matters were presumably decided in secret by the highest political authorities and were never subjected to public debate.

A draft of the proposed Constitution went public on June 4, 1976. There followed one of the most elaborate exercises in Soviet-type political participation ever organized. Over a four-month period, ending in October, the document was studied at 1.5 million meetings involving over 140 million people. Approximately 400,000 amendments were proposed, of which 150 were ultimately accepted by the Constitutional Commission.[47] Commission members made no important changes in the basic document, but they may have succeeded in lending to the process the kind of participatory flavor that the Party leadership seeks diligently to maintain.

Case 2: The Lake Baikal Controversy

Situated in the mountainous region of southern Siberia just north of the Mongolian border, Lake Baikal is one of the natural wonders of the world.[48] Over 400 miles long and 50 miles wide, and well over a mile deep at one point, it contains one-fifth of the world's supply of fresh water in a state of unmatched purity. The region around the lake is host to some 600 types of plant life and twice as many varieties of animals, including some, like the world's only freshwater seals, that are found nowhere else on earth. It is ecologically a fragile area, where the rivers have only one-tenth the capacity to purify themselves as do the great European rivers like the Volga and the Don, and the scar left by a passing bulldozer takes twenty years to heal.[49]

Unfortunately, the Baikal area is also rich in a number of natural resources that have spurred the development of the paper and pulp industries in the past two decades. The two main cities in the area, Ulan-Ude and Irkutsk, have seen waves of new residents pour in to build the factories and dams that now surround the lake. The beginning of the construction of the new Baikal Amur Mainline (BAM) railroad in the early 1970s brought more people and more heavy equipment to the area, intensifying the damage being done to the environment. As the situation worsened, residents of the Baikal region began to protest. Their objections found support among academics, writers, and journalists both in Siberia and elsewhere in the Soviet Union. The struggle to save Lake Baikal had begun.

What triggered the initial protests was a decision made in Moscow in 1957 to build three large factories to produce rayon cord for rubber tires, using a process that required large quantities of pure water and a special softwood tree necessary for the production of viscose. Both were in abundant supply in the Baikal area, so the decision was made to build the plants at that location. The decision also called for expanding the timber industry in the Baikal region to include processing as well as procuring lumber.

Initial attempts by individuals to create a national issue out of the problems of the Baikal region began in 1959 at a meeting of the Moscow Branch of the All-Union Geographical Society, attended by over fifty representatives of scientific and academic institutes as well as government administrators from Gosplan and the USSR State Construction Committee. The concerns expressed at that meeting bore fruit the following year when a law was enacted by the RSFSR Supreme Soviet requiring attention to environmental concerns in the building of new plants. Despite the law, construction of the first plant was completed without an effective means of recycling its poisonous effluents.

In 1960, objections to the industrial development of the Baikal region appeared in two books published in Ulan-Ude. The following year, Gregori Galazii, director of the Limnological Institute of Baikal, published a letter in the mass-circulation newspaper *Komsomolskaia Pravda* decrying the potential damage the plant would do to the lake and urging that recycling facilities be built to protect the water. In the early 1960s, concern was spreading among scientists and interested observers of the area. In 1963 and again in 1965, several major national magazines published lengthy exposes, but these produced no significant political response.

There seem to be two reasons why the increasing volume of negative publicity failed to move the government to action in defense of the Baikal area. One was the fact that the economic need for the products of the new plants was unquestionably great and therefore had strong supporters in the planning agencies and economic ministries involved. The other is that the scientific community was itself divided on the issue. In 1962, as the plants were being constructed, the State Committee for Scientific Research judged the waste-treatment plans of the industry unsound. Yet two years later, the Siberian Department of the Academy of Sciences, from which some of the original warnings had been issued, formally approved the plant designs.

Finally, in 1966, a dramatic appearance by Mikhail Sholokov, one of the Soviet Union's most famous writers, at the 23rd Party Congress seemed to crystalize the sense of impending disaster at Baikal. "Our descendants will not forgive us," he warned, "if we do not preserve this glorious lake, this sacred Baikal."[50] By then the Baikal plant was in operation, no filtration system was working, and the problem had become a national issue that could no longer be avoided by the ministries involved or by the Party leadership.

Immediately following the Party Congress, the national planning agency (Gosplan) formed a commission to study the matter and propose a concrete solution. The resulting recommendations, fully supporting the ministries' position on the issue, was then approved by an even higher-level group, including the leadership of Gosplan, the State Committee on Science and Technology, and the Academy of Sciences. But this attempt to reach a consensus among interested parties failed as the opposition of conservationists to this "whitewash" intensified. Reports in the following year affirmed that the waste effluents pouring into the lake were well above maximum standards. Where that was happening, Pravda reported, from one-third to one-half of the plant and animal life had already died.

As the controversy refused to die out, the State Committee on Science and Technology convened another commission in March 1968, to attempt once again to draft a proposal that would gain general support. This time, after deliberating for more than a year, the commission produced a report that accepted most of the recommendations of the environmentalists. Strict limits were to be placed on logging operations and on waste treatment and the damage already done to the lake was to be repaired. This heartened the environmentalists but generated strong opposition in some of the ministries.

Because the 1969 proposal, like those before it, had failed to achieve a true consensus, the decision made by the Council of Ministers and the Politburo was not the final act in the drama. Despite the decision, conditions at Baikal failed to change much, and objections from academic environmentalists and journalists continued to be published in the national press. This resulted in the need for additional decisions on the matter. In 1971, another and more detailed decree was issued by the Council of Ministers and the Party Central Committee, and in 1974 further regulations designed to implement the 1971 decree were published. In 1975, yet another commission, this time formed by the USSR Academy of Sciences, began deliberations on the matter that lasted for over a year. This produced a comprehensive general plan for the Baikal area that seemed, finally, to have the support of most of the participants in the struggle.

On this basis, the plan could be implemented with some assurance of success.

Accordingly, the USSR State Committee on Hydrometeorology and Environmental Control has organized a nationwide network of technicians responsible for monitoring environmental conditions. They are operating in over 350 cities, at 70 stations that test the chemical composition of the air, at 1,000 bodies of water checking purity and potability, and at many other sites.[51] This represents a substantial victory for those who waged the early struggle for an effective national environmental policy.

On the other hand, economic development continues to be the number-one national priority. In the Baikal region, new processing plants are being constructed, the Baikal-Amur railroad project continues to draw thousands of workers and machines to the area, and the cities in Baikal's basin are still expanding. All this development is now subject to the environmental protection policies of the government, but the momentum of industrial development in the area has not slowed as a result. Environmental protection, in the Soviet Union as elsewhere, seems to be the kind of battle that has to be fought over and over again.

Case 3: The Struggle Against 'Hooliganism'

In Soviet legal parlance, a "hooligan" is a public nuisance, someone who disturbs the peace, offends passersby, or uses foul language in public. Hooliganism is an unspecific violation of the social order. It includes virtually any behavior, not already declared illegal, that offends people, so it is pretty much up to the militiaman on the street to determine when it has occurred.

It is also nothing new in Soviet society. Well before the Russian Revolution, law enforcement authorities and civil leaders complained incessantly about *neculturny* (uncultured) behavior among ordinary Russian citizens. Shortly after the Revolution, hooliganism was formally included in the Criminal Code. As Stalinism took hold, repeated campaigns were launched (in 1925, 1935, and 1940) to crack down on antisocial behavior. By 1940, hooliganism had been officially designated a felony and made subject to imprisonment. Hooliganism is closely associated with drunkenness, and given the problem of alcoholism in the Soviet Union, it is not surprising that hooliganism accounts for more arrests than any other crime. In many cases, it also results in violence and in resistance to lawful authority.

The policy issues involved in the struggle against hooliganism have remained relatively constant over the years:

- Given that some 90 percent of all arrests for hooliganism involve drunkenness as well, is the real problem hooliganism or alcoholism?
- Should hooliganism be considered a crime subject to harsh punishments like imprisonment, or as a misdemeanor better dealt with by public pressures and fines?
- Given the high volume of hooliganism cases, should they be handled through the regular court system or by administrative agencies?

There have been four major participants in the decades-long policy debates over hooliganism: the Party leadership in a decision-making role, the judiciary and its academic institutes, the police establishment allied with the Ministry for the Protection of the Social Order (MOOP), and the general public. We shall look at three periods in the post-Stalin era to see how policy toward hooligans changed and how the various participants were involved.

The 1950s: De-Stalinization. After Stalin's death in 1953, the number of convictions for all types of crimes decreased significantly, and in 1956, "petty" hooliganism became an "administrative crime," to be handled routinely by a single judge. To deal with more severe cases, three new categories of hooliganism were created: "common hooliganism," "malicious hooliganism" (marked by "particular cynicism or impudence" or involving resistance to authority), and "very malicious hooliganism" (involving the use of "firearms, knives and . . . brass knuckles").[52]

In some respects the relaxation of public discipline that attended de-Stalinization involved unpleasant consequences. By the late 1950s, there had been a marked increase in the incidence of youthful rowdyism and delinquency as well as of antisocial adult behavior. As a result, a growing volume of complaining letters from citizens appeared in the newspapers, and Party and police officials expressed increasing exasperation with the situation. There were frequent calls from both quarters for more effective control and harsher penalties for violators. All this led finally to a major reform of the hooliganism laws in 1966.

The 1966 Reform. By 1965, the problem was being addressed more directly. Academic studies were commissioned and practical experiments, especially in Leningrad, were undertaken. The Communist Party leadership instructed various government and academic institutes to begin work on a draft law looking toward a significant reduction in alcoholism, under the assumption that the control of drunkenness would go a long way toward reducing hooliganism. The effort was spearheaded by Professor A.A. Gertsenzon of the Procuracy Institute and B.Z. Anashkin, head of the Criminal Division of the USSR Supreme Court.

This approach was opposed by the forces of "law and order," which called for a direct approach involving harsher measures of apprehension and punishment for hooligans. A prominent spokesman for this point of view was V.S. Tikunov, the Minister for the Defense of the Social Order (MOOP). His speech to a conference of senior police officials in March 1966 was fully reported in *Izvestia,* which called for an open discussion of the issue. Surprisingly, no public discussion emerged, in *Izvestia* or elsewhere. Yet at that moment, the Party leadership was moving toward a decision in favor of the direct approach. Its decision in May 1966 cut short the broad debate on the issues that had been promised. "So far as we know," Peter Solomon concludes, "the adherents of these two approaches did not argue their differences in public or private forums; neither of them even addressed the other's arguments."[53] Thus, the Party leadership demonstrated once more both its willingness to allow, and even to stimulate, public debate on an issue as well as its ability to silence that debate and impose a decision.

In this instance, a basic policy decision had been made by the leadership before a concrete proposal had even been drafted. And an existing proposal, setting forth the indirect approach to the problem favored by most academics and drawn up at the leadership's specific request, had been scratched. Whether this resulted largely from the personal preferences of members of the Politburo or from the greater political influence of MOOP and Minister Tikunov is not known, but either is possible.

In mid-May, officials at MOOP drafted their proposal and forwarded it to an editorial commission for refinement and then to the Presidium of the Supreme Soviet. The latter body formed a subcommission of members of the Legislative Proposals Commissions of both chambers to polish the final draft, considering carefully the legal implications of the proposals. Academics from the Procuracy Institute participated reluctantly in the drafting. Most had opposed a police crackdown as an unworkable solution to the problem.[54]

The public phase of the reform began on July 23, 1966, with a live TV presentation of the trial of a man charged with malicious hooliganism in Riazan Province. The dramatic show produced hundreds of angry letters to the press and to the government condemning the accused. On the basis of this response the Party declared that the people "demanded" action. Three days later, the draft statute that had already been prepared was introduced in the Supreme Soviet and passed unanimously. For several weeks therafter all manner of public organizations held meetings and rallies to discuss the new law and to commit themselves to implementing it to the fullest. The public campaign culminated with a nationally televised press conference of leading officials of the Supreme Court, the Procuracy, and MOOP. In this public exercise, there was very little participation by the scholars and experts who had previously been active in debating the merits of various proposals.

Before the statute could be implemented, it had to be explained in greater detail, a common characteristic of Soviet legislation. Scholars in the Procuracy Institute prepared a number of papers on various aspects of the law for use mainly by administrators charged with carrying it out. The division that continued to exist among scholars on this issue was reflected in a second set of articles published somewhat later that drew attention to difficulties that would be encountered in implementing the law. Obviously in this case, the enactment of the reform statute, in accordance with the leadership's will, had not ended, or silenced, the opposition.

The response to the law on the streets of the USSR was emphatic. In the Belorussian Republic, for example, the number of court sentences for hooliganism in 1967 was nearly double that of 1965.[55] Sentences of short-term deprivation of freedom (up to one year—the maximum sentence for hooliganism)—increased in the same period from 3.2 percent of all sentences to nearly 9 percent.[56]

By 1970, however, convictions for hooliganism had dropped off considerably. The campaign was over and control of hooliganism had returned to a routine police function. Even though hooliganism remained the most common violation of the law, having replaced home distilling of alcohol in 1965. the number of arrests and convictions dropped substantially. This probably reflects both a laxness in reporting such crimes and an unwillingness of both the police and the courts to burden court schedules with a high volume of minor breeches of the law.

The 1977 Reform. By the early 1970s, the pendulum had begun to swing back the other way. Many jurists and police officials, as well as a large group of academic criminologists and lawyers, took up the argument for returning to a more educational and prophylactic approach to hooliganism. The burden on both the police and the courts of treating hooliganism as a full-fledged crime requiring formal trials, appeals, and incarceration had been a heavy one. In 1977, all this culminated in the adoption of a new statute that made two important changes in the treatment of minor crimes including hooliganism: It authorized judges to treat such acts as misdemeanors rather than crimes and to deal with them through administrative procedures rather than court trials.[57]

The reaction to the publication of the new law was immediate. In the first year, in various districts of Odessa Province, for example, between 40 percent and 79 percent of all minor crimes were diverted from the criminal-justice process to the administrative bureaucracy. The negative features of the reform also stimulated a strong response. By late 1977, the press was publishing claims of widespread laxness in the law's implementation. Judges were releasing hardened criminals to administrative agencies, police were misdescribing illegal acts so they could treat them as misdemeanors rather than crimes, and courts were ignoring prior convictions of defendants.

By 1978, leaders of the higher courts were becoming increasingly disturbed by these revelations and by the growing number of letters from citizens condemning the apparent rise in acts of hooliganism on the streets and in public places. In the fall, the USSR Supreme Court held a plenary meeting at which much of this was aired. On September 7, 1978, it issued new guidelines for carrying out the 1977 reform, aimed at tightening up its enforcement. Such guidelines are an important source of judicial behavior distinct from specific laws and Party policy statements.

A year later the Party Central Committee further tightened the leash. It issued a decree demanding more effective law enforcement and an intensification of the influence of collectives on miscreants. Significantly, the leadership did not call for a reversal of the 1977 reform. The principle of administrative jurisdiction for minor crimes was upheld, as had been continuously urged by many specialists and academics. The Party instruction was followed shortly by a directive from the Supreme Court to the lower courts explaining the instruction and, three months later, by a formal decree issued jointly by the Central Committee, the Presidium of the Council of Ministers, and the All-Union Council of Trade Unions.[58]

The long campaign to reduce the prevalence of hooliganism and other antisocial behavior did not end with the latest Party decree on the subject. Nor have the differing views on the subject expressed by the police forces, the courts, academics, lawyers, Party officials, and the mass citizenry been finally reconciled. Policy on the subject of hooliganism has swung in varying directions as one participant or another gained adherents to its views. Overseeing the whole policy debate was the highest Party leadership, which reserved the right both to instigate and to suppress debate on the issue and to step in at any point and make a decision.

As we have seen, the timing of the leadership's decisions did not follow a fixed pattern. Sometimes they preceded, sometimes they followed, other facets of the process, such as academic debate, the drafting of legislative proposals, public discussion and campaigns, and the issuance of directives by non-Party organs such as the Supreme Court. Those other activities themselves appeared in varying sequences. In the 1966 reform, for example, the public discussion came mainly after the fact, while in the late 1970s public outrage at the hooligans stimulated both the courts and the Party leadership to make changes in the policy. This case illustrates the complexity of the policy-making process and the importance of the involvement of participants who, while outside the circles of Party power, nevertheless can exert significant influence on the leadership's decisions.

CONCLUSIONS

These brief case studies and the analysis that preceded them allow us to reach some general conclusions about the Soviet policy-making process. They are offered despite the realization that there is no single process for arriving at policy decisions. The process varies with the subject of the policy (economic, environmental, or foreign policy, for example), with the degree of secrecy imposed by the leadership, and with the personality and style of the General Secretary. Nevertheless, a number of features are common to the Soviet policy-making process:

1. *Origins of Policy Initiatives.* Clearly, the Party leadership is not the only, or even the primary, source of issues that make it to the official agenda, even though the leadership has the ultimate voice in *whether* an issue is to be taken up. Policy initiatives regularly come from ministries, regional and local administrative agencies, academic institutes, journalists and individual scholars, and from the mass public. The main channel for those outside government is the national press, including both newspapers and professional and scholarly journals. Because government censors are imperfect, many complaints and reform proposals find their way into print that are later rejected by the higher leadership.
2. *Striving for Consensus.* Rather than being an exercise in arbitrary decision making by top leaders, the normal policy process is strongly infused with pressures for consensus among all concerned parties. This partly accounts for the long delays that often precede decisions, and for the fact that final decisions are often compromises among various interests rather than clear victories for any side.
3. *The Party Leadership's Role.* This striving for consensus does not diminish the ultimate authority of the top leaders at all. As we have seen, sudden decisions by the Politburo to end debate on an issue or to decide the issue in the midst of or

even before a general discussion has taken place are not uncommon. When this happens, formal and public opposition to the decision ceases, for a while at least. When evidence pointing to defects in the policy begins to mount, those who would call for revisions or for scrapping the policy must carefully judge the leadership's willingness to reopen the discussion. Mistakes can be costly.

4. *Carrying Out the Party's Will.* As two of the cases made clear, policy decisions, even at the top level, do not necessarily solve problems. The implementation of a policy is the ultimate test of its effectiveness. If lower-level administrators cannot, or will not, cooperate in carrying it out, or if the general public remains staunchly opposed to it, the chances of its working well are minimized. In numerous cases in the past several decades, major policy decisions have had to be substantially revised or even rescinded because they could not be effectively implemented.

In the next two chapters we shall examine a single policy area—the economic system—in greater detail to see how, and with what success, the Party leadership's will is carried out. The crucial importance that the leadership has always attached to economic development makes this a valuable area through which to explore the ways in which the Soviet Union is governed.

NOTES

1. Quoted in Flora Lewis, "Changing the Party?", *New York Times,* 2 March 1986, p. E23.
2. See Roger Kanet, "The Rise and Fall of the 'All-People's State': Recent Changes in the Soviet Theory of the State," *Soviet Studies,* 20:1, July 1968, pp. 81–93; on "developed socialism," see Donald Kelley, "Developments in Ideology," in Donald Kelley, ed., *Soviet Politics in the Brezhnev Era* (New York: Praeger, 1980), pp. 182–99.
3. For a detailed study of this phenomenon, see Valerie Bunce, *Do New Leaders Make a Difference?* (Princeton, N.J.: Princeton University Press, 1981).
4. The role of specialists in policy-making is carefully explored by Thane Gustafson in *Reform in Soviet Politics* (Cambridge: Cambridge University Press, 1981).
5. For a summary of current arguments on this subject, see H. Gordon Skilling, "Interest Groups and Communist Politics Revisited, *World Politics,* Vol. 36, October 1983, pp. 1–27.
6. See John Leowenhardt, *Decision Making in Soviet Politics* (New York: St. Martin's Press, 1981), pp. 59–63.
7. Ibid., pp. 48–54.
8. Gustafson, *Reform in Soviet Politics,* pp. 40–46.
9. See Peter H. Solomon, Jr., *Soviet Criminologists and Criminal Policy* (New York: Columbia University Press, 1978), pp. 58–63.
10. See, for example, Franklyn Griffiths, *Images, Politics, and Learning in Soviet Behavior Toward the United States* (Ph.D. Dissertation, Columbia University, 1972; University Microfilms), p. 293.
11. Both terms, "opinion groups" and "policy coalitions," are used by Loewenhardt, *Decision Making in Soviet Politics,* pp. 24–25.
12. Gustafson, *Reform in Soviet Politics,* p. 82.

13. See Bill Keller in the *New York Times*, 27 September 1987, p. 1.
14. See Thane Gustafson, "Soviet Energy Policy: From Big Coal to Big Gas," in Seweryn Bialer and Thane Gustafson, *Russia at the Crossroads* (London: George Allen and Unwin, 1982), pp. 121–39; and David Wilson, *The Demand for Energy in the Soviet Union* (London: Rowman & Allanheld, 1983), chapter 1.
15. Gustafson, "Soviet Energy Policy," pp. 133–34, emphasis added.
16. Philip D. Stewart, James W. Warhola, and Roger A. Blough, "Issue Salience and Foreign Policy Role Specialization in the Soviet Politburo of the 1970's," *American Journal of Political Science*, 28:1, February, 1984, pp. 1–22; also see Arnold Beichman's review essay, "Kremlin Factions and Foreign Policy," *Problems of Communism*, September-October 1984, pp. 95–99.
17. *Pravda*, 13 February 1986, p. 3.
18. Elizabeth Teague, *Radio Liberty Reports* Nos. 242 and 476, 1984.
19. His statement on rents was: "Proposals on fair changes in the system of payments for housing, relating them closely to the size and quality of the apartment occupied, deserve attention." *Pravda*, 26 February 1986, p. 6.
20. For a useful discussion of the importance of locally raised issues, see Philip Stewart, "Soviet Interest Groups and the Policy Process: The Repeal of Production Education," *World Politics*, Vol. XXII, October 1969, pp. 29–50.
21. Robert Miller, *One Hundred Thousand Tractors: The MTS and the Development of Controls in Soviet Agriculture* (Cambridge, Mass.: Harvard University Press, 1970), p. 314.
22. See Peter H. Juviler, "Family Reforms on the Road to Communism," in Peter H. Juviler and Henry W. Morton, eds., *Soviet Policy-Making: Studies of Communism in Transition* (New York: Praeger, 1967), pp. 29–60.
23. On this, see C. Offe, "Political Authority and Class Structures," in P. Connerton, ed., *Critical Sociology* (Harmondsworth England: Penguin, 1976). Offe argues that democratic capitalist systems also have "exclusion rules" that belie claims of political neutrality of capitalist state apparatuses.
24. Gustafson, *Reform in Soviet Politics*, p. 87.
25. Gustafson's term in *Reform in Soviet Politics*, p. 87.
26. For a discussion of unorthodox ideas that have been published by academics in professional journals but not yet accepted for the official agenda, see Ronald Hill, *Soviet Politics, Political Science and Reform* (New York: M.E. Sharpe, 1980.)
27. See Serge Schmemann's analysis of this change in the *New York Times*, 18 February 1986, p. 1.
28. Criticism of ineffective committees is common. See, for example, M.S. Smirtyukov, *Sovetskii Gosudarstvenny Apparat Upravleniya* (Moscow: Izd. Politicheskoi Literatury, 1982), p. 183–84.
29. Both cases are discussed briefly in Loewenhardt, *Decision Making in Soviet Politics*.
30. Darrell Slider, "Reforming the Workplace: The 1983 Soviet Law on Labour Collectives," *Soviet Studies*, XXXVII:2, April 1985, pp. 173–83.
31. George Breslauer, *Khrushchev and Brezhnev as Leaders: Building Authority in Soviet Politics* (London: George Allen and Unwin, 1982), p. 245.
32. See Martin Crouch, "Transport Policy in Britain and the Soviet Union: A Political Paradox," *Policy and Politics*, Vol. 9, No. 4, 1981, pp. 441–42.
33. Jerry F. Hough and Merle Fainsod, *How the Soviet Union Is Governed* (Cambridge, Mass.: Harvard University Press, 1979), p. 383.
34. Gustafson, "Soviet Energy Policy," p. 125.

35. Dietrich A. Loeber, "Legal Rules 'For Internal Use Only,' " *International and Comparative Law Quarterly,* January 1970, p. 77; cited in Gustafson, *Reform in Soviet Politics,* p. 87.
36. Albrecht Martiny, "Housing and Construction in the Period of 'De-Stalinization': The Change in Construction Policy from 1954 to 1957," in Peter J. Potichnyj and Jane Shapiro Zacek, *Politics and Participation Under Communist Rule* (New York: Praeger, 1983), pp. 90–91.
37. Loewenhardt, *Decision Making in Soviet Politics,* p. 47.
38. Slider, "Reforming the Workplace," p. 175–79.
39. *Izvestia,* 18 June 1983.
40. For a thorough examination of this case, see Slider, "Reforming the Workplace," pp. 173–185.
41. Ibid., p. 181.
42. *Komsomolskaya Pravda,* 7 January 1979, p. 3, trans. *Current Digest of the Soviet Press,* XXXI, 1, p. 4.
43. See Jerome M. Gilison, "Khrushchev, Brezhnev and Constitution Reform," *Problems of Communism,* Vol. 21, September-October 1972, p. 73.
44. The restructuring had to do with the role of the Politburo vis-á-vis the Council of Ministers and the position of the General Secretary in the overall system. For a discussion of this point, see D. Richard Little, "The New Soviet Constitution: Does It Matter?", paper presented at the Western Slavic Association Conference, February 16, 1978, pp. 14–16.
45. S. Rusinova and V. Rianzhin, eds., *Sovetskoe Konstitutsionnoe Pravo* (*Soviet Constitutional Law*) (Leningrad: Leningrad State University Press, 1975). For a review of the book and discussion of the issues it raises, see Christopher Osakwe's essay in *Tulane Law Review,* Vol. 51, 1977, pp. 411–22.
46. Robert Sharlet, *The New Soviet Constitution of 1977* (Brunswick, Ohio: King's Court Communications, Inc., 1978), p. 8–10.
47. The statistics are from Boris Topornin, *The New Constitution of the USSR* (Moscow: Progress Publishers, 1980), pp. 14–15.
48. The principal secondary sources used for this case study were the following: Craig Zumbrunnen, "The Lake Baikal Controversy," in Ivan Volgyes, ed., *Environmental Deterioration in the Soviet Union and Eastern Europe* (New York: Praeger, 1974; Slava Lubomudrov, "Environmental Politics in the Soviet Union: The Baikal Controversy," *Canadian Slavonic Papers,* XX, No. 4, December 1978, pp. 529–43; Gustafson, *Reform of Soviet Politics.*
49. *The Soviet Union,* (Alexandria, Va.: Time-Life Books, 1985), pp. 54–55.
50. Quoted in Gustafson, *Reform in Soviet Politics,* p. 41.
51. Iuri A. Izrael, "Toward a Strategy for Protection of the Environment and Rational Use of Nature in the USSR," *Voprosy Filosofii,* No. 6, 1979, trans. *Soviet Sociology,* Winter 1979–80, pp. 81–82.
52. *Great Soviet Encyclopedia,* 3rd ed., English trans. (New York: Macmillan, 1978), Vol. 28, p. 54.
53. Solomon, *Soviet Criminologists,* p. 90.
54. Solomon gleaned this from interviews with officials and academics in the USSR. See Ibid., p. 88.
55. See Ger P. van den Berg, *The Soviet System of Justice, Figures and Policy* (Dordrecht: Martinus Nijhoff Publishers, 1985), Table 100, p. 293. Comparable data for the USSR as a whole are not available.

56. Ibid., Table 114, p. 306.
57. This discussion of the 1977 reform draws mainly on Peter H. Juviler, "Diversion from Criminal to Administrative Justice: Soviet law, Practice, and Conflicts of Policy," in F.J.M. Feldbrugge and William B. Simons, *Perspectives on Soviet Law for the Eighties* (The Hague: Martinus Nijhoff Publishers, 1982), pp. 153–70.
58. *Pravda,* 12 January 1980, p. 1.

CHAPTER 9
Managing the Planned Economy

Rightly or wrongly, people in modern societies tend to hold their governments responsible for their economic well-being. In Western democratic states, economic failure is a serious, but not necessarily fatal, circumstance, for it can usually be blamed on the party in power, rather than on the political system itself. In the USSR, however, the political system is inseparable from rule by the Communist Party, and the successful economic development of the country is one of the Party's principal justifications for holding power.

The importance of economic success is intensified by the USSR's international role as a model of development of third-world states. The Soviet record in developing a modern industrialized society without introducing capitalism or depending heavily on Western financial investment has wide appeal in the non-Western world. To the extent that the contemporary Soviet system exhibits weaknesses and deficiencies in its economic development, its attractiveness as a political model declines, and this affects the international influence of the USSR.

Throughout the post-Stalin years, but especially during the Brezhnev period, the Soviet economy maintained a respectable gross output, comparable to that in other industrialized countries. That fact conceals a host of other problems, however, as a result of which by the early 1980s the Soviet economy was clearly in trouble. The death of Brezhnev in 1982 raised the expectation that new and younger leadership might tackle the problems of the economy more effectively. But three years were to pass, marked by the brief tenure of two successors to Brezhnev (Andropov and Chernenko), before the leadership problem was resolved. In March 1985, Mikhail Gorbachev became the new General Secretary, and within months he made clear his intention to reform the economic system.

For two years thereafter, Gorbachev toured the country attempting to light the fires of economic reform while working to secure his political power in Moscow. By early 1987, it was becoming evident to many observers that his new policy of "restructuring" the economy had become little more than a slogan. The Western press began to write it off as just another propaganda campaign, and Gorbachev himself exhibited growing irritation and impatience at the lack of progress. Finally, at a special plenary session of the Party Central Committee, held in June 1987, Gorbachev launched a direct attack on the deficiencies of the economic system. In a 111-page speech he outlined his plan for a "radical reorganization of economic management."[1] This time, he made clear, there would be real reform.

In this chapter we will assess the new Gorbachev program in light of the basic characteristics of the Soviet economic system. The prospects for success depend not only on how much support Gorbachev can muster in the Politburo or the Central Committee, but on two other factors as well: whether he can overcome the resistance to change that has already been demonstrated by the entrenched and conservative Soviet bureaucracy, and whether he can mobilize the mass of workers and citizens to support a restructured economic system. To evaluate his prospects, a clear understanding of the nature of the present economic system is necessary.

THE PROCESSES OF ECONOMIC MANAGEMENT

The Soviet economy is largely a "planned economy" in the sense that most basic economic decisions—where to invest money, what to produce, how much to charge for goods, how much to pay for labor—are made for the entire society by central governmental authorities in Moscow. The production of goods is a function of orders from planners, not from customers; it is not, therefore, a "market economy." There is also an unplanned, or "second economy," that does resemble a form of market economy. We shall explore that phenomenon in the following chapter.

The Legacy of Stalinism

The planned economy is the creation of Stalin and his colleagues in the early 1930s. Since that time nothing fundamental has changed in the way the planned sector is organized. The first Five-Year Plan, adopted in 1928, was intended to mobilize the entire Soviet population in pursuit of a few clear-cut goals: raw material extraction and the development of new energy sources; construction of dams and railroads; the production of iron, steel, and other basic metals; and industrial machinery that would be used to produce other machines. And, of course, weapons of all types. It was a classic case of an underdeveloped nation striving for modern, industrial status.

By the time of Stalin's death in 1953, the pattern for economic management was well established and its priorities were clear: centralized control over all phases of the economy, a high priority for extractive and basic industries, a strong emphasis on the gross output of products rather than quality or costs of production, a severe restraint on the production of consumer goods, and a clear preference for industry over agriculture as the key to development.[2]

For a nation determined to force a rapid pace of economic and military development, these priorities are at least defensible. They brought about a tremendous surge of economic growth, which, even a decade after Stalin's death, continued at nearly 10 percent a year, one of the highest rates in the world.

Nevertheless, in the 1950s, the defects of the economic system began to show themselves more clearly, and by the time Nikita Khrushchev was securely in power, the "era of reforms" had begun. Ever since then the Party leadership has been struggling with the legacies of the Stalinist economy. One reform has followed another in successive attempts to adapt the Stalinist system to the complexities of a modern, developed economy. Yet throughout this period, the problems have grown more serious.

The Ministerial Apparatus

The economy of the USSR is run by approximately fifty ministries and six state committees.[3] The ministries are divided between all-union ministries, which directly control activities in their jurisdiction wherever they occur in the country, and union-republic ministries, which operate indirectly, working through republic-level ministries below them. The ministerial complex has long been a prime target for reforms, in the hope that some optimal organizational formula can be found. Thus, over the years, many ministries have been divided into two or more, combined with others to form "superministries," or simply abolished.

The six state committees, on the other hand, have remained somewhat more stable even though their functions have also evolved. They are responsible for planning several general facets of the overall economic system. They include the following national agencies:

Gosplan: The State Planning Committee. Gosplan[4] is the highest-level and most comprehensive planning agency in the USSR. Employing thousands of planners, technicians, accountants, and other staff personnel, Gosplan carries overall responsibility for assessing the productive potential of all branches of industry and agriculture and drafting the major national economic plans. It maintains its own bureaus for overseeing each branch of the economy so that it need not depend on ministries or enterprises for accurate assessments of their economic capabilities.

Gossnab: State Committee for Material and Technical Supply. While Gosplan decides on the number and assortment of items to be produced, it is Gossnab's responsibility to provide the raw materials, parts, and components to factories producing the products. As it usually takes numerous inputs to produce a single product, the number of items planned for by Gossnab is far larger—on the order of nine to one—than the number of products planned for by Gosplan.[5]

Gosstroi: State Committee for Construction. This agency oversees all major construction projects in the country, such as dams, railroads, and new factories, as well as the expansion and modernization of existing facilities.

In addition to these three major planning agencies, three other state committees have broad responsibilities for the economy. *Gostsen,* the State Committee for Prices, sets prices for all goods in accordance with elaborate formulae and procedures. *Gostekhnika* coordinates the development of new technologies for the entire economy. It works closely with technical institutes and with the Academy of Sciences and runs a broad array of technological experiments in factories and farms. *Gosbank,* the State Bank, is probably the most powerful of the three; it controls all funds that circulate in the economy except those for capital investment and international trade. Enterprises get their funds for production, wages, materials, and other needs from local branches of Gosbank. Gosbank also handles all sales transactions, paying enterprise bills when they come due. In doing so, Gosbank branches are able to monitor closely the activities of enterprises. They have the power to refuse to pay for goods delivered if the terms of contracts are not met. They can even force an enterprise into bankruptcy.[6]

None of the state committees has operational control over the ministries, so they cannot order ministers to carry out their plans and proposals. But they carry great weight, for they are responsible for working out rational and achievable plans for all phases of the economy.

The Plans

In the Soviet Union there are several economic plans, the most important of which is the Five-Year Plan (FYP). There have been twelve FYPs so far, the twelth running from 1986–1990. Each Five-Year Plan is divided into annual plans, which specify detailed performance requirements for all segments of the economy. Specific plans are drawn up for union-republics, oblasts and raions, for production associations and agricultural complexes, and for individual factories and farms.

Beyond the five-year plans, a number of "perspective plans" are drawn up to fit the FYPs into a longer time frame. These include, for example, the ten-year economic plan drawn up in 1979, a fifteen-year plan covering 1986–2000, and a twenty-year long-term plan for scientific and technical development announced in July 1979.

The task of actually planning an economy the size of the Soviet Union is one of staggering complexity. To enable a factory manager to turn out a given quantity of goods, planners must be sure that other factories, processors, and mines provide the manager with the specific materials needed and that they are delivered when the manager needs them. They must also assure that there will be an adequate labor force for each factory and sufficient machinery to do the job and that firms responsible for the transport, storage, and retailing of products all act in close coordination with the manufacturer. Together Gosplan and Gossnab are involved in the distribution of literally millions of products that are needed by the nation's factories and farms, and by 280 million consumers as well.

Annual plans are not simply imposed on factories and farms; they result from extensive negotiations between Gosplan and these enterprises. These negotiations are crucial for both, for year-end bonuses and career prospects rest heavily on fulfilling the annual plan. Unfortunately for the economy as a whole, what benefits a plant manager or a minister under this system is often detrimental to the country's need for products and services. Yet there are advantages as well to a system of central planning, both in the economic and political spheres.

The Advantages of Central Planning

The heart of this centralized management system is the control over all phases of the production and distribution of goods that is exercised by ministers sitting in Moscow. The most important advantage of this system is that it allows the Communist Party leadership to impose *political* priorities on the economic system directly. In the consumer area, for example, the leadership is able to direct investment into approved collective channels, such as health care, housing and food subsidies, and public transportation, and away from more individual gratifications, such as private automobiles. Central control over prices and wages reinforces this power because they do not have to correspond to the true market values of products and labor. This has important advantages both economically and ideologically. It also has disadvantages, as we shall see below.

Another advantage is that major policy changes can be implemented in a planned economy more easily and quickly than in a market economy. In the late 1960s, for example, the Party leadership decided to launch a massive campaign to raise the productivity of the agricultural sector, tripling its share of the national investment. Similarly, in the early 1980s, the declining output of coal and oil triggered a decision to increase natural gas production by 50 percent during the eleventh FYP (1981–1985). Such sudden shifts in resources and productivity would be virtually impossible in a market economy, no matter how serious the crisis.

Finally, a centrally planned economy ensures that the managerial and technocratic classes are tied firmly to higher political authorities for success in their careers and the benefits that success brings. There are no fortunes to be made through catering to the buying public, at least not legally. The maverick entrepreneur with a radical idea for franchising a chain of fried chicken restaurants has no place in the Soviet planned economy.

With these advantages it is not surprising that successive generations of Soviet leaders have remained committed to the planned economic system established by Stalin. To make it work efficiently and effectively has always been the overriding objective of the Party leadership. But the problems facing the leadership in fulfilling that goal are serious and basic.

PROBLEMS AT THE NATIONAL LEVEL

The main problems on the national level all involve the role of ministries in managing the economy. The most conspicuous problem is the *overcentralization* of authority concentrated in the ministries. Officials with offices in Moscow make countless operational decisions for managers located in all parts of the country. In obtaining supplies and materials for production, for instance, factory managers must deal with the ministries that control those supplies, rather than with the factories that produce them. If those ministries miscalculate the amount of coal or iron or magnesium that will be required by the steel industry, some steel factories are not going to get what they need. And this is often the case.

To anticipate such a diversity of needs and production schedules, the ministries require an almost unimaginably large amount of factual information. Ministry officials base their decisions on all the information they can get from the factories, but in practice neither the quantity nor quality of information moving up the chain of command is sufficient to guarantee correct decisions. Indeed, much of the information is deliberately falsified, for reasons we shall look into shortly.

A second major problem with economic management is a tendency toward *imbalance* in the development of the economy. For the national plan to work, all sectors must fulfill their production quotas on time. To the extent that vital sectors fall short of their quotas, bottlenecks develop that can shut down production lines all over the country. Sometimes new industries are opened in territories where no provision has been made for adequate transportation of products to markets. Cattle herds are increased while construction of barns to house them lags badly. A speed-up of dock loading and handling of goods is ordered, but the production of forklift trucks and conveyor belts languishes.

Sometimes whole industries fail to develop, leaving a segment of the economy in a backward state for decades. In the 1950s, for example, the progress of agricultural development was seriously hindered by the failure of planners to anticipate the importance of an advanced chemical fertilizer industry. No ministry was specifically charged to develop the industry, and ministries normally do not volunteer to take on additional responsibilities. In more recent times, the slow development of computer technology and equipment has greatly handicapped Soviet management and planning agencies.

This independence of ministries from each other produces the third major problem with economic management: the *competitiveness* of individual ministries. Each ministry must meets its annual production quota by ensuring that the factories or farms under its jurisdiction meet their quotas. It is of little importance to a given minister whether another minister meets his planning goals, for each official's salary and career advancement depend only on his own performance. It is true that the Council of Ministers has overall responsibility for economic development, but the council does not exercise operational control to ensure the balanced development of all sectors of the economy. This leaves each ministry relatively free to carry out its individual responsibilities without the burden of integrating its work with that of other ministries.

One consequence of this is a widespread duplication of production facilities. Given the perennial shortages of products and delays in delivery from factories outside their jurisdiction, virtually all ministries set up facilities for producing materials, machines, and so on that are officially the responsibility of some other ministry. None of this extra production is authorized by Gosplan or Gossnab, of course, but without it many ministries would find it impossible to fulfill their production quotas.

The inefficiency and costliness of such practices are obvious, as in this hypothetical case. The Machine Tool Ministry (MTM) might set up a small factory to make metal casters needed in the production of its major products, realizing that the ministry responsible for producing casters has a record of slow deliveries. The MTM then ships its casters to its own machine tool factories all over the country, but refuses to supply casters to a factory in the next town, which is managed by a different ministry, a task for which MTM has not been budgeted. The trucks that carry the casters thousands of miles sometimes return empty because there is no advantage in hauling the goods of some other ministry.

Altogether, the amount of production capacity used in this inefficient way is huge, estimated by one Soviet writer at 18 percent of the total gross output of the economy.[7] Although Gossnab is formally responsible for providing the supplies and materials necessary for production of all kinds, the ministries continue to distribute some 25,000 products compared to only 7,500 for Gossnab.[8]

A costly waste of industrial byproducts results from the same logic. Industries are responsible for their principal products, not for side products that might be useful in other industries. The oil industry, for example, produces byproducts usable in petrochemical operations, but the oil ministry has nothing to gain by concerning itself with the use of its products by another ministry. A department head at Gosplan recently complained publicly that in Sverdlovsk Province six out of seven large mining and ore processing operations extract only iron from the ore. Other valuable minerals are simply discarded because the mines are only charged with the processing of iron.[9] According to another source, "40 percent of the Kola Peninsula's useful minerals are buried in waste banks; in this way intermediate products are turned into useless minerals that are sometimes even harmful to the environment."[10]

Other important defects that ail the Soviet economy can be understood more easily if one looks at the situation from the vantage point of individual factory managers. They are the focal point for all of the contradictory forces that keep the economy in a constant state of fermentation.

PROBLEMS AT THE ENTERPRISE LEVEL

The economic problems facing ministers and high Party leaders are difficult ones, but those officials at least are in a position to change the way things are done, to introduce new procedures, and to modify the administrative structure. On the level of the plant manager or farm director, however, the economic system exists as a given. Managers have no choice but to adapt to it if they wish to avoid trouble and advance their careers.

Because the economic system tends to work at cross-purposes, managers have to adapt to it in ways that often reduce productivity, diminish customer satisfaction, and cause violations of laws and regulations. The system tends to corrupt itself, so that even the most conscientious and public-spirited managers find themselves sometimes acting against the real economic needs of the country.

Successful industrial managers focus on four major concerns: obtaining a workable annual production plan from higher authorities; dealing with the various, often mutually incompatible, planning goals (production indicators) that are sent down by the ministry; keeping production lines running in order to fulfill output quotas; and maintaining a competent labor force. We shall examine each of these briefly to illustrate the dilemmas faced by plant managers almost daily as they attempt to satisfy ministry officials, to conceal unavoidable violations of laws and regulations, and to enhance (or at least not jeopardize) their own careers.

Obtaining a Manageable Plan

For most managers, each year's plan consists of the previous year's level of production plus a small increment to encourage greater effort and efficiency in the future. To ensure year-end bonuses for themselves and their workers, managers must meet production quotas. To do so, they negotiate with ministries to keep the quotas as low as possible, understating the true capacity of their factories in order to maintain a cushion against delays and down-time.

Once managers receive their quotas, they must take care to produce no fewer than the prescribed number of products, but also not many more. If they should have the misfortune to produce, say, 20 percent more than plans calls for, they would be in trouble in two ways: They would have revealed their surplus capacity to the ministry, and they would start next year with plans 20 percent higher than this year's. Therefore, discretion requires that a plant not be too successful in fulfilling the quota. No one can calculate how much output is lost in the USSR every year because of this disincentive to use total plant capacity.

Even when managers obtain reasonable annual plans, they may run into trouble during the year and be unable to fulfill the plans. In that case, they will approach the ministry for a "plan correction" (that is, reduction). Despite a Central Committee resolution in 1975 calling for an end to plan corrections, the practice is still widespread. It has the practical advantage both of saving the factory's bonus and of permitting the ministry to announce successful plan fulfillment, even though it is not the original plan. It also reduces somewhat the manager's incentive to meet the goals of the original plan.

Coping with the "Indicators"

The annual plan comes to the factory manager in the form of "production indicators." These are individual goals and quotas by which the ministry attempts to direct the factory's work, and there are potentially a large number of them. The most important deal with the *output of goods:* overall volume of production, the assortment of sizes, styles, and models of goods, and the proportion of goods that should receive the designation of "high quality."

Other indicators relate to the *efficiency* of the productive process. They set limits on various cost items such as raw materials, capital investment, and energy. They establish the number of workers to be employed and the average wage they are to be paid, as well as the profit margins expected for the goods produced. The final delivery of goods to customers is covered by such indicators as sales volume for the year and the proportion of delivery schedules to be met on time.

In practice it is virtually impossible for most managers to fulfill all twenty or so of the indicators that they most commonly receive. There are too many variables to deal with, too many unforeseen breakdowns, too many supply failures, too much bad weather and human error. For the government to deny a year-end bonus to a manager and his or her staff because of their failure to achieve every single indicator goal would be practically to eliminate bonuses altogether, and with them a large part of the earnings of factory personnel.

What happens, therefore, is that indicators become informally ranked in politically determined priorities. Managers are held responsible for only those deemed most important by the current Party leadership, and they are rewarded even if other goals are not met. In the Stalinist era, sheer volume of production dominated all other indicators because of shortages in every category. By the 1960s, standards of quality, product diversity, and technological sophistication had come to play a much more prominent role in production. In the 1970s, profits became an important indicator, while in the 1980s the principal indicators have been labor productivity, the proportion of output that earns a "top quality" rating from the State Standards Committee, and the percentage of delivery contracts that are fulfilled on time.[11]

Above all of these indicators remains one of overwhelming importance: the volume of goods produced. Despite thirty years of complaint and criticism, volume indicators "continue to be the mandatory indicators that are used to evaluate performance."[12] It is no longer the only important goal, but managers who continuously achieve their volume goal will rarely get into trouble over other failures. The political task for managers is to interpret the priorities of higher authorities and to focus on those indicators that seem most pressing.

The current set of priorities is supported by a sliding scale of penalties for nonperformance. Failure to meet the volume indicator may result in no bonus at all, unless the manager can finagle a last-minute plan correction. But if the wage fund maximum is exceeded, bonuses are only cut in half until the deficit is made up. Exceeding the energy quota or failing to conduct adequate machine maintenance costs managers even less. Thus, managers who decide to run night shifts throughout December in order to fulfill their annual volume indicators may violate both average wage norms and electrical energy limits yet still come out ahead when bonus time rolls around.

Some indicators can be safely ignored altogether. The indicator requiring reduction of costs resulting from the introduction of technological innovations, for example, is so far down the priority list that "every year almost all of the industrial ministries and departments fail to achieve their quotas."[13]

The fact is, so many instructions come down to managers from ministerial officials that many managers become almost immune to direction from above. In a recent survey in an economic journal, managerial attitudes were graphically illustrated:

After getting a decision from the ministry, one-third of the directors immediately begin carrying it out, while half of them await additional instructions and every fifth one experiences an inner need to find grounds for not carrying it out. Such is the retribution for the avalanche of directives.[14]

Aside from the problem of the number and priority of indicators, there is also a problem with the *nature* of an indicator. Volume indicators, for example, can be expressed in more than one way. A factory producing cloth may receive its quota calculated in linear feet or square feet, the width of the cloth, the weight of the material, or its unit value.

Competent managers naturally organize production to accommodate the indicator in the most efficient way. If the ministry orders a factory to produce, say, 10,000 feet of cloth, the manager will concentrate on narrow bolts rather than wide ones, as that requires fewer materials. Likewise, an indicator expressed in square yards rather than length tends to produce very lightweight cloth, perhaps of only one color, for the same reason.

If the ministry, to counter this tendency, orders production to be calculated by weight rather than by length or width, it will get a surplus of heavy, coarse materials and relatively few fine, thin fabrics. Or if it shifts to a plan expressed in terms of the ruble value of all products produced, or *val* (*valovaia produktsia*), the manager's tendency is to use very expensive materials, for increasing the cost of materials raises the *val* of each item. A clever manager (or minister) can show an increase in productivity without producing any more items merely by recording output by its ruble value rather than by its volume. This is what Soviet economists disparagingly call "growth without growth," and it is widespread in the Soviet system.

The oil-drilling business offers another example of that kind of "growth." Quotas for digging wells have long been expressed in terms of the number of meters of drilling completed. This has produced many very shallow wells, for deeper drilling is simply more time-consuming and difficult, and it adds nothing to the fulfillment of the annual quota, not to mention the year-end bonus. As *Pravda* reported,

There are geological expeditions in the Republic of Kazhakstan that have not discovered a valuable deposit for many years but are counted among the successful expeditions because they have fulfilled their assignment in terms of meters. The groups which conscientiously turn up deposits are often financial losers.[15]

Expressing the plan in terms of the *val* of the products resulted in the following situation at the V.I. Lenin Uralsk Fittings Plant in West Kazakhstan. The plant normally

> manufactures plumbing valves that are in short supply. At the same time, the plant is now producing hose valves as well, and producing them over and above its plan. Production capacity is thus being used for a purpose other than the one for which it was intended, just because the hose valves are more expensive. As a result, a line forms outside the director's office, since dozens of customers cannot get plumbing valves. Meanwhile, plant representatives are sending hose valves to every part of the country looking for markets.[16]

When asked what he could do about this situation, the author, who is Gossnab director for the entire Kazakh Republic, responded that he had levied a fine against the plant. But, he admitted, "it continues to produce the hose valves that nobody needs. The USSR Ministry of Chemical and Petroleum Machinery, to which it is subordinate, welcomes this initiative: It is a profitable one!"

The head of a Moscow construction firm put it even more succinctly to a *Pravda* reporter:

> We are, in fact, not "building," but "utilizing funds!" The higher our expenditures, the better the results for us. They would be best of all if we were to build houses out of solid gold. Laying the foundation alone would put us in the front ranks for a decade.[17]

It is tempting to suggest that the central planning agencies could surmount the whole problem of manipulating indicators by demanding compliance with *all* of the indicators they assign. Why not specify to the cloth factory the length, width, weight, value, colors, patterns, and styles of all products needed, rather than leaving most of those decisions up to the plant manager? The reason this cannot be done is twofold. First, this would amount to a ministry's simply taking over direct decision making at the factory level, a task for which the ministry has neither the staff nor the detailed knowledge of the factory's circumstances to carry out effectively.

More importantly, even if this could be done, it would be impossible for the ministry to know what varieties of cloth materials customers really want. As long as the customer is not the ultimate determinant of what is produced, any decision-making structure is bound to fall short in satisfying consumer needs.

Keeping the Lines Running

Given the extreme emphasis on meeting production quotas, the Soviet plant manager's primary concern is keeping the production and assembly lines running. Anything that threatens to shut down a line or a whole facility is a danger to the manager and must be resisted. Unfortunately, the effects of that resistance have serious negative consequences for other facets of the economy.

Among the most common causes of down-time is the failure of needed raw materials, components, and supplies to arrive on schedule and in the correct assortment. This leads managers to produce as many of the necessary components of production as possible in their own plants, whether authorized to do so or not. As a result, Soviet factories tend to be very large and comprehensive. The proportion of factories employing a thousand or more employees in the Soviet Union, for example, is double that in Western Europe.[18]

A second source of potential down-time is the need to repair or replace aging equipment used in production. For this purpose, Gosstroi budgets about one-third of the total capital construction budget each year. In practice, however, much of this money is diverted to the expansion of existing facilities and the building of new ones. This makes sense to factory managers, for their primary goal is keeping the lines running. To renovate an existing line means shutting it down, whereas to construct a new line, while the old line is still running, even if not very efficiently, increases the overall productive capacity of the plant.

It does not make sense, however, for the economy as a whole. It means that a great deal of aging equipment is not being maintained and repaired as it should, because new equipment is so readily available. It means also that as the old equipment gets older, the cost of maintaining it increases. Nationwide, for example, more than 27 percent of all metal-cutting machine tools are being used to repair machinery and equipment, rather than being used in production.[19] This is of little concern to the plant managers for managers are not charged for the metal-cutting machines, but for the nation it constitutes a substantial loss of productive capacity.

Another way for managers to keep the lines running is to warehouse extra machinery and supplies in case a breakdown or shortage occurs. Because the costs of production are far less important than the quantity of output, managers can do this at little cost to their factories. Nationally, this means that a large amount of new production equipment lies idle in warehouses, stashed away to ensure that factories fulfill their production quotas. The volume of such hoarding is necessarily high because up to 80 percent of new production machinery fails to qualify for the "Seal of Quality" and almost a third of it is substandard or obsolete to begin with.[20] To be sure of one good machine, a manager must order two or three.

Perhaps the most damaging consequence of this emphasis on production is its depressing effect on innovation and modernization in the industrial sector. The development by a research institute of an improved production machine tends to be seen by factory managers as a threat to their bonuses, rather than a boost for production. The introduction of a new production machine would probably require shutting down the line for a period of time, retraining workers, and possibly reorganizing other stages of the production process.

Furthermore, managers know that with the new machines in place, the ministry will expect higher output. Yet they cannot even be certain that the new machines will work. On balance, managers are more likely to have a successful year if they reject the innovation altogether. One indication of the seriousness of this problem is the fact that in the past decade applications for new patents on inventions have dropped sharply in several of the most basic industries. Inventors, as *Pravda* reports, "are sometimes viewed not as champions of technological progress but as annoying hindrances in work and life."[21]

The Labor Problem

Until the late-1970s, the USSR had enjoyed a continuous labor surplus ever since the Revolution. But because labor costs have normally not been calculated among the "success indicators" that determine bonuses, managers have been free to hire more workers than they need, pay them the modest state wage, and not work them very hard. This satisfies the constitutional guarantee of a job for everyone able to work, and allows a work pattern of relaxed pace and little discipline.

For the manager, surplus workers provide a cushion against the frequent illness, absenteeism, and drunkenness that characterize so much of the Soviet labor scene. They also enable a manager to maintain a labor reserve for "sponsorship work" without interfering with the factory's output. Sponsorship work is involuntary work performed on state projects in addition to one's regular job. Urban workers are regularly sent "to work at vegetable depots, to tidy up urban areas and Young Pioneer camps, and to construction sites to finish up things that the construction workers were supposed to do themselves."[22] In recent years some 2 percent of all industrial personnel (about 800,000 workers) have been maintained at enterprises solely for this kind of work.

As long as there was an overall labor surplus the arrangement worked well enough. But when the surplus turned into a shortage in the 1970s, the economy felt the effects. Ineffective workers, who could be shunted aside in the past, now are needed on the production lines. The Party leadership has begun to emphasize the "intensification" of the economy as the principal goal, and this means for the workers harder work, fewer rest periods, better training, and stricter discipline.[23]

For plant managers, this creates a number of practical problems. They no longer have much choice in hiring workers but must take what they can get. Turnover rates have climbed to over 30 percent annually in some industries as workers find diminishing satisfaction in the new work rules.[24] Even to keep the workers they have, managers have had to find ways to raise wages beyond what is allowed by the state.

All of these problems contribute to the dilemma that has long faced the Soviet economy. On the one hand, the Party leadership has pressed hard for a continuous expansion of industrial capacity and productivity and has achieved considerable success. On the other hand, it has imposed a command and administrative structure on the economy that tends to minimize the ability of the economy to respond to that pressure. On the whole, the achievements of the Soviet economy have been surpassed by the emergence in recent years of serious deficiencies. Let us look briefly at both the achievements and the deficiencies before attempting to assess the most recent reform program of Mikhail Gorbachev.

How Successful Has the Soviet Economy Been?

How we evaluate the performance of the Soviet economy depends on the criteria we use. Should it be compared with a mature capitalist system like that of the United States, or with that of a developing nation such as Japan in the first half of this century or India since its independence? Should the basis for judgment be the size of the gross national product, the technological sophistication and efficiency of the production processes, the standard of living of the people, or some other criteria? Some would argue that it should not be judged on economic grounds at all, but on political criteria because economic systems primarily serve the political interests of a nation.

We can begin by asking how Soviet spokesmen themselves assess the success of their economic system. The answer is a mixed response, expressing pride in some remarkable achievements as well as disappointment and aggravation over obvious deficiencies.

The Achievements. There is no question that the leaders believe the Soviet Union deserves enormous credit for the achievements of her economic system since the October Revolution. From a state of economic and social backwardness, the Soviet Union has become an industrial giant, a military superpower, and a dominant source of economic support for a network of nations around the world. In the production of some essential industrial products, such as petroleum, steel, and railroad transport, the USSR has become the world's major producer. During the past three decades, Soviet national income has grown at a rate roughly twice that of the United States, as have the volume of production of industrial goods and agricultural products and the rate of increase in labor productivity.[25]

Furthermore, Soviet progress has been accomplished at the same time that a wide range of social benefits has been provided for the Soviet people. There is little involuntary unemployment (except in central Asia where special circumstances exist), as some sort of job is guaranteed to all citizens, including convicted criminals who are regularly used as part of the labor force. Housing takes about 5 percent of an average worker's current income, and government rents have not been raised since 1927. Education at all levels, medical care, day-care centers, and summer camps for most children are provided without direct cost to Soviet citizens. All these represent heavy financial burdens that have been absorbed into the economic life of the country.

The Contemporary Decline. Laudible as these achievements are, they are coming to be seen as glories of the past by many in Soviet society. What increasingly distresses current Soviet leaders is not the overall growth rate, which has not yet dropped to crisis levels, and has in fact been improving marginally in the mid-1980s. Their concern arises from the fact that the economy seems to be weakening while it continues to grow. Many of the indicators that reveal the health of the industrial sector have undergone an alarming decline in recent years. The capital-output ratio, for example, which measures the efficiency with which facilities, equipment, and machines are operating, has been declining for more than a decade.[26]

The growth of labor efficiency has also been disappointing in the past decade. From an increase of about 7 percent a year in the early 1970s, it has dropped to about half that in the early 1980s, and even lower in some areas of production such as transport and agriculture.[27] What increase has occurred has been largely offset in many industries by rising costs of machinery and wage increases.

Raw materials, especially those used for energy, pose additional problems. As older sources of iron ore, coal, and oil in the western USSR become depleted, new mines have had to be opened in western and central Siberia. Not only is this far more expensive, but the quality of the ore is much lower. As a result, the cost of a ton of iron ore has risen in ten years (1970–1980) from 61 to 102 rubles, a trend that is being duplicated in the coal and oil industries.[28]

This problem, too, might be overcome by shifting from fossil fuels to electrical and nuclear energy, as Western nations have done. But the electrical industry has languished in the past decade.[29] Nuclear energy was rapidly being developed in the early 1980s, but it may have suffered a serious setback because of the meltdown of the reactor core at Chernobyl in early 1986.

In the longer term, the supply of human labor is another serious concern. Because of declining birthrates among European Russians, the number of new workers entering the work force is dropping rapidly. During the 11th Five-Year Plan (1981–1985), only one-third as many persons entered the work force as in the previous five years. While the birthrate in the central Asian republics is quite high, this only slightly compensates for the decline in European Russia, for reasons to be discussed in Chapter 11.

If evidence of decline in the Soviet economy is easy to come by, convincing explanations for it are not. A habitual tendency exists among Soviet officials to defend the basic system while blaming incompetent managers, undisciplined workers, and irresolute Party officials. Western observers, on the other hand, tend to see more fundamental causes for the decline. The planned economy itself—the effort to run the economic life of 280 million people from the top—seems to demand greater wisdom, more effective control of human resources, and more command of immense quantities of statistical data than any set of officials can possibly acquire. It also seems to depress, rather than stimulate, the human creativity and initiative that a modern economy demands. Hence, they see production bottlenecks, wasted resources, dissatisfied consumers, and unmet planning quotas as the inevitable results of an unworkable system.

The issue is not wholly an economic one, of course. Often policy decisions that make no economic sense nevertheless satisfy important political or social needs and are fully justifiable on those grounds. For example, the long-term policy of providing bread and meat to Soviet citizens at a fraction of the cost of producing these commodities has a number of negative economic consequences, as we shall see below. But that is a result of Party policy, not a fault of the economic system.

Much of what we have said about the industrial sector of the economy applies as well to agriculture. The farm director faces many of the same difficulties as the factory manager, and the deficiencies in food production parallel those of industrial production. Yet there are special problems as well in Soviet agriculture that bear a closer assessment.

SOCIALIST AGRICULTURE: A CONTINUING DILEMMA

Administering the Farms

Food production in the Soviet Union is done in three organizational settings: *state farms (sovkhozy)*, *collective farms (kolkhozy)*, and *private plots* (which the Soviets prefer to call "personal auxiliary holdings" to avoid the suggestion that there is still private property in the means of production in the USSR). The private plots are a different form of food production, and these will be dealt with in the next chapter.

The two main forms of agriculture—state farms and collective farms—are continuously spoken of by Soviet authors as separate and distinctive. In fact, the distinctions are exclusively theoretical and historical; in practice, no significant differences exist. State farm workers are treated like industrial employees, receiving hourly wages as well as the normal vacation and pension benefits. In earlier years, collective farmers were saddled with the fiction that they exercised independent, collective control over management and shared equally in the profits of their farms. Their "independence" was largely a ruse for denying them the housing, health, vacation, and pension benefits granted to "workers" on *sovkhozy*. In the post-Stalin period, the status and benefits of state and collective farm workers have more or less equalized.[30]

Presently, about 27,000 collective farms and 22,000 state farms are in operation.[31] Collective farms average 16,000 acres in size, whereas state farms average over 43,000 acres. These vast enterprises, far larger than most farms in the United States, are managed by the ministries of agriculture on both the national and republic levels.

Traditionally, the farms have been more or less self-sufficient, each farm engaging in a wide range of activities so that its dependence on other farms or enterprises was minimized. The unreliability of production on farms and factories spurred this need for autarchy, as did the primitive road and rail network that made shipping of products in rural areas difficult.

Administratively, there has also been a long-standing division of agricultural activities among a number of ministries, making overall coordination of food production difficult. State and collective farms, for example, are subordinate to republic ministries of agriculture (except in the Ukraine where there is a separate ministry of *sovkhozy*), food-processing plants to the Ministry of the Food Industry, meat-packing plants to the Ministry of Meat and Dairy Industry, and transportation facilities to the Ministry of Transportation. As in industry, these ministries have traditionally had little incentive to cooperate for the good of the overall economy.

Achievements and Problems in Soviet Agriculture

In agriculture, as in industry, there is a record both of achievement and of disappointment. The achievements include an overall growth rate of agricultural output of well over 3 percent per year since the death of Stalin in 1953. With the population growing at only 1.4 percent per year, the quantity of food available to the population has grown significantly. The Soviet people are eating more meat, vegetables, and fruits and less potatoes and bread, an indication of significant qualitative improvement (although less so in rural areas than in the cities).[32]

On the other hand, the picture is a good deal bleaker when one looks more carefully at agricultural production. The *average* rate of increase in output since 1953 masks the fact that most of it occurred in the first few years of the period: nearly 5 percent a year in the 1950s, down to 3 percent in the 1960s, and less than 1 percent in the 1970s. Furthermore, most of that gain was due to opening up new land and investing more capital rather than to increased productivity per acre. In fact, the productivity of agriculture actually decreased during the 1970s.[33] More recently, the total acreage of land under cultivation has itself begun to diminish, largely due to erosion and the exhaustion of nutrients in the soil. From 1980 to 1984, the total cultivated area in the USSR diminished by over 12 million acres.[34] The loss to erosion alone may be as high as 3 million acres of cropland per year.[35]

Part of the reason for the agricultural problems no doubt lies in the unfavorable climate and terrain of much of the country. The length and severity of the winters, even in European Russia, have a considerable impact on productivity. But even Soviet experts recognize that the major problems with the farms are not natural or climatic.

The chief problem is the same as that with industry: an overconcentration on volume of output and a consequent neglect of many of the conditions that would optimize the use of that output. Because of this, much of the food produced by Soviet farms never reaches the consumer. The shortage of storage facilities, for example, is a chronic deficiency. *Izvestia* reported recently that cattle on most meat combines are kept in open pens winter and summer, causing a loss in slaughter weight of some 100,000 tons a year in the RSFSR alone.[36] Fodder for animals is usually stored in open stacks as well, resulting in losses of 40 to 45 percent in nutritive value and total annual losses of about one-third of the crop.[37] For fruits and vegetables, losses from spoilage range from 20 to 50 percent a year.[38] Potatoes, a major Soviet crop, are planted in acreage fourteen times as large as in the United States, yet the yield is only twice as great.[39]

Transporting edibles to market imposes another great burden. The road system is woefully inadequate, with many roads simply disappearing in the rainy system. Nationwide, only a tenth of the rural settlements are located on paved roads.[40] The hayfields destroyed owing to cars and trucks driving across them because of impassable roads are estimated to be some 10 to 15 percent of the total.[41] Deficiencies in rural electrification and mechanization also plague the agricultural sector.

Surprisingly, the reason for these shortcomings is not mainly a lack of funds. In the mid-1960s, Brezhnev's Politburo nearly tripled the investment in agriculture (to 27 percent of the total versus about 5 percent in the United States). Yet capital productivity declined precipitously over those years, and Soviet agriculture remains heavily labor-intensive, employing about 25 percent of the labor force (compared to 4.6 percent in the United States).[42]

The problem of manpower is equally serious. There has been a strong emigration, anywhere from 10 million to 15 million persons in the 1970s, out of the countryside and into towns and cities.[43] The main reason is the significantly better living conditions and higher incomes offered by urban areas. The result is that the contemporary rural population is increasingly composed of children and older persons, indicating a declining overall capacity for physical labor.

The government has made major strides in educating the rural citizens to work in the increasingly technological environment of modern farming. The proportion of the rural population with a secondary education (complete or incomplete) is today about as high as it is among urban residents.[44] Ironically, the effect of this educational leap has been the opposite of what the leadership had hoped. The more highly educated young rural males have been leaving for cities in even larger numbers, for education is the primary qualification for upward mobility in Soviet society. For example, of the 426,000 combine and tractor drivers who were trained in the RSFSR between 1976 and 1979, only about 50,000 have remained on the farms.[45] Most have found that their mechanical skills command considerably higher wages in urban industries.

To compensate for the manpower shortage, the government transports armies of urban residents to the countryside during harvest time for a month's labor. Since 1960, the number of such workers has doubled to over 15 million annually, half of them industrial workers and half white-collar employees.[46] In addition, some 11,000 foreign students were conscripted to construction projects and farms in the RSFSR in one year (1983).[47] All of this labor is untrained for agricultural tasks, of course. One Soviet study concluded that industrial workers are only about 25 percent as efficient at farm work as they are at their regular jobs.[48]

Recent Reform Efforts

Since 1982, a major reorganization has been underway in Soviet agriculture.[49] One of its objectives is to encourage farms to specialize in a particular crop or processing activity, and to contract with other enterprises for activities that are not economical to do on individual farms.

The farms themselves have also been pressed to form new "interfarm associations." These involve *kolkhozes* and *sovkhozes* subordinating themselves to a new management group, run by a manager appointed by the state and a board of directors composed of the heads of the farms involved. Under this arrangement, various services formerly provided by each farm for itself, such as repair services, construction, transportation, and so on, can be done more efficiently by the association as a whole.

The 1982 reform has only begun to be implemented at this point, so its potential success is difficult to evaluate. However, the potential obstacles to that success are numerous and familiar. The cost of establishing the new administrative structures will be huge, requiring an even higher proportion of the national budget than agriculture presently receives. The 12th Five-Year Plan (1986–1990) provides for an increase, but most of the plans detailing the 1982 reform are conspicuously silent about long-term costs.

In addition, few real incentives exist for individual farm chairmen to welcome the amalgamation of their farms with others. It may mean a reduction in their personal authority with no guarantee of additional benefits to compensate for the loss.

Finally, there exist the usual administrative obstacles as well. The formation of interfarm units crosses ministerial lines in ways that may well threaten the ministers' authority. It would be consistent with the reforms on the lower levels to amalgamate the ministries involved as well, yet this has not been proposed. In fact, as if to ensure against any real change in ministerial powers, the leadership group established to carry out the reform is composed entirely by executives of the ministries themselves. Yet without some adjustment on the top level, the amalgamation of farms and associations on lower levels seems unlikely to succeed. Once again, a "reform" appears to consist of attacking declining economic performance by assigning new powers to higher-level coordinating bodies and then placing those bodies under the existing ministerial structure.

THE GORBACHEV INITIATIVES

Any basic reform of the economic system confronts a major obstacle. For all of its deficiencies, the system as it now works serves some important interests of virtually every segment of the population. Under the system Stalin established, the Party leadership is able to set national economic priorities, and the ministerial elite gets to run the show and is rewarded with the privileges of power. Factory and farm managers are relieved of the pressure to produce high-quality goods, to make a profit, or to concern themselves about their customers. And workers have secure jobs despite acquired habits of indifference, inattention to schedules or standards, and a leisurely pace of work that more or less compensates for the deficiencies of their social status and their standard of living.

Consumers complain incessantly, of course, but the long gradual rise in the general standard of living that followed the Great Patriotic War has kept the level of exasperation within manageable limits. Some elements of the academic community and reformist types in the Party elite have found serious fault with the system, but they have never been able to mount a successful reform.

With Mikhail Gorbachev heading the Politburo, however, the tide may be turning in the direction of real change. In his dramatic presentation to the Central Committee on June 26–27, 1987, he demanded, and got, approval for a comprehensive package of reforms that, if implemented, would certainly transform the Soviet economy. The following week, the new "Draft Law on State Enterprises" was unanimously approved by the Supreme Soviet.

The reform program is to be implemented gradually over a period of several years. In that time some of the major foundations of the Stalinist economic system are to be "restructured" and "democratized." The heart of the reform lies in several fundamental propositions:

1. Centralized control by the ministries and planning agencies is to be sharply reduced; henceforth they are to be concerned with long-range strategic planning and direction of a few critical sectors of the economy. They are to cease exercising direct managerial control over factories and farms.
2. The state will gradually abolish the massive subsidies it has paid to keep consumer prices of basic goods at a minimum. Thus, the costs of food, housing, and transportation will rise to a point relatively close to their actual costs.
3. Gostsen will give up the authority to set retail and wholesale prices for most of the more than 200,000 products it now oversees; prices of most nonmilitary goods will be determined by negotiated contracts between firms and by the general laws of supply and demand.
4. Individual enterprises and farms are to gain sufficient independence from the ministries to make basic economic decisions on their own. Managers will have authority to make the important production decisions, to fire unproductive workers, to export and import materials and products, and even, in some cases, to establish joint enterprises with Western firms. They will also have to face the prospect of bankruptcy if they fail to operate profitably.
5. Small-scale family farming, based on greatly enlarged private plots, will be encouraged through the granting of lifetime leases on land presently used by collective and state farms. If widely adopted, this practice would mean, in the words of a prominent Soviet economist, that "in its traditional form the collective farm will hardly survive."[50]
6. To promote democratization, factory and farm managers will have to stand for election by their employees every five years, and multiple candidacies will be allowed.

The Party leadership argues that the advantages of the reform are obvious: a more efficient economy producing higher-quality goods, greater sensitivity to consumer demand, lower prices for nonbasic goods, and greater opportunity for anyone with a desire to raise his or her standard of living.

The potential risks in these reforms are also obvious and have stimulated broad public concern. The prospect of an end to subsidies for food, housing, and transportation means a dramatic rise in the prices of these goods and a consequent drop in the standard of living of millions of citizens. Widespread unemployment may result from the closing down of unprofitable plants and layoffs of unneeded workers. Those who remain on the job face stricter work regimens, closer supervision, and the possibility of layoffs or even plant closings. In all occupations, the end of wage-leveling and job security portend a new climate in which "pursuit of the ruble" becomes an approved social norm. This may leave a large underclass of low achievers whose lifestyles would suffer increasingly by comparison with those of higher achievers.

Gorbachev and his economic advisers have attempted to reassure the people that these negative consequences will not happen or that they will be effectively handled. Low-income people will be guaranteed basic housing and food supplies at subsidized prices. Workers who are deprived of jobs will receive three months' severance pay, extensive job retraining, and unemployment insurance benefits. Most importantly, the constitutional guarantee of a job for every citizen is to remain in force. The opportunity to increase one's family income, officials say, should not be a cause for alarm but an opportunity for self-advancement. In any case, incomes must still be "earned," as this term is rather narrowly defined in the Soviet context.

How reassuring these arguments are remains to be seen. In the short run, Gorbachev has little to offer the Soviet people in return for their support of the reform. There are no funds for a radical improvement in the standard of living; in fact, in 1985 and 1986, the proportion of the national income devoted to that purpose declined significantly. In any case, subsidizing a higher living standard would contradict the essense of the reform. From now on, Gorbachev is saying, income must be earned by hard work and positive results.

The proposed reform is a radical one by any standards, and many of the consequences cannot be accurately foreseen. In typical Russian and Soviet fashion, the reform is being imposed on Soviet society from the top down. It is not, in Gorbachev's mind, important whether it has public support at this point or not. He has repeatedly defined opponents of "restructuring" as laggards, obstructionists, and saboteurs. He intends to move forward regardless of the opposition.

The nature of that opposition has itself become a matter of public debate. Gorbachev's presentation of his major reform proposals to the Central Committee in early 1987 was, in his words, "a difficult matter." In an unusual admission of opposition within the Party, he revealed that he had had to postpone the Central Committee meeting three times because of an absence of full support for the reforms. On the whole, the economic reform program is a long way from achieving a broad popular or governmental consensus in its favor.

In addition to the planned economic system with which Gorbachev is struggling, there exists another economy, commonly known as the "second economy," with which he will also have to come to terms. This economy has developed over the years as a free market economy, and it satisfies many of the consumer demands for goods and services that go begging in the planned economy. Much of it is carried on illegally or in a gray area of semilegality, yet it has long been the most productive sector of the entire economy. The nature of the second economy and how the current leaders are attempting to handle the issues it raises are the subjects of the next chapter.

NOTES

1. *Pravda,* 26 and 27 June 1987, p. 1.
2. For an excellent discussion of Stalinist economics, see Timothy Dunmore, *The Stalinist Command Economy* (New York: St. Martin's Press, 1980), especially chapter 2.
3. For a full listing of ministries, state committees, and other governmental organs, see David Lane, *Soviet Economy and Society* (Oxford: Basil Blackwell, 1985), pp. 316–19.
4. *Gos* is short for *gosudarstvennie,* which means "state" in Russian.
5. The Soviet source for this figure is from 1975, cited by Alec Nove, *The Soviet Economic System* (London: George Allen and Unwin, 1977), p. 39.
6. See James R. Millar, *The ABCs of Soviet Socialism* (Urbana: University of Illinois Press, 1981), pp. 72ff.
7. Cited in Alice C. Gorlin, "The Power of Soviet Industrial Ministries in the 1980s," *Soviet Studies* XXXVII:3, July 1985, p. 354.
8. Soviet figures for 1981, cited by Gertrude E. Schroeder, "The Soviet Economy in the 1980's: Problems and Prospects," Part I, Papers submitted to the Joint Economic Committee of the United States Congress, (Washington, D.C.: U.S. Government Printing Office, 1982), p. 75.
9. B. Poletayev, in *Planovoye khozyaistvo,* December 1979, p. 60.
10. *Izvestia,* 6 May 1981, p. 2; trans. in *Current Digest of the Soviet Press,* XXXIII, 18, p. 7.
11. See Peter Rutland, *The Myth of the Plan* (London: Hutchinson, 1985), p. 122.
12. Iu. V. Kachanovskii, "Indicators and Their Functions," *Problems of Economics,* January 1986, p. 39.
13. *Ekonomicheskaya Gazeta,* No. 14., April 1984, p. 10.
14. Izvestia, 3 January 1986, p. 3; trans. in *Current Digest of the Soviet Press,* XXXVIII, No. 1, February 5, 1986, p. 22.
15. *Pravda,* 27 January 1978, p. 2; quoted in Marshall I. Goldman, *U.S.S.R. in Crisis* (New York: W.W. Norton & Co., 1983), pp. 38–39.
16. *Pravda,* 9 April 1984, p. 2; trans. in *Current Digest of the Soviet Press,* XXXVI, No. 14, May 2, 1984, p. 18.
17. *Pravda,* 30 June 1986, p. 2.
18. Goldman, *U.S.S.R. in Crisis* p. 37.
19. V. Kamaev, *Problems of Economics,* March 1986, p. 24.
20. V. Pokrovsky, *Ekonomicheskaya Gazeta,* No. 14, April 1984; trans. in *Current Digest of the Soviet Press,* June 6, 1984, p. 7.
21. *Pravda,* 7 January 1986; trans. in *Current Digest of the Soviet Press,* February 19, 1986, p. 23.
22. V. Kostakov, *Sovetskaya kultura,* February 1, 1986; trans. in *Current Digest of the Soviet Press,* February 19, 1986, p. 23.
23. For a thorough discussion of the "intensification" program, announced at the 26th Party Congress in 1981, see S.N. Abdullina, *Intensifikatsia Sotsialisticheskovo Proizvodstva* (Moscow: Izd. Kazanskovo Universiteta, 1985).
24. In fact, turnover rates in the USSR are about the same as in the United States, where it is not considered a significant problem. The rates for the two countries, however, are difficult to compare and, in any case, Soviet writers invariably refer to the turnover rate as a serious problem. For a brief analysis of the difficulty in comparing the two rates, see David E. Powell, "Labor Turnover in the Soviet Union," in Morris Bornstein, *The Soviet Economy, Continuity and Change* (Boulder, Colo: Westview Press, 1981), p. 116, n. 2.

25. These statements are based on Soviet statistics, but the conclusions, if not the specific percentages, are indisputable. It is true, of course, that the USSR started the post–World War II period at a much lower economic base than did the United States. See *Narodnoe Khozyaistvo SSSR za 60 let* (Moscow: Statistika, 1977), pp. 95–97.
26. Kamaev, *Problems of Economics,* p. 24.
27. *Narodnoye Khozyaistvo SSSR v 1984* (Moscow: Financy i Statistiki, 1985), p. 37.
28. Boris Rumer, "Structural Imbalance in the Soviet Economy," *Problems of Communism,* July-August 1984, p. 27.
29. Ibid.
30. The argument that there are no significant differences between *sovkhozes* and *kolkhozes* is made by Michael L. Wyzan, "The Kolkhoz and the Sovkhoz: Relative Performance as Measured by Productive Technology," in Robert C. Stuart, *The Soviet Rural Economy* (Totowa, N.J.: Rowman & Allanheld, 1983), pp. 173–98.
31. *Narodnoye Khozyaistvo,* 1984, p. 223.
32. See Gertrude Schroeder, "Rural Living Standards in the Soviet Union," in Stuart, *Soviet Rural Economy,* p. 246.
33. See James R. Millar, "The Prospects for Soviet Agriculture," in Bornstein, *Soviet Economy,* p. 280.
34. *Narodnoye Khozyiastvo,* 1984, p. 248.
35. *U.S. News and World Report,* October 11, 1982, p. 26.
36. *Izvestiia,* 8 October 1983, cited in John L. Scherer, *USSR: Facts and Figures Annual, Vol. 7* (Gulf Breeze, Fla: Academic International Press, 1984), p. 162.
37. John L. Scherer, (ed.) *USSR: Facts and Figures Annual* Vol. 7 (Gulf, Breeze, Fla: Academic International Press, 1983), p. 161–62.
38. *Literaturnaya Gazeta,* (30), 1983, p. 13; cited in Scherer, *USSR: Facts and Figures Annual,* Vol. 8, 1984, p. 163.
39. Scherer, Vol. 7 1983, p. 162, citing the *Washington Post's* report on a secret Soviet study of agriculture produced by Gosplan and thirty-eight economic ministries.
40. Schroeder, "Rural Living Standards," in Stuart, *Soviet Rural Economy,* p. 254.
41. Scherer, 1982, p. 330.
42. Millar, "Soviet Agriculture," in Bornstein, *Soviet Economy,* p. 281.
43. Estimates of the number of migrants to the cities vary widely. Soviet sources tend to publish lower numbers, Western sources higher numbers.
44. *Narodnoye Khozyaistvo,* 1984, p. 30.
45. *Der Spiegel,* March 15, 1982, p. 138; cited in Scherer, 1983, p. 163.
46. Ye. Manevich, "Ratsionalnoe ispolzovanie rabochei sily," *Voprosy Ekonomiki,* September 1981, p. 60; cited in Scherer, 1983, p. 162.
47. *Pravda,* 7 July 1983; cited in Scherer, 1984, 162.
48. Manevich, "Ratsionalnoe."
49. For analyses of the 1982 reform, see Valentin Litvin, "Agro-Industrial Complexes: Recent Structural Reform in the Rural Economy of the USSR," and Everett M. Jacobs, "Soviet Agricultural Management and Planning and the 1982 Administrative Reforms," both in Stuart, *Soviet Rural Economy,* pp. 258–72 and 273–95, respectively.
50. Nikolai Shmelev, writing in *Novy Mir* in June, 1987; quoted in the *Los Angeles Times,* 27 October 1987, p. 15.

CHAPTER 10
The Political Challenge of the Second Economy

The "second economy" exists in the Soviet Union because the first, or planned, economy has fallen far short of meeting the needs of the population. Although the average standard of living of the Soviet people has improved significantly in the past several decades, it continues to lag well behind even those of some of the East European Communist states. Many of the consumer goods that are provided by the planned economy are rejected by the public because of low quality and unattractive style and lack of modern design. This leaves many people with increasing amounts of unspent income. In 1960, for example, accumulated personal savings were only 20 percent of the total income of the people. By 1970, savings had grown to 40 percent and by 1982 to 70 percent of total income and almost 90 percent of all retail sales.[1]

Stimulated by this vast reserve of personal savings, the second—unplanned—economy has expanded in all directions, often in competition with the planned economy, more often filling needs that are simply neglected. The basis of the second economy is its independence from the ministerial bureaucracy and the planning agencies. Its goods and services are produced by individuals working on their own or in small groups. Products are sold either privately to individuals or in state-authorized free markets. Prices are set by the sellers rather than by the state, and much of the income is concealed from state tax agencies.

The chief value of the second economy to the Soviet population is that it is driven by consumer preferences. The design, production, pricing, and merchandising of goods in the unplanned economy rest squarely on relations between sellers and buyers. Profits are generated only by satisfying customer desires. Over the years, the unplanned economy has been a great success, limited only by the government's long-time resistance to its further expansion. This may be changing, however, in the Gorbachev era, as we shall see shortly.

The success of the second economy rests heavily on the economic plight of the Soviet consumer. The average woman spends nearly two hours a day shopping in state stores, in addition to holding down a full-time job. Because there are no newspaper ads announcing goods in stock, shoppers routinely tour groups of stores hoping to find what they are looking for. In practice, this means buying whatever is available, as it might not be there tomorrow, and standing in any line that has formed, even without knowing what the line is for. If she buys something she has no need for, she can always trade it for something a neighbor has bought under similar circumstances.

State stores almost always have basic foods in stock: dark bread, eggs, potatoes, vodka. Irregularly, they may have butter, milk, fruit, flour, or cabbage, and with a little luck one may find a decent piece of meat as well. More likely, the salesgirls and managers have gone through the supplies beforehand and withdrawn the best-quality items for their own use or for sale "under the counter" to friends.

In recent years, food shortages and rising production costs have resulted in substantial reductions in the quality of the food available. Milk was watered down in the 1970s to the point where only skimmed milk was available in many regions, allowing the government to claim to have doubled the production of milk. Wheat bread is increasingly stretched by the addition of cornmeal and chocolate products with soybeans. Where these economies are not possible, goods that become disadvantageous for factories to produce often simply disappear from the shelves, regardless of public demand.[2] In 1979, Brezhnev himself complained of shortages of "medicine, soap, detergents, toothbrushes and toothpaste, needles, thread, diapers, and other goods produced in light industry."[3]

The plight of the Soviet consumer is mainly the fault of the total economic system and its disinterest, or inability, to satisfy the needs of its people. But it is also the fault of a retail system that has developed its own brand of indifference to customers.

HOW THE RETAIL SYSTEM WORKS

As part of each national economic plan, Gosplan determines, through market research and past sales records, what quantity and variety of, say, cameras should be produced in the coming year. It assigns appropriate quotas to camera factories and designates the specific retail stores that are to be supplied by each factory. These stores enter into contracts with the factories for delivery of specified numbers and types of cameras according to a fixed delivery schedule. A store deposits the money for the cameras in a local branch of the Gosbank, which pays the factory when notified that the cameras have been delivered.

Legally, the store (or a trade association acting for a group of stores) has the right to inspect the goods received and to reject them if they fail to conform to specifications of the delivery contract or if the quality is unacceptable. On the other hand, where a factory manager believes that a store is "systematically" refusing to accept goods without good reason, the producer can demand payment in advance of shipment for a period of six months.[4] A State Arbitration Committee (Gosarbitrazh) exists to adjudicate conflicts between manufacturers and stores, and fines may be levied against either side for failure to comply with contracts.

In law, therefore, producers and retailers would seem to have equal power over the movement of goods, and Soviet writers frequently refer to such "equality."

In practice, however, producers clearly have the upper hand. Soviet writers estimate that some 50 percent of all delivery contracts are not fulfilled on time and about a quarter of the shipments to retail outlets contain an unauthorized mix of products in violation of their contracts.[5] Nevertheless, retail outlets regularly accept goods of low quality, inappropriate assortment, and unattractive styling. The legal remedies open to them to demand quality products from producers are seldom used.

The experience of the Radio and Sporting Goods Trade Association of the city of Penza illustrates the problem.[6] The association employs nearly 100 inspectors and merchandisers to check the quality of its stock. In the past few years, it has been faced with an increasing volume of deficient goods arriving from suppliers, mainly radios and television sets, rising from 6.7 percent of all goods in 1981 to 9 percent in 1982. About half of these goods were returned to manufacturers, while the rest were either repaired in the stores or sold "as is" at discounted prices.

The cost is high either way. The trade association has no budget for the purchase of packing cases and materials or for shipping costs for merchandise returned to the suppliers, an expense of over half a million rubles in one recent year. *Pravda* reported in 1983 that in the previous eighteen months trade associations in Leningrad had required more than 60,000 freight cars and containers to return defective goods to manufacturers.[7]

The association could, of course, challenge its suppliers through the formal arbitration process, but the process is a complicated one that could stretch into months and years before sanctions could be imposed. In addition, the association would have to pay an arbitration fee of 4 percent of the value of the disputed goods, for which it has no budgeted funds. If, in the end, it won the case and a fine were imposed on the producer, the amount of the fine would go not to the association but to the state treasury.

Furthermore, in a producer-dominated system, retailers who become troublemakers often find even fewer of their needs being met by manufacturers. Because retailers may not legally shop around for alternate suppliers, they have little leverage over their own suppliers. All things considered, suing a producer is usually not worth the trouble. In any case, in a society of chronic consumer shortages, retailers know they can sell most of what they receive, regardless of condition. Returning defective or unattractive goods to the factory risks the underfulfillment of their annual sales plan and with it their year-end bonuses. Passing such goods along to customers risks nothing.

The second economy, then, is the product of several conditions: the deficiency in the production of consumer goods, the inadequacy of the retail trade network, the surplus of spending money in the hands of the public, and a willingness of millions of Soviet citizens to engage in economic activities outside their regular job. The types of activities pursued in the second economy are varied and often highly creative.

OPERATING IN THE SECOND ECONOMY

The government's attitude toward the second economy has been one of grudging acceptance of some aspects of it combined with serious efforts to repress others. Much second-economy activity is illegal, yet even some of that is tolerated by officials. Planning agencies have no control over it, yet they include its output as part of the gross national product. This ambivalence is accounted for by one overriding fact: The second economy produces so much that is needed by the nation that to cut it off, even just the illegal part, would trigger serious problems, both economic and political. We shall see this ambivalence in each of the four major forms of the second economy described below.

Private Agricultural Plots

The most important element of the second economy is the network of small privately run farms, or plots, that produces about one-fourth of all Soviet agricultural products. This private agricultural sector has existed since the early days of the Revolution, alongside collective and state farms. Its principal products are meat, milk, eggs, potatoes, vegetables, and wool. Of the output, about three-quarters is consumed by the growers or used for livestock feed and seed, leaving the rest for sale at *kolkhoz* markets.[8]

These are legal enterprises both for peasants already employed by state farms and for urban residents who wish to cultivate small plots on the outskirts of cities. The land belongs to the state, but citizens pay no rent for its use. In all there are about 34 million small family plots, averaging slightly over half an acre each.

To Westerners, considerable mythology shrouds the private plots. The fact that they produce about one-quarter of all agricultural output on only 3 percent of the cultivated land leads many observers to see them as proof that private agriculture is more productive and efficient than collective agriculture. But that image is oversimplified. The fact is, the private plots are relatively inefficient, more costly than is generally assumed, and heavily supported by the collectivized sector of Soviet agriculture.

The inefficiency arises from the wide use of hand labor, owing to the chronic shortage of small farm machinery such as garden tractors, milking machines, and sprinkler systems. It is also increased by the widespread use of marginal labor, such as children and pensioners. Getting products to market is another serious problem. Most rural roads are unpaved and impassable during much of the year. Because there is only about one storage and processing point for every 6,000 private plots, the distances peasants need to travel over such roads pose a major difficulty.

The costs of private food production are often concealed by the fact that a great deal of financial and physical support is given by state and collective farms. These farms provide most of the fodder and grazing land for animals as well as irrigation water for private crops. One economist has calculated that if all state agricultural land used directly or indirectly to support private plots were included with the area of the plots themselves, the total would be about 20 percent of total arable land, rather than the 3 percent so often cited.[9] Furthermore, a sizable amount of the feed, tools, fertilizers, and so on needed for private plots is stolen from state farms by their own employees.

Despite these drawbacks, the private plots offer the state a number of benefits. They produce great quantities of dairy, meat, and vegetable products that keep the free *kolkhoz* markets supplied for most of the year. This relieves some pressure from the planned economy by satisfying an intense popular demand.

There are also disadvantages. Much of the time spent by farmers on their private plots is taken from their normal employment on the collective or state farms. The reason, of course, is that private farming can be highly profitable compared to collective farming. Because prices of goods at rural free markets are uncontrolled, peasants can sell their products for two to three times the state price. Compared to the 6 to 7 rubles ($8 to $9) a day earned by the average collective and state farmer,[10] a peasant who raises a single cow may get 700 rubles for it on the open market, equivalent to more than six months' wages. In one village, an *Izvestia* correspondent reported,

> One could not help marveling at the difference between the well-fed privately owned animals that lazily meandered through the streets of the village and the emaciated appearance of the collective farm's livestock. The village's inhabitants pilfered straw, hay, silage, mixed feeds—whatever they wanted—from the farm's fields and sheds.[11]

Peasants often travel long distances, sometimes by air, to city markets with a couple of bags of tomatoes or pears, or a pot of honey, which they can sell at a profit despite the costs of transportation. On the average, one-quarter to one-half of all peasant income derives from private plots rather than from their primary employers, the state and collective farms.

The Party leadership has long been ambivalent about the private plots. In periods when state and collective farms experience low yields, restrictions on private agriculture are eased in order to increase production. In 1977, and again in 1981, the government formally charged state and collective farm chairmen to encourage private agriculture in a number of ways. It offered peasant families loans for farm improvements and for buying livestock. It also authorized gifts of livestock to newlyweds, partly as a way of encouraging them to stay on the land.[12] The Gorbachev administration has intensified this encouragement of private farming.

Despite this attitude there remains sharp resistance to the private plot. Some officials favor it because of its essential contribution to the current "food program," while others oppose it because of its competition with, and effect on, the socialized sector of agriculture. There are also intangible and ideological objections that find frequent expression in the Soviet press. These focus on the impact of unplanned economic activity—"free enterprise"—on the people involved. As in the industrial sphere, strong opposition exists to the personal profits that are earned, even where they are legal. As one spokesman put it, profiting from private plots can "have an adverse effect on the formation of the Soviet person's psychology, develop a money grabbing attitude and engender speculation."[13]

Because of this attitude and the shortage of equipment and transportation, the share of private agricultural output in overall farm production has been declining steadily over the past two decades in virtually every category: meat and dairy products, vegetable crops, private herd inventories, total acreage cultivated, and so on.[14] Overall, the proportion of agricultural production done on private plots nationwide has fallen from 32.5 percent in 1965 to 25.3 percent in 1983.[15]

Autonomous Work Brigades

With the end of the winter freeze each year, a great exodus from the villages begins, as tens of thousands of men and women move out in brigades to work in the fields. When they first appeared in the late 1960s, the brigades were composed mostly of Koreans from the central Asian republics. More recently they have been formed by Russians, Ukrainians, and other nationalities, who are still popularly known as "Koreans."[16]

These workers leave the farms or factories where they normally work and hire out their labor to the highest bidder. Typically composed of eight to ten people, brigades sign contracts with farms to assist in all phases of food production and to handle construction projects. They work intensively, often ten or twelve hours a day, seven days a week, especially during harvest time. In comparison with the normal output of the farms for which they work, their productivity is enormous, often amounting to two to three times as much as is produced on the same fields by state or collective farms.

The advantage of the brigades to the farms is widely acknowledged. The Belogorsky State Farm in the Kirghiz Republic, for example, had failed to meet its vegetable quota for years. Contacted by a brigade, the farm agreed to lease seven acres of onion fields to the brigade, in exchange for 21 tons of onions, which would fulfill the farm's planned quota. The brigade actually produced 41 tons of onions on the seven acres, turned over the 21 tons to the farm, and sold the rest on the open market. The farm met its quota for the first time, and the brigade made a huge profit. Meanwhile, the collective farm's own peasants spent most of their time working their private plots, thus substantially increasing their own income.[17]

Needless to say, the independent brigade idea is strongly supported by many collective and state farm chairmen and peasants. It is also vehemently opposed by other officials, and even by ordinary citizens, for a variety of reasons. Opposition to the brigades reveals much about the attitudes of Soviet society toward the relationship between the individual and the social order.

Many officials object on the grounds that most brigade work involves illegal activities. Members do not have residency permits in the areas where they work, as temporary residency permits have been outlawed since 1976. Without permits, they are authorized to remain in an area no longer than a month and a half, a rule that is regularly violated. Furthermore, brigades normally hire housewives and pensioners as well as, in the words of one critic, "drunks and vagrants" who are paid five or six rubles a day and their dinner. This is viewed as an illegal exploitation of the labor of these people. To get around this opposition, brigade leaders resort to bribery of local officials on a broad scale. This, of course, intensifies official opposition to the brigades.

A second problem arises from the number of peasants who are drawn off the farms by the attraction of high incomes from brigade work. "Walk through some villages in the spring," one critic reported, "and you will see that every other house is shut up—whole families have gone off on seasonal work." To make up for the absent workers, students, factory workers, and pensioners are ordered into the fields to help with the harvests, despite their inexperience and the loss of their presence on their regular jobs or in school. In the Chechen-Inguisha area in 1984, 26,000 people left for seasonal work. Besieged by local farm chairman for additional labor, the local Party committee drafted 20,000 schoolchildren from the fifth grade up to help out with the vegetable harvest.[18]

Probably the most serious official objection arises from the sheer profitability of brigade work. There are no published statistics on such income and much of it is not declared, so its dimensions can only be guessed at. The head of the RSFSR Department for Combatting the Embezzlement of Socialist Property and Speculation recently made public photographs of a settlement near the Caspian Sea which showed "two-story, single-family houses with 10 to 15 rooms each, decorated with intricate wood carving and roofed with zinc." Pictures of another settlement nearby revealed "private palaces of over 5,000 square feet with swimming pools, wine cellars and garages. . . ." In all these cases, the homeowners turned out to be "a watchman, a driver, a retiree, an 'unemployed' person, a boiler man, and a machinery operator," none of whom earned more than 100 rubles or so a month. "It goes without saying," the writer concluded, "that for them an official confirmation of employment is only a way of waiting out the winter so that, come spring, they can fly off once again to lucrative lands."[19]

Perhaps these are exceptions, but even the possibility of living in such luxury causes waves of official indignation in the daily press. One police official in Stavropol angrily charged seasonal workers with a willingness to do anything for a pile of cash, including "being disciplined, not drinking, working from dawn to dusk, living in swinish conditions or suffering various and sundry deprivations."[20] A nurse from Gudermes wrote that the health of seasonal workers suffers greatly from the hard work. Many, she charged, "are hospitalized with pneumonia, kidney and stomach ailments, etc."[21]

Another writer unleashed her fury on the very appearance of such people. The seasonal workers, she wrote,

> are remarkably similar in appearance: black leather coat, jeans, imported boots, two or three diamond rings on the hand of each woman, and a gold ring for the

men. The total cost of such a human machine, which rushes past you with its motor whining, is 10,000 to 15,000 rubles, not including its house. The house is a special matter, the object of particular concern.[22]

Cooperative Associations

The formation of cooperative associations was one of the major objectives of the Russian Revolution. It offered a form of postcapitalist economic organization that eliminated bosses, shared profits equally, and restored the dignity of work to the participants. In theory, cooperative arrangements were to be voluntarily entered into by individuals, independent of higher control over operating decisions, and managed by their own elected leaders.

During the NEP period in the 1920s, *consumer cooperatives* were set up in cities as well as in the countryside and operated widely as supplements to state retail shops. *Producer cooperatives* were also established. These brought together groups of craftsmen, such as tailors, shoemakers, and cabinetmakers, as well as professionals such as doctors and lawyers. By the end of the 1920s, however, all consumer cooperatives except for the peasant-run food markets had been abolished. They were replaced by state-run retail outlets, although those operating in the countryside continued to be called "consumer cooperatives." Producers' cooperatives continued to exist, despite heavy taxation and very low priorities for resources, until 1960 when they too were largely abolished in favor of state-run associations.[23]

In recent years, the economic difficulties the country has fallen into have reinvigorated the cooperative as a way of supplementing the formally planned output of the economy. A growing number of voluntary cooperatives have been formed to provide services to members who are engaged in some form of individual enterprise. Fishermen, for example, or urban residents who grow fruits and vegetables on small plots of land, or workers who raise fur-bearing animals as a sideline, or groups of city residents who wish to build privately financed apartment complexes—all share common interests that can be served by cooperative economic activity.

Workers at the "Krasky Kut" State Poultry Breeding Plant at Saratov, southwest of Moscow on the Volga River, offer a typical example. They decided to organize a pig farm in their spare time, and to set up a cooperative to which they would all belong. They obtain a large portion of feed for the pigs from their own garbage and food scraps, so the operation is very economical. Each member of the cooperative contributes to the costs and is entitled, in return, to buy 2 pounds of pork a week for just one ruble, a tremendous bargain on a scarce food item. The rest of the pig production is sold by the cooperative for whatever it can get. All work on the farm is done by hired employees in facilities rented from the city or built out of the profits of the collective.

The advantages of such an operation, both for the workers involved and for the state, are considerable. The workers get a prime, scarce food product at a very low price, and the general public gets additional quantities of pork. The state benefits, in addition to the meat production, from the productive use of private funds that would otherwise lie idle or be channeled into less desirable or even illegal activities. It also benefits from the labor of pensioners, housewives, students, and partially disabled people who can put in a few hours in the cooperative enterprise even if they cannot hold down full-time jobs.

Despite these advantages, enterprises like this one are difficult to organize, often resisted by local authorities, and only weakly supported by the top leadership. Although the Politburo itself discussed the issue at length in early 1985 and ordered "that the appropriate measures be taken in order to accommodate people's needs as far as possible and to eliminate needless barriers,"[24] there has been no major improvement in the situation. In the Moscow region, for example, there is a large unmet desire for additional land needed to permit individuals to join existing agricultural cooperatives, despite the fact, as one scholar attests, that the Moscow region has some 300,000 hectares of open land that could be used for this purpose.[25]

The lack of official support means that individual growers have difficulty obtaining seed, fertilizer, and farm machinery and transporting the product to markets. As a result, much of the food produce is left to rot or ends up in the hands of speculators. In recent years, the number of livestock being raised on personal household plots has actually declined, despite a widespread shortage of meat products.[26]

Why the cooperative movement is so sluggish, despite clear benefits and top-level political support, illustrates an important fact about the Soviet political economy. For all of its objective advantages, the idea of consumer collectives rubs against the basic instincts of many planners and administrators. The products of such enterprises are, first of all, outside the national plan. There is no way of knowing how much meat or footwear or furniture will be produced so the effect on the consumer market is unsettling. And the more of these products that reach the market, the less people buy from state stores, which puts the ministries in charge of retail food sales in a bind in trying to fulfill their monthly sales plans.

Cooperatives also unsettle the labor market. Administrators suspect, with good reason, that many people take time off from regular jobs to work in these enterprises. On a national scale the man-hours lost to planned production are substantial. Financially, the cooperatives pose another problem. To expand them significantly would require a large shift of resources for materials, machinery, and transport from state enterprises to cooperatives. Because no ministry gets credit for the cooperatives' output, little incentive exists to divert resources to them.

On a more ideological level, the fact that private labor in the cooperatives can produce products that, in quantity and quality, are superior to much of what is available in state stores is a silent but forceful criticism of the entire economic system. Further, the profit structure involved in cooperatives means that the financial returns to individuals vary widely, depending on their energy and astuteness. This, as one academic worriedly put it, "sometimes leads to the uncontrolled redistribution of the population's earned income."[27]

The Service Industry

From the consumer's point of view, the deficiencies in the Soviet economy are nowhere more visible, and more irritating, than in the lack of services needed for day-to-day living: home repairs, laundry and cleaning, auto repairs, home nursing, and many others. There are official sources for all of these services, but attempting to use them often results in long delays and inefficient work.

For that reason, a large private-service industry has emerged. Some of the services are legal, performed by individuals outside of their normal jobs. One can hire a typist or translator, a tutor for the children, or a doctor to make a house call. Private tailoring and carpentry are legally available, as are minor repairs on housing. The rule is that income from providing such services must be reported for income tax purposes and the charges must be reasonable by official Soviet standards.

Private services in the medical field are widely available. In addition to government-funded free clinics, there are two other forms of medical treatment available to citizens: "polyclinics" that charge small fees for services, and private physicians who charge considerably more. Both are legal, but government health administrators are often accused of neglecting the polyclinics despite their popularity.

In Moscow, for example, there are twenty polyclinics that yield a million rubles a year in net profit, an income that is by government policy intended to be earmarked for improving the clinics. Yet the Chief Administration of Public Health allocates only 20 percent of the profits for that purpose. This despite the fact that the polyclinics are far more popular and crowded with patients than the free state clinics. Consequently, conditions and equipment at the polyclinics are criticized as obsolete and inadequate.

Ironically, the state plans to expand the volume of fee medical services by some 40 percent in the 1986–1990 period.[28] Unless a significant change occurs in the allocation of funds, it is likely that this expansion will fall far short of providing the people with the increased level of service that the plan should provide.

These legal "moonlighting" activities are, however, just the tip of the iceberg. By Soviet estimates, some 20 million individuals are engaged in an almost endless variety of service and retail activities, many of them illegal. Payment is unreported and normally involves rates far above the official scale, or bribes of money or commodities, or both. To get a broken window repaired within a few days frequently costs a sizable fee and a bottle of vodka as incentive. Foreign-language teachers charge high tutoring fees to families whose children are applying for university admission; government chauffeurs use state vehicles as private taxis and delivery trucks during off-duty hours; the driver of a truck transporting lumber for construction offers a few boards to a friend knowing they will never be missed.

Stemming the flood of services being performed illegally for high rates of pay has proved virtually impossible. Recognizing this, the Party leadership recently announced a dramatic reversal of its long-standing prohibition on many of these activities. On May 1, 1987, a new law went into effect that legalized individual production of retail goods and the performance of personal services to the general public.[29] An individual may now produce clothes, furniture, toys, household goods, and other items for sale at whatever price one can get. Personal services such as hairdressing, carpentry, photography, taxi service using private cars, and renting rooms to tourists have been legitimized and encouraged.

There are some important restrictions attached to the legislation, however. Many of the needs of the people that were previously satisfied illegally remain illegal even under the new law. And the scope of the new activities is intended to be modest. Thus, all such work is to be done in addition to one's regular job (although this requirement may be waived in some cases). No one may hire anyone except members of one's family, and all materials, tools, and supplies must be purchased from regular government outlets. There is also a fee, averaging 400 to 600 rubles a year, to be paid for a license to engage in individual business.[30]

Nevertheless, this is potentially an important change of direction for the Party leadership in dealing with the economic dilemma. There is a huge pent-up demand for the services and products that may flow from this now-legalized private sector. Whether the resources necessary to produce the goods will actually be made available is not certain. To what extent this private sector will compete with and undermine the planned sector is another problem. And whether it will significantly reduce the vast array of illegal economic activities—the gray and black markets— is still to be discovered.

The Gray and Black Markets

Among the illegal activities of individuals and groups there are some practical distinctions that are made by the government. Gray-market activities are condemned by officials and the police but are so widespread and small-scale that little effort is made to eliminate them. Dealing on the black market, however, is viewed as an intolerable violation of law and morality, for which prison sentences or even the death penalty may be imposed.

Gray-market activities occur widely in the retail goods trade where opportunities for illegal profits are almost limitless. Some examples: The manager of a fruit store declares a whole shipment of good grapes spoiled, then sells them for a premium price to regular customers; butchers short-weight their customers and take the best cuts of meat home; salesgirls hold choice goods under the counter for friends; a shop foreman arranges with his workcrew to turn out leather purses or sunglasses during part of their shift, the profits to be shared by all; distributors of locally made blue jeans sew in foreign labels and sell them to teenagers at exorbitant prices.

The government exhibits an ambivalent attitude toward these activities. On the one hand, the unofficial circulation of these goods and services somewhat relieves the pressure on the government to increase the supply of consumer goods. On the other hand, the activities are clearly illegal. Many of the materials and tools involved in these operations are stolen from state enterprises. Primitive inventory-control methods and discreet bribery, along with a general attitude that the materials are not owned by anyone, make such pilfering relatively easy and free of risk. And the more widely these activities go on, the less respect people have for the law and the easier it becomes to ignore it.

Because of this ambivalence, the punishment of such entrepreneurs varies with the circumstances and, often, with the judge and the police officials involved. A person may be fined or dismissed from his job, transferred to a lower-paying position, or removed from access to sources of gray-market goods. Persons active in the gray market are not considered criminals in the formal sense. The activities involve so many people that any attempt to incarcerate the wrongdoers would seriously diminish the national work force.[31]

Beyond these activities is a range of illegal acts for which one *can* be sent to prison or to a work camp or, in extreme cases, to the executioner. The black market deals in goods, legal or illegal, that are obtained through theft or clandestine purchase and resold for a substantial profit. The nature of the transaction may range from a single teenager getting 100 rubles for a pair of designer jeans he got from a tourist to a big-time drug dealer operating a network of pushers.

Markets for such goods exist everywhere. In the city of Krasnodar (as in many other cities), there is a park where young people gather every Sunday to do business in illegally acquired tapes and records. Most of them were brought in by tourists, Soviet sailors, and foreign students returning from vacation. They bring 15 to 100 rubles apiece, and business is very good. When officials finally organized a raid of the park, they confiscated 536 records, of which only a dozen were of Soviet manufacture. Most of the rest were recordings of Western rock groups for which there is an enormous demand in the Soviet Union.[32]

Even more elaborate schemes have been uncovered in recent years. In Ryazan Province in 1985, a man approached the head of the Shoemaking and Repair Association with a proposition. He wished to rent the facilities of the association's Konstantinovsky Workshop in exchange for a payment of 200 rubles a month to each of several administrators. With their agreement, he hired workers and began turning out some 400 pairs of shoes per line compared to the planned norm of sixty to seventy. These stylishly designed shoes were sold for premium prices at various outlets, bringing the entrepreneur over 87,000 rubles in the first ten months of operation.[33]

Konstantin Simis, a former trial lawyer and law professor in Moscow (since emigrated), claims that

> tens of thousands of these underground factories scattered throughout the country manufacture knitwear, shoes, sunglasses, recordings of Western popular music, handbags, and many other goods much in demand by customers.[34]

The essence of the black market is profiteering: the selling of goods not produced by the seller, or produced illegally, for prices well above state prices. As with the gray market, it feeds on shortages of consumer goods as well as the whims of taste and style that the Soviet economy is so ill-equipped to satisfy. It is promoted by certain characteristics of the socioeconomic system itself: a set of production indicators that make it unprofitable for a plant to produce more than a few styles of shoes, the government's refusal to import large quantities of foreign consumer goods, and an official mind-set that looks upon the accumulation of "luxuries" as contrary to the Communist ethic.

Not all of the items acquired on the black market are luxuries, however, by anyone's standard. The owner of a 10,000-ruble automobile who needs a new fanbelt or tire in order to drive the vehicle finds no such parts available and seeks them through illegal channels. A parent whose child contracts an infection for which the local clinics have no antibiotics is advised by her doctor where to obtain them on the black market.[35] These are needs that often cannot be satisfied through regular channels, so citizens find themselves forced to violate the law as well as to pay exorbitant prices.

The black market is only a part—the criminal part—of the second economy. The standard of living of the Soviet people is determined by their involvement in both economies, as well as in the system of "privilege" that pervades so much of Soviet life. Because raising the standard of living has for so long been the express policy of the Communist Party leadership, it is important to see how the leadership is addressing each of these factors.

THE STANDARD OF LIVING

The importance of the second economy in the Soviet standard of living makes it difficult to assess that standard accurately. Much of the distribution of goods and the income it generates is never reported in economic statistics. To compare the standard of living of one country to that of another is even more difficult, for economic needs and values vary widely from one culture to another. It is useful, however, to compare at least gross income figures in order to highlight the special features of the Soviet standard of living.

The average gross wage for a factory worker in the Soviet Union is about $213 a month, while his counterpart in the United States earns about $1,620.[36] In the case of the American worker, his employer typically withholds about one-quarter of his gross wage for federal and state income taxes, Social Security, pension contributions, health plans, union dues, and other deductions, whereas in the Soviet case only the income tax is withheld. In the USSR, this ranges from zero for the lowest paid employees ($80 a month) to 22 percent for those earning $500 a month. (Earnings over $575 a month are taxed at the rate of 65 percent.)[37] Thus, the actual take-home pay of the two workers is about $1,200 for the American and $200 for the Soviet, or a ratio of 6:1.

This is misleading, however, because the amount of money the two workers need to live comfortably varies greatly. In fact, the Soviet worker is more likely to end up with a surplus at the end of the month than is the American. There are several reasons for this. First, the American has to pay for a number of expensive items out of his salary that are provided free, or at very low cost, to the Soviet worker. These include housing (the maximum rent in the USSR is about $12 a month for any size apartment); medical care, including catastrophic illness (free); education (free at all levels, plus a government stipend for college and university students); transportation (a subway ride in Moscow still costs about a nickel); and vacations, for which the government maintains a large network of hotels, spas, and resorts provided for the use of Soviet citizens at nominal cost.

On the other hand, this is balanced by the fact that food costs Soviet citizens considerably more of their take-home income, typically 40 to 50 percent, than it does Americans.[38] Furthermore, many of the consumer items that Westerners consider ordinary necessities are viewed as luxuries in the Soviet Union and are priced accordingly by the government. These include such products as coffee, gasoline, automotive spare parts, leather apparel, tobacco products, candy, carpets, and, of course, automobiles, the cheapest of which sells for about what an average worker earns in two years.

There are concealed costs in the Soviet standard of living as well. Moving into a new apartment does not mean higher rent payments, but there are other costs. The quality of Soviet housing construction is so poor that a new tenant typically has to spend up to $1,500 repairing damaged walls and windows, completing the installation of plumbing and electrical outlets, and finishing floors and woodwork.[39] And these people are more fortunate than many others. Considering *urban* housing as a whole, Soviet statistics reveal that nearly one apartment in ten has no indoor water supply, two in ten have no bathroom, and three in ten have no hot water.[40]

Another concealed cost of living is inflation. Soviet spokesmen have always contended that inflation is a capitalist phenomenon and does not exist in the USSR.[41] The fact is, prices do rise in the Soviet Union, along with wages, but they rise in different ways and for different reasons from those in the United States. The simplest sort of price rise results from a government decree setting higher prices for specific goods. Often this is done in order to siphon off excess spending money that builds up in the population because of the shortage of consumer goods. There were, for example, steep increases in the prices of carpets, china, furniture, jewelry, leather apparel, and wines in 1981, and another hike on many of the same goods in 1983.

In addition, there are indirect and sometimes hidden price increases. The costs of necessities such as clothes and home appliances are sometimes raised with the explanation that newer models and advanced styles justify higher prices. Soviet citizens frequently complain that the "advances" are impossible to identify. In basic foodstuffs, higher costs have sometimes been passed along not through price increases but by reducing the quality of the products, as noted above.

The Soviet standard of living described so far is the minimum available to all Soviet citizens. The system also makes it possible for some people to live well above that minimum. This occurs under two circumstances: (1) when an individual or family has considerably higher income than the average worker, and (2) when an individual qualifies for social and economic privileges unavailable to ordinary citizens.

Money is an important determinant of the standard of living despite the social benefits provided to citizens and the subsidized retail prices on many goods. For those willing and able to pay for them, a wide range of special services and products are available. This is particularly evident in two areas: housing and medical care. The government permits individuals to build private apartments through cooperative associations as well as single-family houses. In the country-side, a majority of housing is privately owned, whereas in cities about one-quarter of all housing is private. The government provides up to 70 percent of the financing through twenty-five-year loans at nominal interest (0.5 percent per year).[42]

In comparison with rental housing, the cost of private housing is very expensive—about $170 per square yard of space, compared to an annual rate of under $2 per square yard for rental housing. Nevertheless, if one can afford it, private housing offers the security of ownership as well as an ultimate return on the investment and the right to leave it to one's children. Cooperative housing especially attracts people who are low on the priority lists for state housing, such as single people and childless couples.[43]

Medical care is free to all citizens, but the quality is widely acknowledged to be lamentably low. To satisfy demands for higher-quality care, the private clinics discussed above are permitted to operate and to set relatively high fees. There is also a wide range of other private services offered to those who can afford them, such as academic tutoring and music lessons, house remodeling, custom tailoring, and so on.

The number of people who earn higher than average incomes comprise a fairly large segment of the population. The average wage of about $200 a month is earned by semiskilled factory workers while skilled workers earn $300 to $350 a month. Among higher-level professionals, university professors earn over $500 a month, and more if they hold administrative posts or are members of one of the scientific academies. Junior officials in the Party Central Committee earn about the same, while *oblast* and republic first secretaries earn about $700 a month. General Secretary Gorbachev is reputed to earn over $1,000 a month.[44]

According to a former Soviet official, high political officials who are not on the Politburo earn even more than those who are. The Minister of Defense and the President of the Academy of Sciences earn $2,300 a month in salary alone.[45] The reason for this discrepancy is that the special privileges accorded to Politburo members make greater monetary incomes unnecessary. Thus, long-time foreign minister Andrei Gromyko's promotion to the Politburo in 1973 resulted in a cut in salary (from $1,700 to $900 a month) but a rise in his standard of living.[46]

These are base salaries, however. Party and government officials at the *oblast* level and above are believed to receive additional salary stipends of several varieties. Many receive "thirteenth month" supplements, an extra month's pay each year, which is colloquially known as "hospital" or "cure money." "Valuable officials" at the highest levels receive additional supplements either directly or through well-known subterfuges. Fictitious jobs may be found for wives or part-time extra jobs are provided for the officials. The awarding of academic degrees, often without the usual burden of study, entitles officials to additional income.

In terms of money incomes, not even these officials are the most highly paid Soviet citizens. As in Western countries, fame has its practical rewards. Movie stars, prima ballerinas, widely read authors, and outstanding scientists reap rewards that are often well above those of the highest political leaders. Andrei Sakharov, the physicist and political dissident, once donated over $100,000 to medical research, money he had accumulated through various awards and bonuses. At these levels of income, the standard of living can only be imagined, for it is never publicized in the USSR. But income in rubles, though important, is only a part of the matter. The other, and often more important, part is *privilege,* the enjoyment of perquisites based not on income but on the position one occupies in society.

PRIVILEGE

Privileges are enjoyed by the upper elements of all societies, but the ratio of wages to privilege in the makeup of a standard of living varies widely. In the market economies of the West, employees are compensated almost entirely in wages and salaries, either directly or indirectly through expense accounts or other supplements. They are free to do what they want with their income, and their standard of living is determined almost entirely by that income and the ways they choose to spend it.

In these societies, wages and salaries are steeply graduated but privileges are more or less equally distributed. People earn vastly different amounts of income, but restaurants, theaters, hotels, supermarkets, and department stores are open to all who can afford them. Any citizen with a coat and tie and $50 can eat in the best restaurant in town.

In societies based more heavily on privilege, such as the Soviet Union, the balance shifts the other way. The salary structure is relatively flatter, but access to privilege is sharply graduated. There are many limitations on what people can do with their income, and the amount of money someone earns is not as important a determinant of one's standard of living. The results of this condition are evident throughout Soviet society.

Shops and Restaurants

Everywhere in the Soviet Union there are shops of all kinds that are open to everyone. But there are also shops that are restricted to certain clienteles, offering goods that are not available in the public shops at prices often far below retail. At the highest level, that of the Party Central Committee and the Council of Ministers, special, closed shops, hidden from public view, offer officials and their families the most desirable of consumer items, including gourmet foods, scarce hardgoods, high-tech imports from Japan and the West, and books not available to the public. Shopping is often done by servants or aides, and home delivery of goods is always available.

Eating facilities are equally elegant. In the Central Committee building in Moscow there are three large dining rooms on separate floors, evidently for different classes of officials. Similar facilities have been identified at the Academy of Sciences on Lenin Prospect, the Supreme Court building, and elsewhere around Moscow.

Below the top level, there are hundreds of thousands of officials, scholars, managers, and the like who are served by stores and restaurants specific to their rank and position. Factories provide eating facilities for executives as well as workers, though executive dining rooms generally serve higher-quality food at lower prices. Educational institutes also offer such facilities.

Shopping is eased for these elite groups by a network of "tailors, hairdressers, launderers, cleaners, picture framers, and other retail outlets secretly serving a select clientele," according to an American journalist.[47] Even in stores open to the public, such as the massive GUM department store on Red Square, there are limited-access rooms where the elite can buy goods that are otherwise unavailable.

Groceries

Without special access to food supplies, the average Soviet housewife must endure the daily aggravation of long lines, short supplies, and unfriendly salespeople. Fortunately for many of them, the government makes a great deal of food available through places of work. In a typical office complex, for example, lists of foods, arranged in groups, are posted each week. Employees must order a complete group of items, which will include some desirable items and some that the retail system is having trouble disposing of. As a Western journalist reported, the weekly package at one office complex included

> one kilo of fresh beef, two cans of pressed meat (something like Spam), a length of Finnish sausage, one kilo of hamburger meat, and one kilo of frozen vegetables. . . . [When they arrived] the vegetables were poorly frozen and virtually inedible and the hamburger was turning green inside. But the beef and sausage were both good. Lyuba was happy: she had saved hours of lining up in the snow outside or inside a state shop.[48]

At higher levels of status, green hamburger is much less a problem. In general, the quality and quantity of goods increases, and prices decline, at each higher level of employment.

Medical Care

Like other public services, medical care is available to all and guaranteed by the Soviet Constitution. But also like other services, the quality of care depends on the status and resources of the patient. At the top is the Kremlin Clinic, serving the highest Party and government officials in accordance with a strict pecking order. One Western journalist was told that "the patients wore varied pajamas—stripes, no stipes, etc.—to delineate rank."[49]

The Kremlin Clinic is managed by the Fourth Department of the Ministry of Health, whose major responsibility is to provide high-quality health care for the Soviet elite. Every major city has its Fourth Department facility. According to Robert Kaiser, the Fourth Department publishes a book "which tells its employees exactly what sort of treatment officials at each level of the bureaucracy are entitled to, what kind of room, with what furnishings, and so forth."[50]

At lower levels of officialdom and for the general public there are free clinics and hospitals as well as polyclinics where patients pay fees in anticipation of receiving better care. Access to higher-quality services is especially important in the medical field because the normal level of Soviet health care is notoriously poor. Although there are more doctors and hospital beds per capita in the USSR than in the United States, most Soviet doctors are minimally trained and are paid about the same as skilled factory workers.[51]

In general hospitals and clinics, frequented by those without privileged access to more elegant facilities, standards of sanitation and sterilization are low, and basic equipment is not always available. It is reported that one-third of all Soviet hospitals lack facilities for blood transfusions, while bandages, syringes, thermometers, and other basic items are in short supply. In the city of Novosibirsk it was found that only 11 percent of the 215 standard medicines prescribed for specific illnesses are available.[52] In 1977, the Soviet Minister of Health, Boris Petrovsky, revealed that 75 percent of all Soviet X-ray film is uninterpretable because of its poor quality.[53]

In the free general clinics and hospitals, patients are often shown little sympathy for their discomfort and pain. The food is notoriously bad, forcing most patients to have meals brought from home. Complaints about the unavailability of clean sheets, bedpans, and other items abound in the Soviet press. Doctors and nurses rarely talk to patients about their conditions, keeping them ignorant even about life-threatening diseases. Anesthesia is used sparingly and postoperative care is often neglected. Dentists seldom use novocaine for normal work, saving it for extractions. Pregnant women receive little prenatal care until the last month and rarely have a choice of obstetricians.

For the services they do receive, patients have little choice but to indulge in an endless process of petty bribery. Recently, the newspaper *Izvestia* described the experience of "Citizen K," who was admitted to a hospital with acute appendicitis. Before leaving for the hospital, he stuffed his pockets with one-ruble notes. He used these to bribe the hospital staff to get him quickly to a bed, provide decent food, and ensure the necessary medical services. All went well until his money ran out, after which increasing delays occurred in his medication, food, and even bedpans.[54] For admission to highly regarded clinics or to engage a specialist for an operation, much larger bribes or relatively high privileged status are usually necessary.

The results of a medical establishment that has failed to modernize are evident in the health statistics of the Soviet people. Since 1970, the infant mortality rate in the USSR has risen alarmingly, a finding seemingly confirmed by the fact that the Ministry of Health ceased publishing that statistic a decade ago.[55] Diseases that have been virtually wiped out in Western countries, such as rickets, typhoid, and measles, are still serious threats to the health of Soviet children. Mortality rates for older people, and even for twenty- to forty four-year-old males, are high and still climbing, in contrast to rates in all other major industrialized countries.[56]

Even at its best, the quality of medical care is suspect. When the head of the Academy of Sciences, Mstislav Keldysh, required treatment for heart disease, he used an American specialist rather than Soviet physicians. Many Soviet doctors believe that even the Kremlin Clinic suffers from so high a level of professional conservatism and political timidity that the quality of care is not of the highest.[57]

The Importance of Scarcity

The economic basis for the whole system of privilege is scarcity, and it involves an almost endless variety of commodities that the Soviet people strive to attain: theater and concert tickets, books and magazine, medicines, access to foreign films, imports of all kinds, fashionable clothes, records and tapes, residence permits for cities, restaurant reservations, and on and on. Access to Western cultural events is especially prized. Performances by English rock groups, a concert by the New York Philharmonic, or the showing of a first-run American film trigger an intensive search for tickets among those who know how to work the system.

Those who control such prizes are in a position to enhance their own standard of living. They may distribute them to relatives and friends or to higher officials whom they wish to cultivate. Or they may exchange them for commodities held by others. A ticket to the Bolshoi Theater can usually be traded for a couple of choice steaks. A pharmacist who locates a source of scarce medicines may be able to ensure his family a continuous supply of fresh fruits and vegetables. Every store manager and salesgirl has access to the store's inventory before the shelves are stocked for sales to the public, which helps to explain the shortage of so many needed consumer products. As one citizen told David Willis,

> the people we Russians really love are the meat-counter assistants and all the others who can supply us with *defitsitnyi* (scarce) goods. If everything was plentiful, we might not love them. But nothing is plentiful, and oh, how we love them.[58]

The use of a commodity or a close relationship to secure a benefit is called *blat,* and it is one of the most highly developed practices in Soviet society. When the commodity is money, the action is simple bribery, which is called *vzyatka. Blat* and *vzyatka* are major factors in achieving a higher standard of living for Soviet citizens.

These practices have obvious disadvantages for Soviet society. They promote corruption and criminal activity, and they create a negative image of a privileged elite enjoying luxuries unavailable to ordinary workers. They tend to instill in the public mind the cynical view that the benefits of society are not distributed according to merit or equity but through influence and favoritism. With this view it is not surprising that the lack of incentive to do one's job conscientiously and creatively is a major national problem.

The system of privilege is known to be a source of irritation to ordinary Russians, and this sometimes is reflected in official publications. To quote a *Pravda* correspondent in 1986:

> We cannot close our eyes to the fact that party, state, trade union, economic, and even Komsomol leaders at times objectively deepen social inequality by taking advantage of every kind of special canteen, special store, special hospital, etc. . . . [Let] the leader receive higher pay, but in other matters there should be no privilege. The boss should go together with everyone else into an ordinary store and stand in line with the rest—then maybe these irritating lines would become shorter.[59]

On the other hand, the system of privilege offers real benefits to those who have access to it. At the top level, privilege allows a small elite to live on the grand scale while drawing relatively modest salaries. Much of that lifestyle is carried on out of view of the ordinary citizen and is never reported in the press. This protects the official from undesirable attention but also makes him heavily dependent on higher officials. Privileges that can be given privately can also be taken away privately, without recourse to courts or public accountability.

Furthermore, in an economy of shortages, distributing scarce goods on the basis of privilege rather than income allows the leadership to reward those whose services they value rather than those who merely accumulate wealth. A strict money economy would reward the corruption and illegal incomes that are so widespread in Soviet society.

On lower levels, lesser privileges are enjoyed, according to one Western estimate, by about one-quarter of the population.[60] This constitutes a large segment of the population who benefit from, and are dependent on, the system. In the long run, then, the system of privilege is an effective instrument of political control. Nevertheless, in the brief period in which Mikhail Gorbachev has been in power, there have been attacks on the excessive privileges of the elite and a significant move toward meeting the needs of the population through private enterprise. This may gradually increase the importance of income over status and generate new demands for pay raises on all levels. This too is potentially a troubling problem for the leadership.

Nevertheless, Gorbachev has publicly espoused the individual's right to increase his or her income as long as the person does it by honest labor. In the legalized sectors of the second economy, prices are to be set by negotiation between buyers and sellers. That this may result in some people actually becoming rich is a prospect that disturbs some officials and a segment of the general public. The direction of change in the economic system indicates, however, that this is a problem that the Party is clearly going to face in the near future.

NOTES

1. Data cited in Timothy J. Colton, *The Dilemma of Reform in the Soviet Union* rev. ed. (New York: Council on Foreign Relations, 1986), p. 51.
2. Fyodor I. Kushnirsky, "Inflation Soviet Style," *Problems of Communism*, January-February, 1984, pp. 49–50.
3. *Pravda*, 28 November 1979.
4. The operative law is the Statute on Consumer Goods Deliveries, enacted by the Supreme Soviet in July 1981. See M. Darbinian, "The Population's Demand and Ways of Satisfying It," *Problems of Economics*, March 1986, pp. 82–83.
5. See Darbinian, ibid., p. 87.
6. This example comes from Ia. Orlov, "The Role of Industry and Trade in Satisfying the Population's Demand," *Problems of Economics*, April 1986, pp. 53–54.
7. Cited in John L. Scherer, ed., *USSR: Facts and Figures Annual*, Vol. 8, (Gulf Breeze, Fla: Academic International Press, 1984), p. 131.
8. See Ann Lane, "USSR: Private Agriculture on Center Stage," in *Soviet Economy in the 1980's: Problems and Prospects*, Part 2, Joint Economic Committee, U.S. Congress, 1982, p. 25 note 4.
9. Lane, ibid., p. 28.
10. The average daily income, in 1984, of *kolkhozniks* was 6.63 rubles, and of *sovkhozniks*, 7.71 rubles. See *Narodnoe Khozaistvo SSSR v 1984* (Moscow: Financy i Statistika, 1985), pp. 294, 304.
11. *Izvestia*, 9 June 1985, p. 3; trans. in *Current Digest of the Soviet Press* July 10, 1985, p. 4.
12. The new decree is discussed at length in Lane, "USSR," pp. 29–39.
13. V. Mazur, in *Kommunist*, No. 5, 1981, cited in Lane, "USSR," p. 39.
14. For statistics on these changes, see ibid., pp. 25–29.
15. Alexei Dumov, "Personal Subsidiary Plots and the USSR Economy," *Soviet Panorama*, September 23, 1985; trans. in *Reprints from the Soviet Press*, October 15, 1985, p. 61.
16. They are also known by many other names, including, commonly, *shabashniki*. See Patrick Murphy, "Soviet *Shabashniki*: Material Incentives at Work," *Problems of Communism*, November-December 1985, pp. 48–57.
17. *Izvestia*, 16 June 1985, p. 2.
18. *Pravda*, 13 June 1985, p. 3; trans. in *Current Digest of the Soviet Press*, July 10, 1985, p. 4.
19. Ibid., p. 5.
20. *Izvestia*, 16 June 1985, p. 2.
21. Ibid.
22. Ibid.
23. In 1960, it was reported that 3 percent of the Soviet gross national product was produced by producer cooperatives, but in subsequent years no such data were published. See

Raymond Hutchings, *Soviet Economic Development,* 2d ed. (New York: New York University Press, 1982), p. 103, note 17.

24. V. Marianovskii, "Cooperative Forms of Management Under Socialism," *Problems of Economics,* May 1986, p. 45.
25. Ibid.
26. Ibid., p. 48, note 14.
27. Ibid., p. 45.
28. *Izvestiia,* 21 January 1986, p. 3.
29. The law was passed by the USSR Supreme Soviet on November 20, 1986. See *Pravda,* 21 November 1986, p. 1, for the full text.
30. For a discussion of the implementation of this law, see *Izvestia,* 30 April 1987, p. 6.
31. For a detailed presentation of the normal punishments for a wide range of semilegal and illegal activities, see F.J.M. Feldbrugge, "Government and Shadow Economy in the Soviet Union," *Soviet Studies,* XXXVI:4, October 1984, pp. 533–40.
32. *Komsomolskaya Pravda,* 7 April 1984, p. 2.
33. *Izvestiia,* 13 February 1986, p. 3.
34. Konstantin Simis, *USSR, The Corrupt Society* (New York: Simon & Schuster, 1982), p. 147.
35. David Shipler, *Russia, Broken Idols, Solemn Dreams* (New York: Penguin, 1983), pp. 223–24.
36. The Soviet figure is 185 rubles, cited in *Narodnoe Khoziastvo SSSR v 1984,* p. 428. The American figure is from the U.S. Bureau of Labor Statistics, cited in *The World Almanac, 1986* (New York: Newspaper Enterprise Association, 1985), p. 117. Conversion of rubles to dollars is at the 1986 rate of exchange of 1.15 U.S. dollars to 1 ruble.
37. These figures appear in new tax legislation approved by the Supreme Soviet in April 1987. See *Vedomosti Verkhovnovo Soveta SSSR,* No. 17, April 29, 1987.
38. Soviet sources consistently state that by the mid-1980s, Soviet families were spending no more than 30 percent of their income on food. This is considered by some Western analysts as a substantial understatement. For an analysis, see Kushnirsky, "Inflation Soviet Style," p. 49, note 4.
39. See Scherer, *USSR: Facts and Figures,* Vol. 10, 1986, p. 276.
40. Although these figures seem high, they are only about half as high as they were as recently as 1970, so considerable progress has been made in recent years. See *Narodnoe Khoziastvo,* 1983, p. 427.
41. For an example, see Alexander Birman, "Prices and Demand," *Soviet Life,* October 1979, p. 19.
42. Data are in Scherer, *USSR: Facts and Figures,* 1986, p. 276.
43. See Basile Kerblay, *Modern Soviet Society* (New York: Pantheon, 1977), p. 70.
44. Mervyn Matthews, *Privilege in the Soviet Union,* (London: George Allen and Unwin, 1978), p. 23.
45. See Simis, *The Corrupt Society,* p. 39.
46. Ibid., p. 47.
47. Hedrick Smith, *The Russians* (New York: The New York Times Book Co. 1976), p. 27.
48. David K. Willis, *Klass: How Russians Really Live* (New York: St. Martin's Press, 1985), p. 22–23.
49. Shipler, *Broken Idols,* p. 222.
50. Robert Kaiser, *Russia* (New York: Atheneum, 1976), p. 177.
51. In 1985, the Council of Ministers approved 30 to 40 percent bonuses for certain types of medical personnel, but the general salary scale remains relatively low.

52. See Richard Schifter, "US-Soviet Quality of Life: A Comparison," *Current Policy* No. 713 (1985), United States Department of State, p. 5.
53. William A. Knaus, *Inside Russian Medicine* (Boston: Beacon Press, 1981), p. 106.
54. Ibid., p. 329–30.
55. It has recently been announced that such data will again be published, in line with Gorbachev's new policy of *glasnost* (openness).
56. See the comments of Murray Fesbach in Cullen Murphy's "Watching the Russians," *The Atlantic Monthly,* February 1983, pp. 34–52.
57. Shipler, *Broken Idols,* p. 221.
58. Willis, *How Russians Really Live,* p. 94.
59. *Pravda,* 13 February 1986.
60. Willis, *How Russians Really Live,* p. 311, note 3.

PART 4

Guiding Public Behavior

To Marxist idealists at the turn of the twentieth century, the goal of a socialist revolution was not primarily the seizing of power from the capitalist class. It was not about power at all, but about the human condition and its improvement. Indeed, it was generally assumed that political power and the state that exercised it would disappear once the proletariat had disposed of the former exploiting classes. Simultaneously, the working classes would undergo a renaissance of creativity, social cooperativeness, and brotherly love.

But Lenin was no idealist. As he foresaw, and as has been abundantly demonstrated in all Communist countries since, the end of bourgeois rule does not necessarily transform the human personality. That would require a long process of reeducation and social change. In the meantime, there were pressing demands on the new state: industrializing the country, expanding agricultural output, modernizing the military forces, and educating a largely peasant population. At the speed at which Stalin was determined to move, these tasks required sacrifices almost beyond imagination on the part of ordinary citizens who, because they had no grasp of the deeper theoretical justifications for this new task, were understandably reluctant to make the sacrifices.

Under Stalin's rule, terror became a primary instrument for promoting this transformation. Since Stalin's death, however, the Communist Party has relied far more heavily on other means to shape the minds of the Soviet people. These involve a broad array of state agencies: the educational system, the communications media, the law and the courts, and the state security forces. How public behavior is conditioned and with what success among ordinary citizens is the subject of the present chapter. We shall examine both the techniques of behavioral training and its successes and failures in two critical social areas: ethnic minority populations and the younger generation. In the next chapter we shall consider the coercive elements of state control as manifested in the system of laws and the courts and in the role of the police.

CHAPTER 11
Creating a "New Soviet Person"

Ever since the Russian Revolution, an image of the ideal citizen has been a constant part of the upbringing of Soviet children as well as the conditioning of adults. Curiously, there has never been a firm consensus on the precise qualities of the "new Soviet person." The Communist Party Program offers one definition, but many authors have drawn up their own lists. One scholar offered 140 groups of human qualities derived from 1,300 individual characteristics as a description of the ideal citizen.[1]

The "new Soviet person" is usually described in terms of three types of characteristics. First, there are basic *values* toward the country and its political system. Some of the approved values would be acceptable in any society: patriotism, respect for the family and the individual, a sense of public duty, intolerance of racial and ethnic prejudices, and so on. Others are more narrowly tied to Communist social systems: devotion to the ideal of communism, fraternal solidarity with the international working class, and a commitment to collectivism.[2]

Secondly, the "new Soviet person" is expected to have a set of *beliefs* about the real world that are consistent with the official view. These "images of reality" are produced by all media of communications, written and oral, and are officially declared to be true. They focus on Soviet society as well as on capitalist, Western societies. For both, the attempt is to create an ideal image, positive for Soviet society, negative for the West. Soviet citizens are continually assured that the Soviet standard of living is higher than that in the West, that the USSR is a true democracy, that there is no ethnic disharmony or anti-Semitism in the USSR, and that the Soviet people have no interest in religious beliefs. The negative ideal describes the West as suffering from endemic poverty and unemployment, racial tensions, and class conflict. To the extent that the Soviet system has problems, they tend to be described as temporary and uncharacteristic of true socialism.

The third set of characteristics expected of the "new Soviet person" is a *behavioral* one. He or she is expected not only to adopt official values and beliefs as personal commitments, but also to make a positive contribution to the development of the society and the state. This requires that people work conscientiously at their jobs, obey the laws, accept Party policies and endeavor to carry them out, conduct their private lives in accordance with accepted standards of behavior, and exhibit unrelenting hostility toward those who would harm Soviet society.

The "new Soviet person" is not merely an ideological abstraction. In many practical ways, the Party relies on these qualities to advance its policies and to mobilize mass support for its leadership. The latest Five-Year Plan, for example, relies heavily on increased labor productivity to meet its goals, and this is to come primarily from a higher level of dedication and commitment from the workers to fulfilling the plan. Much of the "restructuring" that General Secretary Gorbachev has called for involves changes in attitude and behavior on the part of the working people.

The enormous effort put forth by the state to develop these three sets of characteristics in the masses is, therefore, of great practical importance. It is not an effort to create merely quiescent, pliable citizens who cause no trouble. On the contrary, the ideal citizen shows initiative and creativity in all activities and displays little patience with the laggards and drones of society.

To appreciate the thoroughness with which the official values are propagated in Soviet society we need to examine each of the major socializing institutions: the family, the school system, the propaganda agencies, the press, and the agencies concerned with literature and the arts. Each has its particular role to play in shaping the Soviet mind, and each has its limitations. These institutions are not, of course, unique to the Soviet system, but they are used there with an intensity and a political content far greater than in Western societies.

THE FAMILY

In much of the prerevolutionary writings of Soviet Marxists, the family was earmarked for the "dustbin of history." It was seen as a haven for class distinctions, religious training, discrimination against women, and parental oppression of the younger generation. With the Revolution, it was argued, the family's functions, especially child-rearing and property-holding, would pass to the social collective and be done in accordance with common, socialist values.

By the end of the 1920s, however, the conservative social orientation of Stalinism had reversed this position, restoring the family to a respectable place in the new socialist society. Since then, the family has remained a basic unit of "socialist construction." In the 1970s, the financial integrity of the family was reinforced, as inheritance laws ensured the protection of family wealth and property.

In recent years, however, the Soviet family has suffered the same kinds of inner weakening as have families in Western societies. Urban divorce rates are rising to two out of every three marriages,[3] the values of young people are shaped increasingly in the streets and courtyards where parental control is absent, and young married couples wait anxiously for private housing away from the family home. With both parents working in most families, children are raised by grandparents or relatives, or attend state nursery schools. However, only about one-third of Soviet children six years old and under are enrolled in preschool institutions, due both to the cost involved and to the lack of such schools in many areas.[4]

The family exists as an institution of relatively low penetration by the state and its propaganda. While Soviet adults tend to accept the dominant values of the society, the special, intimate environment of the family makes it easy for parents to pass on their personal values to their children even where those values contradict those of the state. Interest in religious beliefs and ceremonies, for example, appears to be cultivated primarily in the home. Motivation for higher education, likewise, is largely a product of home environment, which partly accounts for the high proportion of university students who come from upper-income families, contrary to Party policy. Thus, the family operates as a relatively independent ally of the Party, transmitting values that are generally, but not in all respects, consistent with those espoused by the Party.

THE EDUCATIONAL SYSTEM

In most societies, schools reflect the most direct effort by government to turn children into loyal and useful citizens. In the Soviet Union, there has been an unceasing attempt over the years to extend educational opportunities to every sector of the population and to every age group. A primary purpose of that policy has been to elevate the political consciousness of the Soviet people. As Leonid Brezhnev stated,

> The Soviet school does not merely train educated people. It also has the responsibility for seeing to it that the people leaving its walls are politically intelligent, ideologically convinced champions of the communist cause. The school has never stood and cannot stand aside from politics, from the class struggle. The communist world view must be an integral part of the Soviet man.[5]

The Classroom and Politics

In the first four years of schooling (grades K–3), there is no overt political training, but children are given a foundation for the desired "Communist world outlook." They are introduced to Lenin and his family through stories, songs, and artworks. The Communist Party is portrayed as the basic guarantor of peace and progress, and the Party's special interest in young people is emphasized. Children are exposed to major political events, such as Party congresses and meetings of the Supreme Soviet, and participate in organized events celebrating these occasions.

In these early years, children are initiated into the "collective" way of life. They learn that each student is responsible to all others in the collective. If a child misbehaves or fails to do homework, say, he lets his collective down and is made to feel the disappointment and criticism of his classmates. Children interact in numerous collectives, each of which applies rules of behavior and standards of performance. These include, for example, the class at school and even the row in which they sit, the Little Oktobrist organization to which all youngsters belong, and the clubs or groups in which they participate after school.

In the upper grades (4–11), a "Communist world outlook" is promoted in more advanced forms. Normal subjects, such as mathematics, natural sciences, history, and literature, are oriented toward the achievements and advantages of socialist systems and the negative features of capitalist societies. Especially in history classes, which students take from the fourth grade through graduation, the world according to Marx, Lenin, and the current General Secretary is promulgated as the sole legitimate point of view. A major theme is the inevitable triumph of communism over capitalism and the steady progress of world history toward the goal.

Social science classes deal with the role of the Communist Party and the major political institutions, emphasizing the democratic nature of Soviet society. Science classes, especially biology, teach secondary students the impossibility of the existence of God and the harm to scientific social progress that comes from religious belief. "Religion obstructs the inculcation of hatred towards the exploiters and towards the enemies of the workers; by preaching universal love and forgiveness, it supports outmoded customs in the family and in life."[6]

Respect for the military is heavily emphasized at all grade levels. A special "peace lesson" is given to all students on the opening day of each new school year. Veterans in full uniform and bedecked with medals visit each classroom to talk about their experiences in the "Great Patriotic War." Soviet youths are taught that it was the heroic Soviet army that defeated the Germans and saved the world from fascism. The need for an effective defense of the motherland is emphasized along with the patriotic duty of every young man to serve in the armed forces. In recent years, stories of bravery and self-sacrifice in the Afghan war have begun to appear in the press and are discussed in the schools. Beginning in the ninth grade, boys and girls receive formal military training including the use of firearms.

At the upper grade levels, all students take courses in the history of the CPSU, Marxist-Leninist philosophy, political economy, and scientific communism. As a condition of graduation everyone takes a standard examination on these subjects.[7] Instructors in these courses are increasingly trained at "universities of Marxism-Leninism," which are parts of established higher schools.

Training for Work

The "new Soviet person" is expected to develop a love of productive labor and a useful vocational skill. From the earliest grades, schoolchildren are exposed to the world of work, both through classroom studies and through actual work experience. At the end of the ninth grade, young people are directed into one of two broad educational tracks for two years. One track leads to advanced technical training, where students prepare for such vocations as nursing, auto mechanics, carpentry, librarianship, and machine maintenance. The other leads to advanced general education studies in preparation for entry into colleges and higher institutes.

On the technical training track, students continue to receive some additional general education, but the emphasis is primarily on vocational skills. The path to higher education, and to the better jobs and incomes that accompany it, is almost exclusively through the second track: graduation from a general education school. For that reason, the pressures from parents and students to move into this track are intense.

Ample evidence shows that the tracking process exhibits a strong class bias in the Soviet Union. Children of middle-class, educated parents have a much better chance for avoiding vocational schools than do children of workers or peasants. One study of Leningrad youth revealed that of workers' children with average grades (3.5 on a 5-point scale) only 19 percent were directed to general education schools, whereas 77 percent of children of educated parents with average grades were so directed.[8]

A further consequence of the bias in favor of the college preparatory curriculum is the huge overenrollment of students in higher institutes and universities. These institutions regularly graduate far more "engineers" and other specialists than the country needs. In industry alone, over half of those trained as engineers are being used in other, often lesser, capacities.[9] Many applicants who fail to gain admission to higher schools enroll in night schools and correspondence courses in order to obtain the precious diploma.

In 1984, the government enacted a major educational reform whose objectives were to channel a far greater proportion of ninth-graders (up to 70 percent in contrast to the then current 30 percent) into vocational schools and to increase the practical work in factories and farms in which these students participate. Yet the resistance of parents to the change remains high. In the reform's third year, a prominent sociologist concluded that "so far it hasn't had any particular success, one must admit."[10]

Higher Education

On this level, there are two general types of institutions: universities and institutes. Universities offer a broad education in a wide variety of academic areas. Technical institutes, where three-fourths of the higher-education students are enrolled, provide professional curricula in such fields as engineering, law, medicine, foreign service, and education. Admission to these institutions is based mainly on secondary school grade averages and competitive examinations. In 1980, about 12 percent of the eighteen-year-old population entered full-time university study and another 20 percent enrolled on a part-time basis.[11]

Political education in the higher schools varies considerably with the discipline. Far more time is spent on it in the humanities and social sciences and in teacher-education programs than in the natural sciences. Nevertheless, all students must pass general examinations on Marxism-Leninism, the history of the CPSU, and dialectical and historical materialism prior to graduation. Higher-school students are expected to participate in ceremonies honoring veterans and other heroes, to present talks to workers and peasants on political subjects, and to be involved to some extent in the ideological training of lower-school students.

It is widely recognized that as students advance through primary and secondary grades to higher institutes, their acceptance of ideological values and beliefs becomes increasingly tempered by outside influences. Disapproved life-styles that glorify rock music, foreign-made clothes, and avant-garde tastes are sweeping through the younger generations with great force. At the same time, youths in higher institutes and technicums are grasping for career options that will ensure them an acceptable standard of living. The use of influence, bribes, and falsification of records to ensure favorable decisions is so widespread that Party leaders have launched public campaigns against these practices.

Despite decades of official propaganda, few Soviet citizens who have a choice really value manual labor, even where it pays better than some white-collar professions. Recent attitudinal studies of high school and college students consistently show strong career preferences for intellectual rather than physical work. They also show a preference for the "humanistic professions" such as medicine, academics, law, and theater, over technological professions such as engineering.[12] The Party's long-time objective of narrowing the social gap between manual and mental labor appears, in the cities at least, to have failed to divert the post-Khrushchev generation from its pursuit of higher living standards and more congenial occupations. The educational system, therefore, falls short of fulfilling Party goals in both areas: in the furtherance of the qualities of the "new Soviet person" and in channeling students toward employment in accordance with the needs of the economy.

AGITATION AND PROPAGANDA

Beyond the formal school system there is another set of institutions that operates directly to implant the Party's messages into the Soviet mind. These are the agencies of *agitprop,* the apparatus that is responsible for continuing the political education of the Soviet people throughout their lifetimes.

The two activities of agitprop—agitation and propaganda—have different purposes, although the differences are not always clear in practice. Propaganda is intended to inform an audience about a political subject, to create a "reality"consistent with current Party policy. Propagandists ask, and answer, broad questions of public concern: why the capitalist world poses a military threat to the USSR, for example, or why the Party launched the *perestroika* campaign in 1985.

Agitation, on the other hand, seeks to move people to action. Agitators launch campaigns during elections to acquaint voters with current Party policies and to ensure a full turnout. They periodically initiate efforts to fulfill production quotas at individual factories or to drum up enthusiasm for an upcoming Party Congress or session of the Supreme Soviet. The linkage of propaganda and agitation is supposed to ensure that a proper understanding of a subject leads to the appropriate action, leaving as little as possible to spontaneous popular judgment.

The interaction between agitprop instructors and the public takes place in many different settings: evening lectures, political sessions at places of work, correspondence and evening courses of study, election caucuses, and ceremonial occasions such as parades and gatherings on national holidays. The agitprop network is so vast in scale that it is unlikely that any citizen can avoid at least occasional contact with it.

Agitprop activities are normally directed by a senior Party secretary, usually also a member of the Politburo. This official, currently Alexander Yakovlev, heads the Propaganda Department of the Party Central Committee. He directs the work of agitprop officials at all levels down to the most remote rural Party cell.

The Propaganda Department runs a top-level research institute called the Institute of Marxism-Leninism, headquartered in Moscow with branches in several other cities. At this institute, thousands of scholars and writers prepare books, pamphlets, and articles that explain the "Party line" on contemporary political events as well as on historical subjects. The department is editorially responsible for *Kommunist,* the Party's main theoretical monthly journal, as well as for the ideological orientation of its principal newspaper, *Pravda.* The department also runs the (so-called) Academy of Social Sciences, which is in fact an institute for training professional propagandists. The academy contains specialized sections, such as the Institute for Scientific Atheism, in which research and training are also conducted.

Much of the work of propagandists is done through three national organizations that are also run by the Propaganda Department. These are Znaniye (Knowledge Society), People's Universities, and Schools of Communist Labor.

Znaniye Society

Founded in 1947, the Znaniye Society has become a nationwide organization of lecture bureaus that dispenses political and educational information to audiences all over the Soviet Union. Its lecturers, over 3 million strong, are mostly volunteers trained to deliver lectures on a host of topics. In 1980, Znaniye claimed to have presented 28 million lectures to a total audience of 1.5 billion people, an average of 5 or 6 lectures for every man, woman, and child in the country.[13] Many lecturers are teachers or professionals contributing their spare time to the effort. Some of them are paid modest lecture fees, but much of the work is volunteered—a way for the intelligentsia to fulfill a social obligation.

Znaniye lectures are not exclusively political in content. In a study of the Leningrad branch, Barghoorn and Remington concluded that about 60 percent of the lectures dealt with political and social subjects, including a large number of lectures espousing "scientific atheism."[14]

The People's Universities

Established in the 1950s, these institutions have grown into a nationwide system of 131,000 different courses of study enrolling over 18 million students.[15] In contrast to the regular education system, people's universities are financially independent of state budgets, meeting their expenses through fees charged to students. Most of the instructors are volunteers, teaching without pay. About half of them are teachers and higher-school professors who contribute their services in the evenings. Another large group consists of professional people, such as engineers, physicians, and agronomists, who offer courses aimed at upgrading students' skills. Probably two-thirds of the instructors are Communist Party or Komsomol members.

Political courses in the people's universities present interpretations of Party policy, refresher lectures on Marxist-Leninist ideology, and a continuation of the Communist unbringing that began in the early years of childhood. Although official statements emphasize political education as the most important part of the curriculum, in fact only about one-fifth of the students take courses in this area. The most popular subjects are those dealing with popular culture and vocational skills.

Schools of Communist Labor

The major purpose of courses offered in these schools is to increase the knowledge of urban workers about technological developments in their industries. Lectures on production techniques and economic problems as well as on-site visits to innovative factories occupy most of the twice-monthly classes. The political messages are delivered in lectures that deal with general political questions and policy decisions of the Party and government.

By the early 1970s, a large number of these schools were operating in the major cities. Leningrad alone had 3,350 schools with a total enrollment of 80,000 workers. Classes are held outside of working hours in factories or in classrooms.

The effectiveness of the overall agitprop effort is virtually impossible to assess. Soviet scholars rarely attempt more than superficial surveys on the subject, except possibly for the private use of Party leaders. Nevertheless, some judgments can be made from the level of criticism the agitprop business receives in the national press. There are frequent complaints about incompetent lecturers and dull subject matter. Many lecturers are young college students fulfilling manadatory public service requirements. Others are well-intentioned but poorly trained for the task or not effective as public speakers. In the presentation of antireligious lectures, for example, a Soviet official found that "the entire 'scientific baggage' of a large proportion of professional atheists consisted solely of the fact that they did not believe in God."[16]

The rapid turnover of lecturers and the dropout rate are additional concerns. Recently, the Estonian Republic's School for Young Lecturers and the Knowledge Society reveiwed a five-year period to discover that although 300 students had studied to become lecturers, only 50 had graduated and just 15 were working as lecturers. According to the report, the Estonian Komsomol had no idea what the others were doing.[17]

The dissemination of propaganda confronts several contemporary obstacles that are forcing the Party to upgrade the quality of its messages. As the literacy and educational attainments of the population increase, people are less patient with crude attempts at information control and obviously one-sided viewpoints. Competition from Voice of America and other foreign broadcasts gives many people alternative sources of information that tests the credibility of official propaganda. As the Soviet press moves toward greater frankness about the deficiencies of the economy and the society, under the new policy of *glasnost* (discussed below), the standard propaganda messages become less effective. A reexamination of this entire subject is underway in the higher levels of the Party leadership.

THE SOVIET PRESS

Like the school system, the Soviet press has important political and social functions to perform in addition to its normal communications role. "Press, television, radio, verbal propaganda and agitation," a Party resolution states, must increasingly . . . arouse aspirations to contribute to a maximum to the common cause, to the construction of communism."[18]

The Soviet press is a gigantic operation, and a carefully controlled one. It consists of over 8,000 newspapers, 640 of them published daily, along with some 6,000 journals and other periodicals. There are three types of newspapers: (1) all-union papers like *Pravda (Truth)*, the official newspaper of the CPSU with a daily circulation of over 11 million; *Izvestia (News)*, the organ of the Supreme Soviet; and *Komsomolskaya Pravda,* the newspaper of the Young Communist League; (2) regional or municipal newspapers of general circulation; and (3) newspapers servicing specialized audiences, such as *Krasnaya Zvezda (Red Star)*, published by the military establishment; *Trud (Labor)*, representing the national trade union movement; and *Sovetsky Sport,* which covers sports news all over the country.

Of these newspapers, *Pravda* occupies a unique and dominant position, for it speaks for both the Politburo and the Secretariat. It frequently criticizes other publications for errors but is itself beyond criticism. *Pravda* reporters have a status befitting their employer. According to one former Soviet journalist,

> A correspondent of *Pravda* is admitted everywhere at all times. People talk to him with deference and at length, putting aside the most urgent work, conferences and consultation, as do ministers, directors of enterprises, secretaries of Party organizations on the oblast and Republic levels, scientists, artists, deputies of the Supreme Soviet and so forth.[19]

Pravda is printed in forty-six different cities, and much of the news printed in regional and local papers is telexed to them daily from *Pravda's* offices in Moscow. In addition, these newspapers include regional and local news as well as coverage of sports, cultural events, television schedules, and other items. Some classified advertising is carried as supplements to local newspapers, but it is expensive ($5 or $6 for two words and a telephone number) and the delay in getting an ad published can last up to several months.[20] Soviet newspapers seldom run more than four or six pages in length, so the space available for any type of coverage is extremely limited.

Despite that limitation, all Soviet newspapers devote space to letters from readers. *Pravda,* its editor claims, receives 600,000 letters a year, which requires a staff of sixty-five people to handle. The content of the letters, those not published as well as those that are, provides an important sampling of public opinion on a wide range of issues. Newspaper editors are legally obliged to follow up on citizen complaints, although one also reads complaints about the failure of newspapers to do so.

The Soviet press is a controlled press in that Party organs direct and monitor the content of all newspapers as they do that of all other legal communications media. But the "control" is a complex and flexible process and often exhibits flaws and errors. At the highest level, editorial control of the major national newspapers rests with the agitprop staff of the Party Central Committee, headed by the secretary for ideological matters. Day-to-day control is exercised through the State Committee on the Press, which is the central headquarters of a vast collection of censorship agencies operating throughout the country at every level. The most important of these agencies is the Chief Administration for the Preservation of State Secrets in the Press, which is directly subordinate to the Central Committee's Propaganda Department.

Censorship takes various forms in the Soviet press. In dealing with ordinary news and events, newspaper editors consult a multivolume *Index,* informally known as the "Talmud." This contains guidelines for handling various types of stories, interpretations of current Party policies and the emphases to be given them, and specific instructions on a vast array of details. Because Soviet newspapers are far less concerned with late-breaking news stories than is the Western press, the daily "news" is often written days and even weeks before it is published. Editors of the major national papers meet to discuss editorial policy on alternate Tuesdays in the office of the Central Committee Propaganda Department.

In addition to these formal controls, an experienced editor usually knows instinctively what he is expected to publish. Learning to read the political weathervane is one of the critical skills essential to both journalists and editors. As one *Pravda* editor put it to a group of American students:

> The idea that the Kremlin controls the Soviet press is sheer nonsense. I must say that nobody ever tells us what to present. We are our own bosses. When Mr. Andropov [General Secretary at the time] suggests good propositions for the good of our people, of course we write about the value of those good propositions. Nobody has to tell us.[21]

The Soviet press also performs an important communications function between the political leadership and the various layers of bureaucracy that manage the country. The information that is published in the leading newspapers, especially *Pravda,* is intended to give guidance to officials and members of the Communist Party and to countless others whose functions require an understanding of Party policy. While all articles in the press conform to and elaborate on Party policies, front-page editorials in *Pravda* have special importance. They are often addressed to specific ministries or organizations and contain policy statements, criticism of the organization, and directives for overcoming their deficiencies.

The chief Soviet news agency, TASS (Telegraphic Agency of the Soviet Union), also serves to distribute various types of information to those who are authorized to receive it. Ordinary news sufficiently censored for general distribution is called "blue TASS," identified by the color of its cover page. "White TASS" contains more detailed and often critical material that the press is not authorized to publish. It is sent to organizations that deal with public information or with the management of propagandists and agitators, affording them a more penetrating source of information on various matters.

Highly sensitive information is sent around in two forms: as "red TASS," which is distributed by armed messenger to newspaper editors, higher Party and government officials, and others with a demonstrated need to know; and the "Special Bulletin," which is circulated only to members of the Politburo and Secretariat, senior government ministers, and the chief editors of the most important newspapers. These packets often contain anti-Soviet information and details of crisis situations considered too sensitive for release even to the higher levels of the bureaucracy.[22]

How widely and carefully the Soviet press is read by citizens is a difficult question to answer. Raw circulation figures no doubt understate actual exposure to the content of newspapers. Typically, more than one person reads a single newspaper, and major newspapers are posted daily on bulletin boards for all to read. Important articles in *Pravda* are often read over the radio as well as at factories and offices as part of routine agitprop activities.

Since 1966, Soviet officials have shown a keen interest in newspaper readership and have authorized a number of public surveys on the matter.[23] They discovered patterns of readership that corresponded roughly with those of European countries. Most people, for example, prefer local newspapers to the national press. *Pravda,* for all its political importance, is read by only 12 to 13 percent of the people, mainly Party members and including predominantly urban rather than rural residents and Russians rather than non-Russians. Among all age and education groups in the Soviet Union, there is a strong preference for articles dealing with international events and for those offering light human-interest stories.

The impact of the Soviet press on popular thinking is probably high. No opposition press exists, and the consistency of viewpoints presented in the nation's newspapers is extremely high owing to the overall control of the press by the Party. Nevertheless, Soviet readers have been highly critical of some aspects of the press, notably its failure to cover important events and its extensive presentation of rather boring official commentary. As a contributor to the general socialization effort, however, the press undoubtedly has a substantial effect on the knowledge the Soviet people have of both domestic and international affairs.

RADIO AND TELEVISION

By the mid-1980s, nearly every Soviet home had a radio and most had at least a black-and-white television set. Broadcasting has long been a primary means of communicating both information and propaganda, and through the development of satellite transmission capabilities it reaches far more people than does the printed word. The extension of TV broadcasts into rural areas has in fact significantly changed the means of official communication. Rural residents watch many more hours of television, and they read far fewer newspapers and books than do their urban cousins.[24]

Television is the most popular form of entertainment in the USSR, even though, as with all communications media, its official purpose is not entertainment but education. Programming is developed and scheduled centrally, and its content must conform to Party policies and established principles of behavior and morality. Even the lightest fare, such as quiz programs and detective shows, offer guidance for improving social values. As one observer described a popular monthly quiz show, "Let's Go Girls":

> Everyone wins something, a small prize of flowers or books, and the object is not to get rich, but rather to popularize occupations and encourage good work. Recently, a group of policewomen performed on the show, marching and drilling to music, using their nightsticks. They were asked ("quizzed") how to improve traffic rules, and they offered such suggestions as redesigning traffic signs.[25]

The paradox in the attraction of such programs is that even though Soviet citizens, like most people, watch television primarily for entertainment, surveys of viewers almost invariably produce the officially approved view that the most important function of television is to present political subjects and international affairs. This view is characteristic of all age and education groups and of both urban and rural viewers. People appear to know what is expected of them even though they behave differently.

Soviet ideologists prefer television to radio as a medium of propaganda for an obvious reason: Television programming can be almost totally controlled by central offices. The only major exception is in the Estonian Republic, where the native language is similar enough to Finnish that people listen regularly to Finnish TV. Radio reception, on the other hand, is much more difficult to control. In particular, radios provide many citizens with access to the Voice of America and the Radio Liberty/Radio Free Europe networks that broadcast from West Germany to the USSR and Eastern Europe. In 1983, a survey of Soviet tourists abroad (not defectors) indicated that some 11 percent of the Soviet people listen to the Voice of America, while smaller percentages listened to the British Broadcasting Company, Deutsche Welle (West Germany), and Radio Liberty.[26] Soviet authorities have long attempted to jam such broadcasts but without great success. In early 1987, General Secretary Gorbachev ordered jamming of Voice of America to cease, while at the same time increasing the interference directed at Radio Liberty, which is considered to be a CIA operation bent on subversion.

LITERATURE AND THE ARTS

High culture in the Soviet Union, no less than the press, has always been considered an essential instrument of the Communist Party in promoting basic social values. "Literature, the cinema and the arts," a 1930 Pravda editorial intoned, "are levers in the hands of the proletariat which must be used to show the masses positive models of initiative and heroic labor."[27] Artists, writers, sculptors, filmmakers— even architects and city planners—are expected to imbue their works with the "spirit of communism," to create characters and images that motivate Soviet citizens toward higher achievements and guide them in developing Party-approved values and tastes.

Socialist Realism

The guiding concept for Soviet art and literature since the beginning of Stalin's rule has been "socialist realism." A "socialist" orientation demands an enthusiastic preoccupation with "building communism" in the USSR. It decries concern for "mere" individual happiness and the resolution of personal problems. It rests on the assumption that the final victory of true communism in Russia will itself resolve all important personal problems. "Realism" requires rather simple styles of expression and communication so that ordinary people can understand and enjoy their cultural heritage. As Lenin once said,

> I cannot value the works of expressionism, futurism, cubism and other "isms" as the highest expressions of artistic genius. I don't understand them. They give me no pleasure. . . . Art belongs to the people. It must have its deepest roots in the broad mass of workers. It must be understood and loved by them.[28]

Historically, Party control of the arts has mirrored the control structures of other mass functions. A member of the Party Secretariat is in charge of cultural matters and manages a vast network of Party and government agencies and organizations, principally the USSR Ministry of Culture and its branch ministries on the republic level. The state owns all publication media and all theaters, performing studios, and art galleries. It seeks to bring all creative artists into state-run unions where *nomenklatura* officials decide what is to be published and performed.

In the Stalin era, this administrative process was backed up by extremely harsh treatment of nonconformists. Literature and the arts pursued blatantly political objectives with little regard for artistic integrity or quality. The central themes were the glorification of the Leader (Stalin), the state, the Party, the military and other official institutions, and the historic magnificence of the new Soviet society. The message that suffused all media is well expressed in Alexander Zinoviev's masterful satire, *The Yawning Heights:*

> Our society is the most perfect, the most humane, the most free, the best organised, the most . . . the best . . . the most. . . . If you stumble upon anything good anywhere you must know that it is much better done in Ibansk [the U.S.S.R.]. . . . If anywhere you observe an error, you must know that this error does not exist in the doctrines of Ibanism [Marxism-Leninism], since Ibanism excludes error as a matter of principle.[29]

In the typical Soviet novel or film, fictional characters were designed as model citizens, and every work had to have a moral lesson. The "positive hero" was a model of pure dedication to social progress and a paragon of socialist morality, a person with no private life and no concern with personal goals or disappointments. He appeared in an endless stream of novels, poems, plays, and "popular" songs crafted by artists and writers who had learned how to accommodate the regime. Although some works of quality were written in the Stalinist era, the more pervasive consequence of Stalinism was an artistic straitjacket of deadening, conformist mediocrity.

In the post-Stalin era, the most extreme manifestations of socialist realism gradually subsided. During a brief thaw grudgingly allowed by Nikita Khrushchev, an opening toward greater honesty and objectivity in Soviet arts appeared. The Stalin era itself came under scrutiny in such works as Ilya Ehrenburg's novel *The Thaw* (1954) and Alexander Solzhenitsyn's *One Day in the Life of Ivan Denisovich.*

By 1962, however, alarmed conservatives in the Party and the government, headed by the Chairman of the Ideological Commission, Leonid Ilyichev, began to impose heavy controls once again. Liberal writers and artists were denounced in public assemblies and forced to admit their "errors" and recant their "anti-Soviet works." In his last year in power (1964), Khrushchev supported the crackdown and reimposed stricter censorship.

The main problem in the Brezhnev years (1964–1982) was how to establish a middle ground for the arts that would confine artistic products to Party-approved standards of socialist realism, while ensuring that the arts were attractive enough to the general public that their political content was not ignored or rejected. The regime came to rely more heavily on censors and less on the secret police. Writers and artists were freer to create their own works, but the government was equally free to deny them public exposure if they failed to conform to the standards of the Secretariat's censors. This arrangement did not preclude continued police oppression of "anti-Soviet" writers and artists who explored forbidden subjects, attacked basic aspects of the Soviet system, or published their works abroad.

The Current Dilemma

By the end of Brezhnev's time in power, it was clear that this compromise had not worked. Published literature was crammed with stale plots and dehumanized characters whom nobody cared about. The great potential of the arts for social mobilization was being squandered by heavy-handed bureaucrats and hack writers whose literary talents were more or less on a par.

The field of classical and popular music is a good example. For four decades, Tikhon Khrennikov has headed the USSR Composers' Union, an organization of some 1,700 composers and 800 musical historians and critics. The union controls the publication of new compositions largely through "purchase commissions" operating through the Ministry of Culture. According to one Soviet composer, Vladimir Dashkevich,

> Members of these commissions are not responsible for the future life of the compositions; therefore, it is not surprising that 80–90 percent of the compositions they purchase go virtually unperformed. On the other hand, ballyhood reports listing hundreds of new operas, symphonies and quartets regularly shake the air.[30]

The aging Composers' Union leadership has ignored much of the popular music field, roiling against "raucous, bourgeois sounds from untrained hooligans," as well as newer fields such as electronic music and music composed for films. As a result, the union's official journal, *Sovetskaya Musika*, has lost 40 percent of its subscribers in recent years, and the union's influence over the music field has waned in every area.[31]

Outside the Composers' Union, and despite its official monopoly over Soviet music, new compositions and performers have stirred a near renaissance, especially in popular music. Thousands of "amateur" musicians are writing and performing new works, despite the fact that their amateur standing means they are not entitled to professional status, advertised performances, or royalties. On a recently published list of the country's ten most popular composers, only two of those named were members of the Composer's Union. As Vladimir Dashkevich has concluded, "an avalanche of amateur music of all kinds has engulfed today's pop music, and the Composer's Union has lost its grip on the helm controlling the ship of musical life."[32]

In the world of Soviet theater, the picture is similar. Amateur theater groups began performing in the early 1970s, both as a forum for presenting more experimental and appealing works and to accommodate a broader audience. Amateur groups are governed by state commissions, but their nonprofessional status often affords them more lenient treatment in the content and style of their work. At the same time, they must struggle for recognition against the established theater groups. Amateur productions are not publicized in official playbills, so information about performances is largely by word of mouth. The groups usually have no permanent stage facilities and most funding must come from ticket sales. Nevertheless, some of the country's most talented writers and actors, eager to work without the constraints of the conservative union elites, have been attracted to the amateur groups.

The regime's artistic establishment has also been challenged from abroad. Performers, films, and exhibits from the West and Japan have in recent years tended to crowd out Soviet offerings. Celebrated Western musicians, both classical and popular, draw packed audiences wherever they perform in the USSR. Most young people are strongly attracted to Western popular music and to Soviet rock groups that pattern themselves after their foreign heroes.

Local movie houses exhibit the same bias. In a recent survey of movie theaters in several cities, a newspaper found patrons "confronted with a solid wall of foreign films." In Gorky, for example, four of the eight theaters were showing the same Spanish film (*Secret of the Island of Monsters*), while only one was showing a Soviet film.[33] Theater managers, eager to fulfill attendance quotas, are increasingly demanding, and getting, imported films from trade ministries laboring under similar quotas.

The main consequence of these developments has been severely to undermine official Party-approved cultural standards. The unofficial culture that has emerged is more reflective of popular tastes and attracts a significantly higher quality of artistic talent than its established competition. The increasingly well-educated Soviet public has largely turned away from the simplistic and moralistic poses of the "dedicated builder of communism" and the "heroic fighter against fascism" who dominated Soviet novels and films in earlier years. Many reach out instead for more complex emotional and personal stories, for honest reflections of their own problems and ambitions. And they reach increasingly for literary quality as a value superior to ideological conformity.

This is an embarrassment for the Soviet leadership, for the inferiority of so much of contemporary Soviet (official) culture is universally recognized. But the political consequences are even more disturbing. The Party relies heavily on literature and the arts for the proper upbringing of the younger generation and the continuing ideological commitment of adults. The unofficial culture represents, therefore, not only divergent aesthetic values but also a serious ideological challenge. The Party's ability to define reality, and to exclude alternative definitions, cannot be sustained if it loses control of the emotions and sensibilities of its citizens. On the other hand, it cannot reach those emotions if it ignores or rejects the forms of cultural expression—the songs, the plays, the poems, and the novels—that stimulate the greatest public response.

To all of these problems, and to the broader problems of propaganda and information, the Gorbachev regime has proposed a solution that is, in one sense at least, a radical one. Gorbachev calls it *glasnost,* which means "openness" and implies a far higher degree of frankness and objectivity than has ever characterized the Soviet media. It is clearly a calculated risk, and one that has already generated much excitement, confusion, and skepticism, both in the USSR and in the West.

GLASNOST

On the surface at least, *glasnost* has been a sensation in the three years since Gorbachev announced the policy. Words have been written, published, spoken, and sung that, under Brezhnev, would have landed most of their authors in jail.

Newspaper and magazine sales have skyrocketed as each new issue raids another "forbidden zone" of Soviet censorship.

The scope of *glasnost* is truly astonishing compared to the very recent past:

- Boris Pasternak, who was denied his 1958 Nobel Prize for Literature and savagely denounced as anti-Soviet, is now being honored as one of the country's greatest writers. An official commission has been formed to restore his name, and his long-suppressed masterpiece, *Dr. Zhivago,* has finally been published in the Soviet Union;
- A prominent newspaper article sharply criticizes Stalin's inept handling of national defense during World War II, and Leon Trotsky is sympathetically portrayed in a popular play;
- Stories exposing prostitution, homosexuality, drug abuse, and urban youth gangs appear for the first time in national and regional newspapers and on TV;
- President Reagan's Secretary of State, George Shultz, is interviewed live on Soviet TV, and Phil Donahue puts on an uncensored talk show in Moscow;
- Writing in the National magazine *Novy Mir* (*New World*), a prominent economist attacks Gorbachev's proposals for economic reform as unworkable and bound to fail.

It is tempting for Westerners to see in *glasnost* an end to Soviet censorship and the beginnings of "freedom of speech" and artistic spontaneity as they are practiced in Western democratic societies. Clearly there has been a sudden and radical broadening of the limits of expression, and the Party leadership is promoting the change. For Soviet writers with drawers full of unpublished manuscripts, the new orientation must be exhilarating.

It should be recognized, however, that *glasnost* does not represent an abandonment of Party control over communications nor a rejection of the need for censorship. *Glasnost* is a policy, not a cessation of policy. It has been introduced for specific reasons and is expected to produce certain outcomes. Its general purpose is the mobilization of the energy and enthusiasm of the Soviet people in support of the goals of Gorbachev's restructuring campaign. "The main task of journalists today," Gorbachev stated in a recent speech to the Party Central Committee,

> is to help people to better understand and assimilate the ideas of restructuring and to rally the masses in a nationwide struggle for successful fulfillment of the Party's plans.[34]

Literature and literary criticism have vital political roles to play under *glasnost:*

> In conditions of restructuring and the democratization of all aspects of life, the criteria and nature of criticism are also changing. But one thing is certain— criticism should always be Party criticism, and grounded in the truth, and this depends on the editor's Party spirit.[35]

Gorbachev and his associates have spoken repeatedly and at length about the meaning of *glasnost.* Yet an underlying contradiction emerges from their statements. Gorbachev has stressed his determination to present the Soviet people with the whole truth—"an objective, comprehensive vision of reality." There must be "no forgotten names or blank spots in either history or literature," no "lack of objectivity or one-sidedness." Criticism will be effective "only when it is based on the complete truth."

The "truth" of *glasnost,* however, is by definition the Party's version of events, as it has always been. In dealing with the sensitive issue of Stalinism, Gorbachev recognizes that "there have been both joyous and bitter moments" in the Soviet past. But,

> no matter what happened to us, we moved forward, we did not fall under the tank treads of fascism. . . . There was grief in every home, smoldering ruins where our cities had been. The economic blockade. The cold war. But we did not bend. We stood our ground once more and reached out into outer space.[36]

To Gorbachev, this is not merely one of various ways of interpreting the Stalinist era; this is the necessary conclusion one must reach, based on what he has called "the immutable, socialist law of truth. . . ." This "law" ensures that the truth corresponds precisely to the Party's current version of history and its plans for the development of society. *Glasnost* is intended to produce correct messages on all subjects. The Stalinist era, for example, is expected to be discussed in terms of "mistakes" and "miscalculations" with the major emphasis on the achievements of the Party. On the subject of relations among the ethnic minorities, *glasnost* will make clear how a "highly unique phenomenon in human history was established, one in which more than 100 nations and nationalities live . . . harmoniously and well."[37] Any other view would be objectively untrue. Recent anti-Russian riots in Kazakhstan and mass demonstrations in Armenia (described in the following chapter) are somehow to be fitted into this general conclusion.

This impression of Gorbachev's intentions for *glasnost* is reinforced by repeated official warnings against opponents of *glasnost* and reconstruction. Politburo member Y.K. Ligachev has spoken out against "intrigues of lying bourgeois propaganda, which has brought up substantial forces to undermine the Soviet people's faith in the rightness of the Communist Party's course and the reality of the restructuring that has gotten under way. . . ."[38]

Despite the leadership's reassurance on the point, many officials oppose *glasnost* as a threat to their own interests or as a weakening of the overall system of political control. Many government agencies, long identified as "forbidden zones" and thus protected from public scrutiny, are continuing to reject any change. Information about the nation's ecological problems can be published only with the approval of the ministries involved, and that has frequently not been forthcoming. The space program also persists in issuing the same empty responses to inquiries: "The mechanisms are operating normally, the cosmonauts feel fine."[39]

Pravda's editor, Victor Afanaseyev, recently revealed another source of obstruction, which he calls the "forbidden zone game." To initiate it, a regional Party leader rises at a Party conference to criticize the central press for some alleged but nonspecific deficiencies. If the press responds later with criticism of the official or his province, it can be charged with seeking retribution for the earlier criticism. As a result, "a new 'forbidden zone' for criticism comes into being."[40]

To counter any negative publicity that arises, government ministries are launching vigorous public relations campaigns of their own. Press centers have been established in ministry offices to create what one critic called "boastful, rose-colored, cheery reports, losing all sense of objectivity or proportion." This "glorification industry" is often staffed covertly by journalists carried on the ministry books as "engineers, researchers, etc."[41]

In the journalistic trenches, where reporters attempt to apply *glasnost* to the administrative bureaucracy, the work entails considerable risk, as Afanaseyev reveals:

> No sooner is a correspondent sent on assignment . . . than the phone calls begin. Attempts are made to keep the article from appearing, and if this doesn't work, there is a search for an acceptable, glib answer, and phone calls are made to the editors in an effort to find out "who authorized this." We know of a great many instances of the direct or indirect suppression of criticism. "Critics," including journalists, are discredited, removed from their jobs, expelled from the Party, and sometimes even put behind bars.[42]

The controversy over *glasnost* reflects the profound dilemma of a ruling elite that has rested much of its legitimacy and political effectiveness on its ability to define reality for its citizens. In introducing *glasnost,* the leadership has shown no intention of abandoning its right to define reality. It has no plan to open the government or the Party to spontaneous, uncensored criticism. Its objective is to implant the idea that restructuring is not just a new policy but a "new reality" for the Soviet people. "Restructuring has become reality," Gorbachev stated in a speech to newspaper and propaganda officials, and "in this crucial period, we need an objective, comprehensive vision of reality as never before."[43] This view of Party policy as reality provides the leadership with logical grounds for rejecting any criticism of "restructuring" as "unreal" and therefore invalid and even nonsensical.

Despite this constraint, *glasnost* has produced some startling criticisms, for there is much about the present social and economic systems that Gorbachev would like to change. This high level of criticism is a risky policy, however, for several reasons. First, as a practical matter, the policy of *glasnost* offers little guidance to media officials and censors. Editors may err on the side of overstepping the bounds of acceptable criticism or of reacting too conservatively. In either case, considerable confusion has replaced the earlier clarity in the Party's management of the communications media.

Second, many of the revelations of *glasnost* may prove to be irreversible, thus limiting the leadership's ability to alter the official viewpoint at a later date. Once

Stalin has been exposed for the cruelty and incompetence of many of his decisions, it will be difficult ever to restore him to the same pedestal. Once the press reveals that social ills like prostitution, drug abuse, and urban street gangs really do exist in the USSR, future denials will never ring quite true.

Finally, there is the problem of social control. For generations the Party's monopoly of all forms of communications has been used to convince the Soviet people that the entire population, aside from a small number of isolated anti-Soviet individuals, fully supports the Soviet system of government and the policies of the Communist Party. To the extent that *glasnost* reveals real controversies over major issues, individuals with complaints against the government will realize they are not alone. Instead of isolated dissidents and malcontents, "networks of contacts and connections," as exiled writer Vladimir Bukovsky has called them,[44] may emerge as interest groups that the Party leadership will have to deal with. As noted in Chapter 8, this appears already to be under way.

Perhaps the central political question for the Politburo is whether the policy of *glasnost* can be contained in Party-approved channels, and if it cannot whether it can be abandoned without unacceptable costs to the leadership.

CASE STUDIES IN SOCIALIZATION

In most societies the socialization process finds its greatest challenges in the integration of ethnic minorities into the national culture and in the assimilation of youth into adult society. Over the years, the Soviet experience in both areas has appeared to be unusually successful. Until very recently there has been no evidence of a distinct "youth culture" in the USSR nor any significant movements toward ethnic separatism among the minorities. Soviet officials have long maintained that socialism eliminates the causes of group and generational conflict, so that none could possibly arise.

In the 1980s, however, the picture is changing rapidly. *Glasnost* has revealed higher levels of conflict in Soviet society than had earlier been known, or admitted to. In the following two case studies we shall look briefly at the application of socialization processes to ethnic minorities and the younger generation and attempt to assess the results in each case.

Case 1: The Ethnic Minorities

As indicated earlier (see Chapter 1), the Soviet Union is a multinational state. According to the 1979 census, it contains 104 distinct nationalities, each with its own written language. There are another 50 or so ethnic groups with weaker traditions of identity that are largely integrated with the dominant Russian culture. Twenty-two of the major nationalities, including Koreans, Poles, Kurds, and Jews, are "foreign groups," whose natural homeland is outside Soviet borders. Many of the larger ethnic groups have traditions of national independence extending over many generations: Armenians, Georgians, Lithuanians, and a number of Asian Muslim peoples. They represent all the world's major religions, many of which (Islam, for example) are deeply woven into the fabric of daily life in Muslim communities.

How to mold this enormous ethnic diversity into a single, unified national state has been a Russian problem since long before the Revolution. In a Communist system, the problem is complicated further by the stress on ideological uniformity and by the official opposition to religion. In general, Soviet leaders have pursued a policy of combining national Communist values, to which all citizens must adhere, with respect for the particular customs and values of each ethnic minority, but the balance has changed over time.

In the Stalin era, the scales were heavily weighted toward national Communist values. Manifestations of ethnic separatism were brutally repressed. During and after World War II, a number of ethnic groups were forcibly transported on trains from European Russia to the eastern lands of central Asia and Siberia, on the grounds of potential disloyalty to the Soviet regime.[45] A Party official was quoted at the time as stating that Soviet minority policy consisted simply in having enough boxcars ready.[46] In the 1960s and 1970s, the Politburo was still inclined toward the Russification of the national areas, but Brezhnev opposed suggestions that the new 1977 Constitution include the abolition of the union-republics and the adoption of the concept of "one Soviet nation."[47]

In the post-Brezhnev era, the issue of nationalism hangs on the concept of *sblizhenie* (rapprochement, or coming together), a significant step back from the goal of *sliyanie* (fusion) of the earlier era. *Sblizhenie* characterizes a "united Soviet people in which political, economic and social ideals are shared, but ethnic and cultural differences persist."[48] The mandatory shared values include support for Soviet socialism as a philosophy and a system of national government; national patriotism and participation in national defense; and acceptance of a secular education and of Russian as the national language. On the other hand, the policy supports the growth of "regional consciousness" among major ethnic groups. This entitles minorities to respect for their indigenous languages and customs, the right to a fair share in the national wealth for economic development and improved living standards, and the right to a reasonable degree of autonomy in solving problems peculiar to their particular areas. This combination of socialist and ethnic values has proved difficult to work out in practice.

Political Controls. The Party leadership in Moscow engages in two overall mechanisms of control with regard to the non-Russian republics: the appointment of Russians to key Party, government, and police positions, and the maintenance of a broad program of socialization and indoctrination. The two mechanisms operate variously depending on the loyalty and social conformity of the various ethnic republics. The Ukraine and Belorussia behave as "Slavic brothers" in many senses and enjoy the least degree of direct Russian control. The Caucasian republics

(Georgia and Armenia) and the Baltic republics (Estonia, Latvia, and Lithuania) exhibit historically conditioned anti-Russian sentiments but pose no serious problems because of their small size and military vulnerability.

The most difficult control problem lies with the Muslim population, organized mainly in the five central Asian republics, Azerbaijan and several smaller subrepublics. With their rapidly expanding populations and the unifying strength of the Muslim culture, these peoples have, with varying degrees of success, resisted Russian domination since the death of Stalin.

The major political control mechanism in the non-Russian republics is the *nomenklatura,* or appointment process. Typically, the first secretary on the republic and lower levels is a native while the second secretary is a Russian. In the more troublesome republics, the authority of the second secretaries is nearly as great as that of the first. It involves not only keeping watch on the first secretary but also participating in all policy and administrative decisions for the region.

In addition, Russians head key departments such as Party Organs and Internal Security. In Muslim Uzbekistan in 1980, for example, only the republic first secretary was an Uzbek while all of the main departments and lower-level second secretaryships were filled by nonnatives, predominantly Russians. A rare exception is the Georgian Republic, where all of these positions were held by natives. The military districts in Muslim areas are also dominated by Russians. The commander and four out of five deputy commanders of the Central Asian Military District are Russian, along with thirty out of thirty-two known staff members.[49]

Regional government in the Muslim areas, on the other hand, is heavily influenced by traditional clan and tribal loyalties. These are primary factors in appointments to well-paying jobs in the Party and government as well as allocations of scarce housing and admissions to higher schools. At Yakutsk State University, for example, in the 1985–1986 academic year, Yakuts, who constitute only a third of the population in the territory, made up nearly 80 percent of the student body.[50] In Kazakhstan, where only 36 percent of the people are Kazakhs, the proportion of natives in higher schools has climbed in one institution after another from 30 to 40 percent ten years ago to 70 to 80 percent today. The major victims of this trend are Russians living in central Asia, who find opportunities for educating their children sharply declining.[51]

Moving against these ethnic power structures entails certain risks, even for the top Party leadership. When General Secretary Gorbachev announced the firing of Kazakh leader (and Politburo member) Dikmuhammed Kunaev in December 1986 and his replacement by a Russian, the reaction was immediate and violent. That night and for the next forty-eight hours, thousands of demonstrators took control of downtown Alma-Ata, the capital of Kazakhstan. They overturned cars, attacked bystanders, burned buildings, and fought with the police. As subsequent examinations showed, the grievances of the demonstrators, mostly young people, went far beyond the firing of Kunaev. They included the shortage of consumer goods and the low standard of living in Kazakhstan, the presence of Russians in key positions, and the feuds between southern and northern clans that have traditionally divided the

Kazakhs. The capacity of the Russian-dominated Politburo to handle such ethnic conflicts without violence is by no means certain.

Socializing the Non-Russian Peoples. Avoiding such confrontations depends heavily on the creation of a national culture that overrides ethnic differences. The formation, in 1924, of several union-republics in the Muslim central Asian part of the USSR was intended to break up the large, and traditionally anti-Russian, Muslim population, and to reorient the people toward the nation as a whole. Individual republics, rather than ethnic tribes or religious populations, would be the focus of economic development, recruitment of leaders, and cultural growth.

Over the years, all Soviet minorities, but central Asians in particular, have experienced a divided sense of identity. For the Muslim populations it is in part *supernational,* with loyalties to both Islam and their Turkic heritage; *national,* with an orientation toward their respective union-republics and the USSR as a whole; and *subnational,* with a focus on clans and tribes. Soviet policy has emphasized the gradual strengthening of the national consciousness and the waning of both supernational and subnational loyalties.[52]

The socialization process there, as elsewhere, consists primarily of two related objectives: creating a national (that is, Russian) cultural environment in the non-Russian areas, and restricting the growth of Muslim values and traditions. To encourage the spread of Russian values, the Party has promoted the immigration of Russians and other Slavs into central Asia and of Muslims into European Russia and Siberia. The former has been noticeably more successful than the latter. By now there are substantial numbers of Russians living in non-Russian republics, especially in the Muslim areas, ranging in proportion from 2.3 percent of the population of Armenia to over 40 percent in Kazakhstan. In the latter republic, in fact, Russians outnumber Kazakhs by 10 percent. See Table 11.1.

Moscow has attempted to attract Muslim youths to European Russia for education and employment, but without much success. The difficulties arise from the resistance of central Asians to being integrated with non-Muslims, whose habits of food and alcohol consumption are very different and whose reaction to Muslim religious practices is often contemptuous. The Muslims' relatively low level of general education and lack of knowledge of the Russian language have made the educational process difficult and created barriers between them and other students. At home, the families of these youths, often subsisting on low incomes, have been overwhelmingly opposed to out-migration; one survey found that only 13 percent of the Tadjik youths who have gone to European Russia did so with the approval of their families.[53]

In the past several years, in fact, the movement of populations between European Russia and central Asia has turned against the expectations of the Party leadership. The rate at which Russians have been moving into central Asia has been declining, and in some areas more Russians are moving back to European Russia than are moving in. Muslims, on the other hand, are multiplying much more rapidly (about two and a half times the national rate) than are the Slavs. Between 1959

TABLE 11.1 RUSSIANS LIVING IN NON-RUSSIAN UNION REPUBLICS

Republics	Percentage of Total Republic Population
Slavic Republics	
Ukraine	21.1
Belorussia	11.9
Caucasian Republics	
Armenia	2.3
Georgia	7.4
Azerbaijan	7.9
Baltic Republics	
Estonia	27.9
Latvia	32.8
Lithuania	8.9
Central Asian Republics	
Kazakhstan	40.8
Uzbekistan	10.8
Turkmenistan	12.6
Tadjikistan	10.4
Kirghizia	25.9
Moldavia	12.8

Source: *Vestnik Statistiki,* 2, 1980, p. 27.

and 1979, Russians increased by 7 million people, while Muslims increased by 20 million.

This imbalance is intensified by the return to central Asia of many Muslims who have been living in European Russia and Siberia. As this "nativization" continues, more Russians can be expected to return to their European homeland. They are not by nature a migratory people, and they do not get along well outside Russia unless the cultural environment is predominantly Russian. While this is still the case in some of the major central Asian cities, such as Alma-Ata, Tashkent, and Dushanbe, the overall environment is changing in ways that make Russians less comfortable. Further, most of the returning Muslims are moving into rural areas rather than cities, in contrast to the pattern in European Russia.[54] Thus, the Russian cultural influence, which is strongest in the large cities of central Asia, is commensurately weakening.

With ethnic minorities, language is almost always a core issue. Since the early 1970s, the central authorities have intensified efforts to establish Russian as the national language. New schools opening in minority areas are supposed to reflect the language preference of the local residents, but Moscow has been disappointed to find that this policy has produced a substantial rise in the proportion of native-language schools. As a result, knowledge of the Russian language in the non-Russian republics is not advancing. (See Table 11.2).)

TABLE 11.2 MINORITIES WHO SPEAK RUSSIAN

Ethnic Group	Russian-Speaking Percentage	Ethnic Group	Russian-Speaking Percentage
Ukrainians	49.8	Estonians	24.2
Belorussias	57.0	Latvians	56.7
Armenians	38.6	Lithuanians	52.1
Georgians	26.7	Kazakhs	52.3
Azerbaijanis	29.5	Uzbeks	49.3
Moldavians	47.4	Turkmeni	25.4
		Tadjiks	29.6
		Kirghizi	29.4

Source: Vestnik Statistiki, 2, 1980, p. 24.

Newspapers in Kazakhstan have been sharply criticized in *Pravda* for excessive concentration on the Kazakh language and culture. To this, a Kazakh poet responded bluntly in a republic newspaper:

To take pride in one's native tongue, to show concern for its purity and foster its development, is one of the chief duties of every Kazakh, of every Kazakh family, of every person who considers himself a Kazakh, of the entire population.[55]

More forceful efforts to give preference to Russian over native languages have met with sharp resistance in minority areas. In 1978, for example, when Moscow leaders attempted to write new republic constitutions that deleted references to the Georgian, Armenian, and Azerbaijanian languages as the official languages of those republics, thousands of Georgians and Armenians took to the streets to protest. As a result the central authorities backed down.

Ethnic Groups and the Military. One hope for more rapid *sblizhenie* rests with the program of compulsory military service. The induction of non-Russians brings them into a cultural environment dominated by Slavs, mainly Russians. The military uses the Russian language exclusively for oral commands and all forms of written communication. Non-Russians are required to learn enough Russian to function in military units, and they are discouraged from speaking their native languages even off-duty. Political lessons in Russian are given regularly throughout military service.

Existing in this environment for their two-year period of service provides a mixed experience for most non-Russian youths. Learning something of the Russian language and living outside their own national territory increase their exposure to a more national set of values. On the other hand, it soon becomes clear to new recruits that their status is well below that of the dominant Slavic majority. Virtually all officers and most noncoms are Slavs, primarily Russian, and combat units are dominated by Slavs. Non-Slavs are assigned overwhelmingly to construction units and as security forces for the prison and workcamp systems. They receive little military training and only limited access to weapons. The more highly technical fields of military service, such as the Strategic Rocket Forces, the Air Force, and the Navy, are staffed almost exclusively by Slavs.[56]

In the post-Brezhnev era, a gradual change has been under way. Commanders and noncoms are given classes on the problems of interethnic conflict, non-Russians are being offered more intensive Russian-language training, and the recruitment of non-Russian officer candidates is being encouraged.[57] Nevertheless, basic prejudices remain as the heightened ethnic consciousness of the Soviet Union's major minorities presents a continuing challenge to the national Party leadership.

Conclusions. The "nationalities problem" encompasses two sets of relations between ethnic minorities and the dominant Russian culture. Deep-seated anti-Russian feelings no doubt continue to create barriers to the creation of a unified Soviet culture. This does not mean, however, that minority populations are necessarily anti-Soviet. One should not underestimate the value to the minorities of the formation of union-republics, the long-term investments in economic and social development, the recruitment of ambitious young people into leadership positions on the republic and national level, and the general effect of the Soviet Union's international prominence. Sovietization has also brought about the cessation of violent confrontations that have historically marked relations among many Soviet minorities.

The central Soviet leadership itself has long pursued a gradualist approach to the integration of the minority populations. Many of the social and cultural decisions that affect ordinary people have been left up to ethnic leaders as long as national priorities are not openly obstructed. The country depends heavily on non-Russian republics as primary sources for food, raw materials, and energy. It looks toward the growing minority populations as increasingly important components in the national labor force and in the military. And it is highly sensitive to the impact of its own majority-minority relations on third-world countries.

The problems that exist between the center and the provinces are likely to force major adjustments in national policies in the coming decades if present trends continue. As recent events in Kazakhstan, Georgia, and elsewhere have demonstrated, the potential for violent protest along ethnic lines is present in Soviet society. It is unlikely, however, that such activities could pose any threat to the country as a whole. On that level, the system remains highly stable.

Case 2: Soviet Youth

In one sense, there has never been a "younger generation" in the Soviet Union until recently. Soviet children have always been perceived, officially, as adults-in-training rather than a separate generation with its own legitimate values. To the extent that a young person's values conflict with adult standards, something in the socialization process has gone wrong: A school has failed, or a parent, or the local Komsomol organization. As an official publication stated, when asked about a "generation gap":

> In a society that has proclaimed as its main objective the complete satisfaction of man's requirements and a constant improvement in his material and cultural standards, there can never be any gap between the wisdom and experience of the older generation and the energy of youth.[58]

The Komsomol is officially in charge of Soviet youth. It controls most young people's clubs and recreational facilities and has broad responsibility for their activities and behavior, both at school and work and during their free time. Its mission is to "bring up the young generation in the spirit of Communism," to guide them along a straight and narrow path to "socially useful labor" and dedicated service to society. Along the way, "it is important that young men and women not indulge in shallow amusements in their free time and that all forms of leisure-time activity facilitate their ideological enrichment and physical development."[59]

That most Soviet teenagers have rejected this course of development is by now widely recognized, both abroad and in the USSR. The pursuit of "shallow amusements" has become a national passion. Westerners used to Brezhnevian conservatism are surprised to see young Muscovites wind-surfing and hang-gliding, cruising on skateboards, scribbling graffiti on public walls, and eating pizza at a local pizza parlor. High-school kids clad in Levi's and camouflage flak-jackets gyrate to the music of Western rock bands blaring from their portable stereos. The temptations of alcohol and drugs are constantly at hand, and the black market in imported clothes and high-tech goods flourishes.[60]

In Soviet cities, large and small, huge apartment complexes that now house most Soviet families surround "courtyards" where the younger crowds hang out. Parents, peering out of seventh-floor windows, can only hope that their children are staying out of trouble.

In many cities, street gangs have become more numerous and more visible. They include the *fanaty*, avid fans of particular sports teams; *urla*, strong-arm groups of working-class youths who control areas of urban parks and streets; and *fashisty*, upper-class youths who don black leather jackets and swastikas and parade their admiration for Adolf Hitler.[61]

In the past several years, the most widely publicized youth gangs have come from the Moscow suburb of Lyubertsy. These "Lyubers" are mostly members of informal weightlifting clubs who come into downtown Moscow in their checkered pants looking for action. They seek out hippies, skinheads, punk rockers, and other nonconformists who, they claim, offend public taste and morality.[62]

In the judgment of a Soviet journalist, "the young people's environment in suburban Moscow has formed its own style of behavior, its own fashions, its own laws of brotherhood and friendship based on geographic origin."[63] Much of this style and fashion is based on Western culture and supported by foreign goods that pour across the borders through the gray and black markets. Much of it is also provided legally by a government that has somewhat relaxed its opposition to Western music, dress styles, and hard goods. And the whole phenomenon is by no means confined to Moscow.

The root problem is not so much the intrusion of Western culture into the USSR, although there is a strong conservative element in the political elite that opposes just that. The more serious problem is the extent to which young people have defected from the traditional values of their own society. Sociological surveys have demonstrated repeatedly that the younger generation has little interest in manual labor or collectivist projects, little respect for the Komsomol as a source of values, and little confidence in grand Party plans for a bright future.[64]

Conflicting theories abound about the causes of this decline in Communist values, but there is some consensus as well. Life for a Soviet teenager suffers, in the words of one of them, from "elementary, acute boredom." For years, the Party has invested in family-oriented, adult-run facilities and activities consistent with its concept of a wholesome environment for children's nonschool hours. When the evidence of defection began to mount, it intensified this investment. It organized more family picnics and school outings, more music lessons and evening courses, more "red corners" in apartment complexes, and more folk concerts and hobby clubs.

To combat unwholesome street gatherings, the Komsomol formed "pedagogical detachments" of young workers and students, whose job was "to become the real masters of the street."[65] Despite the recruitment of nearly 2 million youths for this effort, little has come of it. In Leningrad, stronger measures have been introduced. A law enacted in 1984 imposed strict rules for teenagers: No one under sixteen could be on the streets without an adult after 9 P.M.; youths arrested twice for drunkenness may have their money (including wages) confiscated and managed by a city agency; children under fourteen may not ride bikes on the streets; and parents may be fined for any violations by their children.[66]

The results of these tactics have been disappointing to Party leaders. In the past several years, a different approach to youth has appeared alongside, and often in competition with, the traditional one. It offers a somewhat modernized image of the Soviet teenager, in which youthful fancies, such as hard rock music, innovative hair styles and colors, and Western clothes, are no longer seen as evidence of depravity. Since 1986, consistent with *glasnost,* there has been a sharp increase in the types of entertainment and amusements that seem to appeal to Soviet youth. The government-owned recording firm, Melodia, is issuing tapes and records of many Soviet groups that had been shunned in the past, and popular Western groups are touring the Soviet Union in increasing numbers. Dancing is still forbidden at rock concerts, and Soviet rock groups avoid the political and sexual themes that characterize much of Western popular music.

This relaxation of official standards is criticized frequently in the press as a retreat from Communist standards for the upbringing of Soviet youth. On the personal level, there is little tolerance among adults for the youth culture that is developing, but growing recognition that there is no way to stop it. Even the Komsomol has been infiltrated with the "new wave" of youthful values and interests, as manifested in part by a growing reluctance to punish members who run afoul of the authorities. In one recent year, only 38.8 percent of Komsomol members who were convicted of crimes were expelled from the organization.[67]

CONCLUSIONS

Assessing the effectiveness of the socialization process is a task that Soviet scholars have never seriously undertaken. The inclination to deny any evidence of failure is so strong in the CPSU that sociological research that might produce such evidence is generally prohibited, or at least concealed from public scrutiny. In addition, Soviet citizens are conditioned to giving approved answers to questions put by strangers. Therefore, any conclusions to be drawn will be at best tentative and disputable.

Our initial discussion in this chapter suggested the usefulness of looking at Soviet social orientation in terms of basic values, beliefs, and behavior. The socialization process aims at affecting all three, of course, but it is not equally successful in all. On the level of basic values, there are clearly areas of consensus that are shared not only by Soviet citizens but even by defectors and refugees. A commitment to the social welfare programs of the country—job security, free medical care, and education, and a gradually rising standard of living—is widely shared, for example.[68]

Nevertheless, the level of commitment to the system as a whole may be considerably lower. Western studies repeatedly point to a general and long-term decline of civic morale, an increasing disillusionment in all age groups toward the values of the regime. A Soviet sociologist who defected in the 1970s has argued that "almost all members of the society, except a few old Stalinists and some parts of the elite, are in complete opposition to official values and to Soviet ideology as a whole."[69]

It is at least clear from persistent complaints in the Soviet press that the creation of the "new Soviet person" is not proceeding according to official expectations. Manifestations of aberrant social behavior continue to increase, and glasnost is serving to give them heightened publicity and, in a way, legitimacy. To some extent, the ideological apparatus has tended to retreat before these developments, unable either to stem the tide or to rechannel it in ideologically approved directions.

As a result, the images of reality, or beliefs, that are promulgated by the ideological apparatus are increasingly confronting a more realistic, and negative, picture of Soviet society. Years of denial that there is unemployment in the USSR, that drug addiction and prostitution are serious problems, or that relations between Russians and non-Russians are antagonistic have been challenged by recent revelations in the Soviet press. Under the policy of *glasnost,* Soviet citizens are acquiring a sounder basis for drawing their own conclusions about the quality of Soviet life. The political danger to the Party in all this is the potential loss of its ability to define reality for its citizens.

On still another level, that of behavior, Soviet citizens, especially the younger generation, have already moved well beyond the limits of traditional Party prescriptions. In the economic sphere, the widespread indulgence in the second economy, the lack of discipline at work, and the indifference to quality and service reflect an environment in which conservative Party values hold little sway. Outwardly, public behavior adheres to the general standards, but this patina of conformity conceals a great deal of behavioral diversity.

In general, the socialization of the Soviet people creates a dual character to the mass personality. On the one hand, people come to understand and assimilate the official values and behavioral expectations of the political system. On the other hand, they act in ways that promote their personal interests even where these contradict the dictates of the Party. These divergent qualities are not necessarily in conflict with one another. It is, in fact, one of the most important characteristics of Soviet communism that the official conception of society can so sharply diverge from the reality of everyday life without producing any significant degree of social unrest. The Soviet people have learned to tolerate a relatively high degree of discontent without threatening the stability of the political system. To that extent, at least, the socialization process has not failed.

NOTES

1. V.E. Semenov. *Sotsial'no-Psikhologicheskiie Problemy Nravstvennogo Vospitanniia Lichnosti* (Leningrad: Leningradskogo Universiteta, 1984), p. 23.
2. These are excerpted from a longer list in Seymour M. Rosen, *Education and Modernization in the USSR* (Menlo Park, Calif.: Addison-Wesley, 1981, p. 137–38.
3. See Peter Juviler, "The Soviet Family in Post-Stalin Perspective," in Stephen F. Cohen, Alexander Rabinowitch, and Robert Sharlet, *The Soviet Union Since Stalin* (Bloomington: Indiana University Press, 1980), p. 243.
4. Nursury schools are free to families who earn 60 rubles a month or less.
5. Quoted in V.P. Eliutin, *Higher Education in a Country of Developed Socialism,* trans. in *Soviet Education,* December 1984, p. 63.
6. Studenikin, *Kommunisticheskoe vospitanie,* p. 31; quoted in John Morison, "The Political Content of Education in the USSR," in J.J. Tomiak, ed., *Soviet Education in the 1980s* (London: St. Martin's Press, 1983), p. 160.
7. For a detailed look at the higher school curriculum in Communist subjects, see Eliutin, *Higher Education,* chapter 3.
8. *Sotsiologicheskiye Issledovaniya, No. 2,* 1981; cited in David Shipler, *Russia, Broken Idols, Solemn Dreams* (New York: Times Books, 1983), p. 196.
9. M. Rutkevich, in *Sovetskaya Rossia,* October 24, 1986; trans. in *Current Digest of the Soviet Press,* December 24, 1986, p. 3.

10. Ibid., p. 1.
11. Statistics are from Mervyn Matthews, "Long Term Trends in Soviet Education," in J.J. Tomiak, ed., *Soviet Education in the 1980's* (London: St. Martin's Press, 1983), p. 6.
12. See E. Saar and A. Yunti, "Shkala Prestizha Professii Sredi Studenchestva Estonskoi SSR," in *Sotsialno-Professionalnaya Orientatsia Studenchestva* (Vilnius: 1981), pp. 29–43.
13. N.N. Bokarev, *Sotsiologicheskie issledovaniia effektivnosti lektsionnoi propagandy* (Moscow: Znanie, 1980), cited in David C. Lee, "Public Organizations in Adult Education in the Soviet Union," *Comparative Education Review*, Vol. 30, No. 3, August 1986, p. 345.
14. Frederick C. Barghoorn and Thomas F. Remington, *Politics, USSR* (Boston: Little, Brown, 1986), p. 173.
15. See Lee, "Public Organizations," p. 346, 350.
16. Cited in David E. Powell, *Antireligious Propaganda in the Soviet Union: A Study of Mass Persuasion* (Cambridge, Mass.: MIT Press, 1975), p. 107.
17. *Sovetskaya Estonia*, October 21, 1984.
18. CPSU Central Committee Resolution, "On the Further Improvement of Ideological and Political Educational Work," April 26, 1979; quoted by Valerij S. Korobeinikov, "The Role of Mass Media in a Developed Socialist Society," in Walter M. Brasch and Dana R. Ulloth, *The Press and the State: Sociohistorical and Contemporary Studies* (New York: University Press of America, 1986), p. 354.
19. Quoted in Daniel Tarschys, *The Soviet Political Agenda* (Armonk, N.Y.: M. E. Sharpe, 1979), p. 46.
20. *Izvestia*, 11 July 1985, p. 3.
21. *Los Angeles Times*, 4 May 1983, p. 2.
22. See Gayle Durham Hollander, *Soviet Political Indoctrination, Developments in Mass Media and Propaganda Since Stalin* (New York: Praeger, 1972), p. 33.
23. Findings on this subject come primarily from Ellen Propper Mickiewicz, *Media and the Russian Public* (New York: Praeger, 1981), chapter 5; and Tarschys, *Soviet Political Agenda*, pp. 47–50.
24. See Mickiewicz, *Media and the Russian Public*, pp. 18–31.
25. Ibid., p. 20.
26. Radio Liberty publication, cited in John L. Scherer, (ed.) *USSR: Facts and Figures Annual*, (Vol. 9), (Gulf Breeze, Fla.:Academic International Press, 1985), p. 317.
27. Quoted in David MacKenzie and Michael W. Curran, *A History of Russia and the Soviet Union* (Homewood, Ill.: Dorsey Press, 1982), p. 550.
28. Quoted in Jesse D. Clarkson, *A History of Russia* (New York: Random House, 1961, p. 733.
29. Quoted in Martin Crouch and Robert Porter, eds., *Understanding Soviet Politics Through Literature* (London: George Allen and Unwin, 1984), p. 7.
30. V. Dashkevich, *Izvestia*, 1 March 1987; trans. in *Current Digest of the Soviet Press*, XXXIX:9, p. 4.
31. Ibid., p. 3.
32. Ibid.
33. Lyudmila Kasyanova, *Sovietskaya Rossia*, July 18, 1985; trans. in *Current Digest of the Soviet Press*, XXVII:40, October 30, 1985.
34. *Pravda*, 14 February 1987; trans. in *Current Digest of the Soviet Press*, XXXIX:7, March 18, 1987, p. 8.
35. Ibid., p. 6.
36. *Izvestia*, 15 February 1987; trans. in *Current Digest of the Soviet Press*, XXXIX:7, March 18, 1987, p. 6.

37. Ibid., p. 7.
38. *Izvestia,* 25 February 1987; trans. in *Current Digest of the Soviet Press,* XXXIX:7, March 18, 1987, p. 8. See also the statement by *Pravda's* editor, V. G. Afanaseyev, in *Pravda,* 15 March 1987, p. 1,3–4.
39. Ibid., p. 7.
40. Ibid.
41. Yu. Makhrin, *Pravda,* 27 February 1987, p. 3; trans. in *Current Digest of the Soviet Press,* XXXIX:9, April 1, 1987, p. 24.
42. Afanaseyev, *Pravda.*
43. Speech to news and propaganda officials, *Pravda,* 14 February 1987, p. 1–2; trans. in *Current Digest of the Soviet Press,* XXXIX:7, p. 8.
44. Vladimir Bukovsky, "Glasnost, Genuine or Illusory?" *The World and I,* June 1987, p. 28.
45. See Alexander M. Nekrich, *The Punished Peoples* (New York: W.W. Norton & Co., 1978).
46. Paul A. Goble, "Managing the Multinational USSR," *Problems of Communism,* July-August 1985, p. 83.
47. Alexander Shtromas, "The Building of a Multi-National Soviet 'Socialist Federalism:' Success and Failures," *Canadian Review of Studies in Nationalism,* Spring 1986, p. 91.
48. Martha Brill Olcott, "Yuri Andropov and the 'National Question,' *Soviet Studies,* January 1985, p. 106.
49. Michael Rywkin, *Moscow's Muslim Challenge* (London: M.E. Sharpe, 1982), pp. 126, 136.
50. *Pravda,* 13 February 1987, p. 2.
51. *Izvestia,* 24 January 1987, p. 3.
52. For a discussion of this phenomenon, see Alexandre Bennigsen and Marie Broxup, *The Islamic Threat to the Soviet State* (New York: St. Martin's Press, 1983), pp. 135ff.
53. For a discussion of this program, see P. Gurshumov and R.L. Kogai, *Sotsiologicheskie Issledovania,* No. 2, April-June 1985, pp. 94–98.
54. In the past two decades, the rural population of the RSFSR has dropped by 27 percent, while it has increased by 75 percent in Uzbekistan, 83 percent in Turkmenistan, and 97 percent in Tadzhikistan. *Narodnoye Khoziastvo SSSR v 1980,* 1981, pp. 10–11; cited in John L. Scherer, *USSR, Facts and Figures Annual,* Vol. 9, 1985, p. 52.
55. T. Yesilbayev, *Pravda,* 11 February 1987, p. 2; trans. in *Current Digest of the Soviet Press,* XXXIX:7, p. 4.
56. S. Enders Wimbush and Alex Alexiev, "The Ethnic Factor in the Soviet Armed Forces: Preliminary Findings," *A Rand Note,* N-1486-NA, May 1980, p. 53.
57. Goble, "Managing the Multinational USSR," p. 80–81.
58. G. Zhuravlev, et al, *Soviet Youth, Questions and Answers* (Moscow: Novosti Press Agency, 1974), p. 66.
59. Resolution of the CPSU Central Committee, *Pravda,* 7 July 1984, pp. 1–2; trans. in *Current Digest of the Soviet Press,* XXXVI:27, August 1, 1984, p. 3.
60. In 1984, 46,000 people were officially listed as drug adicts; 80 percent were under thirty years of age. *Pravda,* 6 January 1987, p. 3.
61. Richard Tempest gives a fuller description of these groups in "Youth Soviet Style," *Problems of Communism,* May/June, 1984, pp. 63–64.
62. See Vladimir Yakovlev, "The Office of the Lyubery," *Ogonyok,* January 1987, pp. 20–21; and *Sovetskaya Rossia,* March 4, 1987, p. 6, for another view.
63. A. Kupriyanov, *Sobesednik,* February 1987; trans. in *Current Digest of the Soviet Press,* XXXIX:10, April 8, 1987, p. 4.
64. See, for example, Vladimir Shlapentokh, *Sociology and Politics, The Soviet Case* (Falls

Church, Va.: Delphic Associates, 1985), p. 49; and V. M. Saturin, Molodozh: Doverie i Otvetstvennost] (Kiev: Naykova Dumka, 1984).

65. *Sovetskaya Rossiya,* 1 February 1984; trans. in *Current Digest of the Soviet Press,* XXXVI:5, February 29, 1984, p. 2.

66. *Leningradskaya Pravda,* 9 February 1984, p. 2.

67. *Bakinsky Rabochy,* 30 September 1984.

68. See Zvi Gitelman, "Soviet Political Culture: Insights from Jewish Emigres," *Soviet Studies,* October, 1977, pp. 543–64; and Stephen White, "Continuity and Change in Soviet Political Culture: An Emigre Study," *Comparative Political Systems,* October, 1978, pp. 381–95.

69. Vladimir Shlapentokh, "The Study of Values as a Social Phenomenon: The Soviet Case," *Social Forces,* December 1982, p. 406.

CHAPTER 12
Guarding the Social Order

In a society as intensively socialized to a single set of values as the Soviet Union, it is an odd paradox that a high level of state coercion also seems necessary in order to shape and control public behavior. The explanation lies not so much in the failure of the socialization process as in the impossible job it has been asked to do. The Communist Party has attempted through the socialization process to persuade highly religious peoples to give up their faith, land-hungry peasants to submit to state-run collectives, an increasingly well-educated population to accept without question the official version of everything, however implausible, and a younger generation to do only what their elders think is best for them. It seems unlikely that any society in human history has successfully accomplished such a revolution in values by persuasion alone.

To enforce adherence to its rules and policies where voluntary obedience has failed, the Communist Party leadership maintains two overlapping structures of police power: the regular police and the judiciary to administer ordinary criminal and tort law; and a special police apparatus to deal with activities that constitute, in the Party's mind, a threat to the political system. The latter apparatus is managed mainly by the Committee for State Security (KGB), although other agencies are involved as well.

In this chapter we shall examine both structures of police power, seeking to understand the difference between them and the significance of those differences for the political system as a whole. The focus will be on those citizens who choose to operate outside the rules of society, especially those who, for religious, political, ethnic, or personal reasons, challenge the Soviet system on the issue of individual rights.

THE ROLE OF LAW

The effective management of the Soviet Union requires far more than the mere issuance of edicts and policies by the Party Politburo. It requires, above all, a high degree of predictable behavior, which in turn requires that people understand clearly what is expected of them. In the absence of Stalinist terror, this predictability can only be achieved through the application of general rules in a consistent manner to the entire population. The Party leadership, therefore, has a strong commitment to a system of laws as a way of structuring the behavior of its citizens as well as directing the activities of the government and Party bureaucracies.

On the other hand, the Party Politburo reserves the right to act in any way it chooses on any matter it decides to consider. There is neither in the practice nor in the theory of the Soviet state any effective constraint on the authority of the Politburo. The Soviet Constitution (Article 6) does provide that "all Party organizations are required to operate within the framework of the USSR Constitution." Yet the Constitution itself was written by and is frequently amended by decisions of the Party leadership. Legislation is enacted by the same authority, as are the major directives of the Council of Ministers and all regional and local governments.

Two characteristics of Soviet law stand out under these circumstances. First, the law is an important instrument of rule by the Party Politburo, perhaps its most important. Secondly, the Party Politburo is above the law and the Constitution, answerable presumably only to history. In practice, this means that the party enforces the laws of the land except in cases where the application of a given law would contravene the wishes of the leadership in that instance. It also means that government and Party officials at all levels must be sensitive not only to the written laws and regulations under which they work but also to the inclinations of the Party leadership. In any given instance, either one may be the controlling factor.

It is also important to understand that many policies and decisions of the Party leadership are not issued as laws at all. Party organs, especially the Central Committee, issue resolutions that have the standing of law and must be enforced. Party leaders often launch "campaigns" against some social or economic evil, which mobilize countless officials and voluntary organizations against malefactors. Such campaigns generate volumes of ministerial regulations and impose standards that are expected to be adhered to by everyone concerned.[1]

Policies that are given the form of legal enactments are issued in three main forms: formal laws (*zakony*) enacted by the legislature; edicts (*ukazy*) issued by the Presidium of the Supreme Soviet, and regulatory decrees (*postanovleniye*) issued in vast numbers by all governmental agencies in their areas of jurisdiction. As guidelines for behavior, many of these enactments are deficient and difficult to understand. Most laws are incompletely written, containing cross-references to other laws and directives. Phrases such as "provided there is no infringement of this or that" or "specific provisions are defined in such-and-such a resolution" abound, leaving citizens confused while local administrators find ample grounds to forbid activities that higher authorities may have wanted to encourage. *Izvestia* recently offered a typical example involving the USSR Law on the Protection and Utilization of Historical and Cultural Landmarks:

> More than half of its articles were in cross-reference form. The USSR Council of Ministers was supposed to make the law specific. But the regulations in question were not adopted by the USSR government until September 16, 1982—six years after the law had taken effect. It was more detailed than the 1976 law, but it, in turn, contained many cross-references of its own—this time, cross-references to departmental rulings . . . [many of which] had not only not been adopted but had not even been drawn up.[2]

In other cases, laws are left intentionally vague so as to maximize the discretionary authority of administrators or Party officials. Many laws used against political dissidents appear in this form, as illustrated in the discussion below. The disadvantage for the Party leadership in vague laws is that when the leadership does wish to give clear directions to the public, it often finds that legal statutes prove an ineffective means. In the recently approved Law on Individual Enterprises, a centerpiece of Gorbachev's "reconstruction" program, the crucial clauses identifying the types of activities permitted and those prohibited were so heavily cross-referenced and surrounded with conditions that both administrators and citizens were confused.

An additional source of confusion arises from the fact that a large majority of the decrees cross-referenced in laws are never published.[3] They reside in ministerial files and are used largely at the discretion of government administrators. For the citizen, it is difficult to argue against a bureaucrat who claims to be following legal procedures that are nowhere available to the citizen.

The major problem with enforcing the law arises in this context: What must be enforced are not only written statutes but also edicts and decrees that may not have been published; written laws containing references to unpublished decrees; and Party policies articulated partly in laws and partly in other formats—decrees, speeches, resolutions of Party meetings, and long-standing attitudes of the ruling elite. Among those responsible for enforcement, there is an understandable uncertainty as to what the rules of Soviet society actually are and therefore whether someone has actually violated one of them. Obviously, the individual citizen has the same problem. The long-term result is a strong tendency on everyone's part to consider every act that is not specifically authorized to be a violation of a rule or policy. In other words, what is not permitted is prohibited.

With these difficulties in mind, we shall consider the two structures of police power as they affect the behavior of Soviet citizens. We begin with the enforcement of ordinary laws and policies and then consider those laws and policies that are applied to various categories of "anti-Soviet," or "dissident" behavior. They overlap to a certain extent, but in major respects they operate separately and under different rules of procedure.

ENFORCING ORDINARY LAWS AND POLICIES

The Procuracy

The Procuracy of the USSR is a ministerial-level government organ that employs over 15,000 lawyers, about one-eighth of the entire legal profession. It is run by a Procurator-General and a Collegium of eight senior administrators, all of whom are appointed by the Party leadersip for indefinite terms. The Procuracy is an independent agency, not subordinate at any level to the government or the courts, and it is subordinate to the CPSU only at the highest level. This is intended to protect it from local interference by Party or government agencies.[4]

The Procuracy has a very broad mandate. It is responsible for ensuring that government agencies, economic firms, and other establishments do not violate the laws. It institutes civil suits against individuals or collectives, acts as state prosecutor in all criminal trials, investigates potential violations of the law, and oversees the processing of citizen complaints. In addition to its law enforcement responsibilities, the Procuracy also supervises the legal organs of the government, including the uniformed militia and (to a limited degree) the agencies of the Committee of State Security (KGB) as well as the prison system.

This supervisory role (*nadzor*) does not give the Procuracy unlimited power over the government, however. Unlike the court system, it cannot order or forbid any action by a government agency or official. It is limited to issuing protests, warnings, and findings, and to recommending penalties for noncompliance. Nevertheless, the Procuracy is a powerful body with well-established authority to see that the laws are carried out.

In the day-to-day business of law enforcement, Procuracy lawyers are the principal authority. They oversee the conduct of criminal investigations, examine civil accusations, bring indictments against suspects, carry out the prosecution of defendants in court, and, if they think it warranted, appeal court decisions to higher courts. The Procuracy also has general responsibility for the entire court system. In this capacity, it must ensure that court procedures comply with the law and that defendants are provided with an adequate defense.

Soviet Lawyers

Most Soviet lawyers are employed either in private practice (*advokaty*)[5] or as counselors to economic firms and government offices (*iurisconsults*).[6] *Advokaty* are organized into colleges of advocates, of which there are 153 in the USSR. Moscow and Leningrad each have both a city and a regional college of advocates, where several hundred lawyers are employed. Each college is managed by a presidium, whose members are elected by the college attorneys for three-year terms. These elections, according to most sources, are relatively free, and debates on policy issues are often heated.[7] Nevertheless, colleges of advocates operate under the general supervision of justice sections of local soviets or branches of the Ministry of Justice, as well as Party committees.

Large cities have legal offices at various locations to serve clients. Some of their business is on a drop-in basis, and citizens have the right to request specific attorneys. Fees for legal services are fixed by the Ministry of Justice, and they are, by Western standards, extremely low. In fact, many legal services, such as assisting in the recovery of alimony and the evaluation of workers' compensation claims, are made available without charge. In cases of financial hardship, fees can be waived by the presidium of the college.

Partly in response to a recent government campaign urging people to utilize their legal rights more fully, the amount of legal business undertaken by advocates and legal counselors is growing rapidly. Recent legislation has enabled lawyers to represent clients before administrative boards and government agencies as well, and this should open a broad avenue of new legal activity for *advokaty*.

Citizens in Law Enforcement

As with other aspects of the political system, law enforcement involves masses of citizens in a variety of ways. Soviet citizens have both the responsibility to report violations of the law that come to their attention and the right to complain against employers, officials, and others who they believe have violated their rights. They also serve as volunteers in several mass organizations whose responsibility is to monitor the fulfillment of government directives by social and economic institutions and to observe and correct improper behavior by individuals. The largest organizations utilizing citizen volunteers are the organs of People's Control, Komsomol and trade union inspectorates, and the Volunteer People's Guards (*druzhiny*).

Organs of People's Control. These organs mobilize a vast army of volunteers, over 10 million strong and organized into more than a million groups and centers. Their function is to monitor the fulfillment of the Party's economic plans, the observance of laws relating to the citizen complaints, and the exposure of corruption and bureaucratism. They are prohibited from getting involved with matters that are under investigation by the Procuracy or the police, and they have no authority to make arrests. They can, however, exercise lesser powers: reprimanding errant officials, publicly exposing violations of regulations and policies, and recommending fines and dismissal from employment for officials who are derelict in their duties.[8]

The organs of People's Control are headed by a national People's Control Committee, which is formed and maintained by the USSR Supreme Soviet. At the local level, the organs operate under dual subordination: to the local soviet and to the higher-level People's Control office. In addition, they are under the general authority of the local Party committee and are required to work with individual ministries whenever an investigation touches the ministries' concerns. In practice, then, the organs of people's control are subject to supervision by a whole range of Party and government agencies, ensuring that the organs' activities will remain within acceptable bounds.[9]

Komsomol Searchlight. In a tradition dating back to the Revolution, the Party's youth organization maintains a corps of volunteer inspectors called "Searchlight" (*Prozhektor*). Formed at factories, farms, offices, and schools, Searchlight inspectors seek out waste and inefficiency in the economy, violations of labor discipline by young workers, and instances of petty theft and absenteeism. Searchlight groups often work with, or under the supervision of, People's Control agencies, and they have little independent authority.

Trade Union Inspectors. Trade union committees in workplaces normally form control groups that monitor many of the activities of employees on the job and of management as well. They engage in periodic inspections of the use of public funds in the workplace, fulfillment of housing and recreational facilities for workers, and the operation of restaurants, stores, warehouses, and depots.

In the relatively structured environment of the factory or office, observing and influencing individual behavior is a fairly routine process, backed up by the economic sanctions available to management and state agencies. Outside of the workplace, however—in the streets, the home, the parks, and recreational facilities—the task is more difficult. To maintain approved standards of behavior, Soviet leaders have formed a network of social organizations focusing on the individual during his or her free time. Such organizations include the Volunteer People's Guards (*druzhiny*), residential and neighborhood committees, and local committees formed for special purposes, such as combatting hooliganism and public drunkenness.

Volunteer People's Guards—Druzhiny. Subordinate to the Procuracy, *druzhiny* units are formed by volunteers acting to assist the police in maintaining order in public places. Numbering over 7 million and wearing their customary red armbands, *druzhiniki* are commonly found directing traffic, controlling street brawls, containing hooliganism, and identifying violators of the laws. They function mainly to extend the control of public behavior without the direct involvement of police or other formal authorities. They are widely used to discipline citizens who, while violating no laws, are acting in unapproved ways.

Druzhiny have the authority to demand identification of citizens, to place people under arrest, and to enter any office or public place in pursuit of a suspect. Reports of abuses of their authority by *druzhiniki* occasionally appear in the press, but there is also evidence that they make some difference in controlling street crime and maintaining order. *Druzhiniki* are protected by law against attack and resistance to arrest just as regular police officers are.[10]

Residence Committees. The *residence committee* that operates in every apartment building has several functions. It monitors the physical condition of the building, ensures that apartments are properly assigned and used for legitimate purposes, and receives complaints from residents about conditions in the apartment. One of its major jobs is to control the movement of people into and out of apartment buildings. All Soviet citizens must carry internal passports that indicate their name, nationality, place of authorized residence, previous residences, present and previous employment, and other information. All residents must be registered with the police of their communities and must reregister whenever they move. Some of the larger cities, including particularly Moscow and Leningrad, are closed to new residents without special permission; thus, checking residential documents is a major task of the residence committees. Despite this control, the number of illegal residents in Moscow and Leningrad alone has been estimated in the millions.

In addition to established networks of volunteer controllers, state and Party organizations frequently form special groups to monitor and correct specific types of antisocial behavior. Groups such as the Komsomol's "pedagogical detachments" (described in the previous chapter) are formed with specific objectives—in this case to curb youth-gang activities in city streets and parks.

Taken together, these various forms of public participation in law enforcement engage an army of volunteer citizens numbering somewhere over 40 million people. The effective integration of this army into the regular law enforcement and judicial processes is an almost overwhelming task. The vast majority of volunteers have little training for their activities. Thus, the potential both for the ineffective use of their authority and the abuse of that authority is apparent. On the whole, volunteer groups find themselves carefully guided in their activities by regular administrative agencies. The CPSU also keeps a close watch on them. In the People's Control agencies, for example, over 50 percent of the volunteers are Party members.[11]

Public support of these social organizations is often criticized as lukewarm, and official membership figures are frequently exaggerated.[12] Nevertheless, it is likely that the link between individuals and local authorities that is created by these volunteers is an accepted and approved one. The atmosphere of genuine participation of citizens in the management of their immediate environment is often commended in surveys and interviews. The endless monitoring of people's activities, both public and private, tends to be viewed not so much as a police activity but rather as a normal expression of mutual responsibility in maintaining the social order. In their everyday lives, the Soviet people spontaneously monitor the behavior of their neighbors and co-workers and even strangers on the street, and they are quick to point out deviations from accepted standards.

Citizen Complaints. Soviet citizens have numerous and well-developed channels for submitting formal complaints to the government. In addition to lending a sense of democracy to the political process, citizen complaints serve an important law enforcement purpose. Individuals who believe that their rights have been violated or that they have been treated unfairly by a government official may complain either orally or in writing to the agency involved. That agency must investigate, notify the complainant of its decision, and implement its decision, all within restrictive time limits.[13] Citizens have the right to appeal if not satisfied with the response, and these appeals are often directed to the Procuracy, which is also legally obliged to take action on the complaints. In fact, according to one study, nearly two-thirds of the local activities of procurators is generated by citizen complaints.[14]

As one might expect, officials subject to such complaints have ways to protect themselves, and the system as a whole has placed some operational limits on the effectiveness of citizen complaints. Once an initial complaint is made, for example, a citizen is allowed no further involvement with the process. If the agency or official to whom the complaint is directed declines to act, the citizen has no recourse, except to appeal to another agency. If one can enlist the aid of the Procuracy or one's trade union or a local soviet, one's chances for a satisfactory outcome improve considerably. Unfortunately, it is likely that these agencies will be more concerned with maintaining good relations with each other than they are with satisfying the complaint of an individual citizen.

The right of a citizen to sue a government agency or official was finally granted in legislation that took ten years to write. Implemented on January 1, 1988, the law "On Procedures for Appealing to the Courts Unlawful Actions by Officials that Infringe the Rights of Citizens" appeared to provide at last a legal remedy for aggrieved citizens. However, because of intense lobbying by government agencies against the principle of legal challenges by citizens, and by the courts against the anticipated increase in their workload, the new law was emasculated before even being implemented. The final wording limited the actions that can be appealed in court to "actions carried out *individually* by officials on their own account or on behalf of the agency they represent. . . ." However, in the words of a senior Soviet legal scholar, "the overwhelming majority . . . of the decisions that citizens dispute as infringing their rights are adopted collectively. According to the law's text then, all such actions have been deliberately placed outside the sphere of judicial monitoring."[15]

The importance of citizen complaints to law enforcement agencies is undeniable. Citizens often reveal corruption, malfeasance, and incompetence in officials that formal monitoring procedures fail to uncover. The Procuracy pays close attention to citizen complaints, not so much out of a spirit of public service as for the information they provide about the workings of the state bureaucracy. Control of this bureaucracy is one of the Procuracy's major responsibilities.

The Judicial Process

Soviet courts are organized in a four-tier system, headed by the USSR Supreme Court and including the republic Supreme Courts, the provincial courts, and the broad network of "peoples' courts." The Supreme Court consists of thirty-four judges, including the presidents of the union-republic supreme courts, and forty-five people's assessors. The latter participate only in actual trials conducted by the court, but their presence on the court conforms to the general principle that ordinary citizens be involved at all levels of the judiciary process. All members of the Supreme Court are appointed by the Party leadership, then formally elected by the Supreme Soviet for five-year renewable terms. The Court is organized into criminal, civil, and military panels before which cases are heard both on appeal and in original jurisdiction. There is also a system of "special courts" to hear cases involving secret state information.[16]

Although the Supreme Court has no power to judge the constitutionality of laws, it exercises considerable influence over their interpretation. Because most laws (*zakony*) are stated in general terms, the application of laws to specific cases is normally left to the judiciary and the procuracy. The Supreme Court is authorized to develop "guiding explanations" of laws, which are binding on lower courts and the procuracy. This gives it an important quasi-legislative role.[17]

By far the most numerous courts are the people's courts, which handle 96 percent of all judicial activity. A people's court consists of a judge and two lay assessors. The assessors, selected by the Ministry of Justice with Party approval (followed by popular election), have the same rights as the judge and are present at all phases of a trial. However, in practice, they are almost wholly subordinate to the judge, rarely raising objections or participating verbally.

In dealing with a court of law, a Soviet citizen faces an institution that is heavily stacked in favor of the state. An individual arrested on suspicion of a criminal act enters a maze of procedures, most of which are posited on the assumption of almost certain guilt. After arrest, the accused is placed in the custody of the Procuracy (that is, the police) throughout the entire investigation of the matter. In complex cases, this may take months, during which investigators interview witnesses, gather evidence, interrogate the accused, and prepare the case for trial. During this time, the accused is confined to jail, as there is no provision for bail. He cannot demand an appearance before a judge on grounds of *habeus corpus,* nor is he entitled to the services of a lawyer at this stage. Often, communication with family members and friends is forbidden until the trial.

Despite the requirement of the RSFSR Criminal Code (Article 77) that a confession must be corroborated by evidence in order to convict, guilty judgments based on confessions alone are standard practice. The tendency, therefore, of investigators to extract confessions at all costs is well known. Judges often treat the absense of a confession from the accused as a delaying tactic, indicating a refusal to cooperate with the court or to repent one's "crime." The legally required "presumption of innocence" has not become the operating rule in either the Procuracy or the courts. The presumption of guilt is so strong in fact that judges and prosecutors tend to see acquittal as a failure of the judicial process.[18]

Rather than admit failure, judges facing cases that involve charges too blatantly absurd to justify a conviction normally return them for "additional investigation," during which they can be quietly dropped. Unfortunately for the accused, the suspicion of guilt often remains in the community long after the case is settled. Under the circumstances, people against whom charges have been dismissed for lack of evidence sometimes demand a public court trial and acquital as the only way to convince the community of their innocence.[19]

The suspicion of guilt attached to anyone who has been arrested produces a second casualty as well: the defense attorney who speaks for the accused and who therefore tends to be seen as spokesman for a criminal. The right of an accused to see his attorney is determined mainly by the Procurator's office (that is, the *prosecuting* attorney), and the confidentiality of conversations between attorney and client is an often-violated principle. Prosecutors sometimes attempt to force defense attorneys to take the stand as witnesses in order to learn what clients have revealed in confidence.[20]

Accusations against individuals often arise from anonymous letters mailed to the police or the courts. Traditionally, the right to do so has been protected so that aggrieved persons need not fear retribution from the accused. In practice, the right has been grossly abused. For years, critics have complained of the harm done by unjust anonymous accusations, often lodged out of personal enmity. In 1985, amendments to the RSFSR Criminal Code finally outlawed anonymous accusations and sought to protect accusers by prosecuting anyone attempting to silence fair criticism.[21] Yet a year later, an *Izvestia* correspondent was unable to discover, after extensive research, a single example of the new law being applied to an anonymous letter-writer.[22]

Although the Soviet Constitution requires criminal trials to be open to the public, the right is often ignored. Journalists are subjected to document checks and even expelled from trials if the judge so decides.[23] The other two members of the court, the lay assessors, rarely do more than nod agreeably in support of the judge's decisions. To challenge the judge's rulings would cause difficulties for them outside the courtroom.

Individuals who feel their investigation or trial has not been conducted fairly have the right to appeal the decision. There is little hope of reversal, however, as the appeals court has only the written report of the investigator and the transcript of the trial to review. No one involved in the case is involved in the review. Consequently, unless the violation appears clearly in the written record, the higher court has no basis to act.

In this case, the person has one other avenue of appeal: He or she may lodge a protest (as opposed to an appeal) with the procuracy or a higher court and hope for a review of the case. The chances of a reversal through this procedure are also slim, as the complaint process is loaded with bureaucratic obstacles. As described recently by A. Move, chairman of the criminal law and procedure sections of the Moscow Province Defense Lawyers' Collegium, the Russian Republic Supreme Court offers a typical example. Citizens wishing to file protests or other complaints line up the night before to get on a list for appointment with a court official the next day. Only twenty fortunate applicants will be given appointments. The official hears the complaint, but there is usually nothing the official can do about it because the records of the trial are stored in the court's archives, some of which are located in provinces far from Moscow. The chances of some archive employee giving any particular case serious attention, when this person has no contact with the individuals involved, are modest at best. As Move notes, "Most often the complainant receives the laconic response: 'Your complaint has been reviewed and denied. The right to lodge a protest is denied. The sentence is justified and legal.' "[24]

The deficiencies in the Soviet judiciary process described in these pages have evoked widespread popular dissatisfaction in recent years. They have antagonized segments of the legal and judicial communities even longer. The USSR Supreme Court itself has condemned every one of the abuses that we have described here,[25] yet reforms are rarely forthcoming. As one law professor put it:

> The need for the defense lawyer to participate in the initial stage of the investigation has been discussed so much in our legal press, and the benefits arising from such participation are so obvious, that the lack of progress in this problem simply saps my enthusiasm to talk about it once more.[26]

Ultimately the Party leadership must initiate legal reforms. The absence of reforms therefore leads to the assumption that the Party is more or less satisfied with the existing system. The extent to which Party organs are directly involved in the operation of the judicial system can only be guessed at. The settled policy of the Party is that, although overall supervision of the judiciary is a major Party responsibility, interference in the disposition of individual cases is strictly prohibited. Party officials have sometimes been publicly disciplined for such interference.[27] Nevertheless, Party officials have the authority to "make inquiries" into the conduct of court cases. In the nature of the Soviet political system, this becomes a useful means of closely monitoring the judiciary. Many of the decisions in such cases are made in accordance not with legislation but with what is commonly known as "telephone law," which guides judicial decisions in accord with politicians' orders. The process has become so mechanized, in fact, that

> in some judges' chambers there is a direct intercom line to the district leadership for "urgent consultation." Technology has its own effect; "telephone law" (the term has become notorious) can now be called "intercom law." What will it be tomorrow? Relay or computer law?[28]

The Gorbachev administration has encouraged debate on complaints regarding the judicial process, and much has been forthcoming. It would be consistent with other aspects of his new domestic program for him to respond more positively to arguments for reform than his predecessors did. Still, there have so far been no significant changes in the process.[29]

Popular Participation in the Judicial Process

The involvement of citizens in law enforcement is complemented by an even more intensive involvement in the judicial process. In fact, in all phases of trial procedures, both in and out of court, laypeople outnumber professional judges. This is consistent with the Soviet principle of democratic procedures in all phases of government. The fact that these laypeople rarely exert any independent influence over judicial procedings is also consistent with a Soviet principle: that the public requires constant guidance by government and Party officials in carrying out its democratic responsibilities. Nevertheless, millions of Soviet citizens are engaged daily in the administration of justice. The main forms that this involvement takes are the following.

People's Assessors. In the conduct of trials in people's courts, there are two roles that lay citizens play that do not exist in Western courts. The more important is that of *people's assessor,* two of whom sit with the judge in every trial of original jurisdiction right up to the USSR Supreme Court itself. Each assessor is elected to a local panel of assessors for a term of two and a half years, during which the assessor spends not more than two weeks in court. The purpose is to lend a popular flavor to court procedings, which it no doubt does. In reality, however, assessors almost never contradict judges in specific rulings or in final verdicts.[30]

Social Prosecutors and Defenders. The other courtroom role for laypeople is that of *social prosecutor* or *social defender.* The law permits a representative of any social organization or economic collective to send a representative to a trial to speak either for the defendant or for the prosecution. These representatives have the same rights to question witnesses, introduce evidence, and deliver a peroration as do the attorneys in the case. Again, the idea behind this role is to ensure that the public will is expressed in individual trials. As social prosecutors and defenders rarely have any legal training, they serve mainly to attest to (or deride) the character of the defendant and to introduce emotional and sometimes moral arguments into the deliberations. The rules of admissible evidence in Soviet trials are, by Western standards, extremely lax. Social and moral characteristics of defendants are given considerable weight, especially in the sentencing phase of a trial and lay influences can be effective at this point.

Comrades' Courts. The direct administration of justice by one's peers without the participation of judges, lawyers, or police has long been a tradition of Soviet justice. The *comrades' courts* were an early experiment in popular justice that was discontinued by Stalin and then revived by Khrushchev in the 1960s. In spirit, they represent the imposition of a community's will on its own members, holding them to account for violations of community standards and meting out mild punishments. The worker whose repeated absence from work hinders a production line or the mother whose neglect of her children alarms her neighbors are prime candidates for comrades' courts.

Members of the courts are elected by the local community and operate under the supervision of the plant management and trade union leadership in economic settings and of the local soviet in residential areas. In recent years, official enthusiasm for comrades' courts appears to have declined. New administrative procedures have been developed to deal with the kinds of issues traditionally handled by these gatherings, and their powers in imposing penalties have diminished.[31]

Work Collectives. These are another form of popular control over individuals. Ever since the enactment of the Law on Labor Collectives in 1983, employees at individual work sites have been given increased authority over labor discipline. This appears to have diminished the jurisdiction of the comrades' courts even further, for the jurisdiction of the work collectives overlaps that of the comrades' courts. The collective has greater disciplinary power as well, including the right to fire an employee. Like comrades' courts, labor collectives are closely supervised by local authorities, so they do not function as independent sources of popular control. Nevertheless, the active involvement of a person's friends and fellow workers in judging his or her behavior has always been viewed by Soviet leaders as an important form of social control.[32]

All of these modes of popular participation are part of the Party's elaborate effort to mobilize social pressure against individuals who violate the normal rules and mores of Soviet society. Their objective is the containment of a range of *social* evils, such as crime, corruption, drunkenness and juvenile delinquency. In the *political* sphere, the mode of operation is quite different. The public is not involved except to give general support to the Party's efforts to root out all political opposition from the society. Actions against political opponents are carried out largely without publicity and often without the involvement of the courts or the regular police. In controlling political and other forms of dissident behavior, there is a different set of rules.

CONTROLLING DISSIDENT BEHAVIOR

For substantial segments of the Soviet population, some of the basic principles of the Communist system have never been acceptable. Millions of Soviet citizens defy the official atheism of the state and continue to practice their religion either openly or in private. Millions of others persist in valuing their own ethnic culture and language above the national (Russian) culture. In smaller numbers, other nonconformists reject the official censorship of the arts, the restrictions on emigration, and the severe limitations on individual rights characteristic of Soviet society.

For a very small segment of these people, nonacceptance of these principles has forced them into active opposition, either privately in their own lives and among friends and associates or openly in the public arena. Some of these dissidents, like Andrei Sakharov and Roy Medvedev, Nathan (Anatoly) Sharansky and Yuri Orlov, have achieved international attention, whereas many others are identified only on the rosters of the KGB and of Western human rights organizations. All of them have endured the full force of official repression, including for most incarceration for a number of years in the forced labor camps of the "Gulag Archipeligo."

Soviet dissidents have many objectives—religious, political, ethnic, socioeconomic—a fact that creates considerable diversity among them, both in terms of goals to be pursued and tactics to be used.[33] Nevertheless, the sense of a common cause permeates many of the separate groupings, in part because of the development of a remarkable communications network that operates despite the KGB's constant efforts to monitor and infiltrate dissident circles.

The most common form of communication is through personal contact. A group of friends gathers in someone's apartment to hear a reading of a new poem or a tape of some banned singer. Foreign books and tapes brought into the the country by tourists and returning Soviet travelers are copied and shared with others or sold on the black market. Members of a forbidden religious sect gather secretly in the woods for services.

As the frequency of such exchanges increased in the post-Stalin era, more formal channels of communication were developed. Poems and short stories, political essays, ethnic manifestos, and later whole novels began to be typed on private typewriters with three or four carbon copies and circulated among trusted acquaintances. This came to be known as *samizdat* (*sam* self, *izdat* publishing), a phenomenon that greatly helped to advance the unity and effectiveness of many of the dissident elements operating in isolation. *Samizdat* was augmented by *radizdat*, a printed record of material recorded from foreign radio broadcoasts such as the Voice of America and the British Broadcasting Corporation; *tamizdat*, material printed abroad and smuggled into the Soviet Union; and *magnitizdat*, which produces homemade tape recordings.

One of the most significant early *samizdat* publications was the *Political Diary*, published and edited by dissident historian Roy Medvedev from 1964 to 1971. It was the first regularly issued journal of uncensored political and social commentary since the Revolution and it had wide influence. It had a very small circulation—not more than fifty people—but they included both other dissidents and a few Party officials. Medvedev developed unique sources of information through his Party contacts, which *Political Diary* made available to the broader readership of *samizdat*.[34]

Another *samizdat* publication, *Chronicle of Current Events,* has had a continuing influence ever since its appearance in 1968.[35] Begun by Natalia Gorbanevskaya on an aging typewriter in her Moscow apartment, the *Chronicle* became within a decade the principal voice of the diverse elements that made up the Soviet "democratic movement." It is the only publication in the Soviet Union to report regularly and without censorship about the record of human rights violations. Despite the most strenuous efforts of the KGB to close down the *Chronicle,* and the arrest and imprisonment of successive contributors (Gorbanevskaya herself was arrested in 1970 and sentenced to an indefinite term in a special psychiatric hospital), the *Chronicle* has continued to be issued inside the Soviet Union.

Aside from providing information to other dissidents, *samizdat* reaches two other important audiences. It is read closely by the political leadership, to whom in fact many of its articles are specifically directed. Additionally, *samizdat* reaches a huge audience outside the Soviet Union. Excerpts are frequently published in

Western newspapers and magazines, and collections of articles have appeared in book form. International agencies, such as Amnesty International and the United Nations Commission on Human Rights, make extensive use of this information, as do foreign governments. Perhaps its greatest impact, however, is on the Soviet people itself, not through direct access but by means of foreign radio broadcasts. Agencies like Radio Liberty and the Voice of America broadcast a great deal of *samizdat* information back to the Soviet Union, and for many citizens this has become an important alternative to the official press.[36]

The KGB versus the Dissidents

Whatever their differences in objectives and personal involvement, dissidents share one overriding experience: the need to deal with the intrusive presence of the KGB in their lives. The relationship is a symbiotic one: Dissidents must be extremely sensitive to the likely reaction of the police to their activities; at the same time, the KGB tends to respond to some extent to the activities of the dissidents.

This is evident in the tactics used by the KGB over the years to deal with dissident groups. In the early post-Stalin years, the KGB utilized court trials extensively to impose sentences on dissidents as well as to provide a deterrent to other citizens. However, public trials had disadvantages for the authorities. Dissidents tend to attract the attention of the foreign press, which covers the trials closely. Putting a man or woman on trial for exercising his or her constitutional rights to attend church or to exercise free speech creates a highly negative image of the alleged democratic nature of Soviet society. Taking advantage of their right to make concluding statements in their defense, dissidents on trial frequently deliver scathing denunciations of the government and the KGB, detailing the illegalities of their treatment and the injustices they see in Soviet society.

To avoid negative publicity, the KGB moved in the 1970s toward the wider use of administrative measures in dealing with dissidents. For this it pursues a course of "graduated, incremental reprisals."[37] KGB officers apply pressure against selected targets through a series of escalating tactics: verbal warnings, surveillance, interception of mail and phone calls, repeated "invitations" to meet with KGB officers, written reprimands, the creation of pretexts for disciplining people at work and for firing them, removal to less desirable housing, denial of educational opportunities to one's children, and the occasional rescinding of an academic degree.[38] These measures can be taken quietly because few employers or officials are willing to interfere with the KGB's pursuit of "political criminals." In general, the KGB prefers to handle dissident behavior with as little coercion as possible, as a matter of efficiency and to avoid damaging publicity. Individuals who respond positively to KGB warnings can sometimes resume their normal activities without further difficulties.

The legal authority of the KGB to prohibit dissident activities exists in republic criminal law codes (there is no national criminal law code). The codes provide vague, catch-all statutes that lend themselves to whatever interpretation the state wishes to put on them. The two most commonly used statutes, especially against civil rights and free speech advocates, are the following:[39]

> *Article 70: Anti-Soviet Agitation and Propaganda.* This article prohibits "the spreading of slanderous fabrications defaming the Soviet state and social system" and possessing and circulating "literature of such content." It requires proof that an individual committed these acts "for the purpose of subverting and weakening Soviet power." This latter clause long posed a problem for both the government and the dissident. The government consistently refused to admit that a single dissident writing poetry could challenge the power of the Soviet state, and the dissident agreed, thus undercutting the basis for prosecution.
>
> *Article 190-1: Circulation of Fabrications Known to Be False Which Defame the Soviet State and Social System.* Developed partly in response to the above problem, this article covers the same offenses as Article 70 but without the requirement of intent. Violations carry a lesser sentence (up to 3 years in a labor camp, compared to 7 years plus 5 years of internal exile for Article 70) and are easier to prove in court.

Other statutes are used against religious believers, dissatisfied workers, ethnic patriots, and other targets. Article 190-3 prohibits group activities that "entail a disturbance of the work of transport and of state or social enterprises, instituitons, and organizations." This effectively prohibits labor strikes and the formation of employee organizations other than those authorized by the state. Article 142 prohibits the "violation of the laws on the separation of church from state and of school from church." The fact that there are no such laws leaves the authorities free to interpret this article as they wish. Article 227 makes illegal the infringement of citizens' rights "under the appearance of performing religious rites," and has been applied especially to the offering of religious training to minors. The selling of religious artifacts is prohibited under Article 162, "Engaging in a Prohibited Trade."

When warnings and other moderate measures do not suffice, the KGB may decide to remove a dissident from his or her social environment. In doing so, it has three choices of action. It can force the dissident into exile, either by relocating him within the Soviet Union, as was done when Andrei Sakharov was removed from Moscow to Gorky, or by expelling him from the country; it can confine the person to a prison or labor camp; or it can commit him to a psychiatric hospital as a mental incompetent.

The Gulag. Most dissidents eventually serve time in labor camps, referred to collectively as the "gulag," an acronym for the Russian term for Main Administration of Camps. Alexander Solzhenitsyn has described in terrifying detail the network of forced-labor camps that were set up by Stalin and which stretch across the entire country.[40] Non-Soviet experts estimate that there are currently some 1,100 labor camps in the Soviet Union, which house somewhere around 2 million prisoners, including 8,000 to 10,000 prisoners of conscience.[41] Of the latter group, the breakdown of causes of confinement, according to a report made to the U.S. Congress, includes the following:[42]

Activists for civil and political rights	17.7%
Applicants for emigration (mainly Jews and Germans)	14.2%
Ethnic rights movements (mainly Ukrainian, Lithuanian, and Estonian)	27.8%
Religious believers (88% are Baptists)	23.5%

The labor camps are administered by the Ministry of Internal Affairs (MVD) rather than the KGB, but KGB troops and other employees constitute most of the enforcement personnel. Convicted felons are assigned to one of several different categories of treatment, ranging from standard regime to special regime. Under *special regime*, extremely harsh conditions are maintained, severely limiting prisoners' receipt of mail and visitors, rest periods, physical comforts, and living conditions. Prisoners who violate camp rules or refuse to cooperate with KGB officers may be sentenced to additional terms of incarceration, according to Article 188-3, which was added to the republic criminal codes in 1983. Prisoners work primarily on major construction and natural resource projects, such as the Baikal to Amur Railroad (BAM) and the mining of gold and other minerals in eastern Siberia.

Soviet Psychoprisons. The other possible disposition of a political prisoner is confinement in a mental institution, usually for an indefinite period. The Ministry of Internal Affairs administers a number of "special" psychiatric hospitals, separate from ordinary mental institutions administered by the Ministry of Health. These institutions have long been used in part to isolate political dissidents under the pretext that they are mentally ill. Doctors regularly use drugs, restraints, and psychological pressures to deal with these "patients."

Individuals can be confined to such hospitals without a court trial or the permission of family members and may be kept for indefinite periods. As to their mental states, there is abundant evidence that the deviant quality for which they are confined is political in nature. In the case of Pyotr Grigorenko, a former general and early dissident, the medical diagnosis was "paranoid development of the personality with reformist ideas arising in the personality. . . ."; for Vaclav Sevruk, a sociologist who had written for the *Chronicle of Current Events*, the illness was "a mania of Marxism and truth-seeking"; Nadezhda Gaidar was confined in 1976 as a result of "nervous exhaustion brought on by her search for justice."[43] In 1984, Zoya Petrovna, a high school math and computer teacher, was characterized as one who "stubbornly defends delirious ideas of truth-seeking" for repeatedly charging malpractice against a physician who, she claims, neglected her tumor until it became malignant.[44]

In recent years, the Ministry of Health has applied the concept of "zealotry delirium" to a kind of mental illness sometimes found in otherwise quite normal individuals. In the words of one Soviet physician, a person could be obsessed by any pathological idea. He might think he is a psychic, a prophet, a messiah, or perhaps a rights activist. And in any of these cases, he could transmit his pathological reformative ideas, which are the fruit of a morbid process, as they say, to the masses. More than that, he may acquire pupils, followers, defenders—people who have deluded themselves into believing in him, as well as some who seek to profit from the situation. However, if a professional psychiatrist sees such a person, he'll realize that the person is ill.[45]

The utility of this kind of formulation in the handling of political dissidents is obvious. It can be applied even to relatively mild situations of individual discontent. In 1984, for example, the Ministry of Public Health amended the instructions for initial psychiatric examinations to authorize a finding of mental illness for "persons who disorganize the work of institutions with numerous letters of absurd content."[46]

Underlying these rationales for dealing with socially unacceptable behavior is an elaborate body of psychiatric theory developed mainly by the dominant figure in Soviet psychiatry for the past quarter century, Andrei Snezhnevsky. As head of the USSR Academy of Medicine's Institute of Psychiatry, founder of the Academy's All-Union Mental Health Research Center, and editor of the major scholarly journal in psychiatry, Snezhnevsky spawned a generation of psychiatrists who adhered to his theories. One of his main contributions was the expansion of the symptoms of schizophrenia to include forms of individual behavior that are not recognized by most Western psychiatrists.[47]

Snezhnevsky argued that conditions of schizophrenia tend to get progressively worse over the patient's lifetime, during which time symptoms range from mild, or "sluggish," as he called them, to severe. At the severe end, one observes the hallucinations, delusions, and escapes from reality normally attributed to schizophrenics. But at the mild end of the scale are, according to Snezhnevsky, symptoms that to a Western psychiatrist evidence little more than eccentricity or at worst some form of neurosis. These have often included, in the diagnoses of dissidents, qualities such as stubbornness in pursuing unusual goals, refusal to conform to social norms, an unwillingness to be restrained by warnings or disciplinary measures, preoccupation with minor social flaws, and intense personalities.

Snezhnevsky also argued that schizophrenia is biological in origin and therefore hereditary, rather than environmentally caused. Once it was diagnosed in a patient, it was considered to be permanent, subject perhaps to modification by treatment and periods of remission but ultimately incurable.

This combination of "mild" symptoms and incurability provided the state security forces with a medical concept that proved ideal in dealing not only with political dissidents but also with other social deviants. Once diagnosed as a schizophrenic, an individual is entered on a permanent list that shapes his or her future treatment. Any involvement with proscribed activities can invoke a judgment of mental illness. This has two important advantages in dealing with dissidents. It legitimizes the KGB's objection to dissident activities, for these activities can all be defined as evidence of mental illness. More importantly, it permits the system to deal with dissidents through medical, rather than judicial, procedings. Public trials, with the inevitable negative foreign publicity, can be avoided while dissidents are quietly removed from circulation through indefinite confinement in psychiatric hospitals.

There is no reason to believe that Snezhnevsky was merely a tool of the KGB in his activities. Probably he and his adherents genuinely believe in the concept of "mild schizophrenia," and in any case the concept has been applied throughout Soviet society, not just to political dissidents.[48] Nevertheless, the international psychiatric community has condemned the Soviet use of "medical discipline" over the past decade. In 1983, facing almost certain expulsion by the World Psychiatric Association, the Soviet Union withdrew from the organization. Since then, especially during 1986/1987, there have been indications that the Party leadership is moving to respond to the criticisms and that Soviet reentry in the association is being sought. With the death of Andrei Snezhnevsky in July 1987, the field of Soviet psychiatry may be freer to respond to changing conditions both within the Soviet Union and outside. In the meantime, Soviet dissidents continue to be shunted into psychiatric hospitals on diagnoses of mental incompetence whether or not objective medical diagnoses would identify symptoms of genuine illness. This remains a primary tactic of the KGB for dealing with dissidents.

Although the oppressive measures of the KGB have succeeded in preventing the formation of well-organized national dissident movements, dissent in three major areas remains active and poses a continuing challenge to the Party leadership: political dissent involving civil and human rights issues, religious freedom, and the homeland issue for ethnic minorities. We shall look at each of these areas briefly.

POLITICAL DISSENT

Dissenters in the cause of civil and human rights pose the most serious challenge to the Party leadership because the issues directly challenge the nature of the political system itself. Political dissidents demand the right to speak and write freely, to communicate their ideas with others and to organize to protect their interests, to demonstrate and protest publicly against government policies, to be secure against covert police activity and against arrest and imprisonment for exercising rights guaranteed to them in the Soviet Constitution. Such demands constitute a rejection of the Party's assumed right to control human thought and public communication, and thus strike at the foundation of much of the Party's political power.

Political dissent is a post-Stalin phenomenon whose emergence coincided with the end of overt terror as an instrument of Party control. The Khrushchev years had seen the repression of some dissidents but also a modest expansion of the limits of political rights. After Khrushchev was forced to resign from the Politburo in October 1964, the new leadership headed by Leonid Brezhnev began to crack down on those elements of the intelligentsia who had taken advantage of Khrushchev's more tolerant policies.

The new leadership instituted court trials for a number of early dissidents, and the patent injustice of these procedings sparked a wave of negative reaction among elements of the intelligentsia. In February 1965, Joseph Brodsky, a poet and translator in his mid-twenties, was arrested and tried as a "social parasite" on the grounds that he was not employed in "real labor"—he only wrote poetry. After his conviction, a copy of the transcript of the trial was published in the West, and its demonstration of procedural violations and overall injustice sparked widespread denunciation of the Soviet leadership.[49]

Despite the unfavorable publicity, the Brezhnev regime soon launched a further attack by arresting Andrei Sinyavsky and Yuli Daniel, two writers living in Moscow, on the charge of violating Article 70 of the RSFSR Criminal Code, which prohibits "anti-Soviet agitation and propaganda," with the intent of weakening Soviet authority. The charges arose as a result of the publication of several of their works abroad under assumed names.[50] Daniel was little known, but Sinyavsky was a respected literary critic and essayist, a university professor and staff member at the presitigious Gorki Institute of World Literature. He was the first prominent member of the Soviet Writers' Union to be arrested since the end of the Stalinist era.

The trial of Sinyavsky and Daniel was a farce in judicial terms. It generated a flood of letters to the press protesting the injustice of the charges and the procedings (along with other letters praising the verdicts). Even some Western Communist leaders criticized the procedings. On the other hand, the blatant injustice of the trial brought forth a period, from 1965 to the late 1970s, of struggle by Soviet intellectuals against the restraints of the government on the exercise of constitutionally guaranteed human rights. Marked by repeated demonstrations, letters to the press and to high officials, and the formation of protest groups, the period saw also the persistent attack on these dissidents by the KGB and the government.

In this period, also, were formed several small illegal organizations devoted to the defense of human rights. In 1969, the Initiative Group for the Defense of Human Rights was formed after a prominent civil rights leader, Peter Grigorenko, was arrested. The following year Andrei Sakharov, Valery Chalidze, and several others formed the Moscow Human Rights Committee, which sparked similar committees in several other cities. In 1973, the first chapter of Amnesty International was founded in Moscow.

With the signing in 1975 of the Helsinki Accords on Human Rights by a large number of nations, including the Soviet Union, a renewed effort on the part of Soviet dissidents was undertaken. In 1976, the first of several Helsinki Watch Groups was formed in Moscow by Yuri Orlov.[51] Its purpose was to monitor Soviet compliance with the Helsinki Human Rights Accords, publicizing violations to the world press. Many letters and petitions were directed at Soviet officials, calling for respect for the Soviet Constitution's protection of individual rights. The KGB fought a running battle with members of the Watch Groups who, nevertheless, continued to proclaim their objectives and to publish information in *samizdat.*

By the late 1970s, the number of protest groups was increasing along with the anger of the regime toward them. In 1977, a Working Commission to Investigate the Abuse of Psychiatry for Political Purposes was formed. Its efforts led to formal condemnation of the Soviet Union by the International Congress of Psychiatrists later that year and a wave of international protest. In 1978, the Initiative Group for the Defense of the Rights of Invalids was created, and an independent trade union, the Free Interprofessional Association of Workers, also came into being. There followed in 1979 the creation of a group called the Right to Emigrate and another called Elections 79. The purpose of the latter was to nominate candidates for the March 1979 election to the Supreme Soviet, an exercise of the constitutional right of workers to nominate candidates. The group was refused permission to do so, ostensibly on procedural grounds.

Although the number of people involved in all these efforts is small, probably no more than a few hundred, there is considerable diversity in their prescriptions for change in the Soviet Union. One orientation, long represented by Roy Medvedev, argues for reform within the general framework of a "Leninist" system of government. He sees the greatest opportunity for reform in a presumed "liberal element" within the Party leadership and views the reemergence of a Stalinist orientation as the greatest danger the country faces. Stalinism itself, he argues, was a form of "pseudo-socialism" rather than a natural evolution of Marxism-Leninism.[52]

Other dissidents argue that the monopoly of power held by the Communist Party leadership will never permit the development of true democracy. Therefore, the Communist system must evolve in the direction of Western parliamentary institutions and abandon censorship, central economic controls, the *nomenklatura,* and the privileges of the Party elite. The champion of these views has long been Andrei Sakharov, Soviet physicist and Nobel Prize laureate and co-founder in 1970 of the Moscow Committee for Human Rights. Although strongly influenced by Roy Medvedev in the 1960s, Sakharov shared the dismay of many of his colleagues at the Soviet invasion of Czechoslovakia in 1968 and the crushing of the Czech democratic socialist experiment.[53]

The dispute between Medvedev and Sakharov is paralleled in more recent times by that between two of the most prominent dissident leaders of the Gorbachev era. Lev Timofeyev, "leader of Press Club Glasnost, argues that the movement should seek a 'constructive dialogue' with all elements of Soviet life, including the ruling Communist Party." But Sergei Grigoryants, editor of the dissident publication *Glasnost,* "asserted that the Soviet Government 'has absolutely no use for us,' and that conciliation can only muddy the movement's 'purity and clarity'."[54]

A third strain of dissident opinion emerged in the 1970s in the writings, mostly from exile, of Alexander Solzhenitsyn. In his "Letter to the Soviet Leaders," transmitted to Brezhnev in September 1973, Solzhenitsyn advocated the abolishment of communism in Russia and a return to a form of national-religious authoritarianism. He believes that the Soviet people are unprepared for true democracy and need to be insulated from Western influences in order to develop a genuine Russian character.[55]

The advent of Gorbachev's reform program in the mid-1980s had a strong effect on the dissident community, especially in the major cities. Both Sakharov and Medvedev welcomed and supported *glasnost* and the reforms of *perestroika* though reserving judgment as to the permanence of the changes.[56] The emergence of unofficial groups in Moscow and Leningrad advocating greater freedom and justice has clearly heartened much of the dissident community, but there are many skeptics as well. The release of some 200 prisoners of conscience by Gorbachev in 1987 appeared neither to confirm nor deny the adoption of a new attitude by the Politburo. The many dissidents still being held in labor camps, prisons, and mental hospitals offer mute evidence of the absence of a thorough change of policy in this area.

RELIGIOUS DISSENT

Although officially atheistic, the Soviet Union contains a large population of religious believers. The government estimates that some 20 percent of the population are believers, but the true figure is impossible to say for several reasons.[57] Numerous religious sects are illegal so their members are forced to practice in secret. Many citizens identify with the rites and ceremonies of one church or another without having a strong theistic orientation. Still others, especially young people raised without formal religious education, see religion as a means of developing a philosophy of life, of answering the age-old Russian question, *Kak zhit?* (How should one live?)

The evident decline in popular adherence to Marxist values in the Soviet Union has generated a search for new values among some elements of the population, and this has heightened the general interest in religious teachings. By the estimates of Western scholars, based admittedly on such sketchy evidence as Soviet public opinion surveys, unofficial records of baptisms and religious funerals, and even counting the candles sold in churches, the proportion of religious believers in the Soviet Union may be as high as 50 percent of the population.[58]

Constitutionally, the Soviet government protects religious belief as an expression of individual conscience. Article 52 of the Constitution grants citizens "the right to profess or not to profess any religion," as well as the right "to conduct religious services." It also forbids the "incitement of hostilities or hatred on religious grounds." The USSR is a signatory to both the 1973 International Covenant on Civil and Political Rights and the 1975 Helsinki Agreement on Security and Cooperation in Europe. The latter obliges nations to "recognize and respect the freedom of the individual to process and practice, alone or in community with others, religion or belief in accordance with the dictates of his own conscience."[59]

Despite these commitments, the Communist Party leadership has never been supportive, or even neutral, concerning the practice of religion. The Marxist roots of Soviet communism convey the idea that religious belief attracts people only as an opiate, a form of consolation and comfort in the face of capitalist oppression. Pre-Revolutionary intellectuals long castigated the Orthodox Church as a regressive supporter of czarism, and Bolshevik revolutionaries vowed to abolish its influence in Russian life. They intended not only to bring down the religious establishment but also to root out all traces of religious belief from the minds of the masses. In this they have been singularly unsuccessful.

The relationship between the Communist Party and organized religion in the Soviet Union today rests on an uneasy compromise. All churches are required to be registered with the Council on Religious Affairs, a government agency attached to the USSR Council of Ministers. Those permitted to register may exercise a limited number of religious functions. Church activity is confined to religious rites and services conducted within the walls of the church itself. Clergy may perform rituals that cannot be done by laypeople, but they have no voice in the management of the church. They are not ordained on a permanent basis but only for a specific church for as long as they are employed there. The church building itself may be used only for formal religious services open to the entire congregation. It may not be used for educational purposes or cultural activities or for social events such as charitable activities, choral singing except at services, baptisms, or outdoor funerals. Churches may not proseletyze new members nor publish religious treatises, or engage in any activity that has the effect of encouraging religious belief in nonmembers.[60]

Restrictions on churchgoers are also numerous despite the "freedom of conscience" provision of the Soviet Constitution. Religious belief is incompatible with membership in the Communist Party and can be a hindrance in the pursuit of many non-Party careers. Work is often scheduled on religious holidays, and careful records may be kept of absenteeism on those days. Harassment of believers and interference with religious services are fairly common. One reporter observed young men circling a church on motorcycles, attempting to drown out the voices of the clergy. In another case, a military unit set up an artillery range next to an ancient church building, which began to disintegrate because of the noise and concussion of the firings.

Religious Denominations

Most religious denominations have bowed to Party controls as the price of remaining active. The rest are outlawed and constitute one of the major dissident factions among the Soviet population. The legal churches (see Table 12.1) represent five major religious groupings and several smaller denominations active in limited areas of the country.

**TABLE 12.1 MEMBERSHIP IN REGISTERED
SOVIET RELIGIOUS ORGANIZATIONS**[61]

	Believers (in millions)	Churches
Russian Orthodox	30–35	7,500
Protestant evangelicals	1.2	5,300
Moslims	40–50	400
Jews	1.8	200
Catholics	2.8	245
Georgian Orthodox	3	40
Armenian Apostolic	4.5	40

Russian Orthodox Church. With an estimated 40 million to 50 million adherents, the Russian Orthodox Church is the largest denomination in the Soviet Union. The Church leadership has long maintained a cooperative relationship with the Communisty Party, accepting its domination and offering visible support for its policies. Church leaders publicly supported the Soviet invasions of Czechoslovakia and Afghanistan, and they frequently discipline their own clergy for violations of Party policies. They have had little choice in the matter because the grudging tolerance of the regime for the Church is in constant danger of turning into harsher measures of repression. In the early 1980s, for example, restrictions on several of the surviving Orthodox monasteries were increased. The present abbot of the Monastery of the Caves near Pskov, believed to be a KGB appointment, has closed the catacombs of the Caves to pilgrims and restricted the open hours of all the monastery's churches to times of actual church services.[62]

Protestant Evangelicals. In a move to bring all of the diverse Protestant sects into an organizational framework that the state could control. Stalin formed the All-Union Council of Evangelical Christians and Baptists in 1944. Baptists formed the largest segment, but the council also represented Mennonites who originally emigrated from Germany, Seventh-Day Adventists, and Pentecostals. Aside from the Russian Orthodox Church, the council is the only national organization of churches. Other Protestant churches, including Lutherans, Presbyterians, and Methodists, operate legally but are denied an all-union organization to unite and integrate their parishes.[63]

Moslems. Soviet Moslems are perhaps the most difficult to describe in religious terms because the Islamic religion is so intimately conjoined with the cultural and social practices of Moslem communities.[64] Inhabiting primarily the five central Asian republics, the nation's 43 million Moslems share, almost without exception, certain Islamic customs such as abstention from pork, circumcision, and the celebration of religious holidays. Widespread prejudices also exist, for example, against intermarriage with non-Moslims or the education of women and in favor of payment of bride-prices. This closeness between religion and culture has induced Soviety authorities to proceed cautiously in its antireligious campaign. While gradually reducing the number of mosques and the authority of the mullahs over the years, the regime recognizes Islam as a legal religion. Moscow's interest in not offending Arab allies in the Middle East has also caused it to abstain from outright oppression of Islamic religious observance.[65]

Jews. Soviet Jews present both a religious problem and a homeland issue (to be discussed below) to Soviet authorities. As a religion, Judaism is probably the most oppressed major faith in the USSR. The Hebrew language was prohibited in the Stalin era, and the approved language of Soviet Jews, Yiddish, is spoken by very few of them. There are fewer than 200 synagogues remaining for nearly 2 million Soviet Jews, and only one national periodical is published. Anti-Semitism has a long history among some elements of the Russian people. In recent years, as Soviet Jews have become more insistent on their right to emigrate, this prejudice seems to have hardened.

Catholics. Roman Catholicism is more closely associated with Western culture than any other Soviet religion. About half of the 5 million Catholics live in the republic of Lithuania, where they constitute three-fourths of the population, the rest inhabiting parts of Belorussia, the Ukraine, and Moldavia. In Lithuania, Catholicism is deeply rooted in society and attracts a large majority of young people to religious services and ceremonies.[66] As a cultural bulwark against Russification, the Lithuanian Catholic Church has experienced some of the most strenuous antireligious efforts of the Communist Party.

In addition to these major denominations, there are a number of other large denominations that exist almost entirely in individual republics. These include the Georgian Orthodox Church, the Armenian Apostolic Church, the (illegal) Catholic Uniate Church in the Ukraine, and Lutheran denominations in Latvia and Estonia. Like Lithuanian Catholicism, these religious organizations have been heavily restricted as much because of their potential for stimulating ethnic separatist feelings as because of their religious activities.

Religious Dissenters

It is useful to distinguish between religious believers and religious dissenters in the Soviet context. Believers may or may not attend church, and if they do they attend legal churches registered with the Council on Religious Affairs. Dissenters attend unregistered churches or engage in forbidden religious practices outside church buildings. They exist in all of the major denominations and are officially disowned by those denominations. In the Russian Orthodox Church, dissident believers have formed the Christian Seminar, which has attracted a number of young intellectuals who seek to explore their religion in greater depth than the mother church allows.[67] A dissident element of the Baptist church formed the Council of Churches in 1960s, although most of its members were eventually arrested.[68]

Dissident Catholics operate in Lithuania a branch of the illegal Christian Committee for the Defense of the Rights of Religious Believers. They publish the influential *Chronicle of the Catholic Church in Lithuania,* a *samizdat* publication of fairly wide distribution.[69] Among Muslims, the quiescent and cooperative Islamic church in central Asia is countered by militantly religious orders called *Tarikats.*[70] These groups are found mainly in Azerbaidjan and parts of central Asia.

Religious dissidents are subject to prosecution under several articles of the republic criminal codes. Article 142 prohibits any religious activity not specifically permitted by law, and it provides a penalty of up to three years in a labor camp for violation. Article 227 make it unlawful to encourage people to separate themselves from Soviet society under the appearance of performing religious rites. A refusal to serve in the armed forces is punishable under Articles 80 and 249, because conscientious objection is not recognized in Soviet law. To inhibit the publication of religious materials, Article 162, which proscribes engaging in a prohibited trade, is sometimes used. Michael Rowe cites an example of an Orthodox nun who was arrested under this article for making and selling belts embroidered with a biblical text. She was committed to a psychiatric hospital for an indefinite period.[71]

On strictly political grounds, the attitude of the Party leadership toward dissident sects and churches is somewhat ambivalent. Internationally, the harsh repression of denominations that exist also in foreign countries sometimes presents a foreign-policy problem for the leadership. This is clearly a factor in Soviet treatment of both Jews and Moslems, given the delicacy of relationships with the United States and the Arab world. Internally, there is a different problem. Increasing the pressure on legal churches to prevent them from expanding encourages greater involvement of believers with illegal sects and congregations where state control is far less effective. Thus, the Party is inclined to soften its campaign against illegal sects somewhat in order to ensure effective control over the legal ones. This concern has enabled the legal Baptists, for example, to enjoy considerably greater autonomy in religious matters than they could expect without the silent presence of the illegals.

Under these pressures, some illegal groups have even attained a measure of toleration in recent years.[72] Unregistered churches hold services in many parts of the country, while *samizdat* publications on religious topics circulate fairly widely. Leaders of dissident groups have developed contacts with Western journalists and officials, and occasionally they hold press conferences and issue statements to the Western news media. Some groups have addressed letters to Party and government leaders detailing state violations of the constitutionally guaranteed separation of church and state. The impact of *glasnost* has been felt in this area as well.

THE HOMELAND ISSUE

In a multiethnic nation like the USSR, the desire of ethnic minorities to live together in lands that have been their historic home is very strong. Most Soviet citizens enjoy this right, but there are a number of large minority populations that do not for various reasons. Among these peoples, the desire for repatriation has been a continuing issue for the Communist Party, one that has led to protests and violence on many occasions.

Ethnic minorities seeking emigration fall into two categories: populations whose traditional homeland is within the present boundaries of the USSR but which were forcibly deported to other locations during World War II, and populations whose natural homeland is outside the country. In one additional case, Armenia, most of the population lives in its historic homeland but for a variety of reasons there is a strong impetus toward emigration.

The Deported Nations

During the course of World War II, the defection of small numbers of non-Russian Soviet citizens to the German side, or in some cases in opposition both to Germany and the Soviet Union, was used by Stalin as a justification for mass deportations of non-Russian minorities. In August 1941, two months after the German invasion of the Soviet Union, the Presidium of the Supreme Soviet issued a decree asserting that there were "thousands upon thousands of spies and saboteurs among the Volga Germans" who were eagerly awaiting the appearance of the German army.[73] To forestall mass sabotage and espionage, the government abolished the autonomous republic of the Volga Germans and exiled Germans from all parts of the western Soviet Union eastward to the Urals and central Asia.

In February 1944, the Chechkin and Ingush peoples of the northern Caucasus area were routed out of their homes and forcibly transported northward and eastward. In May, a similar scene, even more brutally played out, occurred in the Crimea. On a single day, with little advance warning, more than 200,000 Crimean Tatars were loaded on trucks and trains and deported from lands they had occupied for over seven centuries.[74] In November 1944, a further expulsion occurred. The Meskhi people, a Muslim sect who previously lived in the Georgian Republic along the Turkish border, were deported to central Asia, purportedly to protect them from the advancing German armies. Elsewhere, other non-Russian peoples—Karachais, Balkars, Kalmyks—met a similar fate.[75] In most of these cases, the charge was the same: collaboration with the enemy and betrayal of the homeland.

For the duration of the war and sometime after, many of these people were used as conscript work battalions. They built irrigation systems in central Asia and manned the thousands of factories that had been moved east to keep them out of German hands. After the war, pressures by the deported peoples for repatriation to their homelands were violently repulsed. The aura of treason surrounded entire populations and little was done by the government to correct the record. It was not until the mid-1960s that the government acted to rehabilitate some of these peoples and restore them to full citizenship. Several minorities were permitted to return to their homelands after that, but in three cases—Volga Germans, Crimean Tatars, and Meskhis—exile was to become their permanent status.

The Tatars waged the most extensive campaign for repatriation. In the 1960s, Tatar leaders directed petitions to the central government from their settlement areas in Uzbekistan. On several occasions these petitions were signed by almost the entire adult Tatar population. Tatars established a permanent if unofficial delegation in Moscow to promote their interests and lobbied government and Party leaders strenuously. They received little support, however, and in more recent times, discouragement over their prospects for repatriation has led many to give up the effort. Others have attempted to move back to the Crimea illegally or have joined underground groups to continue the struggle.[76]

The Volga Germans also began to press for repatriation to their homeland in the mid-1960s. Scattered as they are throughout the RSFSR and central Asia, Volga Germans suffer greatly from Soviet memories of World War II. Although the bulk of the Volga German population was belatedly acclaimed as patriotic defenders of their country during the war, ethnic Germans continue to be objects of discrimination and ill-will. There are virtually no schools, publications, or cultural institutions supporting the German people, and the absence of a common homeland greatly inhibits the rebuilding of their ethnic identity. By 1979, only 57 percent of Soviet Germans still considered German to be their native tongue.[77]

There is little popular support in the USSR for the repatriation of these minorities. The land they left is fully occupied now. Making room for large numbers of minorities with dissimilar cultural and linguistic characteristics has little appeal to established communities. In two of the cases—the Tatars and Meskhis—there is also no foreign constituency to take up the cause or to provide a destination for emigration. The Volga Germans are in a more fortunate position. Emigration to West Germany has been permitted on a small scale (see below), and this has somewhat reduced the pressure for repatriation.

The Emigration Issue

The Soviet government recognizes no general right of emigration. Where it has permitted individuals to depart permanently from the country, it has been mainly for reasons of foreign policy or to suggest compliance with international political and human rights agreements. In the case of the Volga Germans, a limited opportunity to emigrate has resulted from the Soviet Union's efforts to cultivate better relations with the Federal Republic of Germany. Beginning in the 1960s, the flow of German emigrants reached nearly 10,000 persons annually by 1976. In the early 1980s, reflecting heightened tensions between the Soviet Bloc and the NATO countries, the numbers were sharply reduced. By 1987, however, the tide had turned again: In that year some 15,000 Soviet Germans received exit visas.[78]

Unlike the Germans, Soviet Armenians have a full union-republic as a homeland, although only about 60 percent of its 4 million people live in the republic. Another million Armenians live outside the Soviet Union. The desire to emigrate is based mainly on long-standing grievances Armenians have against the Russians, some of them going back well into the czarist period.[79] Although they lack a homeland abroad, large settlements of Armenians exist in France, Canada, and the United States. In the latter country, more than 200,000 Armenians have settled in the Los Angeles area, and this is the destination of most emigrants. In the early 1980s, the Soviet quota for Armenian emigration to the United States fell sharply, from over 6,000 in 1980 to fewer than 2,000 the following year.[80] By 1987, however, the number of exit visas granted was again between 5,000 and 6,000.[81]

The most widely publicized emigration problem in the Soviet Union involves the Jewish population. Numbering nearly 2 million people,[82] Soviet Jews have had an unusual status among the nationalities that comprise the Soviet people. There is a Jewish autonomous republic, but very few Jews live there. Located in Birobidjan in the Soviet far east, the republic lies thousands of miles from the urban centers of European USSR where most Soviet Jews reside.

Despite a long history as a beleaguered minority, Soviet Jews have achieved considerable social success since the Revolution. In terms of social class, they have higher status than any other ethnic group. Of the twenty-four major ethnic groups, Jews have by far the smallest percentages of peasants and workers and the highest proportion of white-collar employees (76.8 percent as compared with 26.2 percent of the Russian population).[83] Educationally, a similar condition exists. In the Russian Republic, where most Jews live, the proportion of Jews who had completed some type of higher education was, in the 1970s, eight times as high as that of Russians. In the nation as a whole, the ratio of Jewish students in higher educational institutions per 1,000 population was well over twice as high as that of Russians.[84]

Politically, Jews are at least numerically well represented. In 1976, they comprised nearly 2 percent of the total membership of the Communist Party, more than twice their proportion of the general population. In the Party Central Committee as well as in the Supreme Soviet, Jews have been represented at or above their proportion of the population.[85] In all these categories, however, the proportion of Jews may have declined in the late 1970s. A dissident Soviet writer points, for example, to evidence in *samizdat* that indicates the imposition of more highly restrictive quotas for Jews in Soviet Universities in the past several years.[86] Soviet sources ceased publishing such data about Jews at that time so this is difficult to confirm.

Whether anti-Semitism, seen as hostility toward Jews as individuals and communities, is a conscious policy of the Party leadership, despite their vehement denials, is difficult to ascertain. One prominent dissident, Valery Chalidze, argues that "no particular nationality in the USSR seems to be persecuted as such. This is confirmed by Soviet history. National persecutions have for the most part been carried out when the regime feared the political disloyalty of that nationality."[87] Dissident Roy Medvedev has made the opposite argument, that anti-Semitism was "the chief factor and main reason" for the emergence of anti-Zionism in the USSR.[88]

Unfortunately for Soviet Jews, both Judaism and Zionism raise the specter of disloyalty in the minds of the Party leadership. As a religion, Judaism is criticized for the implication that Jews are superior to others, that their birthright makes them the "chosen people." Official hostility toward Zionism lies mainly in its insistence that Israel is the natural homeland for all the world's Jews (Zion is the biblical name for Jerusalem) and in the charge that the international Zionist movement is capitalist controlled and anti-Soviet. Intended or not, the regime's virulent anti-Zionist and anti-Judaism policies tend to stir up popular anti-Semitic feelings as well. These feelings are particularly aggravated over the issue of Jewish emigration.

Beginning in the 1960s, applications for emigration to Israel increased dramatically after the Israeli victory in the Six-Day War, a positive incentive, and the Soviet invasion of Czechoslovakia in 1968, a negative one.[89] With President Nixon's visit to the USSR in 1972 and the beginning of detente between the two countries, the Party eased restrictions on Jewish emigration and the numbers of emigrants began to climb rapidly, rising to a peak of 51,320 people in 1979. As detente soured in the wake of the Soviet invasion of Afghanistan, emigration visas became increasingly scarce, numbering only 896 in 1984. Since Gorbachev's emergence as Soviet leader, there have been mixed signals on the issue. Emigrations rose in 1985 to 1,140, fell in 1986 to 945, then rose again in 1987 to over 6,000.[90] The latter increase coincided with increased emigration of Volga Germans and Armenians during 1987.

The emigration picture is unsettled, however. Amendments to the 1970 Emigration Law, which went into effect on January 1, 1987, appear to restrict emigration more tightly than before.[91] Applicants must have close relatives living abroad with whom they wish to be reunited, except that no one who left the country illegally can serve in that capacity. And the state reserves the right to deny anyone an exit visa even for a brief visit abroad if that is "in the interests of safeguarding public order or the health or morality of the population. . . ." (Section 25). For the estimated 380,000 Soviet Jews who have applied to emigrate, those conditions leave little room for optimism.[92]

In other areas, the Gorbachev administration seems to be moving toward greater accommodation of Soviet Jews. Restrictions on the admission of Jews to the better universities and institutes appear to be easing, several Moscow synagogues have reopened, Jewish cultural centers are opening in Minsk and Leningrad, and there is even to be a kosher Jewish restaurant in Moscow. For many religious Jews, however, the key issues are unrestricted emigration and the Hebrew language. Long banned in the Soviet Union as the national language of a hostile state (Israel), Hebrew embodies a culture and a literature without which the maintenance of Judaism in the Soviet Union is hard to imagine. At present, a true revision in Soviet policy toward Jews is not yet in evidence.[93]

CONCLUSIONS

The most significant characteristic of the Soviet Communist Party leadership's effort to enforce its policies is the dual system of justice that exists for all citizens. The Party has drawn a firm line between two categories of illegal behavior. One side is governed by a network of "ordinary laws," the violation of which invokes the normal processes of the Procuracy and the courts. This process, as we have seen, is weighted heavily in favor of the state and against the individual, but it is also subject to rules and procedures that constrain the actions of those who hold the power.

On the other side of the line lie behaviors that the Party has declared to be intolerable threats to the Soviet system itself. For these, there is another system of "justice," largely independent of the rules and personnel of the first and administered mainly by the KGB. Ordinary citizens rarely come in contact with this phase of law enforcement, and many are unaware of its activities. Soviet citizens themselves appear to accept the line as legitimate, condemning dissidents for many of the same reasons the Party condemns them. In a recent poll, for example, run by a joint Soviet-French research team, 42 percent of Soviet respondents said they disapproved of releasing dissidents from prison or exile, whereas only 27 percent approved.[94]

For the average citizen, the possibility of coming into conflict with the system looms large, for most people are engaged in some activities that are either illegal or at least not specifically authorized. But it is unlikely that this situation generates any real fear of the regime. More likely it breeds caution and cynicism—a realization that many of the "rules" of Soviet society do not really mean what they say.

For dissidents, there is always fear, for the possibility of arrest is always present. In the era of *glasnost*, there seem to be conflicting emotions among both dissidents and nonconformists. Old-line dissidents, such as *refuseniks* and human rights advocates, may be the most sensitive to the changes because they have been closest to past repression. One Jewish spokesman spoke positively of the present situation:

> Before we had to operate underground. Now even though nobody's giving us anything, we can try and do something for ourselves and not necessarily have to fear getting thrown into jail. That's the basic difference: the fear has eased and more people are trying to get involved in Jewish life.[95]

Between the ordinary citizen and the dissident, a third element of the population may be emerging in response to the Gorbachev reforms—those who have decided to give *glasnost* and *rekonstruktsia* a chance. They are testing the waters of the proposed new order. Individuals who rarely if ever expressed complaints publicly in the past are attending meetings of newly formed clubs and seminars and speaking openly of matters that only recently could not be mentioned. Such people have traded the security of silence for the risks of public exposure, and this has created an anxious mood among many of them.

In the press, a wider and more critical range of opinions is being expressed in letters from readers, but the proportion of letters that are unsigned is also increasing.[96] People are anxious to express their views but wary of identifying themselves. The humiliation of Boris Yeltsin, former Party leader of Moscow, in November 1987, in part for proceeding too rapidly with the revival of uncensored speech, was interpreted as an "ominous sign" by many of those who had followed Yeltsin's lead.[97] Whether a turning point in the Gorbachev reform program was signified by that event is as yet not clear.

NOTES

1. For details of a recent Party campaign to "clean up" popular music, see "The Nature of Official Documents Concerning Control of Vocal/Instrumental Groups and Discotheques," *Arkhiv Samizdata* (Radio Liberty), No. 34, October 18, 1985; trans. in *Survey,* Summer 1985, pp. 172–79.
2. *Izvestia,* 23 September 1987, p. 3; trans. in *Current Digest of the Soviet Press,* October 21, 1987, p. 28.
3. Dietrich A. Loeber, "Legal Rules: For Internal Use Only," *The International and Comparative Law Quarterly,* January 1970, p. 76.
4. See Gordon B. Smith, *The Soviet Procuracy and the Supervision of Administration* (Amsterdam, Netherlands: Sijthoff and Noordhoff, 1978).
5. A richly detailed account of the life of an advocate, written by a former Soviet advocate, is in Dina Kaminskaya, *Final Judgment* (New York: Simon & Schuster, 1982).
6. For an extensive study of *iurisconsults,* see Louise I. Skelley, *Lawyers in Soviet Work Life* (New Brunswick, N.J.: Rutgers University Press, 1984).
7. See E. Huskey, "The Limits to Institutional Autonomy in the Soviet Union: The Case of the *Advokatura,*" *Soviet Studies,* XXXIV, 1982.
8. W.E. Butler, *Soviet Law* (London: Butterworths, 1983), p. 124.
9. See E.V. Shorina, "Soviets and the Organs of People's Control, *Soviet Law and Government,* Fall 1986, pp. 42–54.
10. Theodore H. Friedgut, *Political Participation in the USSR* (Princeton, N.J.: Princeton University Press, 1979), pp. 257–62; and Butler, *Soviet Law,* pp. 131–32.
11. Jan S. Adams, *Citizen Inspectors in the Soviet Union: The People's Control Committees* (New York: Praeger, 1977), p. 150.
12. See Friedgut, *Political Participation,* p. 283, for evidence of this.
13. See Smith, *Soviet Procuracy,* chapter 4.
14. Walter Gellhorn, *Ombudsmen and Others* (Cambridge, Mass.: Harvard University Press, 1966), p. 359.
15. The text of the law appears in *Current Digest of the Soviet Press,* August 19, 1987, pp. 12–13. The comments of the legal scholar are from *Izvestia,* 29 September 1987, p. 3; trans. in *Current Digest of the Soviet Press,* November 11, 1987, p. 14.
16. See Ger van den Berg, *The Soviet System of Justice: Figures and Policy* (Dordrecht: Martinus Nijhoff Publishers, 1985), pp. 17–31.

17. See Olympiad S. Ioffe and Peter B. Maggs, *Soviet Law in Theory and Practice* (London: Oceana, 1983), pp. 58.
18. For an interesting discussion of this and related issues, see *Lituraturnaya Gazeta*, April 15, 1987, p. 11.
19. Interview with Aleksandr Yakovlev, professor and head of the department of the theory and sociology of criminal law at the USSR Academy of Sciences' Institute of State and Law, *Literaturnaya Gazeta,* September 24, 1986, p. 13; trans. in *Current Digest of the Soviet Press*, XXXVIII:42, p. 4
20. On the problems of lawyers, see V. Savitsky, *Pravda*, 22 March 1987.
21. *Literaturnaya Gazeta*, January 1, 1986, p. 11.
22. *Izvestia*, 5 October 1986, p. 3.
23. *Izvestia*, 4 October 1986, p. 3
24. *Pravda*, 1 August 1987, p. 6.
25. See the report on the Supreme Court's plenary session held in December 1986, in *Izvestia*, 12 December 1986, p. 3.
26. Yakovlev, *Current Digest.*
27. See J.N. Hazard, W.E. Butler, and P.B. Maggs, *The Soviet Legal System*, 3d ed., (Dobbs Ferry, N.Y.: Oceana Publications, 1977), p. 67.
28. Arkady Vaksberg, *Literaturnaya Gazeta*, May 7, 1986, p. 3; trans. in *Current Digest of the Soviet Press*, November 19, 1986, pp. 6–7.
29. For an interesting discussion of the Soviet judicial process, see Robert Sharlet, "The Communist Party and the Administration of Justice in the USSR," in Donald Barry, George Ginsburgs, and Peter Maggs, eds., *Soviet Law Under Stalin*, Part 3: *Soviet Institutions and the Administration of Law* (Amsterdam, Netherlands: Sijthoff and Noordhoff, 1979), pp. 321–92.
30. For an in-depth study of the judicial process, see Kaminskaya, *Final Judgment.*
31. See Paul B. Stephen, "Comrades' Courts and Labor Discipline Since Brezhnev," in Olympiad S. Ioffe and Mark W. Janis, *Soviet Law and Economy* (Dordrecht: Martinus Nijhoff Publishers, 1987), pp. 213–32.
32. See ibid., pp. 222–24.
33. Robert Sharlet has offered the concept of "contra-system" to incorporate all facets of the dissident population. See his "Soviet Dissent Since Brezhnev," *Current History*, October 1986, pp. 321–24, 340, and sources cited there.
34. For an analysis of and numerous excerpts from *Political Diary* see Stephen F. Cohen, ed., *An End To Silence* (New York: W. W. Norton & Co., 1982).
35. See Mark Hopkins, *Russia's Underground Press: The Chronicle of Current Events* (New York: Praeger, 1983).
36. See Howard L. Biddulph, "Protest Strategies of the Soviet Intellectual Opposition," in Rudolf L. Tokes, ed., *Dissent in the USSR* (Baltimore: The Johns Hopkins University Press, 1975), pp. 110ff.
37. Frederick C. Barghoorn, "The Post-Khrushchev Campaign to Suppress Dissent: Perspectives, Strategies, and Techniques of Repression," in Rudolf L. Tokes, *Dissent in the USSR*, p. 63.
38. Ioffe and Maggs, *Soviet Law*, pp. 244–45.
39. For the text of all statutes referred to here, see W.E. Butler, ed., *Basic Documents on the Soviet Legal System* (New York: Oceana Publications, 1983).
40. Alexander Solzhenitsyn, *The Gulaq Archipeligo, 1918–1956: An Experiment in Literary Investigation*, 2 vols. (New York: Harper & Row, 1975).

41. Estimates on the number of prisoners vary widely and there is no official data from the Soviet Union. See John L. Scherer, *USSR: Facts and Figures Annual*, Vol. 8, (Gulf Breeze, Fla.: Academic International Press, 1984), p. 287, for several estimates.

42. Compiled by Cronid Lubarsky, Commission on Security and Cooperation in Europe, in a report to the U.S. Congress, *Implementation of the Final Act of the Conference on Security and Cooperation in Europe: Findings and Recommendations Seven Years After Helsinki* (1982), pp. 255–58. Based on an analysis of 848 prisoners in 1982.

43. Harvey Fireside, *Soviet Psychoprisons* (New York: W. W. Norton & Co., 1979), pp. 19, 141.

44. *Izvestia*, 11 July 1987, p. 1; trans. in *Current Digest of the Soviet Press*, August 19, 1987, p. 3.

45. Ibid, p. 5.

46. Ibid., p. 3.

47. The following is based partly on Walter Reich's informative article, "Diagnosing Soviet Dissidents," *Harper's Magazine*, August 1978, pp. 31–37.

48. Ibid., p. 37.

49. The transcript was published in the *New Leader*, August 31, 1964, pp. 6–17. In 1987, Joseph Brodsky, by then an American citizen, won the Nobel Prize in literature for his poetry and essays.

50. On the Sinyavsky/Daniel case, see Joshua Rubenstein, *Soviet Dissidents, Their Struggle for Human Rights* 2d ed. (Boston: Beacon Press, 1985), chapter 2.

51. See Ludmilla Alexeyeva, *Soviet Dissent* (Middletown, Conn: Wesleyan University Press, 1985), pp. 335–49.

52. See Roy Medvedev, *Let History Judge* (New York: Random House, 1971), chapters 15 and 16.

53. See his *Progress, Coexistence and Intellectual Freedom* (New York: Alfred A Knopf, 1968); and *Alarm and Hope* (New York: Alfred A. Knopf, 1978).

54. The *New York Times*, December 16, 1987, p. 3.

55. See his "Letter to Soviet Leaders," *Kontinent* (New York: Anchor Press, 1976), which also carries reactions to Solzhenitsyn's views by Sakharov.

56. *New York Times*, 28 December 1986, p. 9.

57. Soviet statistics on religious believers tend to be based on categories that maximize the number of atheists reported. Among Muslims, for example, researchers list those who only "perform Muslin rites" and those who "perform Muslim rites under the influence of their relatives" as nonbelievers. See Michael Rywkin, "National Symbiosis: Vitality, Religion, Identity, Allegiance," in Yaacov Ro'i, ed., *The USSR and the Muslim World* (London: George Allen and Unwin, 1984), p. 9.

58. This is John Lawrence's conclusion in his "Religion in the USSR," in Curtis Keeble, ed., *The Soviet State: the Domestic Roots of Soviet Foreign Policy* (Boulder, Colo.: Westview Press, 1985), p. 59. For an analysis of the problem of numbers, see William C. Fletcher, *Soviet Believers: The Religious Sector of the Population* (Lawrence: The Regents Press of Kansas, 1981), chapter 4.

59. Quoted in Albert Boiter, *Religion in the Soviet Union*, The Washington Papers, No. 78 (Beverly Hills, Calif.: Sage Publications, 1980), p. 5.

60. Ibid., pp. 34ff.

61. These statistics have been summarized from data compiled by S.P. Hanchett, Keston College, Kent, England, and by B.R. Bociurkiw, Carleton University, Ottawa, Canada. Published in Scherer, *USSR: Facts and Figures*, Vol. 5, 1981, pp. 324–26.

62. Lawrence, in Keeble, *The Soviet State*, p. 65.

63. For a historical survey of the evangelicals, or "sectarians" as the author calls them, see

Andrew Blane, "Protestant Sectarians and Modernization in the Soviet Union," in Dennis J. Dunn, ed., *Religion and Modernization in the Soviet Union* (Boulder, Colo.: Westview Press, 1977, pp. 382–407.

64. See Alexandre Bennigsen, "Several Nations or One People? Ethnic Consciousness among Soviet Central Asian Muslims," *Survey*, Summer 1979.

65. See Michael Rywkin, *Moscow's Muslim Challenge* (London: M.E. Sharpe, 1982).

66. Dunn, *Religion and Modernization*, p. 359.

67. Alexeyeva, *Soviet Dissent*, pp. 259–60.

68. Michael Rowe, "Soviet Policy Towards Religion," in Scherer, *USSR: Facts and Figures*, Vol. 5, 1981, p. 323.

69. Alexeyeva, *Soviet Dissent*, pp. 255–59.

70. See Michael Rywkin, *Moscow's Muslim Challenge*, p. 88.

71. This case and information on the Articles appears in Rowe, "Soviet Policy Towards Religion," p. 322.

72. See Peter Reddaway, "Policy Towards Dissent Since Khrushchev," in T.H. Rigby, Archie Brown, and Peter Reddaway, *Authority, Power and Policy in the USSR* (New York: St. Martin's Press, 1980), p. 182–83.

73. Quoted in Alexeyeva, *Soviet Dissent*, p. 168.

74. Crimean Tatars should not be confused with the far larger populaton of Kazan Tatars who occupy an autonomous republic east of Moscow. The two branches of the Tatar peoples differ somewhat in both language and culture. See Helene d'Encausse, *Decline of an Empire* (New York: Harper & Row, 1978), pp. 191–192.

75. For a brief history of the deportation of all these peoples, see Isabelle Kreindler, "The Soviet Deported Nationalities: A Summary and an Update," *Soviet Studies*, July 1986, pp. 387–405.

76. The Tatar case is discussed in Alexeyeva, chapter 7; see also Aleksandr M. Nekrich, *The Punished Peoples* (New York: W.W. Norton & Co., 1978), chapter 1. Both of these books also deal with the Meskhi situation and other aspects of the deported peoples.

77. Alexeyeva, *Soviet Dissent*, p. 171.

78. Statistics are from the Consulate General of the Federal Republic of Germany, May 20, 1985; published in Scherer, *USSR: Facts and Figures*, Vol. 10, 1986, p. 335. The 1987 figure is from *The New York Times*, December 6, 1987, p. 8.

79. See Alexeyeva, *Soviet Dissent*, pp. 121–33.

80. Scherer, *USSR: Facts and Figures*, Vol. 8, 1984, p. 290.

81. *New York Times*, 2 November 1987, p. 6.

82. Sources differ on the number of Soviet Jews. The 1979 Soviet census reports 1,811,000 Jews; d'Encausse puts the figure, based on several sources, at somewhere between 2 million and 3.5 million. See d'Encausse, *Decline of an Empire*, p. 203.

83. See Darrel Slider, "A Note on the Class Structure of Soviet Nationalities," *Soviet Studies*, October 1985, p. 536.

84. Zev Katz, Rosemarie Rogers and Frederic Harned, eds., *Handbook of Major Soviet Nationalities* (New York: Free Press, 1975), p. 377.

85. Al Szymanski, *Human Rights in the Soviet Union* (London: Zed Books, Ltd., 1984), p. 94.

86. Alexeyeva, *Soviet Dissent*, p. 179.

87. Valery Chalidze, *To Defend These Rights* (New York: Random House, 1974), p. 165.

88. Quoted in William Korey, "Anti-Zionism in the USSR," *Problems of Communism*, November–December 1978, p. 69.

89. See Rubenstein, *Soviet Dissidents*, pp. 157–78.

90. The latter figure is cited in the *New York Times*, 24 November 1987, p. 3.
91. See *Current Digest of the Soviet Press*, February 11, 1987, pp. 13–14.
92. See V. Fulmacht, "The New Emigration Law," *Glasnost*, (Moscow), July, 1987, p. 13–14. The exact number of applicants for exit visas is not known, and Soviet authorities deny there are anywhere near that many. The National Conference on Soviet Jewry claims that there are 380,000 pending exit applications. See the *New York Times*, 11 January 1987, p. 4.
93. See Arthur Hertzberg, "Glasnost and the Jews," *New York Review of Books*, October 22, 1987, pp. 20–23.
94. *New York Times*, 1 November 1987, p. 12.
95. *New York Times*, 21 November 1987, p. 3.
96. See Vladimir Nedein in *Izvestia*, 3 October 1987, p. 3.
97. See the *New York Times*, 29 November, 1987, p. 8.

CHAPTER 13
Prospects for Reform

If there has been a constant factor throughout the history of the Russian nation, it may be the absence of significant reform in the system of government. While European states were churning through the upheavals of the Renaissance, the Protestant Reformation, the rise of mass political movements in the eighteenth and nineteenth centuries, and the emergence of liberalism and democracy, the Russian nation was clinging steadfastly to czarist absolutism and religious orthodoxy. The Revolution of 1917, which destroyed the old system, proved to be no exception to the pattern. There began anew the absolutist politics of a ruling elite that was just as intolerant of the dissident forces of gradual reform as was its predecessor.

It is not that past leaders were unaware of the need for reform. As pointed out in Chapter 2, the Russian system was often in critical straits, and all strong czars attempted to cope with them. Yet the political system failed to *evolve*, despite these crises and despite the repeated efforts at reform. Nicholas II resisted no less vigorously in the twentieth century, than did Alexander I in the nineteenth, the pressures for modernization and social justice that were rampant in the land. In the contemporary period, a new leader has once again called for drastic reforms in response to critical deficiencies in the political, economic, and social systems. Whether the chances for genuine reform of the system have improved in this century is a question that remains to be answered.

What General Secretary Gorbachev intends to do for his country is by now relatively clear. He has campaigned all over the country for the "new thinking" that he deems necessary. He has caused his reform plans, generally referred to as *perestroika*, to be adopted by Communist Party assemblies and enacted into law by the Supreme Soviet, and he has set forth his ideas in a 1987 book addressed both to his own people and to the world at large. The book offers an unusual format for the Soviet leader to make the case for his brand of reform.

Gorbachev insists in his book that the Soviet Union is not in a state of crisis. He sharply disagrees with those who argue that *perestroika* "has been necessitated by the disastrous state of the Soviet economy and that it signifies disenchantment with socialism and a crisis for its ideals and ultimate goals."[1] "Nothing," he says, "could be further from the truth than such interpretations, whatever the motives behind them."

On one level, his point is defensible, for there is much about the system that works as well as it ever did. The Communist Party leadership remains firmly in control of the country, and there are no organized forces on any horizon that could pose a challenge to that dominance. The system has proved capable, time after time, of choosing new leadership without provoking either popular or elite protest. Militarily, the country is secure, surrounded as it is by subordinate buffer states and commanding what is possibly the world's greatest arsenal of weapons and armies. Economically, the system provides a moderate standard of living for its people with no extremes of wealth and poverty, no significant elements suffering from unemployment or homelessness, and no serious imbalance between the resources, human and material, that are available and the economic goals of the system. Finally, the society itself provides an overwhelming majority of the people with physical protection, minimum basic human needs such as food, housing, and medical care, upward mobility, and educational opportunity for their children at least on a par with other industrialized countries. Measured by internal conditions fifty, or even twenty, years ago, the Soviet Union in the late-1980s is far better off, and there is widespread recognition of this fact among the Soviet people.

Compared to the rest of the industrialized world, however, the USSR presents a very different picture, and the people are increasingly aware of this fact as well. The USSR has proved chronically incapable of competing with the Western world in economic terms, while in cultural terms the contrast is even sharper. *Glasnost* is beginning to reveal to the Soviet people what outsiders—and many inside—have long known: that the "official truth" about the Soviet system constitutes one of the great coverups of modern history. Seventy years of denying the existence of poverty, anti-Semitism, police brutality, and elite privileges has not ensured Soviet society against those very evils. Seventy years of insisting that the people are unanimously behind every initiative of the Party leadership has not made it so. What it has produced instead is a cynical indifference to "officialdom" that pervades all avenues of social interaction in the USSR—a "credibility gap" as Gorbachev describes it in his book.[2]

There is, therefore, a crisis of performance and a crisis of confidence in the Soviet Union of the 1980s, and these crises feed upon each other. The failure of the system to perform adequately in the fulfillment of human needs has diminished public confidence in the Party and its ideology. At the same time, the Party's failure to solve social and economic problems has led most Soviet people to seek other ways of enhancing their circumstances. These include involvement with both the gray and black markets; bribery of officials, shopkeepers, doctors, and others; and widespread violation of approved standards of behavior.

The central question is whether the Gorbachev reforms—*perestroika, glasnost*, and *demokratizatsia*—can achieve both significantly higher performance levels and a restoration of public confidence in the Communist Party leadership. Lying across the path of such achievements are a number of obstacles that reflect intrinsic characteristics of the Soviet political system. Three such obstacles seem of greatest importance in considering the Gorbachev reforms: the absence of organized support for the reforms, either among the masses or among the intelligentsia; the problem of squaring the reforms with Soviet ideology; and the need to deal with those who go beyond the permitted limits of the reforms.

POPULAR AND ELITE SUPPORT FOR THE REFORMS

The reform program, according to Gorbachev, "started on the Communist Party's initiative, and the Party leads it. . . . *Perestroika* is not a spontaneous, but a governed process."[3] What saves it from being merely another "reform from above," he argues, is the fervent support it has engendered from the Soviet people. *Perestroika* could not work "if the masses had not regarded it as their program, a response to their own thoughts and a recognition of their own demands; and if the people had not supported it so vehemently and effectively."[4]

Gorbachev seems convinced that such support exists. "In my talks with people in the street or at the workplace," he states, "I constantly hear: 'Everybody supports *perestroika* here.' I am convinced of the sincerity of these words. . . ."[5] There is, however, little objective evidence to support that conviction. The Soviet press regularly reports indications of skepticism and opposition to *perestroika*, especially those core aspects of the reform that appear to call for tighter discipline for workers, less job security, and higher prices for basic consumer items.

The belief in mass support of *perestroika* arises from a perspective characteristic of Soviet politics. It incorporates several elements: (1) the leaders' assumption that Party policies are rational and necessary, so that any opposition to them must be based on irrational or deliberately anti-Soviet attitudes; (2) the assurance that whether popular support is present at the outset of a new policy or not, it can be quickly manufactured by means of the resources of agitprop, the press, and the Party; and (3) the readiness of the Soviet people to express publicly whatever views the Party wishes to hear. These tendencies of the Soviet system pervade the dialogue on reform that has been underway ever since Gorbachev came to power.

The paucity of mass support is compounded by the weakness of support offered by the political and economic elite of the country. There appear, in fact, to be no major groups in Soviet society with a strong commitment to the reform. The only constituencies in favor of it, as economist Joseph Berliner has pointed out, "are some economists, some scientists and liberal intellectuals, and some Party and military officers."[6] The career interests of many of the governmental bureaucrats who must implement the reforms are at considerable risk if the reforms should succeed.

THE IDEA OF "SOVIET SOCIALISM"

Perestroika poses an ideological challenge as well. The Marxist foundations of the Soviet system are embedded in values that have met wide acceptance in Soviet society. As a practical matter, the Soviet people understand "socialism" to mean security of employment, relative equality of income, progressively shorter workweeks and a standard of living based on extremely low prices for basic necessities such as food, housing, transportation, and leisure. The Gorbachev reforms appear to threaten all of these perquisites in favor of more demanding working conditions, a shift to a semimarket economy, and the prospect of inflation and unemployment, all of which may well create a lower standard of living for many people in the short run. This raises a question as to whether Soviet society is truly progressing to ever higher planes of socialism, as the regime continues to insist, or has tacitly admitted that such progress is impractical and must be reexamined.

The question of whether socialism is compatible with even a semimarket economy is far from settled among Soviet authorities. The conservative view is well expressed in a recent issue of *Novy Mir*:

> Socialism—and this is my firm belief—is incompatible with the market by its essense, by its founders' design, by the instinct of those who embodied and continue to embody in life the appropriate principles and procedures. In the most varied periods of Soviet history the most varied policies and theories have tried to turn the country onto a market direction, but it did not take even one step along. Is this accidental?[7]

In the short run, the issue of ideological conformity is far less important to the Soviet population than are the practical implications of the reform for personal income, working conditions, and job security. But in some Party circles, including elements at the highest level, adherence to a plausible theory of progressive socialism is highly important. Gorbachev's drive for economic efficiency based on profit and competition poses a challenge to the established idea of socialism in the USSR.

MAINTAINING PARTY CONTROL OF THE REFORMS

As *perestroika, glasnost,* and *demokratizatsia* take hold in Soviet society, Gorbachev and his supporters must increasingly walk a narrow line. Many forms of individual and group behavior that were previously prohibited are now encouraged, but there are new limits to which the leadership is determined to hold fast. Educating an army of bureaucrats, procurators, and police officers to administer these new standards effectively is a huge task, and one that has barely begun.

In the meantime, Soviet society is rife with "excesses" in the implementation of the reforms. Greater economic freedom for plant managers encourages them to shift production lines to more profitable goods, fire unproductive workers, seek raw materials outside regular channels, and ignore planning quotas. *Glasnost* has already produced such excesses as the reestablishment of the human rights movement, the open publication of uncensored and highly critical pamphlets, and a host of small-scale protest demonstrations in Red Square and elsewhere. The encouragement of *demokratizatsia* has prompted unrecognized groups, including dissidents, to organize openly against some Party policies and to demand the right to run anti-Party candidates in local elections.

These "excesses" pose a threat to the success of the general policy of *perestroika* for several reasons. They provide Gorbachev's opponents in the Party and government with arguments for abandoning or at least curtailing *perestroika*. They also force the regime into an apparent contradiction: They must deal harshly with the excesses as a lesson to citizens, while encouraging the basic policies, a distinction that may well be lost on many ordinary citizens. And in dealing with the excesses, the specter of a more visible and aggressive KGB clearly belies the image of an increasingly open and democratic society. Internationally, such contradictions make it more difficult for Western leaders and the Western press to accept Soviet claims of genuine reform.

Unfortunately, the Gorbachev Politburo has little choice but to crush the excesses of *perestroika* if it wishes to retain its dominant political position. The excesses will not disappear on their own, for they clearly express the pent-up desires of many Soviet individuals and particularly of many within the intelligentsia. In crushing the excesses, the leadership may chill the overall reform program as well, for citizens and administrators alike will be wary of overstepping the shifting and uncertain limits of acceptable behavior.

Underlying these immediate obstacles to the Gorbachev reforms is an additional and more general factor. Reform has always been difficult for Russian and Soviet regimes because of the historic prohibition against a legitimate opposition to the government. Between major policy changes, the full weight of the state and Party is turned to stamping out any deviation from the current standards and policies. Opposition to those standards among the populace and the intelligentsia that might illuminate their weaknesses and help move the system gradually toward the evolution of new standards is ruthlessly stamped out. When a Gorbachev or a Khrushchev or a Lenin decrees that the old ways were wrong and empties the jails of all those whom the previous leader had arrested for saying the same thing, the result is mass confusion and an overwhelming tendency to wait out the newest "reform." What is missing in the Soviet political process is the right of organized groups to mobilize public opinion in favor of changes that the current leadership has not yet accepted. In political systems where this does happen, new leaders take power with widespread support for new programs, and real reform becomes possible.

For that to happen, however, requires a tolerance for political opposition and the emergence of an opposition leadership capable of mobilizing popular and elite support against the present rulers. Democracies accomplish this through opposition political parties and elections. The Soviet Union, like czarist Russia before it, has never permitted this process to occur. Thus, its leadership is forced to start each new reform essentially from scratch and against the settled patterns of popular behavior that were imposed, often at horrendous cost, by previous leaders.

"Revolutions from above," such as the Gorbachev reforms, are not necessarily doomed to fail, as the history of Turkey under Ataturk, Japan under the Meijis and later under General MacArthur, and Spain under Juan Carlos have shown. In the Soviet case, the international position of the USSR imposes urgent priorities on the

Gorbachev Politburo, which were less salient in previous eras. The pressures for reform are therefore greater than before, and this gives Gorbachev something of a running start. But based on a long history of aborted reforms, one should not expect very much. Gorbachev himself has pointed to the underlying paradox of Soviet reform movements: "This society is ripe for change. It has long been yearning for it. . . . [Yet] generations must pass for us to really change. Generations must pass."[8] He may well be right on both counts.

NOTES

1. Mikhail Gorbachev, *Perestroika: New Thinking for our Country and the World* (New York: Harper & Row, 1987), p. 10.
2. Ibid., p. 22.
3. Ibid., p. 55.
4. Ibid., p. 56.
5. Ibid., p. 105.
6. Joseph Berliner, *Los Angeles Times*, 7 November 1987, p. 20. A Soviet commentator agrees, arguing that "because of the absence of experience with and forms of political self-reliance, there are no organized forces behind the restructuring." He advocates the formation of a "National Front of Advocates of Restructuring" to fill the gap. See *Glasnost*, No. 1, 1987, p. 12.
7. L. Polkova, "Where Are the Pirogi Flakier?" *Novy Mir*, No. 5, 1987; trans. in *Glasnost*, No. 1, 1987, p. 11.
8. The first part of the quotation is from Gorbachev, *Perestroika*, p. 17; the second part is quoted in the *New York Times*, 18 December 1986, p. 8.

Select Bibliography

The following list includes scholarly books in English that will assist readers in pursuing individual subjects further. There are several valuable sources of Soviet documents in translation. The chief source is the *Current Digest of the Soviet Press*, a weekly journal of translations covering the major Soviet newspapers and magazines. *Reprints from the Soviet Press*, published biweekly, contains speeches by Soviet officials, documents, and periodical excerpts. Other publications of translations particularly related to the subject of this text are *Soviet Law and Government, Problems of Economics, Soviet Sociology, Soviet Statutes and Decisions, Soviet Education,* and *Soviet Military Review*. Since 1987, an English translation of the daily newspaper *Pravda* has also been available.

CHAPTER 1: INTRODUCTION

Howe, G. Melvyn. *The Soviet Union: A Geographical Survey*, 2d ed. Plymouth, Devonshire, England: Macdonald and Evans, 1983.
Mellor, Roy E. H. *The Soviet Union and Its Geographical Problems.* London: Macmillan Press, 1982.
Symons, Leslie, Dewdney, J. C., Hoosen, D. J. M., Mellor, R. E. H., Newey, W. W., *The Soviet Union: A Systematic Geography*. Totowa, N.J.: Barnes & Noble, 1983.

CHAPTER 2: THE ORIGINS OF SOVIET AUTOCRACY

Beazley, Raymond, et al. *Russia from the Varangians to the Bolsheviks.* Oxford: Clarendon Press, 1918.
Black, Cyril E. *Understanding Soviet Politics: The Perspective of Russian History.* Boulder, Colo.: Westview Press, 1986.
Blum, Jerome. *Lord and Peasant in Russia from the Ninth to the Nineteenth Century.* Princeton, N.J.: Princeton University Press, 1961.
Clarkson, Jesse. *A History of Russia.* New York: Random House, 1961.
Cowles, Virginia. *The Romanovs.* New York: Harper & Row, 1971.
Crankshaw, Edward. *The Shadow of the Winter Palace.* New York: Viking, 1976.
Halperin, Charles J. *Russia and the Golden Horde.* Bloomington: Indiana University Press, 1985.
Hosking, Gerald. *The Russian Constitutional Experiment.* Cambridge: Cambridge University Press, 1973.

Pushkarev, Sergei. *Self-Government and Freedom in Russia.* Boulder, Colo.: Westview Press, 1988.
Yaney, George. *The Systematization of Russian Government.* Urbana: University of Illinois Press, 1973.

CHAPTER 3: THE RUSSIAN REVOLUTION

Conquest, Robert. *The Harvest of Sorrow.* New York: Oxford University Press, 1986.
Florinsky, Michael T. *The End of the Russian Empire.* New York: Howard Fertig, 1973.
Geyer, Detrich. *The Russian Revolution: Historical Problems and Perspectives.* New York: St. Martin's Press, 1987.
Lewin, Moshe. *Lenin's Last Struggle.* New York: Pantheon Books, 1968.
Lincoln, W. Bruce. *In War's Dark Shadow.* New York: Dial Press, 1983.
Meyer, Alfred G. *Leninism.* New York: Praeger, 1957.
Pares, Bernard. *Russia and Reform.* Westport, Conn: Hyperion Press, 1907.
Vassili, Paul. *Behind the Veil at the Russian Court.* London: Cassell, 1913.
Von Laue, Theodore H. *Why Lenin? Why Stalin?* 2d. ed. Philadelphia: Lippincott, 1971.
Wilson, Edmund. *To the Finland Station.* New York: Farrar, Straus & Giroux, 1972.
Wolfe, Bertram D. *Three Who Made a Revolution.* New York: Dell Publishing Co., 1948.

CHAPTER 4: STALINISM

Avtorkhanov, Abdurakhman. *Stalin and the Soviet Communist Party.* New York: Praeger, 1959.
Campeanu, Pavel. *The Origins of Stalinism: From Leninist Revolution to Stalinist Society.* New York: St. Martin's Press, 1986.
Carrere d'Encausse, Helene. *Stalin.* New York: Longman, 1981.
Djilas, Milovan. *Conversations with Stalin.* New York: Harcourt, Brace & World, 1962.
Hingley, Ronald. *Joseph Stalin, Man and Legend.* New York: McGraw-Hill, 1974.
Medvedev, Roy. *Let History Judge.* New York: Random House, 1971.
Nove, Alec. *Stalinism and After.* London: George Allen and Unwin, 1975.
Reiman, Michael. *The Birth of Stalinism.* Bloomington: Indiana University Press, 1987.
Trotsky, Leon. *Stalin.* New York: Harper & Row, 1941.
Tucker, Robert C. *Stalin as Revolutionary.* New York: W.W. Norton & Co., 1973.

CHAPTER 5: THE COMMUNIST PARTY

Avtorkhanov, Abdurakhman. *The Communist Party Apparatus.* Chicago: Henry Regnery, 1966.
Bialer, Seweryn. *Stalin's Successors: Leadership, Stability and Change in the Soviet Union.* Cambridge: Cambridge University Press, 1980.
Harasymiw, Bohdan. *Political Elite Recruitment in the Soviet Union.* New York: St. Martin's Press, 1984.
Hazan, Baruch A. *From Brezhnev to Gorbachev.* Boulder, Colo.: Westview Press, 1987.

Hill, Ronald J., and Frank, Peter. *The Soviet Communist Party.* 2d. ed. London: George Allen and Unwin, 1983.

Loewenhardt, John. *The Soviet Politburo.* New York: St. Martin's Press, 1978.

Narkiewicz, Olga A. *Soviet Leaders: From the Cult of Personality to Collective Rule.* New York: St. Martin's Press, 1986.

Schapiro, Leonard. *The Communist Party of the Soviet Union.* New York: Random House, 1960.

CHAPTER 6: THE GOVERNMENTAL STRUCTURE

Avidar, Yosef. *The Party and the Army in the Soviet Union.* University Park: Pennsylvania State University Press, 1983.

Colton, Timothy J. *Commissars, Commanders, and Civilian Authority.* Cambridge, Mass.: Harvard University Press, 1979.

Carrere d'Encausse, Helene. *Confiscated Power: How Soviet Russia Really Works.* New York: Harper & Row, 1982.

Harding, Neal, ed. *The State in Socialist Society.* Albany, N.Y.: SUNY Press, 1984.

Rigby, T. H., and Harasymiw, Bohdan, eds. *Leadership Selection and Patron-Client Relations in the USSR and Yugoslavia.* London: George Allen and Unwin, 1983.

Savas, E. S., and Kaiser, J. A. *Moscow's City Government.* New York: Praeger, 1985.

Voslensky, Michael. *Nomenklatura: The Soviet Ruling Class, An Insider's Report.* Garden City, N.Y.: Doubleday, 1984.

Williams, E. S. *The Soviet Military: Political Education, Training and Morale.* New York: St. Martin's Press, 1986.

CHAPTER 7: THE SOVIET PARLIAMENT

Jacobs, Everett M., ed. *Soviet Local Politics and Government.* London: George Allen and Unwin, 1983.

Minagawa, Shugo. *Supreme Soviet Organs.* Tokyo: The University of Nagoya Press, 1985.

Mote, Max. *Soviet Local and Republic Elections.* Stanford, Calif.: Stanford University Press, 1965.

Siegler, Robert S. *The Standing Commissions of the Supreme Soviet.* New York: Praeger, 1982.

Taubman, William. *Governing Soviet Cities.* New York: Praeger, 1973.

Vanneman, Peter. *The Supreme Soviet: Politics and the Legislative Process in the Soviet Political System.* Durham, N.C.: Duke University Press, 1977.

CHAPTER 8: HOW NATIONAL POLICIES ARE MADE

Chung, Han-ku. *Interest Representation in Soviet Policymaking.* Boulder, Colo.: Westview Press, 1986.

Gustafson, Thane. *The Soviet Gas Campaign: Politics and Policy in Soviet Decision-Making.* Santa Monica, Calif.: Rand Report No. R-3036-AF, June 1983.

Juviler, Peter, and Morton, Henry, eds. *Soviet Policy-Making.* New York: Praeger, 1967.

Loewenhardt, John. *Decision Making in Soviet Politics.* New York: St. Martin's Press, 1981.

Moses, Joel C. *Regional Party Leadership and Policy-Making in the USSR.* New York: Holt, Rinehart & Winston, 1974.

Potichnyj, Peter J., and Zacek, Jane Shapiro. *Politics and Participation Under Communist Rule.* New York: Praeger, 1983.

Pryde, Philip R. *Conservation in the Soviet Union.* London: Cambridge Univesity Press, 1972.

Skilling, H. Gordon, and Griffiths, Franklyn, eds. *Interest Groups in Soviet Politics.* Princeton, N.J.: Princeton University Press, 1971.

Valenta, Jiri, and Potter, William C., eds. *Soviet Decisionmaking for National Security.* London: George Allen and Unwin, 1984.

CHAPTER 9: MANAGING THE PLANNED ECONOMY

Bergson, Abram, and Levine, Herbert S., eds. *The Soviet Economy: Toward the Year 2000.* London: George Allen and Unwin, 1983.

Berliner, Joseph S. *The Innovation Decision in Soviet Industry.* Cambridge, Mass.: MIT Press, 1976.

Bernstein, Morris. *The Soviet Economy, Continuity and Change.* Boulder, Colo.: Westview Press, 1981.

Dunmore, Timothy. *The Stalinist Command Economy.* New York: St. Martin's Press, 1980.

Goldman, Marshall I. *U.S.S.R. in Crisis.* New York: W.W. Norton & Co., 1983.

Lane, David. *Soviet Economy and Society.* Oxford: Basil Blackwell, 1985.

Leites, Nathan. *Soviet Style in Management.* New York: Crane, Russak, 1985.

Nove, Alec. *The Soviet Economic System.* London: George Allen and Unwin, 1977.

Rutland, Peter. *The Myth of the Plan.* London: Hutchinson, 1985.

Stuart, Robert C. *The Soviet Rural Economy.* Totowa, N.J.: Rowman and Allanheld, 1983.

CHAPTER 10: THE POLITICAL CHALLENGE OF THE SECOND ECONOMY

Gregory, Paul, and Stuart, Robert C. *Soviet Economic Structure and Performance,* 2d ed. New York: Harper & Row, 1981.

Hutchings, Raymond. *Soviet Economic Development,* 2d ed. New York: New York University Press, 1982.

Johnson, D. Gale, and Brooks, Karen M. *Prospects for Soviet Agriculture in the 1980's.* Bloomington, Ind: Indiana University Press, 1983.

Knaus, William A. *Inside Russian Medicine.* Boston: Beacon Press, 1981.

Matthews, Mervyn. *Privilege in the Soviet Union.* London: George Allen and Unwin, 1978.

Nove, Alec. *The Economics of Feasible Socialism.* London: George Allen and Unwin, 1983.

Simis, Konstantin. *USSR, the Corrupt Society.* New York: Simon & Schuster, 1982.

Soviet Economy in a Time of Change (prepared for the Joint Economic Committee, U.S. Congress). Washington D.C.: U.S. Government Printing Office, 2 vols., October 10, 1979.

Willis, David K. *Klass, How Russians Really Live.* New York: St. Martin's Press, 1985.

CHAPTER 11: CREATING A NEW SOVIET PERSON

Crouch, Martin, and Porter, Robert, eds. *Understanding Soviet Politics Through Literature.* London: George Allen and Unwin, 1984.

Hammer, Darrell P. *Russian Nationalism and Soviet Politics.* Boulder, Colo.: Westview Press, 1987.

Hollander, Gayle Durham. *Soviet Political Indoctrination: Developments in Mass Media and Propaganda Since Stalin.* New York: Praeger, 1972.

Mickiewicz, Ellen Propper. *Media and the Russian Public.* New York: Praeger, 1981.

Rosen, Seymour M. *Education and Modernization in the USSR.* Reading, MA: Addison-Wesley Publishing, 1981.

Shlapentokh, Vladimir. *Sociology and Politics: The Soviet Case.* Falls Church, Va.: Delphic Associates, 1985.

Simon, Gerhard. *Nationalism and Policy Towards the Nationalities in the Soviet Union.* Boulder, Colo.: Westview Press, 1988.

Tomiak, J. J., ed. *Soviet Education in the 1980s.* London: St. Martin's Press, 1983.

Tumarkin, Nina. *Lenin Lives! The Lenin Cult in Soviet Russia.* Cambridge, Mass.: Harvard University Press, 1983.

CHAPTER 12: GUARDING THE SOCIAL ORDER

Bennigsen, Alexander, and Broxup, Marie. *The Islamic Threat to the Soviet State.* New York: St. Martin's Press, 1983.

Butler, W. E. *Soviet Law.* London: Butterworths, 1983.

Cohen, Stephen F., ed. *An End to Silence.* New York: W.W. Norton & Co., 1982.

Fletcher, William C. *Soviet Believers.* Lawrence: The Regents Press of Kansas, 1981.

Hopkins, Mark. *Russia's Underground Press.* New York: Praeger, 1983.

Ioffe, Olympiad S., and Maggs, Peter B. *Soviet Law in Theory and Practice.* London: Oceana, 1983.

Kadarkay, Arpad. *Human Rights in American and Russian Political Thought.* Lanham, Md.: University Press of America, 1982.

Kaminskaya, Dina. *Final Judgment.* New York: Simon & Schuster, 1982.

Nekrich, Alexander M. *The Punished Peoples.* New York: W.W. Norton & Co., 1978.

Powell, David E. *Antireligious Propaganda in the Soviet Union: A Study of Mass Persuasion.* Cambridge, Mass.: MIT Press, 1975.

Reddaway, Peter, and Block, Sidney. *Soviet Psychiatric Abuse.* Boulder, Colo.: Westview Press, 1985.

Rubenstein, Joshua. *Soviet Dissidents: Their Struggle for Human Rights,* 2d ed. Boston: Beacon Press, 1985.

Rywkin, Michael. *Moscow's Muslim Challenge.* Armonk, N.Y.: M.E. Sharpe, 1982.

Shanor, Donald R. *Behind the Lines: The Private War Against Soviet Censorship.* New York: St. Martin's Press, 1985.

Skelley, Louise I. *Lawyers in Soviet Work Life.* New Brunswick, N.J.: Rutgers University Press, 1984.

Smith, Gordon B. *The Soviet Procuracy and the Supervision of Administration*. Amsterdam, Netherlands: Sijthoff and Noordhoff, 1978.
Spechler, Dina R. *Permitted Dissent in the USSR*. New York: Praeger, 1982.

CHAPTER 13: PROSPECTS FOR REFORM

Colton, Timothy J. *Reform in the Soviet Union*, rev. ed. New York: Council on Foreign Relations, 1986.
Friedberg, Maurice, and Isham, Heyward, eds. *Soviet Society Under Gorbachev: Current Trends and Prospects for Reform*. New York: St. Martin's Press, 1987.
Gorbachev, Mikhail. *Perestroika: New Thinking for Our Country and the World*. New York: Harper & Row, 1987.
Menze, Ernest A., ed. *Totalitarianism Reconsidered*. Port Washington, N.Y.: Kennikat Press, 1981.
Zaslavsky, Victor. *The New-Stalinist State: Class, Ethnicity, and Consensus in Soviet Society*. Armonk, N.Y.: M. E. Sharpe. 1982.

APPENDIX A

Constitution (Fundamental Law)
of the Union
# of Soviet Socialist Republics*

The Great October Socialist Revolution, made by the workers and peasants of Russia under the leadership of the Communist Party headed by Lenin, overthrew capitalist and landowner rule, broke the fetters of oppression, established the dictatorship of the proletariat, and created the Soviet state, a new type of state, the basic instrument for defending the gains of the revolution and for building socialism and communism. Humanity thereby began the epoch-making turn from capitalism to socialism.

After achieving victory in the Civil War and repulsing imperialist intervention, the Soviet government carried through far-reaching social and economic transformations, and put an end once and for all to exploitation of man by man, antagonisms between classes, and strife between nationalities. The unification of the Soviet Republics in the Union of Soviet Socialist Republics multiplied the forces and opportunities of the peoples of the country in the building of socialism. Social ownership of the means of production and genuine democracy for the working masses were established. For the first time in the history of mankind a socialist society was created.

The strength of socialism was vividly demonstrated by the immortal feat of the Soviet people and their Armed Forces in achieving their historic victory in the Great Patriotic War. This victory consolidated the influence and international standing of the Soviet Union and created new opportunities for growth of the forces of socialism, national liberation, democracy, and peace throughout the world.

Continuing their creative endeavours, the working people of the Soviet Union have ensured rapid, all-round development of the country and steady improvement of the socialist system. They have consolidated the alliance of the working class, collective-farm peasantry, and people's intelligentsia, and friendship of the nations and nationalities of the USSR. Socio-political and ideological unity of Soviet society, in which the working class is the leading force, has been achieved. The aims of the dictatorship of the proletariat having been fulfilled, the Soviet state has become a state of the whole people. The leading role of the Communist Party, the vanguard of all the people, has grown.

---

* Source: Moscow: Novesti Press, 1987

In the USSR a developed socialist society has been built. At this stage, when socialism is developing on its own foundations, the creative forces of the new system and the advantages of the socialist way of life are becoming increasingly evident, and the working people are more and more widely enjoying the fruits of their great revolutionary gains.

It is a society in which powerful productive forces and progressive science and culture have been created, in which the well-being of the people is constantly rising, and more and more favourable conditions are being provided for the all-round development of the individual.

It is a society of mature socialist social relations, in which, on the basis of the drawing together of all classes and social strata and of the juridical and factual equality of all its nations and nationalities and their fraternal cooperation, a new historical community of people has been formed—the Soviet people.

It is a society of high organisational capacity, ideological commitment, and consciousness of the working people, who are patriots and internationalists.

It is a society in which the law of life is concern of all for the good of each and concern of each for the good of all.

It is a society of true democracy, the political system of which ensures effective management of all public affairs, ever more active participaton of the working people in running the state, and the combining of citizens' real rights and freedoms with their obligations and responsibility to society.

Developed socialist society is a natural, logical state on the road to communism.

The supreme goal of the Soviet state is the building of a classless communist society in which there will be public, communist self-government. The main aims of the people's socialist state are: to lay the material and technical foundation of communism, to perfect socialist social relations and transform them into communist relations, to mould the citizen of communist society, to raise the people's living and cultural standards, to safeguard the country's security, and to further the consolidation of peace and development of international co-operation.

The Soviet people,

guided by the ideas of scientific communism and true to their revolutionary traditions,

relying on the great social, economic, and political gains of socialism,

striving for the further development of socialist democracy,

taking into account the international position of the USSR as part of the world system of socialism, and conscious of their internationalist responsibility,

preserving continuity of the ideas and principles of the first Soviet Constitution of 1918, the 1924 Constitution of the USSR and the 1936 Constitution of the USSR,

hereby affirm the principles of the social structure and policy of the USSR, and define the rights, freedoms and obligations of citizens, and the principles of the organisation and the socialist state of the whole people, and its aims, and proclaim these in this Constitution.

I. PRINCIPLES OF THE SOCIAL STRUCTURE AND POLICY OF THE USSR

Chapter 1 The Political System

ARTICLE 1. The Union of Soviet Socialist Republics is a socialist state of the whole people, expressing the will and interests of the workers, peasants, and intelligentsia, the working people of all the nations and nationalities of the country.

ARTICLE 2. All power in the USSR belongs to the people.

The people exercise state power through Soviets of People's Deputies, which constitute the political foundation of the USSR.

All other state bodies are under the control of, and accountable to, the Soviets of People's Deputies.

ARTICLE 3. The Soviet state is organised and functions on the principle of democratic centralism, namely the electiveness of all bodies of state authority from the lowest to the highest, their accountability to the people, and the obligation of lower bodies to observe the decisions of higher ones. Democratic centralism combines central leadership with local initiative and creative activity and with the responsibility of each state body and official for the work entrusted to them.

ARTICLE 4. The Soviet state and all its bodies function on the basis of socialist law, ensure the maintenance of law and order, and safeguard the interests of society and the rights and freedoms of citizens.

State organisations, public organisations and officials shall observe the Constitution of the USSR and Soviet laws.

ARTICLE 5. Major matters of state shall be submitted to nationwide discussion and put to a popular vote (referendum).

ARTICLE 6. The leading and guiding force of Soviet society and the nucleus of its political system, of all state organisations and public organisations, is the Communist Party of the Soviet Union. The CPSU exists for the people and serves the people.

The Communist Party, armed with Marxism-Leninism, determines the general perspectives of the development of society and the course of the home and foreign policy of the USSR, directs the great constructive work of the Soviet people, and imparts a planned, systematic and theoretically substantiated character to their struggle for the victory of communism.

All party organisations shall function within the framework of the Constitution of the USSR.

ARTICLE 7. Trade unions, the All-Union Leninist Young Communist League, co-operatives, and other public organisations, participate, in accordance with the aims laid down in their rules, in managing state and public affairs, and in deciding political, economic, and social and cultural matters.

ARTICLE 8. Work collectives take part in discussing and deciding state and public affairs, in planning production and social development, in training and placing personnel, and in discussing and deciding matters pertaining to the management of enterprises and institutions, the improvement of working and living conditions, and the use of funds allocated both for developing production and for social and cultural purposes and financial incentives.

Work collectives promote socialist emulation, the spread of progressive methods of work, and the strengthening of production discipline, educate their members in the spirit of communist morality, and strive to enhance their political consciousness and raise their cultural level and skills and qualifications.

ARTICLE 9. The principal direction in the development of the political system of Soviet society is the extension of socialist democracy, namely ever broader participation of citizens in managing the affairs of society and the state, continuous improvement of the machinery of state, heightening of the activity of public organisations, strengthening of the system of people's control, consolidation of the legal foundations of the functioning of the state and of public life, greater openness and publicity, and constant responsiveness to public opinion.

Chapter 2 The Economic System

ARTICLE 10. The foundation of the economic system of the USSR is socialist ownership of the means of production in the form of state property (belonging to all the people), and collective farm-and-co-operative property.

Socialist ownership also embraces the property of trade unions and other public organisations which they require to carry out their purposes under their rules.

The state protects socialist property and provides conditions for its growth.

No one has the right to use socialist property for personal gain or other selfish ends.

ARTICLE 11. State property, i.e. the common property of the Soviet people, is the principal form of socialist property.

The land, its minerals, waters, and forests are the exclusive property of the state. The state owns the basic means of production in industry, construction, and agriculture; means of transport and communication; the banks; the property of state-run trade organisations and public utilities, and other state-run undertakings; most urban housing; and other property necessary for state purposes.

ARTICLE 12. The property of collective farms and other co-operative organisations, and of their joint undertakings, comprises the means of production and other assets which they require for the purposes laid down in their rules.

The land held by collective farms is secured to them for their free use in perpetuity.

The state promotes development of collective farm-and-co-operative property and its approximation to state property.

Collective farms, like other land users, are obliged to make effective and thrifty use of the land and to increase its fertility.

ARTICLE 13. Earned income forms the basis of the personal property of Soviet citizens. The personal property of citizens of the USSR may include articles of everyday use, personal consumption and convenience, the implements and other objects of a small-holding, a house, and earned savings. The personal property of citizens and the right to inherit it are protected by the state.

Citizens may be granted the use of plots of land, in the manner prescribed by law, for a subsidiary small-holding (including the keeping of livestock and poultry), for fruit and vegetable growing or for building an individual dwelling. Citizens are required to make rational use of the land allotted to them. The state, and collective farms provide assistance to citizens in working their small-holdings.

Property owned or used by citizens shall not serve as a means of deriving unearned income or be employed to the detriment of the interests of society.

ARTICLE 14. The source of the growth of social wealth and of the well-being of the people, and of each individual, is the labour, free from exploitation, of Soviet people.

The state exercises control over the measure of labour and of consumption in accordance with the principle of socialism: "From each according to his ability, to each according to his work". It fixes the rate of taxation on taxable income.

Socially useful work and its results determine a person's status in society. By combining material and moral incentives and encouraging innovation and a creative attitude to work, the state helps transform labour into the prime vital need of every Soviet citizen.

ARTICLE 15. The supreme goal of social production under socialism is the fullest possible satisfaction of the people's growing material, and cultural and intellectual requirements.

Relying on the creative initiative of the working people, socialist emulation, and scientific and technological progress, and by improving the forms and methods of economic management, the state ensures growth of the productivity of labour, raising of the efficiency of production and of the quality of work, and dynamic, planned, proportionate development of the economy.

ARTICLE 16. The economy of the USSR is an integral economic complex comprising all the elements of social production, distribution, and exchange on its territory.

The economy is managed on the basis of state plans for economic and social development, with due account of the sectoral and territorial principles, and by combining centralised direction with the managerial independence and initiative of individual and amalgamated enterprises and other organisations, for which active use is made of management accounting, profit, cost, and other economic levers and incentives.

ARTICLE 17. In the USSR, the law permits individual labour in handicrafts, farming, the provision of services for the public, and other forms of activity based exclusively on the personal work of individual citizens and members of their families. The state makes regulations for such work to ensure that it serves the interest of society.

ARTICLE 18. In the interests of the present and future generations, the necessary steps are taken in the USSR to protect and make scientific, rational use of the land and its mineral and water resources, and the plant and animal kingdoms, to preserve the purity of air and water, ensure reproduction of natural wealth, and improve the human environment.

Chapter 3 Social Development and Culture

ARTICLE 19. The social basis of the USSR is the unbreakable alliance of the workers, peasants, and intelligentsia.

The state helps enhance the social homogeneity of society, namely the elimination of class differences and of the essential distinctions between town and country and between mental and physical labour, and the all-round development and drawing together of all the nations and nationalities of the USSR.

ARTICLE 20. In accordance with the communist ideal—"The free development of each is the condition of the free development of all"—the state pursues the aim of giving citizens more and more real opportunities to apply their creative energies, abilities, and talents, and to develop their personalities in every way.

ARTICLE 21. The state concerns itself with improving working conditions, safety and labour protection and the scientific organisation of work, and with reducing and ultimately eliminating all arduous physical labour through comprehensive mechanisation and automation of production processes in all branches of the economy.

ARTICLE 22. A programme is being consistently implemented in the USSR to convert agricultural work into a variety of industrial work, to extend the network of educational, cultural and medical institutions, and of trade, public catering, service and public utility facilities in rural localities, and transform hamlets and villages into well-planned and well-appointed settlements.

ARTICLE 23. The state pursues a steady policy of raising people's pay levels and real incomes through increase in productivity.

In order to satisfy the needs of Soviet people more fully social consumption funds are created. The state, with the broad participation of public organisations and work collectives, ensures the growth and just distribution of these funds.

ARTICLE 24. In the USSR, state systems of health protection, social security, trade and public catering, communal services and amenities, and public utilities, operate and are being extended.

The state encourages co-operatives and other public organisations to provide all types of services for the population. It encourages the development of mass physical culture and sport.

ARTICLE 25. In the USSR there is a uniform system of public education, which is being constantly improved, that provides general education and vocational training

for citizens, serves the communist education and intellectual and physical development of the youth, and trains them for work and social activity.

ARTICLE 26. In accordance with society's needs the state provides for planned
development of science and the training of scientific personnel and organises
introduction of the results of research in the economy and other spheres of life.

ARTICLE 27. The state concerns itself with protecting, augmenting and making
extensive use of society's cultural wealth for the moral and aesthetic education of
the Soviet people, for raising their cultural level.

In the USSR development of the professional, amateur and folk arts is
encouraged in every way.

Chapter 4 Foreign Policy

ARTICLE 28. The USSR steadfastly pursues a Leninist policy of peace and stands for
strengthening of the security of nations and broad international cooperation.

The foreign policy of the USSR is aimed at ensuring international conditions
favourable for building communism in the USSR, safeguarding the state interests of
the Soviet Union, consolidating the positions of world socialism, supporting the
struggle of peoples for national liberation and social progress, preventing wars of
aggression, achieving universal and complete disarmament, and consistently
implementing the principle of the peaceful coexistence of states with different
social systems.

In the USSR war propaganda is banned.

ARTICLE 29. The USSR's relations with other states are based on observance of the
following principles: sovereign equality; mutual renunciation of the use or threat of
force; inviolability of frontiers; territorial integrity of states; peaceful settlement of
disputes; nonintervention in internal affairs; respect for human rights and fundamental freedoms; the equal rights of peoples and their right to decide their own
destiny; co-operation among states; and fulfilment in good faith of obligations
arising from the generally recognised principles and rules of international law, and
from the international treaties signed by the USSR.

ARTICLE 30. The USSR, as part of the world system of socialism and of the socialist
community, promotes and strengthens friendship, co-operation, and comradely
mutual assistance with other socialist countries on the basis of the principle of
socialist internationalism, and takes an active part in socialist economic integration and the socialist international division of labour.

Chapter 5 Defence of the Socialist Motherland

ARTICLE 31. Defence of the Socialist Motherland is one of the most important
functions of the state, and is the concern of the whole people.

In order to defend the gains of socialism, the peaceful labour of the Soviet people, and the sovereignty and territorial integrity of the state, the USSR maintains armed forces and has instituted universal military service.

The duty of the Armed Forces of the USSR to the people is to provide reliable defence of the Socialist Motherland and to be in constant combat readiness, guaranteeing that any aggressor is instantly repulsed.

ARTICLE 32. The state ensures the security and defence capability of the country, and supplies the Armed Forces of the USSR with everything necessary for that purpose.

The duties of state bodies, public organisations, officials, and citizens in regard to safeguarding the country's security and strengthening its defence capacity are defined by the legislation of the USSR.

II. THE STATE AND THE INDIVIDUAL

Chapter 6 Citizenship of the USSR. Equality of Citizens' Rights

ARTICLE 33. Uniform federal citizenship is established for the USSR. Every citizen of a Union Republic is a citizen of the USSR.

The grounds and procedure for acquiring or forfeiting Soviet citizenship are defined by the Law on Citizenship of the USSR.

When abroad, citizens of the USSR enjoy the protection and assistance of the Soviet state.

ARTICLE 34. Citizens of the USSR are equal before the law, without distinction of origin, social or property status, race or nationality, sex, education, language, attitude to religion, type and nature of occupation, domicile, or other status.

The equal rights of citizens of the USSR are guaranteed in all fields of economic, political, social, and cultural life.

ARTICLE 35. Women and men have equal rights in the USSR.

Exercise of these rights is ensured by according women equal access with men to education and vocational and professional training, equal opportunities in employment, remuneration, and promotion, and in social and political, and cultural activity, and by special labour and health protection measures for women; by providing conditions enabling mothers to work; by legal protection, and material and moral support for mothers and children, including paid leaves and other benefits for expectant mothers and mothers, and gradual reduction of working time for mothers with small children.

ARTICLE 36. Citizens of the USSR of different races and nationalities have equal rights.

Exercise of these rights is ensured by a policy of all-round development and drawing together of all the nations and nationalities of the USSR, by educating citizens in the spirit of Soviet patriotism and socialist internationalism, and by the possibility to use their native language and the languages of other peoples of the USSR.

Any direct or indirect limitation of the rights of citizens or establishment of direct or indirect privileges on grounds of race or nationality, and any advocacy of racial or national exclusiveness, hostility or contempt, are punishable by law.

ARTICLE 37. Citizens of other countries and stateless persons in the USSR are guaranteed the rights and freedoms provided by law, including the right to apply to a court and other state bodies for the protection of their personal property, family, and other rights.

Citizens of other countries and stateless persons, when in the USSR, are obliged to respect the Constitution of the USSR and observe Soviet laws.

ARTICLE 38. The USSR grants the right of asylum to foreigners persecuted for defending the interests of the working people and the cause of peace, or for participation in the revolutionary and national-liberation movement, or for progressive social and political, scientific or other creative activity.

Chapter 7 The Basic Rights, Freedoms, and Duties of Citizens of the USSR

ARTICLE 39. Citizens of the USSR enjoy in full the social, economic, political and personal rights and freedoms proclaimed and guaranteed by the Constitution of the USSR and by Soviet laws. The socialist system ensures enlargement of the rights and freedoms of citizens and continuous improvement of their living standards as social, economic, and cultural development programmes are fulfilled.

Enjoyment by citizens of their rights and freedoms must not be to the detriment of the interests of society or the state, or infringe the rights of other citizens.

ARTICLE 40. Citizens of the USSR have the right to work (that is, to guaranteed employment and pay in accordance with the quantity and quality of their work, and not below the state-established minimum), including the right to choose their trade or profession, type of job and work in accordance with their inclinations, abilities, training and education, with due account of the needs of society.

This right is ensured by the socialist economic system, steady growth of the productive forces, free vocational and professional training, improvement of skills, training in new trades or professions, and development of the systems of vocational guidance and job placement.

ARTICLE 41. Citizens of the USSR have the right to rest and leisure.

This right is ensured by the establishment of a working week not exceeding 41 hours, for workers and other employees, a shorter working day in a number of trades and industries, and shorter hours for night work; by the provision of paid annual holidays, weekly days of rest, extension of the network of cultural, educational and health-building institutions, and the development on a mass scale of sport, physical culture, and camping and tourism; by the provision of neighbour-hood recreational facilities, and of other opportunities for rational use of free time.

The length of collective farmers' working and leisure time is established by their collective farms.

ARTICLE 42. Citizens of the USSR have the right to health protection.

This right is ensured by free, qualified medical care provided by state health institutions; by extension of the network of therapeutic and health-building institutions; by the development and improvement of safety and hygiene in industry; by carrying out broad prophylactic measures; by measures to improve the environment; by special care for the health of the rising generation, including prohibition of child labour, excluding the work done by children as part of the school curriculum; and by developing research to prevent and reduce the incidence of disease and ensure citizens a long and active life.

ARTICLE 43. Citizens of the USSR have the right to maintenance in old age, in sickness, and in the event of complete or partial disability or loss of the breadwinner.

This right is guaranteed by social insurance of workers and other employees and collective farmers; by allowances for temporary disability; by the provision by the state or by collective farms of retirement pensions, disability pensions, and pensions for loss of the breadwinner; by providing employment for the partially disabled; by care for the elderly and the disabled; and by other forms of social security.

ARTICLE 44. Citizens of the USSR have the right to housing.

This right is ensured by the development and upkeep of state and socially-owned housing; by assistance for co-operative and individual house building; by fair distribution, under public control, of the housing that becomes available through fulfilment of the programme of building well-appointed dwellings, and by low rents and low charges for utility services. Citizens of the USSR shall take good care of the housing allocated to them.

ARTICLE 45. Citizens of the USSR have the right to education.

This right is ensured by free provision of all forms of education, by the institution of universal, compulsory secondary education, and broad development of vocational, specialised secondary, and higher education, in which instruction is oriented toward practical activity and production; by the development of extramu-ral, correspondence and evening courses; by the provision of state scholarships and grants and privileges for students; by the free issue of school textbooks; by the opportunity to attend a school where teaching is in the native language; and by the provision of facilities for self-education.

ARTICLE 46. Citizens of the USSR have the right to enjoy cultural benefits.

This right is ensured by broad access to the cultural treasures of their own land and of the world that are preserved in state and other public collections; by the development and fair distribution of cultural and educational institutions throughout the country; by developing television and radio broadcasting and the publishing of books, newspapers and periodicals, and by extending the free library service; and by expanding cultural exchanges with other countries.

ARTICLE 47. Citizens of the USSR, in accordance with the aims of building communism, are guaranteed freedom of scientific, technical, and artistic work. This freedom is ensured by broadening scientific research, encouraging invention and innovation, and developing literature and the arts. The state provides the necessary material conditions for this and support for voluntary societies and unions of workers in the arts, organises introduction of inventions and innovations in production and other spheres of activity.

The rights of authors, inventors and innovators are protected by the state.

ARTICLE 48. Citizens of the USSR have the right to take part in the management and administration of state and public affairs and in the discussion and adoption of laws and measures of All-Union and local significance.

This right is ensured by the opportunity to vote and to be elected to Soviets of People's Deputies and other elective state bodies, to take part in nationwide discussions and referendums, in people's control, in the work of state bodies, public organisations, and local community groups, and in meetings at places of work or residence.

ARTICLE 49. Every citizen of the USSR has the right to submit proposals to state bodies and public organisations for improving their activity, and to criticise shortcomings in their work.

Officials are obliged, within established time-limits, to examine citizens' proposals and requests, to reply to them, and to take appropriate action.

Persecution for criticism is prohibited. Persons guilty of such persecution shall be called to account.

ARTICLE 50. In accordance with the interests of the people and in order to strengthen and develop the socialist system, citizens of the USSR are guaranteed freedom of speech, of the press, and of assembly, meetings, street processions and demonstrations.

Exercise of these political freedoms is ensured by putting public buildings, streets and squares at the disposal of the working people and their organisations, by broad dissemination of information, and by opportunity to use the press, television, and radio.

ARTICLE 51. In accordance with the aims of building communism, citizens of the USSR have the right to associate in public organisations that promote their political activity and initiative and satisfaction of their various interests.

Public organisations are guaranteed conditions for successfully performing the functions defined in their rules.

ARTICLE 52. Citizens of the USSR are guaranteed freedom of conscience, that is, the right to profess or not to profess any religion, and to conduct religious worship or atheistic propaganda. Incitement of hostility or hatred on religious grounds is prohibited.

In the USSR, the church is separated from the state, and the school from the church.

ARTICLE 53. The family enjoys the protection of the state.

Marriage is based on the free consent of the woman and the man; the spouses are completely equal in their family relations.

The state helps the family by providing and developing a broad system of childcare institutions, by organising and improving communal services and public catering, by paying grants on the birth of a child, by providing children's allowances and benefits for large families, and other forms of family allowances and assistance.

ARTICLE 54. Citizens of the USSR are guaranteed inviolability of the person. No one may be arrested except by a court decision or on the warrant of a procurator.

ARTICLE 55. Citizens of the USSR are guaranteed inviolability of the home. No one may, without lawful grounds, enter a home against the will of those residing in it.

ARTICLE 56. The privacy of citizens, and of their correspondence, telephone conversations, and telegraphic communications is protected by law.

ARTICLE 57. Respect for the individual and protection of the rights and freedoms of citizens are the duty of all state bodies, public organisations, and officials.

Citizens of the USSR have the right to protection by the courts against encroachments on their honour and reputation, life and health, and personal freedom and property.

ARTICLE 58. Citizens of the USSR have the right to lodge a complaint against the actions of officials, state bodies and public bodies. Complaints shall be examined according to the procedure and within the time-limit established by law.

Actions by officials that contravene the law or exceed their powers, and infringe the rights of citizens, may be appealed against in a court in the manner prescribed by law.

Citizens of the USSR have the right to compensation for damage resulting from unlawful actions by state organisations and public organisations, or by officials in the performance of their duties.

ARTICLE 59. Citizens' exercise of their rights and freedoms is inseparable from the performance of their duties and obligations.

Citizens of the USSR are obliged to observe the Constitution of the USSR and Soviet laws, comply with the standards of socialist conduct, and uphold the honour and dignity of Soviety citizenship.

ARTICLE 60. It is the duty of, and a matter of honour for, every able-bodied citizen of the USSR to work conscientiously in his chosen, socially useful occupation, and strictly to observe labour discipline. Evasion of socially useful work is incompatible with the principles of socialist society.

ARTICLE **61.** Citizens of the USSR are obliged to preserve and protect socialist property. It is the duty of a citizen of the USSR to combat misappropriation and squandering of state and socially-owned property and to make thrifty use of the people's wealth.

Persons encroaching in any way on socialist property shall be punished according to the law.

ARTICLE **62.** Citizens of the USSR are obliged to safeguard the interests of the Soviet state, and to enhance its power and prestige.

Defence of the Socialist Motherland is the sacred duty of every citizen of the USSR.

Betrayal of the Motherland is the gravest of crimes against the people.

ARTICLE **63.** Military service in the ranks of the Armed Forces of the USSR is an honourable duty of Soviet citizens.

ARTICLE **64.** It is the duty of every citizen of the USSR to respect the national dignity of other citizens, and to strengthen friendship of the nations and nationalities of the multinational Soviet state.

ARTICLE **65.** A citizen of the USSR is obliged to respect the rights and lawful interests of other persons, to be uncompromising toward anti-social behaviour, and to help maintain public order.

ARTICLE **66.** Citizens of the USSR are obliged to concern themselves with the upbringing of children, to train them for socially useful work, and to raise them as worthy members of socialist society. Children are obliged to care for their parents and help them.

ARTICLE **67.** Citizens of the USSR are obliged to protect nature and conserve its riches.

ARTICLE **68.** Concern for the preservation of historical monuments and other cultural values is a duty and obligation of citizens of the USSR.

ARTICLE **69.** It is the internationalist duty of citizens of the USSR to promote friendship and co-operation with peoples of other lands and help maintain and strengthen world peace.

III. THE NATIONAL-STATE STRUCTURE OF THE USSR

Chapter 8 The USSR—a Federal State

ARTICLE **70.** The Union of Soviet Socialist Republics is an integral, federal, multinational state formed on the principle of socialist federalism as a result of the free self-determination of nations and the voluntary association of equal Soviet Socialist Republics.

The USSR embodies the state unity of the Soviet people and draws all its nations and nationalities together for the purpose of jointly building communism.

ARTICLE 71. The Union of Soviet Socialist Republics unites:

- the Russian Soviet Federative Socialist Republic,
- the Ukrainian Soviet Socialist Republic,
- the Byelorussian Soviet Socialist Republic,
- the Uzbek Soviet Socialist Republic,
- the Kazakh Soviet Socialist Republic,
- the Georgian Soviet Socialist Republic,
- the Azerbaijan Soviet Socialist Republic,
- the Lithuanian Soviet Socialist Republic,
- the Moldavian Soviet Socialist Republic,
- the Latvian Soviet Socialist Republic,
- the Kirghiz Soviet Socialist Republic,
- the Tajik Soviet Socialist Republic,
- the Armenian Soviet Socialist Republic,
- the Turkmen Soviet Socialist Republic,
- the Estonian Soviet Socialist Republic.

ARTICLE 72. Each Union Republic shall retain the right freely to secede from the USSR.

ARTICLE 73. The jurisdiction of the Union of Soviet Socialist Republics, as represented by its highest bodies of state authority and administation, shall cover:

1. the admission of new republics to the USSR; endorsement of the formation of new autonomous republics and autonomous regions within Union Republics;
2. determination of the state boundaries of the USSR and approval of changes in the boundaries between Union Republics;
3. establishment of the general principles for the organisation and functioning of republican and local bodies of state authority and administration;
4. the ensurance of uniformity of legislative norms throughout the USSR and establishment of the fundamentals of the legislation of the Union of Soviet Socialist Republics and Union Republics;
5. pursuance of a uniform social and economic policy; direction of the country's economy; determination of the main lines of scientific and technological progress and the general measures for rational exploitation and conservation of natural resources; the drafting and approval of state plans for the economic and social development of the USSR, and endorsement of reports on their fulfilment;
6. the drafting and approval of the consolidated Budget of the USSR, and endorsement of the report on its execution; management of a single

monetary and credit system; determination of the taxes and revenues forming the Budget of the USSR; and the formulation of prices and wages policy;

7. direction of the sectors of the economy, and of enterprises and amalgamations under Union jurisdiction, and general direction of industries under Union-Republican jurisdiction;

8. issues of war and peace, defence of the sovereignty of the USSR and safeguarding of its frontiers and territory, and organisation of defence; direction of the Armed Forces of the USSR;

9. state security;

10. representation of the USSR in international relations; the USSR's relations with other states and with international organisations; establishment of the general procedure for, and co-ordination of, the relations of Union Republics with other states and with international organisations; foreign trade and other forms of external economic activity on the basis of state monopoly;

11. control over observance of the Constitution of the USSR, and ensurance of conformity of the Constitutions of Union Republics to the Constitution of the USSR;

12. and settlement of other matters of All-Union importance.

ARTICLE 74. The laws of the USSR shall have the same force in all Union Republics. In the event of a discrepancy between a Union Republic law and an All-Union law, the law of the USSR shall prevail.

ARTICLE 75. The territory of the Union of Soviet Socialist Republics is a single entity and comprises the territories of the Union Republics.

The sovereignty of the USSR extends throughout its territory.

Chapter 9 The Union Soviet Socialist Republic

ARTICLE 76. A Union Republic is a sovereign Soviet socialist state that has united with other Soviet Republics in the Union of Soviet Socialist Republics.

Outside the spheres listed in Article 73 of the Constitution of the USSR, a Union Republic exercises independent authority on its territory.

A Union Republic shall have its own Constitution conforming to the Constitution of the USSR with the specific features of the Republic being taken into account.

ARTICLE 77. Union Republics take part in decision-making in the Supreme Soviet of the USSR, the Presidium of the Supreme Soviet of the USSR, the Government of the USSR, and other bodies of the Union of Soviet Socialist Republics in matters that come within the jurisdiction of the Union of Soviet Socialist Republics.

A Union Republic shall ensure comprehensive economic and social development on its territory, facilitate exercise of the powers of the USSR on its territory, and implement the decisions of the highest bodies of state authority and administration of the USSR.

In matters that come within its jurisdiction, a Union Republic shall co-ordinate and control the activity of enterprises, institutions, and organisations subordinate to the Union.

ARTICLE 78. The territory of a Union Republic may not be altered without its consent. The boundaries between Union Republics may be altered by mutual agreement of the Republics concerned, subject to ratification by the Union of Soviet Socialist Republics.

ARTICLE 79. A Union Republic shall determine its division into territories, regions, areas, and districts, and decide other matters relating to its administrative and territorial structure.

ARTICLE 80. A Union Republic has the right to enter into relations with other states, conclude treaties with them, exchange diplomatic and consular representatives, and take part in the work of international organisations.

ARTICLE 81. The sovereign rights of Union Republics shall be safeguarded by the USSR.

Chapter 10 The Autonomous Soviet Socialist Republic

ARTICLE 82. An Autonomous Republic is a constituent part of a Union Republic.

In spheres not within the jurisdiction of the Union of Soviet Socialist Republics and the Union Republic, an Autonomous Republic shall deal independently with matters within its jurisdiction.

An Autonomous Republic shall have its own Constitution conforming to the Constitutions of the USSR and the Union Republic with the specific features of the Autonomous Republic being taken into account.

ARTICLE 83. An Autonomous Republic takes part in decision-making through the highest bodies of state authority and administration of the USSR and of the Union Republic respectively, in matters that come within the jurisdiction of the USSR and the Union Republic.

An Autonomous Republic shall ensure comprehensive economic and social development on its territory, facilitate exercise of the powers of the USSR and the Union Republic on its territory, and implement decisions of the highest bodies of state authority and administration of the USSR and the Union Republic.

In matters within its jurisdiction, an Autonomous Republic shall co-ordinate and control the activity of enterprises, institutions, and organisations subordinate to the Union or the Union Republic.

ARTICLE 84. The territory of an Autonomous Republic may not be altered without its consent.

ARTICLE 85. The Russian Soviet Federative Socialist Republic includes the Bashkir, Buryat, Daghestan, Kabardin-Balkar, Kalmyk, Karelian, Komi, Mari, Mordovian, North Ossetian, Tatar, Tuva, Udmurt, Chechen-Ingush, Chuvash, and Yakut Autonomous Soviet Socialist Republics.

The Uzbek Soviet Socialist Republic includes the Kara-Kalpak Autonomous Soviet Socialist Republic.

The Georgian Soviet Socialist Republic includes the Abkhasian and Adzhar Autonomous Soviet Socialist Republics.

The Azerbaijan Soviet Socialist Republic includes the Nakhichevan Autonomous Soviet Socialist Republic.

Chapter 11 The Autonomous Region and Autonomous Area

ARTICLE 86. An Autonomous Region is a constituent part of a Union Republic or Territory. The Law on an Autonomous Region, upon submission by the Soviet of People's Deputies of the Autonomous Region concerned, shall be adopted by the Supreme Soviet of the Union Republic.

ARTICLE 87. The Russian Soviet Federative Socialist Republic includes the Adygei, Gorno-Altai, Jewish, Karachai-Circassian, and Khakass Autonomous Regions.

The Georgian Soviet Socialist Republic includes the South Ossetian Autonomous Region.

The Azerbaijan Soviet Socialist Republic includes the Nagorno-Karabakh Autonomous Region.

The Tajik Soviet Socialist Republic includes the Gorno-Badakhshan Autonomous Region.

ARTICLE 88. An Autonomous Area is a constituent part of a Territory or Region. The Law on an Autonomous Area shall be adopted by the Supreme Soviet of the Union Republic concerned.

IV. SOVIETS OF PEOPLE'S DEPUTIES AND ELECTORAL PROCEDURE

Chapter 12 The System of Soviets of People's Deputies and the Principles of Their Work

ARTICLE 89. The Soviets of People's Deputies, i.e. the Supreme Soviet of the USSR, the Supreme Soviets of Union Republics, the Supreme Soviets of Autonomous Republics, the Soviets of People's Deputies of Territories and Regions, the Soviets of People's Deputies of Autonomous Regions and Autonomous Areas, and the Soviets of People's Deputies of districts, cities, city districts, settlements and villages shall constitute a single system of bodies of state authority.

ARTICLE 90. The term of the Supreme Soviet of the USSR, the Supreme Soviets of Union Republics, and the Supreme Soviets of Autonomous Republics shall be five years.

The term of local Soviets of People's Deputies shall be two and a half years.

Elections to Soviets of People's Deputies shall be called not later than two months before the expiry of the term of the Soviet concerned.

ARTICLE 91. The most important matters within the jurisdiction of the respective Soviets of People's Deputies shall be considered and settled at their sessions.

Soviets of People's Deputies shall elect standing commissions and form executive-administrative, and other bodies accountable to them.

ARTICLE 92. Soviets of People's Deputies shall form people's control bodies combining state control with control by the working people at enterprises, collective farms, institutions, and organisations.

People's control bodies shall check on the fulfilment of state plans and assignments, combat breaches of state discipline, localistic tendencies, narrow departmental attitudes, mismanagement, extravagance and waste, red tape and bureaucracy, and help improve the working of the state machinery.

ARTICLE 93. Soviets of People's Deputies shall direct all sectors of state, economic, and social and cultural development, either directly or through bodies instituted by them, take decisions and ensure their execution, and verify their implementation.

ARTICLE 94. Soviets of People's Deputies shall function publicly on the basis of collective, free, constructive discussion and decision-making, of systematic reporting back to them and the people by their executive-administrative and other bodies, and of involving citizens on a broad scale in their work.

Soviets of People's Deputies and the bodies set up by them shall systematically inform the public about their work and the decisions taken by them.

Chapter 13 The Electoral System

ARTICLE 95. Deputies to all Soviets shall be elected on the basis of universal, equal, and direct suffrage by secret ballot.

ARTICLE 96. Elections shall be universal: all citizens of the USSR who have reached the age of 18 shall have the right to vote and to be elected, with the exception of persons who have been legally certified insane.

To be eligible for election to the Supreme Soviet of the USSR a citizen of the USSR must have reached the age of 21.

ARTICLE 97. Elections shall be equal: each citizen shall have one vote; all voters shall exercise the franchise on an equal footing.

ARTICLE 98. Elections shall be direct: deputies to all Soviets of People's Deputies shall be elected by citizens by direct vote.

ARTICLE **99.** Voting at elections shall be secret: control over voters' exercise of the franchise is inadmissible.

ARTICLE **100.** The following shall have the right to nominate candidates: branches and organisations of the Communist Party of the Soviet Union, trade unions, and the All-Union Leninist Young Communist League; co-operatives and other public organisations; work collectives, and meetings of servicemen in their military units.

Citizens of the USSR and public organisations are guaranteed the right to free and all-round discussion of the political and personal qualities and competence of candidates, and the right to campaign for them at meetings, in the press, and on television and radio.

The expenses involved in holding elections to Soviets of People's Deputies shall be met by the state.

ARTICLE **101.** Deputies to Soviets of People's Deputies shall be elected by constituencies.

A citizen of the USSR may not, as a rule, be elected to more than two Soviets of People's Deputies.

Elections to the Soviets shall be conducted by electoral commissions consisting of representatives of public organisations and work collectives, and of meetings of servicemen in military units.

The procedure for holding elections to Soviets of People's Deputies shall be defined by the laws of the USSR, and of Union and Autonomous Republics.

ARTICLE **102.** Electors give mandates to their Deputies.

The appropriate Soviets of People's Deputies shall examine electors' mandates, take them into account in drafting economic and social development plans and in drawing up the budget, organise implementation of the mandates, and inform citizens about it.

Chapter 14 People's Deputies

ARTICLE **103.** Deputies are the plenipotentiary representatives of the people in the Soviets of People's Deputies.

In the Soviets, Deputies deal with matters relating to state, economic, and social and cultural development, organise implementation of the decisions of the Soviets, and exercise control over the work of state bodies, enterprises, institutions and organisations.

Deputies shall be guided in their activities by the interests of the state, and shall take the needs of their constituents into account and work to implement their electors' mandates.

ARTICLE **104.** Deputies shall exercise their powers without discontinuing their regular employment or duties.

During sessions of the Soviet, and so as to exercise their deputy's powers in other cases stipulated by law, Deputies shall be released from their regular employment or duties, with retention of their average earnings at their permanent place of work.

ARTICLE 105. A Deputy has the right to address inquiries to the appropriate state bodies and officials, who are obliged to reply to them at a session of the Soviet.

Deputies have the right to approach any state or public body, enterprise, institution, or organisation on matters arising from their work as Deputies and to take part in considering the questions raised by them. The heads of the state or public bodies, enterprises, institutions or organisations concerned are obliged to receive Deputies without delay and to consider their proposals within the time-limit established by law.

ARTICLE 106. Deputies shall be ensured conditions for the unhampered and effective exercise of their rights and duties.

The immunity of Deputies, and other guarantees of their activity as Deputies, are defined in the Law on the Status of Deputies and other legislative acts of the USSR and of Union and Autonomous Republics.

ARTICLE 107. Deputies shall report on their work and on that of the Soviet to their constituents, and to the work collectives and public organisations that nominated them.

Deputies who have not justified the confidence of their constituents may be recalled at any time by decision of a majority of the electors in accordance with the procedure established by law.

V. HIGHER BODIES OF STATE AUTHORITY AND ADMINISTRATION OF THE USSR

Chapter 15 The Supreme Soviet of the USSR

ARTICLE 108. The highest body of state authority of the USSR shall be the Supreme Soviet of the USSR.

The Supreme Soviet of the USSR is empowered to deal with all matters within the jurisdiction of the Union of Soviet Socialist Republics, as defined by this Constitution.

The adoption and amendment of the Constitution of the USSR; admission of new Republics to the USSR; endorsement of the formation of new Autonomous Republics and Autonomous Regions; approval of the state plans for economic and social development, of the Budget of the USSR, and of reports on their execution; and the institution of bodies of the USSR accountable to it, are the exclusive prerogative of the Supreme Soviet of the USSR.

Laws of the USSR shall be enacted by the Supreme Soviet of the USSR or by a nationwide vote (referendum) held by decision of the Supreme Soviet of the USSR.

ARTICLE 109. The Supreme Soviet of the USSR shall consist of two chambers: the Soviet of the Union and the Soviet of Nationalities.

The two chambers of the Supreme Soviet of the USSR shall have equal rights.

ARTICLE 110. The Soviet of the Union and the Soviet of Nationalities shall have equal numbers of deputies.

The Soviet of the Union shall be elected by constituencies with equal populations.

The Soviet of Nationalities shall be elected on the basis of the following representation: 32 deputies from each Union Republic, 11 deputies from each Autonomous Republic, five deputies from each Autonomous Region, and one deputy from each Autonomous Area.

The Soviet of the Union and the Soviet of Nationalities, upon submission by the credentials commissions elected by them, shall decide on the validity of Deputies' credentials, and, in cases in which the election law has been violated, shall declare the election of the Deputies concerned null and void.

ARTICLE 111. Each chamber of the Supreme Soviet of the USSR shall elect a Chairman and four Vice-Chairmen.

The Chairman of the Soviet of the Union and of the Soviet of Nationalities shall preside over the sittings of the respective chambers and conduct their affairs.

Joint sittings of the chambers of the Supreme Soviet of the USSR shall be presided over alternately by the Chairman of the Soviet of the Union and the Chairman of the Soviet of Nationalities.

ARTICLE 112. Sessions of the Supreme Soviet of the USSR shall be convened twice a year.

Special sessions shall be convened by the Presidium of the Supreme Soviet of the USSR at its discretion or on the proposal of a Union Republic, or of not less than one-third of the Deputies of one of the chambers.

A session of the Supreme Soviet of the USSR shall consist of separate and joint sittings of the chambers, and of meetings of the standing commissions of the chambers or commissions of the Supreme Soviet of the USSR held between the sittings of the chambers. A session may be opened and closed at either separate or joint sittings of the chambers.

ARTICLE 113. The right to initiate legislation in the Supreme Soviet of the USSR is vested in the Soviet of the Union and the Soviet of Nationalities, the Presidium of the Supreme Soviet of the USSR, the Council of Ministers of the USSR, Union Republics through their highest bodies of state authority, commissions of the Supreme Soviet of the USSR and standing commissions of its chambers, Deputies of the Supreme Soviet of the USSR, the Supreme Court of the USSR, and the Procurator-General of the USSR.

The right to initiate legislation is also vested in public organisations through their All-Union bodies.

ARTICLE 114. Bills and other matters submitted to the Supreme Soviet of the USSR shall be debated by its chambers at separate or joint sittings. Where necessary, a bill or other matter may be referred to one or more commissions for preliminary or additional consideration.

A law of the USSR shall be deemed adopted when it has been passed in each chamber of the Supreme Soviet of the USSR by a majority of the total number of its Deputies. Decisions and other acts of the Supreme Soviet of the USSR are adopted by a majority of the total number of Deputies of the Supreme Soviet of the USSR.

Bills and other very important matters of state may be submitted for nationwide discussion by a decision of the Supreme Soviet of the USSR or its Presidium taken on their own initiative or on the proposal of a Union Republic.

ARTICLE 115. In the event of disagreement between the Soviet of the Union and the Soviet of Nationalities, the matter at issue shall be referred for settlement to a conciliation commission formed by the chambers on a parity basis, after which it shall be considered for a second time by the Soviet of the Union and the Soviet of Nationalities at a joint sitting. If agreement is again not reached. the matter shall be postponed for debate at the next session of the Supreme Soviet of the USSR or submitted by the Supreme Soviet to a nationwide vote (referendum).

ARTICLE 116. Laws of the USSR and decisions and other acts of the Supreme Soviet of the USSR shall be published in the languages of the Union Republics over the signatures of the Chairman and Secretary of the Presidium of the Supreme Soviet of the USSR.

ARTICLE 117. Deputy of the Supreme Soviet of the USSR has the right to address inquiries to the Council of Ministers of the USSR, and to Ministers and the heads of other bodies formed by the Supreme Soviet of the USSR. The Council of Ministers of the USSR, or the official to whom the inquiry is addressed, is obliged to give a verbal or written reply within three days at the given session of the Supreme Soviet of the USSR.

ARTICLE 118. A Deputy of the Supreme Soviet of the USSR may not be prosecuted, or arrested, or incur a court-imposed penalty, without the sanction of the Supreme Soviet of the USSR or, between its sessions, of the Presidium of the Supreme Soviet of the USSR.

ARTICLE 119. The Supreme Soviet of the USSR, at a joint sitting of its chambers, shall elect a Presidium of the Supreme Soviet of the USSR, which shall be a standing body of the Supreme Soviet of the USSR, accountable to it for all its work and exercising the functions of the highest body of state authority of the USSR between sessions of the Supreme Soviet, within the limits prescribed by the Constitution.

ARTICLE 120. The Presidium of the Supreme Soviet of the USSR shall be elected from among the Deputies and shall consist of a Chairman, First Vice-Chairman, 15 Vice-Chairmen (one from each Union Republic), a Secretary, and 21 members.

ARTICLE 121. The Presidium of the Supreme Soviet of the USSR shall:

1. name the date of elections to the Supreme Soviet of the USSR;
2. convene sessions of the Supreme Soviet of the USSR;
3. co-ordinate the work of the standing commissions of the chambers of the Supreme Soviet of the USSR;
4. ensure observance of the Constitution of the USSR and conformity of the Constitutions and laws of Union Republics to the Constitution and laws of the USSR;
5. interpret the laws of the USSR;
6. ratify and denounce international treaties of the USSR;
7. revoke decisions and ordinances of the Council of Ministers of the USSR and of the Councils of Ministers of Union Republics should they fail to conform to the law;
8. institute military and diplomatic ranks and other special titles; and confer the highest military and diplomatic ranks and other special titles;
9. institute orders and medals of the USSR, and honorific titles of the USSR; award orders and medals of the USSR; and confer honorific titles of the USSR;
10. grant citizenship of the USSR, and rule on matters of the renunciation or deprivation of citizenship of the USSR and of granting asylum;
11. issue All-Union acts of amnesty and exercise the right of pardon;
12. appoint and recall diplomatic representatives of the USSR to other countries and to international organisations;
13. receive the letters of credence and recall of the diplomatic representatives of foreign states accredited to it;
14. form the Council of Defence of the USSR and confirm its composition; appoint and dismiss the high command of the Armed Forces of the USSR;
15. proclaim martial law in particular localities or throughout the country in the interests of defence of the USSR;
16. order general or partial mobilisation;
17. between sessions of the Supreme Soviet of the USSR, proclaim a state of war in the event of an armed attack on the USSR, or when it is necessary to meet international treaty obligations relating to mutual defence against agression;
18. and exercise other powers vested in it by the Constitution and laws of the USSR.

ARTICLE 122. The Presidium of the Supreme Soviet of the USSR, between sessions of the Supreme Soviet of the USSR and subject to submission for its confirmation at the next session, shall:

1. amend existing legislative acts of the USSR when necessary;
2. approve changes in the boundaries between Union Republics;

3. form and abolish Ministries and State Committees of the USSR on the recommendation of the Council of Ministers of the USSR;
4. relieve individual members of the Council of Ministers of the USSR of their responsibilities and appoint persons to the Council of Ministers on the recommendation of the Chairman of the Council of Ministers of the USSR.

ARTICLE 123. The Presidium of the Supreme Soviet of the USSR promulgates decrees and adopts decisions.

ARTICLE 124. On expiry of the term of the Supreme Soviet of the USSR, the Presidium of the Supreme Soviet of the USSR shall retain its powers until the newly elected Supreme Soviet of the USSR has elected a new Presidium.

The newly elected Supreme Soviet of the USSR shall be convened by the outgoing Presidium of the Supreme Soviet of the USSR within two months of the elections.

ARTICLE 125. The Soviet of the Union and the Soviet of Nationalities shall elect standing commissions from among the Deputies to make a preliminary review of matters coming within the jurisdiction of the Supreme Soviet of the USSR, to promote execution of the laws of the USSR and other acts of the Supreme Soviet of the USSR and its Presidium, and to check on the work of state bodies and organisations. The chambers of the Supreme Soviet of the USSR may also set up joint commissions on a parity basis.

When it deems it necessary, the Supreme Soviet of the USSR sets up commissions of inquiry and audit, and commissions on any other matter.

All state and public bodies, organisations and officials are obliged to meet the requests of the commissions of the Supreme Soviet of the USSR and of its chambers, and submit the requisite materials and documents to them.

The commissions' recommendations shall be subject to consideration by state and public bodies, institutions and organisations. The commissions shall be informed, within the prescribed time-limit, of the results of such consideration or of the action taken.

ARTICLE 126. The Supreme Soviet of the USSR shall supervise the work of all state bodies accountable to it.

The Supreme Soviet of the USSR shall form a Committee of People's Control of the USSR to head the system of people's control.

The organisation and procedure of people's control bodies are defined by the Law on People's Control in the USSR.

ARTICLE 127. The procedure of the Supreme Soviet of the USSR and of its bodies shall be defined in the Rules and Regulations of the Supreme Soviet of the USSR and other laws of the USSR enacted on the basis of the Constitution of the USSR.

Chapter 6 The Council of Ministers of the USSR

ARTICLE **128.** The Council of Ministers of the USSR, i.e. the Government of the USSR, is the highest executive and administrative body of state authority of the USSR.

ARTICLE **129.** The Council of Ministers of the USSR shall be formed by the Supreme Soviet of the USSR at a joint sitting of the Soviet of the Union and the Soviet of Nationalities, and shall consist of the Chairman of the Council of Ministers of the USSR, First Vice-Chairmen and Vice-Chairmen, Ministers of the USSR, and Chairmen of State Committees of the USSR.

The Chairmen of the Councils of Ministers of Union Republics shall be *ex officio* members of the Council of Ministers of the USSR.

The Supreme Soviet of the USSR, on the recommendation of the Chairman of the Council of Ministers of the USSR, may include in the Government of the USSR the heads of other bodies and organisations of the USSR.

The Council of Ministers of the USSR shall tender its resignation to a newly elected Supreme Soviet of the USSR at its first session.

ARTICLE **130.** The Council of Ministers of the USSR shall be responsible and accountable to the Supreme Soviet of the USSR and, between sessions of the Supreme Soviet of the USSR, to the Presidium of the Supreme Soviet of the USSR.

The Council of Ministers of the USSR shall report regularly on its work to the Supreme Soviet of the USSR.

ARTICLE **131.** The Council of Ministers of the USSR is empowered to deal with all matters of state administration within the jurisdiction of the Union of Soviet Socialist Republics insofar as, under the Constitution, they do not come within the competence of the Supreme Soviet of the USSR or the Presidium of the Supreme Soviet of the USSR.

Within its powers the Council of Ministers of the USSR shall:

1. ensure direction of economic, social, and cultural development; draft and implement measures to promote the well-being and cultural development of the people, to develop science and engineering, to ensure rational exploitation and conservation of natural resources, to consolidate the monetary and credit system, to pursue a uniform prices, wages, and social security policy, and to organise state insurance and a uniform system of accounting and statistics; and organise the management of industrial, constructional, and agricultural enterprises and amalgamations, transport and communications undertakings, banks, and other organisations and institutions of All-Union subordination;
2. draft current and long-term state plans for the economic and social development of the USSR and the Budget of the USSR, and submit them to the Supreme Soviet of the USSR; take measures to execute the state plans and Budget; and report to the Supreme Soviet of the USSR on the implementation of the plans and Budget;

3. implement measures to defend the interests of the state, protect socialist property and maintain public order, and guarantee and protect citizens' rights and freedoms;
4. take measures to ensure state security;
5. exercise general direction of the development of the Armed Forces of the USSR, and determine the annual contingent of citizens to be called up for active military service;
6. provide general direction in regard to relations with other states, foreign trade, and economic, scientific, technical, and cultural co-operation of the USSR with other countries; take measures to ensure fulfilment of the USSR's international treaties; and ratify and denounce intergovernmental international agreements;
7. and when necessary, form committees, central boards and other departments under the Council of Ministers of the USSR to deal with matters of economic, social and cultural development, and defence.

ARTICLE 132. A Presidium of the Council of Ministers of the USSR, consisting of the Chairman, the First Vice-Chairmen, and Vice-Chairmen of the Council of Ministers of the USSR, shall function as a standing body of the Council of Ministers of the USSR to deal with questions relating to guidance of the economy, and with other matters of state administration.

ARTICLE 133. The Council of Ministers of the USSR, on the basis of, and in pursuance of, the laws of the USSR and other decisions of the Supreme Soviet of the USSR and its Presidium, shall issue decisions and ordinances and verify their execution. The decisions and ordinances of the Council of Ministers of the USSR shall be binding throughout the USSR.

ARTICLE 134. The Council of Ministers of the USSR has the right, in matters within the jurisdiction of the Union of Soviet Socialist Republics, to suspend execution of decisions and ordinances of the Councils of Ministers of Union Republics, and to rescind acts of ministries and state committees of the USSR, and of other bodies subordinate to it.

ARTICLE 135. The Council of Ministers of the USSR shall co-ordinate and direct the work of All-Union and Union-Republican ministries, state committees of the USSR, and other bodies subordinate to it.

All-Union ministries and state committees of the USSR shall direct the work of the branches of administration entrusted to them, or exercise inter-branch administration, throughout the territory of the USSR directly or through bodies set up by them.

Union-Republican ministries and state committees of the USSR direct the work of the branches of administration entrusted to them, or exercise inter-branch administration, as a rule, through the corresponding ministries and state committees, and other bodies of Union Republics, and directly administer individual enterprises and amalgamations of Union subordination. The procedure for transferring enterprises and amalgamations from Republic or local subordination to Union subordination shall be defined by the Presidium of the Supreme Soviet of the USSR.

Ministries and state committees of the USSR shall be responsible for the condition and development of the spheres of administration entrusted to them; within their competence, they issue orders and other acts on the basis of, and in execution of, the laws of the USSR and other decisions of the Supreme Soviet of the USSR and its Presidium, and of decisions and ordinances of the Council of Ministers of the USSR, and organise and verify their implementation.

ARTICLE 136. The competence of the Council of Ministers of the USSR and its Presidium, the procedure for their work, relationships between the Council of Ministers and other state bodies, and the list of All-Union and Union-Republican ministries and state committees of the USSR are defined, on the basis of the Constitution, in the Law on the Council of Ministers of the USSR.

VI. BASIC PRINCIPLES OF THE STRUCTURE OF THE BODIES OF STATE AUTHORITY AND ADMINISTRATION IN UNION REPUBLICS

Chapter 17 Higher Bodies of State Authority and Administration of a Union Republic

ARTICLE 137. The highest body of state authority of a Union Republic shall be the Supreme Soviet of that Republic.

The Supreme Soviet of a Union Republic is empowered to deal with all matters within the jurisdiction of the Republic under the Constitutions of the USSR and the Republic.

Adoption and amendment of the Constitution of a Union Republic; endorsement of state plans for economic and social development, of the Republic's Budget, and of reports on their fulfilment; and the formation of bodies accountable to the Supreme Soviet of the Union Republic are the exclusive prerogative of that Supreme Soviet.

Laws of a Union Republic shall be enacted by the Supreme Soviet of the Union Republic or by a popular vote (referendum) held by decision of the Republic's Supreme Soviet.

ARTICLE 138. The Supreme Soviet of a Union Republic shall elect a Presidium, which is a standing body of that Supreme Soviet and accountable to it for all its work. The composition and powers of the Presidium of the Supreme Soviet of a Union Republic shall be defined in the Constitution of the Union Republic.

ARTICLE 139. The Supreme Soviet of a Union Republic shall form a Council of Ministers of the Union Republic, i.e. the Government of that Republic, which shall be the highest executive and administrative body of state authority in the Republic.

The Council of Ministers of a Union Republic shall be responsible and accountable to the Supreme Soviet of that Republic or, between sessions of the Supreme Soviet, to its Presidium.

ARTICLE 140. The Council of Ministers of a Union Republic issues decisions and ordinances on the basis of, and in pursuance of, the legislative acts of the USSR and of the Union Republic, and of decisions and ordinances of the Council of Ministers of the USSR, and shall organise and verify their execution.

ARTICLE 141. The Council of Ministers of a Union Republic has the right to suspend the execution of decisions and ordinances of the Councils of Ministers of Autonomous Republics, to rescind the decisions and orders of the Executive Committees of Soviets of People's Deputies of Territories, Regions, and cities (i.e. cities under Republic jurisdiction) and of Autonomous Regions, and in Union Republics not divided into regions, of the Executive Committees of district and corresponding city Soviets of People's Deputies.

ARTICLE 142. The Council of Ministers of a Union Republic shall co-ordinate and direct the work of the Union-Republican and Republican ministries and of state committees of the Union Republic, and other bodies under its jurisdiction.

The Union-Republican ministries and state committees of a Union Republic shall direct the branches of administration entrusted to them, or exercise inter-branch control, and shall be subordinate to both the Council of Ministers of the Union Republic and the corresponding Union-Republican ministry or state committee of the USSR.

Republican ministries and state committees shall direct the branches of administration entrusted to them, or exercise inter-branch control, and shall be subordinate to the Council of Ministers of the Union Republic.

Chapter 18 Higher Bodies of State Authority and Administration of an Autonomous Republic

ARTICLE 143. The highest body of state authority of an Autonomous Republic shall be the Supreme Soviet of that Republic.

Adoption and amendment of the Constitution of an Autonomous Republic; endorsement of state plans for economic and social development, and of the Republic's Budget; and the formation of bodies accountable to the Supreme Soviet of the Autonomous Republic are the exclusive prerogative of that Supreme Soviet.

Laws of an Autonomous Republic shall be enacted by the Supreme Soviet of the Autonomous Republic.

ARTICLE 144. The Supreme Soviet of an Autonomous Republic shall elect a Presidium of the Supreme Soviet of the Autonomous Republic and shall form a Council of Ministers of the Autonomous Republic, i.e. the Government of that Republic.

Chapter 19 Local Bodies of State Authority and Administration

ARTICLE 145. The bodies of state authority in Territories, Regions, Autonomous Regions, Autonomous Areas, districts, cities, city districts, settlements, and rural communities shall be the corresponding Soviets of People's Deputies.

ARTICLE 146. Local Soviets of People's Deputies shall deal with all matters of local significance in accordance with the interests of the whole state and of the citizens residing in the area under their jurisdiction, implement decisions of higher bodies of state authority, guide the work of lower Soviets of People's Deputies, take part in the discussion of matters of Republican and All-Union significance, and submit their proposals concerning them.

Local Soviets of People's Deputies shall direct state, economic, social and cultural development within their territory; endorse plans for economic and social development and the local budget; exercise general guidance over state bodies, enterprises, institutions and organisations subordinate to them; ensure observance of the laws, maintenance of law and order, and protection of citizens' rights; and help strengthen the country's defence capacity.

ARTICLE 147. Within their powers, local Soviets of People's Deputies shall ensure the comprehensive, all-round economic and social development of their area; exercise control over the observance of legislation by enterprises, institutions and organisations subordinate to higher authorities and located in their area; and co-ordinate and supervise their activity as regards land use, nature conservation, building, employment of manpower, production of consumer goods, and social, cultural, communal and other services and amenities for the public.

ARTICLE 148. Local Soviets of People's Deputies shall decide matters within the powers accorded them by the legislation of the USSR and of the appropriate Union Republic and Autonomous Republic. Their decisions shall be binding on all enterprises, institutions, and organisations located in their area and on officials and citizens.

ARTICLE 149. The executive-administrative bodies of local Soviets shall be the Executive Committees elected by them from among their deputies.

Executive Committees shall report on their work at least once a year to the Soviets that elected them and to meetings of citizens at their places of work or residence.

ARTICLE 150. Executive Committees of local Soviets of People's Deputies shall be directly accountable both to the Soviet that elected them and to the higher executive and administrative body.

VII. JUSTICE, ARBITRATION, AND PROCURATOR'S SUPERVISION

Chapter 20 Courts and Arbitration

ARTICLE 151. In the USSR justice is administered only by the courts.

In the USSR there are the following courts: the Supreme Court of the USSR, the Supreme Courts of Union Republics, the Supreme Courts of Autonomous Republics, Territorial, Regional, and city courts, courts of Autonomous Regions, courts of Autonomous Areas, district (city) people's courts, and military tribunals in the Armed Forces.

ARTICLE 152. All courts in the USSR shall be formed on the principle of the electiveness of judges and people's assessors.

People's judges of district (city) people's courts shall be elected for a term of five years by the citizens of the district (city) on the basis of universal, equal and direct suffrage by secret ballot. People's assessors of district (city) people's courts shall be elected for a term of two and a half years at meetings of citizens at their places of work or residence by a show of hands.

Higher courts shall be elected for a term of five years by the corresponding Soviet of People's Deputies.

The judges of military tribunals shall be elected for a term of five years by the Presidium of the Supreme Soviet of the USSR and people's assessors for a term of two and a half years by meetings of servicemen.

Judges and people's assessors are responsible and accountable to their electors or the bodies that elected them, shall report to them, and may be recalled by them in the manner prescribed by law.

ARTICLE 153. The Supreme Court of the USSR is the highest judicial body in the USSR and supervises the administration of justice by the courts of the USSR and Union Republics within the limits established by law.

The Supreme Court of the USSR shall be elected by the Supreme Soviet of the USSR and shall consist of a Chairman, Vice-Chairmen, members, and people's assessors. The Chairmen of the Supreme Courts of Union Republics are *ex officio* members of the Supreme Court of the USSR.

The organisation and procedure of the Supreme Court of the USSR are defined in the Law on the Supreme Court of the USSR.

ARTICLE 154. The hearing of civil and criminal cases in all courts is collegial; in courts of first instance cases are heard with the participation of people's assessors. In the administration of justice people's assessors have all the rights of a judge.

ARTICLE 155. Judges and people's assessors are independent and subject only to the law.

ARTICLE 156. Justice is administered in the USSR on the principle of the equality of citizens before the law and the court.

ARTICLE **157.** Proceedings in all courts shall be open to the public. Hearings *in camera* are only allowed in cases provided for by law, with observance of all the rules of judicial procedure.

ARTICLE **158.** A defendant in a criminal action is guaranteed the right to legal assistance.

ARTICLE **159.** Judicial proceedings shall be conducted in the language of the Union Republic, Autonomous Republic, Autonomous Region, or Autonomous Area, or in the language spoken by the majority of the people in the locality. Persons participating in court proceedings, who do not know the language in which they are being conducted, shall be ensured the right to become fully acquainted with the materials in the case; the services of an interpreter during the proceedings; and the right to address the court in their own language.

ARTICLE **160.** No one may be adjudged guilty of a crime and subjected to punishment as a criminal except by the sentence of a court and in conformity with the law.

ARTICLE **161.** Colleges of advocates are available to give legal assistance to citizens and organisations. In cases provided for by legislation citizens shall be given legal asisstance free of charge.

The organisation and procedure of the bar are determined by legislation of the USSR and Union Republics.

ARTICLE **162.** Representatives of public organisations and of work collectives may take part in civil and criminal proceedings.

ARTICLE **163.** Economic disputes between enterprises, institutions, and organisations are settled by state arbitration bodies within the limits of their jurisdiction.

The organisation and manner of functioning of state arbitration bodies are defined in the Law on State Arbitration in the USSR.

Chapter 21 The Procurator's Office

ARTICLE **164.** Supreme power of supervision over the strict and uniform observance of laws by all ministries, state committees and departments, enterprises, institutions and organisations, executive-administrative bodies of local Soviets of People's Deputies, collective farms, co-operatives and other public organisations, officials and citizens is vested in the Procurator-General of the USSR and procurators subordinate to him.

ARTICLE **165.** The Procurator-General of the USSR is appointed by the Supreme Soviet of the USSR and is responsible and accountable to it and, between sessions of the Supreme Soviet, to the Presidium of the Supreme Soviet of the USSR.

ARTICLE **166.** The procurators of Union Republics, Autonomous Republics, Territories, Regions and Autonomous Regions are appointed by the Procurator-General of the USSR. The procurators of Autonomous Areas and district and city procurators are appointed by the Procurators of Union Republics, subject to confirmation by the Procurator-General of the USSR.

ARTICLE 167. The term of office of the Procurator-General of the USSR and all lower-ranking procurators shall be five years.

ARTICLE 168. The agencies of the Procurator's Office exercise their powers independently of any local bodies whatsoever, and are subordinate solely to the Procurator-General of the USSR.

The organisation and procedure of the agencies of the Procurator's Office are defined in the Law on the Procurator's Office of the USSR.

VIII. THE EMBLEM, FLAG, ANTHEM, AND CAPITAL OF THE USSR

ARTICLE 169. The State Emblem of the Union of Soviet Socialist Republics is a hammer and sickle on a globe depicted in the rays of the sun and framed by ears of wheat, with the inscription "Workers of All Countries, Unite!" in the languages of the Union Republics. At the top of the Emblem is a five-pointed star.

ARTICLE 170. The State Flag of the Union of Soviet Socialist Republics is a rectangle of red cloth with a hammer and sickle depicted in gold in the upper corner next to the staff and with a five-pointed red star edged in gold above them. The ratio of the width of the flag to its length is $1:2$.

ARTICLE 171. The State Anthem of the Union of Soviet Socialist Republics is confirmed by the Presidium of the Supreme Soviet of the USSR.

ARTICLE 172. The Capital of the Union of Soviet Socialist Republics is the city of Moscow.

IX. THE LEGAL FORCE OF THE CONSTITUTION OF THE USSR AND PROCEDURE FOR AMENDING THE CONSTITUTION

ARTICLE 173. The Constitution of the USSR shall have supreme legal force. All laws and other acts of state bodies shall be promulgated on the basis of and in conformity with it.

ARTICLE 174. The Constitution of the USSR may be amended by a decision of the Supreme Soviet of the USSR adopted by a majority of not less than two-thirds of the total number of Deputies of each of its chambers.

Index